Crime Prevention

Crime Prevention
Programs, Policies, and Practices

Steven E. Barkan
University of Maine

Michael Rocque
Bates College

Los Angeles | London | New Delhi
Singapore | Washington DC | Melbourne

FOR INFORMATION:

SAGE Publications, Inc.
2455 Teller Road
Thousand Oaks, California 91320
E-mail: order@sagepub.com

SAGE Publications Ltd.
1 Oliver's Yard
55 City Road
London, EC1Y 1SP
United Kingdom

SAGE Publications India Pvt. Ltd.
B 1/I 1 Mohan Cooperative Industrial Area
Mathura Road, New Delhi 110 044
India

SAGE Publications Asia-Pacific Pte. Ltd.
18 Cross Street #10-10/11/12
Chine Square Central
Singapore 048423

Copyright © 2021 by SAGE Publications, Inc.

Printed in the United States of America

Library of Congress Cataloging-in-Publication Data

Names: Barkan, Steven E., 1951- author. | Rocque, Michael, author.

Title: Crime prevention : programs, policies, and practices / Steven E. Barkan, University of Maine, Michael Rocque, Bates College.

Identifiers: LCCN 2019045633 | ISBN 9781483375083 (paperback) | ISBN 9781483375106 (epub) | ISBN 9781483375090 (epub) | ISBN 9781483375076 (ebook)

Subjects: LCSH: Crime prevention.

Classification: LCC HV7431 .B357 2020 | DDC 364.4—dc23

LC record available at https://lccn.loc.gov/2019045633

This book is printed on acid-free paper.

Acquisitions Editor: Jessica Miller
Editorial Assistant: Sarah Manheim
Production Editor: Myleen Medina
Copy Editor: Megan Granger
Typesetter: Hurix Digital
Proofreader: Barbara Coster
Indexer: Robie Grant
Cover Designer: Dally Verghese
Marketing Manager: Jillian Ragusa

20 21 22 23 24 10 9 8 7 6 5 4 3 2 1

BRIEF CONTENTS

DETAILED CONTENTS

PREFACE

Welcome to this new text on crime prevention! Although crime in the United States has declined significantly since the early 1990s, it continues to affect millions of Americans every year. Parents still worry when their children venture outside, and households everywhere lock their doors and take other security measures.

To combat crime, the United States since the 1970s has used a punitive approach that emphasizes tougher and more certain sentencing. This approach ushered in the era of mass incarceration that has cost the nation tens of billions of dollars. Despite this great expenditure, this approach has had only minimal effects on reducing crime, and it has generated many collateral consequences for the nation as a whole and especially for the people of color who disproportionately inhabit America's prisons and jails and its probation and parole rolls.

Amid these developments, the idea of crime prevention has become both more urgent and more salient. Relying on an impressive amount of sound research, criminologists, public health scholars, and other parties can now point to policies, programs, and practices that show great promise for reducing crime, and at a much lower cost than mass incarceration and other punitive strategies. This text discusses these strategies.

Four thematic features distinguish this text. First, it is grounded squarely in criminological theory, as crime prevention strategies that ignore such theory will be less likely to succeed. Conversely, strategies rooted in criminological theory are more likely to reduce crime. Early chapters thus discuss theory extensively, and later chapters return to it repeatedly.

Second, the text emphasizes the need to address poverty and other decidedly social roots of crime in addition to the criminal justice–related strategies that commonly come to mind when crime and crime prevention are discussed.

Third, the text is purposely not encyclopedic so that it can be shorter, more affordable, and more understandable to the advanced undergraduates and other readers who the authors hope will be learning much from it. Accordingly, rather than discussing every this-and-that policy, program, and practice aimed at crime prevention, the text instead discusses illustrative efforts that represent the range of these strategies.

Fourth, the text ends with a short epilogue chapter that reminds readers what they have learned from the book, presents crime prevention in other Western democracies as a model for the United States to emulate, and reminds readers of the importance of theory, social context, and evidence for successful crime prevention.

Several pedagogical features in the text will enhance reader comprehension:

- Learning questions begin each chapter to highlight important elements of the chapter.

- Selected tables in certain chapters summarize a chapter's theoretical or programmatic discussion.

- Each chapter ends with a conclusion, summary, and list of key terms.

- Each chapter includes an extensive list of references that readers may consult for further information.

ACKNOWLEDGMENTS

The authors would like to acknowledge the assistance of several people. We thank Jerry Westby and Jessica Miller of SAGE Publishing for their interest in this text—Jerry for his help and encouragement in the initial stages, and Jessica for her help and encouragement later on. The SAGE staff did an efficient job during all phases of production, and we thank them, too, for their assistance. The many reviewers of our manuscript helped greatly to improve it, and we thank them for their comments and keen insight. Any faults remaining, of course, are ours alone. Their names are

Keith J. Bell, *West Liberty University*

Leanne Brecklin, *University of Illinois Springfield*

Byung Jun Cho, *Westfield State University*

Nicholas Corsaro, *University of Cincinnati*

John Hazy, *Youngstown State University*

Eugene Hughley, Jr., *S.P.E.C.T.R.U.M. (Systems of Professional Education, Consultation, Training, Research and Utilization Management)* and *Southern University and A&M College*

Kimberly A. Kampe, *University of Central Florida*

YongJei Lee, *University of Colorado*

Philip D. McCormack, *Fitchburg State University*

James Murphy-Aguilu, *Ashford University*

Wendy Perkins, *Marshall University*

Daniel W. Phillips III, *Campbellsville University*

Christopher M. Sedelmaier, *University of New Haven*

Mahendra Singh, *Grambling State University*

Michael W. Weissberg, *Florida International University*

We also thank our many colleagues and teachers over the years, too numerous to mention by name, for helping us learn about crime and criminal justice and for helping us appreciate the need for sound theory and research to guide crime prevention.

Saving the best for last, our final thanks and deep appreciation go to our respective families. Steven Barkan owes a heartfelt debt to Barbara; David, Kelly, and Avery; and Joel and Stephanie. Michael Rocque owes the same debt to Andi, Teddy, and Cam. We thank our families for their love and support as we wrote this book, for the cheer and love they bring to our lives, and for making everything possible.

ABOUT THE AUTHORS

Steven E. Barkan is professor of sociology at the University of Maine. His published works include several textbooks and numerous journal articles in criminology, criminal justice, law and society, and sociology. He served as president of both the Society for the Study of Social Problems (SSSP) and the Textbook and Academic Authors Association, as chair of the Law and Society Division of SSSP, and as a council member for the Sociology of Law Section of the American Sociological Association (ASA). Strongly committed to undergraduate education, he currently serves on the advisory board of the ASA Honors Program and served on the council of Alpha Kappa Delta, the sociology undergraduate honorary society.

Michael Rocque is an associate professor in the Bates College Department of Sociology and the senior research advisor at the Maine Department of Corrections. His research focuses on life-course criminology, as well as race and justice. He is the author of three books: *The Criminal Brain*, *2nd Edition* (2016, NYU Press), with Nicole H. Rafter and Chad Posick, *Desistance From Crime* (2017, Palgrave-Macmillan), and *Great Debates in Criminology* (2018, Routledge) with Chad Posick. He was the recipient of the American Society of Criminology's Division of Developmental and Life-Course Criminology's Early Career Award in 2016.

PART I

INTRODUCTION
Why Crime Prevention?

1

THE CRIME PROBLEM IN THE UNITED STATES

Have you ever been a victim of a crime? Do you know someone who has been a crime victim? Do you ever worry about your personal safety or about protecting your property? Even if you might have answered no to all these questions, you are presumably still interested in learning how crime can be reduced. This book, then, is intended for any readers who are concerned about crime, whether or not it has touched them personally.

When we think about crime in the United States, there is both good news and bad news. The good news is that crime has fallen dramatically since the early 1990s. The bad news is that the U.S. crime rate remains higher than the rate in many other democracies, with the homicide rate higher than any other democracy's. Compared with other democracies, then, the U.S. crime rate is hardly anything to cheer about despite its drop since the 1990s.

Along with its troublesome crime rate, the United States also leads the world's nations in its incarceration rate. This high rate reflects the so-called **get-tough approach** that has guided U.S. criminal justice policy since the 1970s. Under this approach, the United States has fought crime with increased law enforcement and, especially, longer and more certain prison sentences. As this approach took hold, the nation's prisons and jails filled up and many more prisons and jails were built. The consequence has been **mass incarceration**: the confinement of an incredibly large volume of people, more than 2 million on any given day, inside the nation's

Chapter Outline

Learning Questions

1. Why is crime a continuing problem in the United States?

2. Why did the get-tough approach begin several decades ago?

3. How effective is mass incarceration in reducing crime?

4. What are the collateral consequences of mass incarceration?

3

prisons and jails. Many criminologists say mass incarceration does more harm than good while helping only a little to lower the crime rate, if that. They advocate many types of other strategies, some involving the criminal justice system and some involving other efforts, to achieve this goal. These wide-ranging policies, programs, and practices are the subject of this book on how to prevent crime. To set the stage for discussing these strategies, this opening chapter critically examines the U.S. crime problem and policy of mass incarceration.

THE AMOUNT AND COST OF CRIME

The United States has a lot of crime, but how much crime does it have? And how costly is it to its victims and to society as a whole? Answers to these important questions will help us understand the nature and seriousness of crime in American society.

The Amount of Crime

Our knowledge of the amount of crime comes primarily from two sources. The first is the **Uniform Crime Reports (UCR)** system of the Federal Bureau of Investigation (FBI). Police districts around the country transmit crime information to the FBI monthly. Police acquire their crime information mostly from reports by individuals of crimes they have experienced or of crimes they have witnessed. The FBI then compiles all the numbers it receives and issues an annual document in the fall called *Crime in the United States* (https://ucr.fbi.gov/ucr-publications). This document focuses on so-called **Part I crimes**, which include violent crime (homicide, aggravated assault, and rape) and property crime (burglary, larceny, motor vehicle theft, and arson). The FBI reports the number of these crimes; the number of arrests for these crimes; and the gender, race, and age of those arrested. *Crime in the United States* also reports the number of arrests for **Part II crimes**, which include fraud, embezzlement, vandalism, prostitution, drug abuse, disorderly conduct, and other offenses. According to the UCR, more than 1.2 million violent crimes and nearly 7.2 million property crimes occurred in 2018, or more than 8.9 million crimes overall (FBI 2019).

As high as it is, this figure underestimates the true number of crimes. A major reason for this is that almost 60% of all violent and property crime victims overall fail to report their crimes to the police. They may think the crime was a personal matter or that the police can do nothing to help them, they may feel their victimization was not very serious, or they may fear retaliation from an offender (Langton et al. 2012). These possible reasons aside, the bottom line is that much crime occurs that the police and thus the FBI never hear about. These unknown crimes are called **hidden crimes** or the **dark figure of crime**. Homicide data are fairly reliable, because almost all homicides do come to the attention of the police (from a witness report or discovery of a corpse), but other UCR crime data underestimate the actual number of offenses.

This problem leads criminologists to also consider data on the amount of crime from a second source of crime information, the **National Crime Victimization Survey (NCVS)** of the U.S. Bureau of Justice Statistics (BJS). The BJS surveys a random sample of people from tens of thousands of households nationwide every 6 months. Among other questions, these respondents are asked whether they have experienced various types of crimes within the past half year. These crimes include *violent crime* (aggravated and simple assault, rape and sexual assault, and robbery) and *property crime* (burglary, personal theft, and motor vehicle theft). The NCVS does not ask about commercial crime victimization such as shoplifting and store burglaries, and neither does it ask about homicide (because homicide victims lose their lives). Overall, though, the NCVS provides more accurate estimates than the UCR of the violent crime that individuals experience and the property crime that they or their households experience.

The NCVS reports that almost 20 million violent and property victimizations occurred in 2018 (see Figure 1.1). Most of these, some 13.3 million, were property offenses, while more than 5.6 million were violent offenses.

The NCVS also provides the **prevalence rate** for victimization, defined as the percentage of people 12 and older who experienced at least one victimization during the past year. For 2018, the prevalence rate for violent crime was 1.18%, meaning that 11.8 of every 1,000 people experienced at least one violent victimization. This rate translates to about 3.1 million people. Because most of these people were victims of simple assault,

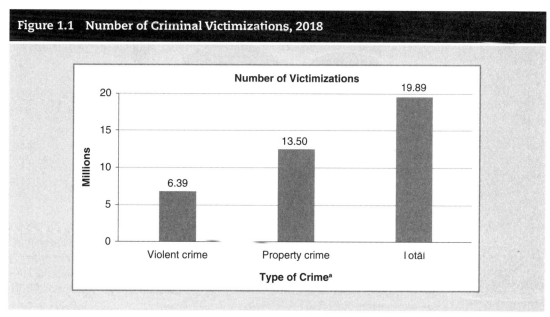

Figure 1.1   Number of Criminal Victimizations, 2018

a Violent crime: rape/sexual assault, robbery, aggravated and simple assault; property crime: personal larceny, household burglary and larceny, motor vehicle theft

Source: Morgan and Oudekerk (2019).

the NCVS also reports the prevalence rate for serious violent crime (rape/sexual assault, robbery, and aggravated assault, but not simple assault). In 2018, this rate was 0.50% (or 50 of every 1,000 people), equal to more than 1.2 million victims of serious violent crime. Meanwhile, 7.27% of all households (equal to 9.1 million households) in 2018 experienced at least one property victimization.

Because many of these individuals and households experience more than one victimization annually, the total number of victimizations in 2018 reached almost 20 million, as reported in Figure 1.1. U.S. victimization rates for violent and property crime are higher than those in many of the world's democracies.

The Cost of Crime

All these crimes are very costly for their victims. Here we should talk about three kinds of costs. The first cost involves *emotional health*. Crime victims often become fearful of additional victimization. Violent crime victims may limit their movements outside of home, and property crime victims may buy home security measures to reduce their chances of new victimization. Victims of rape, sexual assault, and other kinds of assault may experience many emotional effects, including post-traumatic stress disorder and depression. The second cost involves *physical health*. Homicide victims lose their lives, and victims of nonfatal violent crime often suffer injuries, both serious and minor, that require them to seek medical care and to be hospitalized. Many books, studies, and reports describe in detail the emotional and physical harms that crime victims experience (Daigle 2018; Karmen 2016).

The third cost is *economic*. Violent crime victims may miss work because of their physical injuries or emotional trauma, and the families of homicide victims lose any earnings that the victim may have acquired had the homicide not occurred. Many violent crime victims also incur medical bills that are not totally covered by any medical insurance they may have. Property crime victims lose the value of whatever items are stolen from them; many do not have homeowner or rental insurance that covers all their losses. These tangible costs of criminal victimization are estimated at about $100 billion annually (Wright and Vicneire 2010). Taking into account all these emotional, physical, and economic costs, it becomes very clear how costly crime is to Americans across the nation.

The Cost of Criminal Justice

In addition to the cost of crime to victims, there is another huge cost, and that is the cost of the criminal justice system: police and other law enforcement, the criminal courts, and corrections (jails and prisons). The U.S. criminal justice system costs the federal, state, and local governments tens of billions of dollars annually. Using the latest figures available at the time of this writing, Figure 1.2 summarizes these costs for the three stages of the criminal justice system: *law enforcement*, *judicial and legal* (criminal courts), and *corrections* at all levels of government (federal, state, local) combined. These costs, more than $283 billion annually, are staggering.

Figure 1.2 The Economic Cost of the Criminal Justice System (2015 data)

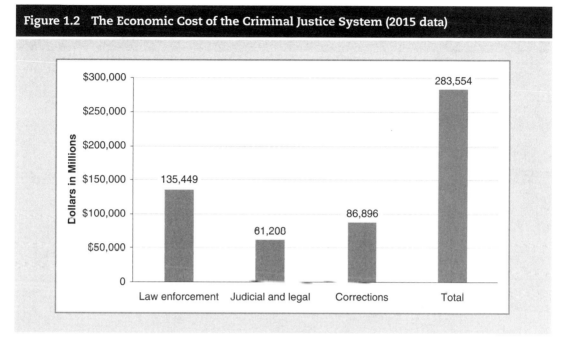

Source: Bronson (2018).

Note: Most recent data available at publication.

The increase in these costs is also staggering. Figure 1.3 shows how criminal justice expenditures have risen since the early 1980s, reflecting the nation's commitment to the get-tough approach. Adjusting for inflation, total expenditures in 2015 were 3 times greater than in 1982.

After the U.S. economy went into a deep recession in 2008, elected officials began taking a new look at the cost of criminal justice. In a rare moment of consensus, conservative and liberal politicians at the state and national levels began agreeing that too many Americans are behind bars (Keller 2015). Because incarceration is so expensive, many states began handing out sentences such as fines, probation, and community service to property offenders and other nonviolent offenders, such as people arrested for drug possession (Porter 2015). Texas, a state not known for being soft on crime, was the first state to implement such reforms on a large scale (Wilson 2014).

As Texas and the other sentencing-reform states recognize, public officials need to think beyond mass incarceration as they ponder how to reduce crime in the best ways possible. Fortunately, a wide body of social science research points to alternatives that would allow the nation to achieve greater "bang for the buck" in reducing crime as it spends its precious dollars. This body of research, of course, is the subject of this book.

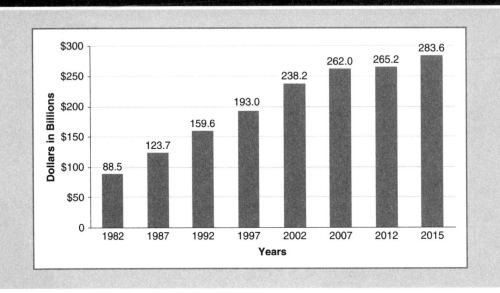

Source: Bronson (2018), Kyckelhahn (2011, 2015).

Note: Most recent data available at publication.

UNAFFORDABLE JUSTICE: THE FAILURE OF MASS INCARCERATION

Because crime has dropped dramatically after peaking in the early 1990s, it is tempting to conclude that the get-tough approach produced the crime decline. If so, perhaps mass incarceration is working and the get-tough approach's huge costs are justified. Unfortunately, this cause-and-effect scenario is more myth than reality, for the get-tough approach has almost certainly *not* reduced crime beyond at most a small degree. If so, the huge costs of this approach are not very cost-effective. In fact, it makes more sense to consider them, as well as the get-tough approach underlying them, as very cost-*ineffective*.

This provocative conclusion reflects a large body of social science evidence pointing to the failure of the get-tough approach and mass incarceration to reduce crime significantly and cost-effectively. To quote the title of this section, this means that the United States currently has a situation of "unaffordable justice." Mass incarceration and the get-tough approach are unaffordable not only for economic reasons but also because they have produced many types of social costs damaging the lives of millions of Americans, many of them people of color. Social science evidence again documents these social costs, which are termed **collateral consequences**.

To help reinforce why alternatives to mass incarceration are necessary, it will be useful to review two kinds of evidence: (1) the evidence on mass incarceration's failure to reduce crime significantly and cost-effectively and (2) the evidence on mass incarceration's collateral consequences. To provide a context for this review, we first discuss how and why the United States developed its get-tough approach and mass incarceration policy.

The Growth of Incarceration

Once upon a time, the United States had incarceration rates that were about average for the world's democracies. This was before the early 1970s, which was when incarceration began exploding in the United States. Therein lies a tale that is worth recounting.

Before the 1970s, the U.S. prison incarceration rate (the number of prison inmates per 100,000 U.S. population) had been stable since the 1930s (Travis et al. 2014). The rate throughout this four-decade period hovered around 110 inmates per 100,000 population. As UCR-measured crime rates rose and fell somewhat at various times during this period, the incarceration rate chugged along, never changing by more than a very small amount from year to year. Even when the crime rate doubled during the 1960s, the incarceration rate did not rise. In fact, it did the opposite, falling from 117 at the beginning of that decade to 97 at the end of the decade.

The U.S. incarceration rate of this early period was about average among the world's democracies: somewhat higher than many nations' rates but somewhat lower than other nations' rates. This was because the United States followed the same correctional policies as did the other democracies. These policies involved reasonable (i.e., not overly long) prison terms for the worst offenders and most dangerous criminals, along with the use of non-*carceral* (the adjective for *incarceration*) sentences whenever possible. In the area of correctional policy, the United States was not at all exceptional among the world's democracies.

This situation began to change during the 1970s. Although, as just noted, the incarceration rate declined somewhat during the 1960s even though crime doubled during the 1960s, incarceration rates began to climb after 1972 as crime continued to rise. As Figure 1.4 shows, the incarceration rate soared into the first decade of this century before declining a bit recently due to the prison reforms described earlier.

The United States had more than 2.2 million prison and jail inmates in 2017 (about 1.44 million state and federal prisoners and 745,200 jail inmates), compared with only 360,000 inmates in 1972 (Kaeble and Cowhig 2018). The current number translates to a rate of 698 inmates per 100,000 population and means that about 1% of American adults are now behind bars. Even with the recent slight decrease in incarceration, the current rate of 698 is still the highest of any nation in the world and almost 5 times higher than the rate for other Western democracies and 10 times higher than the rate for some democracies (see Figure 1.5).

In fact, although the United States has only 5% of the world's population, it confines 25% of all the world's prisoners. This is true even though the U.S. crime rate is only

Figure 1.4 Incarceration Rate, 1972 to 2016 (number of prisoners per 100,000 population)

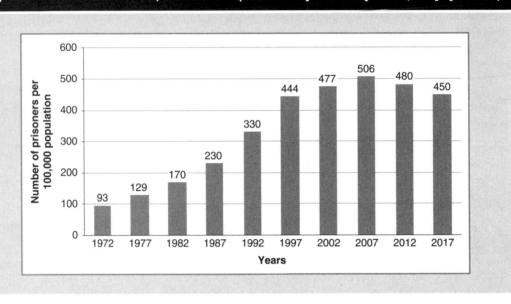

Source: Bronson and Carson (2019), Bureau of Justice Statistics (1982, 2018).

Figure 1.5 Incarceration Rates for Selected Western Democracies (number of inmates per 100,000 population)

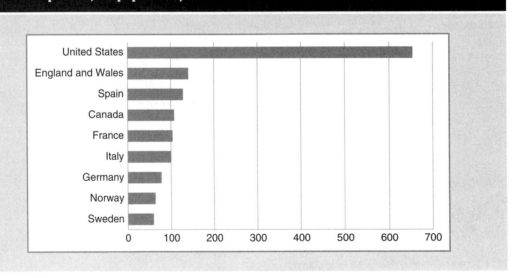

Source: International Centre for Prison Studies (2019).

about average or perhaps slightly higher than average among democracies. A report by the National Research Council underscores the exceptional nature of the U.S. prison boom: "The growth in incarceration rates in the United States over the past 40 years is historically unprecedented and internationally unique" (Travis et al. 2014:2).

In addition to its 2.2 million prison and jail inmates, the United States has another 3.8 million American adults on probation and 870,000 on parole. The total number of adults under *correctional supervision*—in prison or jail or on probation or parole—exceeds 6.7 million (Kaeble and Cowhig 2018). This number equals about 3% of all adults, a percentage that is again far, far higher than any other nation.

Explaining the Prison Boom

The terms **prison boom** and **incarceration boom** are commonly used to describe the huge increase in incarceration since the 1970s. Why did the prison boom occur? An immediate answer is that the prison boom resulted from rising crime during the 1970s. Because crime was rising, correctional policy became more punitive and the get-tough approach developed. This approach involved mandatory imprisonment and mandatory minimum prison sentences for a variety of crimes and, more generally, longer prison terms than were imposed previously (Pfaff 2017). It is fair to say that the 1970s' rising crime rate created the impetus for this change in correctional policy and thus for the prison boom.

However, the situation is more complicated than this simple account suggests, because the get-tough approach and prison boom were *not* inevitable consequences of the rising crime rate. Historically speaking, rising crime sometimes produces rising incarceration, and sometimes it does *not* produce rising incarceration. In this regard, recall that U.S. incarceration decreased somewhat during the 1960s even though crime rose during the 1960s. During that decade, the United States chose to continue to follow the rehabilitation ideal guiding correctional policy. Since the 1970s, crime rates rose and fell at various times, and yet incarceration continued to rise steadily before its recent slight decline. These patterns suggest that there is no clear link between crime rates and incarceration rates (Raphael 2009). As the National Research Council report cited earlier explained, "Over the four decades when incarceration rates steadily rose, U.S. crime rates showed no clear trend: the rate of violent crime rose, then fell, rose again, then declined sharply. The best single proximate explanation of the rise in incarceration is not rising crime rates, but the policy choices made by legislators to greatly increase the use of imprisonment as a response to crime" (Travis et al. 2014:3). As this explanation suggests, the rising crime rate of the 1970s may have indeed led to the get-tough approach and prison boom, but this consequence was by no means inevitable.

Evidence for this conclusion comes from the experience of other democracies. Crime rate trends in most of these nations mirrored the U.S. trend: Crime rates rose from the 1960s into the mid-1990s. Even so, incarceration rates in these nations generally did not rise, and some nations' rates even declined (Lappi-Seppälä 2008).

In the face of rising crime rates, then, the United States consciously chose to follow a more punitive correctional policy, while other democracies chose not to do so. This history led criminologist Michael Tonry (2007:3) to observe, "Any assumption or hypothesis, therefore, that there is a simple, common, or invariant relationship between crime patterns that befall a country and the number of people it confines is wrong. Faced with similar crime trends, different countries react in different ways." Reflecting this argument, criminologist William Spelman (2009:73) says that "nothing was inevitable about the prison buildup in the United States" because crime could have been "dealt with through alternative means."

Because the United States followed a different path than other democracies in dealing with rising crime after the 1960s, the key question then becomes *why* the United States made this choice. Criminologists' answer to this question highlights the role played by racial prejudice (Gottschalk 2006; Hinton 2016; Simon 2007). According to this account, Richard Nixon and other Republican Party officials used racially coded, alarmist statements to paint African Americans as violent criminals in an effort to win votes from fearful whites (Travis et al. 2014). The news media covered these statements heavily and also carried many stories about violent crime committed by African Americans against whites. These developments aroused whites' racial prejudices, heightened public concern about crime, and created an atmosphere that led to the get-tough approach and the prison boom. During the 1980s, politicians' statements and news media coverage about crack cocaine similarly highlighted African American involvement. This racialized treatment provoked harsh sentencing of drug offenders, contributing further to mass incarceration (Alexander 2012; Mauer 2006; Provine 2007).

In sum, the growing crime rate of the 1960s and 1970s set the stage for the get-tough approach, prison boom, and mass incarceration in the United States, but this result was not inevitable, as other nations reacted to their own growing crime rates quite differently. Racial prejudice led the United States to adopt a more punitive reaction to its growing crime rate, and this reaction in turn led to the prison boom and mass incarceration.

Beyond this regrettable origin of the prison boom, mass incarceration has proven damaging in the ways mentioned earlier. To recall, these problems include the following:

- Mass incarceration has not reduced crime beyond at most a small degree.

- The small impact of mass incarceration on the crime rate has not been cost-effective.

- Mass incarceration has created collateral consequences affecting millions of Americans, with a disproportionate effect on African Americans and Latinos.

The next section discusses the limited crime-reduction impact of mass incarceration and this limited impact's huge expense, the first two problems just listed. After discussing these problems, we then summarize the evidence on collateral consequences.

The Limited Crime-Reduction Impact of Mass Incarceration

In assessing whether and to what degree mass incarceration has led to the crime decline of the past few decades, we first need to introduce two criminological concepts, *incapacitation* and *deterrence*. **Incapacitation** refers to any impact of mass incarceration (or imprisonment generally) on the crime rate because convicted offenders are behind bars and not able to commit crimes against the public. If mass incarceration has reduced the crime rate, then, it may be because mass incarceration prevents more than 2.2 million offenders every year from being free to victimize the public. If so, mass incarceration may have a significant *incapacitation effect*. Meanwhile, **deterrence** refers to any impact on the crime rate because potential offenders do not want to risk being arrested, convicted, and incarcerated. If deterrence works, longer and more certain prison terms should deter potential offenders from committing crime.

With so many people behind bars, it might make sense to think that mass incarceration must be having a strong incapacitation effect. Because almost no one wants to go to prison, it also might make sense to think that mass incarceration should have a strong deterrent effect. However, certain conceptual issues suggest that any incapacitation or deterrent effect of mass incarceration must be small at best. We discuss these issues for incapacitation here but reserve our discussion of deterrence issues for the next chapter's review of cognitive processes and criminal behavior.

Conceptual Issues Regarding Incapacitation

Four issues point to only a small incapacitation effect, if that, of mass incarceration. A first issue is one of numbers, or rather two sets of numbers: the number of annual crimes and the number of people incarcerated for these crimes. Simply put, only a small fraction of all serious violent and property crimes leads to someone going to prison. This situation is called the **funnel effect** in criminal justice. Many crimes enter the top of the funnel, and only a few offenders enter prison at the bottom of the funnel (Walker 2015).

For example, in 2017 the United States experienced almost 15.4 million violent and property crime felonies according to the NCVS (rape/sexual assault, aggravated assault, robbery, burglary, motor vehicle theft, theft) and UCR (homicide) (FBI 2018; Morgan and Truman 2018). Yet only about 244,000 people entered state prisons that year for these felonies (Bronson and Carson 2019). Doing a little math, about 1.6% of all the felonies led to someone entering state prison, meaning that about 98.4% of the felonies did *not* result in imprisonment. Because each new prisoner has committed an estimated 20 felonies per year on average (Piquero and Blumstein 2007), the new state prisoners in 2017 may have accounted for about 30% to 32% of annual felonies. This new figure still implies that some 70% of felonies do *not* result in anyone going to prison. If at least 7 out of every 10 felonies do not lead to prison incarceration, the incapacitation effect of mass incarceration cannot be very high, as most offenders are still not behind bars and still committing new crimes.

A second issue concerns the fact that the worst, *chronic offenders* (also called *habitual offenders*) are already likely to be imprisoned, because they commit so many crimes that they eventually get arrested and incarcerated. As the prison boom locked up so many more criminals, lower-level intermittent offenders increasingly became the new people entering prison. This means that any incapacitation effect of mass incarceration became smaller over time because new prisoners were more likely to have committed fewer offenses. As criminologist Samuel Walker (2015:172) observes, "As we lock up more people, we quickly skim off the really high-rate offenders and begin incarcerating more of the less serious offenders. Because they average far fewer crimes per year, . . . we get progressively lower returns in crime reduction."

A third issue involves the fact that groups of offenders commit much crime, particularly drug crimes. If one of these offenders is imprisoned, the remaining offenders are still free to continue committing their group crimes. They may even recruit a new person to replace their incarcerated colleague. This so-called *replacement effect* reduces any incapacitation effect for these group crimes. For this reason, incarceration may actually have no incapacitation effect for drug crimes (Piquero and Blumstein 2007).

The final issue involves the age of prisoners. Because the get-tough approach involved longer prison terms, the average age of prisoners is now much older than before mass incarceration developed. However, offenders tend to "age out" of crime. Criminal offending peaks when people are in their late teens and early 20s and then declines as they grow older (Goldstein 2015), with many inmates staying in prison far beyond the prime offending ages. These prisoners no longer pose a threat to society because they are simply too old to be committing new crimes. Criminologist Daniel Nagin (1998:364) calls these inmates "poor candidates for incarceration from an incapacitation perspective."

All these issues mean that any incapacitation effect of mass incarceration should be modest at best. Research on the actual impact of mass incarceration on the crime rate confirms this pessimistic appraisal, as we will now discuss.

The Actual Impact of Mass Incarceration: Small and Expensive

Many criminological studies assess the impact of mass incarceration on the crime rate. Much of this research focuses on the huge drop in U.S. crime beginning in the early 1990s and lasting for the next two decades. Because the incarceration rate was climbing during this period, many observers said that mass incarceration was playing a large role in the crime drop. However, several kinds of evidence suggest otherwise (Travis et al. 2014).

First, even though incarceration rates rose constantly after the 1970s through the end of the 2000s, crime did not constantly decline during this period. Instead, it rose in the 1970s, fell in the early 1980s, rose again in the late 1980s and early 1990s, and then began plummeting. These trends show that incarceration rates and crime rates do not always track in the way they should if rising incarceration is reducing crime. The fact that incarceration rates and crime rates finally began tracking in the way they "should" after the early 1990s thus does not prove that crime was falling because incarceration was rising.

Second, state incarceration rates and crime rates during the 1990s also did not track well. In fact, crime rates tended to decline *less* in the states where incarceration rates rose the most (Gainsborough and Mauer 2000). Conversely, the states with smaller increases in their incarceration rates tended to have the largest crime declines. During the 2000s, incarceration and crime rates again did not track well. Three states—California, New Jersey, and New York—decreased their prison populations by about 25% and still saw their crime rates decline more than the national average (Mauer and Ghandnoosh 2014).

Third, Canada's crime rate also fell after the early 1990s, even though Canada did *not* increase its incarceration rate (Webster and Doob 2007). Canada's experience suggests that some other set of factors was leading to the crime drop in North America during the 1990s, and it even suggests that crime would have declined even if the United States had not been practicing mass incarceration (Zimring 2006).

Finally, and perhaps most significantly, several highly technical studies find that mass incarceration has only a small impact on crime and that this impact is very expensive for the small amount of crime reduced. These studies find that a 10% increase in the national incarceration rate produces, because of deterrence or more likely incapacitation, a decrease in crime rate between only about 1% and 4% (Levitt 1996; Marvell and Moody 1994; Spelman 2006; Western 2006). Other studies conclude that rising incarceration actually has no effect on the crime rate (DeFina and Arvanites 2002; Kovandzic and Vieraitis 2006).

If a 10% increase in the incarceration rate produces at most a crime decline of between 1% and 4%, this conclusion can be used to construct a cost-benefit analysis of mass incarceration and crime rates. For example, there are now almost 1.5 million state and federal prisoners. If we increase this number by 10%, or nearly 150,000 inmates, we can reduce crime between 1% and 4%. Because each prisoner costs a national average of about $31,300 for all prison-related expenses (Mai and Subramanian 2017), adding 160,000 inmates would cost the state and federal governments almost $5 billion annually. Prison overcrowding would necessitate the building of new prisons to house these 150,000 inmates. If 150 new prisons with 1,000 beds were built at $100 million each, construction costs would total $15 billion (assuming simplistically that this could be done without construction loans and their interest charges). Thus, an expenditure of many billions of dollars would be needed to achieve a crime decline of at most 4% and perhaps as little as 1%. This is not a cost-effective impact.

Focusing on the 1990s, criminologists conclude that the rising incarceration of that decade accounted for at most one-fourth of the crime decline during that decade and perhaps as little as one-tenth (Rosenfeld 2006; Spelman 2006; Western 2006). This limited impact came at such a high economic cost that these criminologists call incarceration "an incredibly inefficient means of reducing crime" and say that mass incarceration takes dollars away from crime prevention measures involving education and employment opportunities and other areas that would reduce crime more effectively and cost-efficiently (Rosenfeld 2006; Spelman 2006:124). In this regard, one researcher calculated that mass incarceration prevented 100 homicides annually during the 1990s at an annual corrections cost of $1 billion, or $10 million for each prevented homicide. Commenting on this high cost, the researcher asked, "Would we be better off if the $1 billion were spent on preschool programs, parent training, vocational training, drug treatment, and other promising prevention programs?" (Rosenfeld 2006:151).

Drawing on the kinds of evidence just presented and on its own new analysis of data since 2000, a report by the Brennan Center for Justice at the New York University

School of Law found that increasing incarceration actually "has had no effect on the drop in violent crime in the past 24 years" and has accounted for "*less than 1 percent* of the decline in property crime this century" (Roeder et al. 2015:15; emphasis in original). The report concluded that "incarceration in the U.S. has reached a level where it no longer provides a meaningful crime reduction benefit" (p. 15).

Collateral Consequences of Mass Incarceration

We have seen that mass incarceration reduces crime by at most a very small amount, and perhaps not at all, and does so at an incredibly high economic cost. As noted earlier, mass incarceration also has social costs called *collateral consequences* (Kirk and Wakefield 2018). These consequences reinforce the need to develop alternatives to mass incarceration.

The Opportunity Cost of Mass Incarceration

Opportunity cost is an economics term that refers to the loss of some potential gain or advantage when one alternative is pursued instead of other, more promising and cost-effective alternatives. Mass incarceration has a huge opportunity cost. The U.S. correctional system costs some $87 billion annually and imprisons Americans at a rate almost 5 times higher than any other democracy and 10 times higher than some democracies (see Figure 1.5). Because the United States imprisons many hundreds of thousands of offenders more than it needs to imprison to ensure public safety, mass incarceration costs billions of dollars more annually than it needs to cost. These dollars could instead be spent far more wisely on the crime prevention policies, programs, and practices that are this book's focus. Because incarceration reduces crime by at most a very small amount, every dollar spent on prevention strategies reduces crime by a much larger amount than every dollar spent on corrections (Greenwood 2006). In short, mass incarceration has diverted much money from efforts that would be more effective in preventing crime.

Families and Communities

Mass incarceration harms families and communities (Kirk and Wakefield 2018). Recall that new prisoners today are more likely than those in the past to be lower-level intermittent offenders. These prisoners are more likely than their earlier counterparts to be suitable spouses, partners, and parents. The loved ones they leave behind when they enter prison or jail suffer from the loss of their companionship and influence. More than 1.5 million children have had a parent behind bars, and the experience of having a parent in prison affects these children tremendously. They are more likely to commit delinquency, to have problems in school, and to experience anxiety and other psychological problems.

Urban communities also suffer from the imprisonment of so many of their residents (mostly young males) and from the return to their streets of offenders from prison. Some 600,000 prisoners are released back to their communities every year (Carson and Golinelli 2014). They arrive home with few prospects for employment, mental health problems, and alcohol and/or other drug problems. Many have a history of being physically and/or sexually abused. This wave of released prisoners adds to their communities' poverty and unemployment rates and weakens them in other ways. To quote the subtitle of a book on this subject, "Mass incarceration makes disadvantaged neighborhoods worse" (Clear 2007).

Racial and Ethnic Inequality

More than 3% of African American males are currently in prison, a figure that rises to almost 7% of African American males in their early 30s (Carson and Anderson 2016). About 1% of Latino males of all ages are in prison. By contrast, only 0.5% of white males of all ages are in prison. African American males are thus 6 times more likely than white males to be incarcerated in prison, and Latino males are twice as likely to be incarcerated. Although women compose only about 7% of all prisoners, African American women are still 2.2 times more likely than white women to be incarcerated, and Latinas are 1.3 times more likely to be incarcerated. As these comparisons suggest, the get-tough approach and mass incarceration, and perhaps especially the legal war against drugs, have disproportionately affected African Americans and Latinos (Alexander 2012; Tonry and Melewski 2008). African Americans use illegal drugs at an overall rate equal to or lower than whites but are far more likely than whites to be arrested, convicted, and imprisoned for drug offenses.

In addition to subjecting so many African Americans and Latinos to the corrections system, mass incarceration has other racial/ethnic impacts. First, because so many African Americans and Latinos now have prison records, mass incarceration makes it more difficult for them to find employment and thus worsens their race-related economic inequality (Western 2006).

Second, almost every state prohibits convicted felons from voting while in prison, and many states prohibit them from voting even after release from prison. This problem is called **felony disenfranchisement** (Manza and Uggen 2008). Some 6.1 million Americans cannot vote for these reasons, compared with fewer than 1.2 million in 1980. This problem again has a disproportionate racial impact, as nearly 8% of African Americans (equal to 2.2 million people) cannot vote because of their criminal records. In a few states, more than one-fifth of African American adults cannot vote (Chung 2016). Because African Americans are very likely to vote for Democratic Party candidates, their felony disenfranchisement has probably affected the outcomes of several U.S. Senate elections and even the 2000 presidential election that Republican George W. Bush won by beating Democrat Al Gore in Florida by an extremely narrow margin. Because disenfranchisement marginalizes ex-convicts and contributes to their social isolation and alienation, it may also make them more likely to commit new crimes (Uggen and Manza 2004), a result that again disproportionately involves African American offenders.

In view of the high cost of mass incarceration, its low or null impact on the crime rate, and its many collateral consequences, a reasonable alternative to the get-tough approach is sorely needed. The public health model, discussed in the next chapter, offers such an alternative. This model holds great promise for achieving crime reduction more effectively and cost-efficiently than the get-tough approach and without collateral consequences.

CONCLUSION

Crime continues to be a significant problem in the United States despite a large crime drop since the early 1990s. The nation spends nearly $300 billion annually dealing with crime. By following its get-tough approach, the United States has implemented a policy of mass incarceration that is unique in the democratic world. Mass incarceration is not cost-effective and has incurred many collateral consequences.

A final word is in order before moving on. As you probably realize, this book focuses on violent crime and property crime, as do most discussions of crime prevention. Along with certain other offenses such as illegal gun possession and illegal drug use and selling, violent and property crime are commonly called **street crime** (a term that includes violent and property crimes that do not literally occur on a street) or **conventional crime**. These terms distinguish these offenses from another type of crime, commonly called **white-collar crime**, that is committed by corporations; physicians, attorneys, and other professionals; and many other individuals in the course of their occupations.

Space limitations prevent a detailed discussion of white-collar crime, which is covered fully in other books (Payne 2017; Van Slyke et al. 2016). Still, the cost of white-collar crime to American society is considerable. Some estimates put the annual economic cost of white-collar crime at almost $600 billion and the annual number of deaths from white-collar crime (e.g., from dangerous or unhealthy workplaces) at almost 100,000 (Barkan 2018). Recalling from our earlier discussion that the annual tangible cost of street crime is "only" $100 billion, it becomes clear that white-collar crime is far more costly in economic terms than street crime. The annual number of estimated deaths from white-collar crime also far exceeds the number of homicides, which was 17,284 in 2017.

In both these respects, white-collar crime is far more costly to the nation than street crime. Because the nation is much more concerned about street crime than white-collar crime, though, most studies and discussions of crime prevention focus on street crime. Reflecting this focus, this book also concerns itself with the prevention of street crime, while acknowledging the need to also prevent and reduce white-collar crime.

SUMMARY

1. The costs of crime and victimization continue to be considerable even though the crime rate is much lower than its peak in the early 1990s.

2. The United States spends nearly $300 billion annually on the components of its criminal justice system: law enforcement, the judicial system, and corrections. Crime victims incur $100 billion in tangible costs annually.

3. To fight crime, the United States has followed a get-tough approach since the 1970s involving longer and more certain prison sentences for violent and property crime and for drug offenses.

4. This approach has led to a rate of incarceration that is the highest in the world and at least 5 times higher than that of other democracies.

5. Mass incarceration has only a small impact on the crime rate, and this impact is not cost-effective.

6. Mass incarceration also has caused many types of collateral consequences involving negative impacts for families, children, and communities. These impacts have fallen disproportionately on African Americans and Latinos.

KEY TERMS

collateral consequences 8

conventional crime 18

dark figure of crime 4

deterrence 13

felony disenfranchisement 17

funnel effect 13

get-tough approach 3

hidden crimes 4

incapacitation 13

incarceration boom 11

mass incarceration 3

National Crime Victimization Survey (NCVS) 5

Part I crimes 4

Part II crimes 4

prevalence rate 5

prison boom 11

street crime 18

Uniform Crime Reports (UCR) 4

white-collar crime 18

REFERENCES

Alexander, Michelle. 2012. *The New Jim Crow: Mass Incarceration in the Age of Colorblindness*. New York, NY: The New Press.

Barkan, Steven E. 2018. *Criminology: A Sociological Understanding*. Upper Saddle River, NJ: Pearson.

Bronson, Jennifer. 2018. *Justice Expenditure and Employment Extracts, 2015—Preliminary*. Washington, DC: Bureau of Justice Statistics. Retrieved August 25, 2019 (https://www.bjs .gov/index.cfm? ty=pbdetail&iid=6310).

Bronson, Jennifer, and E. Ann Carson. 2019. *Prisoners in 2017*. Washington, DC: Bureau of Justice Statistics, U.S. Department of Justice.

Bureau of Justice Statistics. 1982. "Prisoners 1925–81." Retrieved August 25, 2019 (https:// www.bjs.gov/content/pub/pdf/p2581.pdf).

Bureau of Justice Statistics. 2018. "Corrections Statistical Analysis Tool (CSAT)—Prisoners." Retrieved August 25, 2019 (http://www.bjs .gov/index.cfm? ty=nps).

Carson, E. Ann, and Elizabeth Anderson. 2016. *Prisoners in 2015*. Washington, DC: Bureau of Justice Statistics.

Carson, E. Ann, and Daniela Golinelli. 2014. *Prisoners in 2012: Trends in Admissions and Releases, 1991–2012*. Washington, DC: Bureau of Justice Statistics, U.S. Department of Justice.

Chung, Jean. 2016. *Felony Disenfranchisement: A Primer*. Washington, DC: The Sentencing Project.

Clear, Todd R. 2007. *Imprisoning Communities: How Mass Incarceration Makes Disadvantaged*

Neighborhoods Worse. New York, NY: Oxford University Press.

Daigle, Leah E. 2018. *Victimology: The Essentials.* Thousand Oaks, CA: Sage.

DeFina, Robert H., and Thomas M. Arvanites. 2002. "The Weak Effect of Imprisonment on Crime: 1971–1998." *Social Science Quarterly* 83: 635–653.

Federal Bureau of Investigation. 2019. *Crime in the United States, 2018.* Washington, DC: Author.

Gainsborough, Jenni, and Marc Mauer. 2000. *Diminishing Returns: Crime and Incarceration in the 1990s.* Washington, DC: The Sentencing Project.

Goldstein, Dana. 2015. "Too Old to Commit Crime?" The Marshall Project. March 20. Retrieved August 25, 2019 (https://www .themarshallproject.org/2015/03/20/too-old-to-commit-crime).

Gottschalk, Marie. 2006. *The Prison and the Gallows: The Politics of Mass Incarceration in America.* Cambridge, UK: Cambridge University Press.

Greenwood, Peter W. 2006. *Changing Lives: Delinquency Prevention as Crime-Control Policy.* Chicago, IL: University of Chicago Press.

Hinton, Elizabeth. 2016. *From the War on Poverty to the War on Crime: The Making of Mass Incarceration in America.* Cambridge, MA: Harvard University Press.

International Centre for Prison Studies. 2019. *World Prison Brief.* Retrieved August 25, 2019 (http:// www.prisonstudies.org/world-prison-brief).

Kaeble, Danielle, and Mary Cowhig. 2018. *Correctional Populations in the United States, 2016.* Washington, DC: Bureau of Justice Statistics, U.S. Department of Justice.

Karmen, Andrew. 2016. *Crime Victims: An Introduction to Victimology.* Belmont, CA: Cengage.

Keller, Bill. 2015. "Prison Revolt." *The New Yorker.* June 29. Retrieved August 25, 2019 (http:// www.newyorker.com/magazine/2015/06/29/ prison-revolt).

Kirk, David S., and Sara Wakefield. 2018. "Collateral Consequences of Punishment: A Critical Review and Path Forward." *Annual Review of Criminology* 1: 171–194.

Kovandzic, Tomislav V., and Lynne M. Vieraitis. 2006. "The Effect of County-Level Prison Population Growth on Crime Rates." *Criminology & Public Policy* 5: 213–244.

Kyckelhahn, Tracey. 2011. *Justice Expenditures and Employment, FY 1982–2007—Statistical Tables.* Washington, DC: Bureau of Justice Statistics.

Kyckelhahn, Tracey. 2015. *Justice Expenditure and Employment Extracts, 2012—Preliminary.* Washington, DC: Bureau of Justice Statistics. Retrieved August 25, 2019 (http://www.bjs.gov/ index.cfm? ty=pbdetail&iid=5239).

Langton, Lynn, Marcus Berzofsky, Christopher Krebs, and Hope Smiley-McDonald. 2012. *Victimizations Not Reported to the Police, 2006–2010.* Washington, DC: Bureau of Justice Statistics, U.S. Department of Justice.

Lappi-Seppälä, Tapio. 2008. "Trust, Welfare, and Political Culture: Explaining Differences in National Penal Policies." *Crime and Justice: A Review of Research* 37: 313–387.

Levitt, Steven. 1996. "The Effect of Prison Population Size on Crime Rates: Evidence From Prison Overcrowding Litigation." *Quarterly Journal of Economics* 111: 319–351.

Mai, Chris, and Ram Subramanian. 2017. *Price of Prisons 2015: Examining State Spending Trends, 2010–2015.* New York, NY: Vera Institute of Justice.

Manza, Jeff, and Christopher Uggen. 2008. *Locked Out: Felon Disenfranchisement and American Democracy.* New York, NY: Oxford University Press.

Marvell, Thomas B., and Carlisle E. Moody Jr. 1994. "Prison Population Growth and Crime Reduction." *Journal of Quantitative Criminology* 10(2).

Mauer, Marc. 2006. *Race to Incarcerate.* New York, NY: New Press.

Mauer, Marc, and Nazgol Ghandnoosh. 2014. "Fewer Prisoners, Less Crime: A Tale of Three States." Washington, DC: The Sentencing Project.

Morgan, Rachel E., and Barbara A. Ouderkerk. 2019. *Criminal Victimization, 2018.* Washington, DC: Bureau of Justice Statistics, U.S. Department of Justice.

Nagin, Daniel S. 1998. "Deterrence and Incapacitation." Pp. 345–368 in *The Handbook of Crime and Punishment*, edited by M. Tonry. New York, NY: Oxford University Press.

Payne, Brian K. 2017. *White-Collar Crime: The Essentials.* Thousand Oaks, CA: Sage.

Pfaff, John. 2017. *Locked In: The True Causes of Mass Incarceration and How to Achieve Real Reform.* New York, NY: Basic Books.

Piquero, Alex R., and Alfred Blumstein. 2007. "Does Incapacitation Reduce Crime?" *Journal of Quantitative Criminology* 23: 267–285.

Porter, Nicole D. 2015. *The State of Sentencing 2014: Developments in Policy and Practice.* Washington, DC: The Sentencing Project.

Provine, Doris Marie. 2007. *Unequal Under Law: Race in the War on Drugs.* Chicago, IL: University of Chicago Press.

Raphael, Steven. 2009. "Explaining the Rise in U.S. Incarceration Rates." *Criminology & Public Policy* 8: 87–95.

Roeder, Oliver, Lauren-Brooke Eisen, and Julia Bowling. 2015. *What Caused the Crime Decline?* New York: Brennan Center for Justice, New York University School of Law.

Rosenfeld, Richard. 2006. "Patterns in Adult Homicide: 1980–1995." Pp. 130–163 in *The Crime Drop in America*, edited by A. Blumstein and J. Wallman. Cambridge, UK: Cambridge University Press.

Simon, Jonathan. 2007. *Governing Through Crime: How the War on Crime Transformed American Democracy and Created a Culture of Fear.* New York, NY: Oxford University Press.

Spelman, William. 2006. "The Limited Importance of Prison Expansion." Pp. 97–129 in *The Crime Drop in America*, edited by A. Blumstein and J. Wallman. Cambridge, UK: Cambridge University Press.

Spelman, William. 2009. "Crime, Cash, and Limited Options: Explaining the Prison Boom." *Criminology & Public Policy* 8: 29–77.

Tonry, Michael. 2007. "Determinants of Penal Policies." *Crime and Justice: A Review of Research* 365: 1–48.

Tonry, Michael, and Matthew Melewski. 2008 "The Malign Effects of Drug and Crime Control Policies on Black Americans." *Crime and Justice: A Review of Research* 37: 1–44.

Travis, Jeremy, Bruce Western, and Steve Redburn, eds. 2014. *The Growth of Incarceration in the*

United States: *Exploring Causes and Consequences.* Washington, DC: National Academies Press.

Uggen, Christopher, and Jeff Manza. 2004. "Voting and Subsequent Crime and Arrest: Evidence From a Community Sample." *Columbia Human Rights Law Review* 36: 193–215.

Van Slyke, Shanna, Michael Benson, and Francis Cullen, eds. 2016. *The Oxford Handbook of White-Collar Crime.* New York, NY: Oxford University Press.

Walker, Samuel. 2015. *Sense and Nonsense About Crime, Drugs, and Communities.* Stamford, CT: Cengage Learning.

Webster, Cheryl Marie, and Anthony N. Doob. 2007. "Punitive Trends and Stable Imprisonment Rates in Canada." *Crime and Justice: A Review of Research* 26: 297–369.

Western, Bruce. 2006. *Punishment and Inequality in America.* New York, NY: Russell Sage Foundation.

Wilson, Reid. 2014. "Tough Texas Gets Results by Going Soft on Crime." *Washington Post.* November 27. Retrieved August 25, 2019 (http://www.washingtonpost.com/blogs/govbeat/wp/2014/11/27/tough-texas-gets-results-by-going-softer-on-crime/).

Wright, Emily M., and Malanie J. Vicneire. 2010. "Economic Costs of Victimization." Pp. 344–348 in *Encyclopedia of Victimology and Crime Prevention,* edited by B. S. Fisher and S. P. Lab. Thousand Oaks, CA: Sage.

Zimring, Franklin E. 2006. *The Great American Crime Decline.* New York, NY: Oxford University Press.

2

PUBLIC HEALTH AND THE STUDY OF CRIME PREVENTION

Chapter 1 pointed out several problems with the nation's get-tough policy of crime control that has involved mass incarceration. In response to these problems, many criminologists emphasize the need to prevent crime with alternative strategies that focus on the roots of crime and the many problems (including histories of drug and alcohol abuse, physical and sexual victimization, and mental illness) that offenders already have when they enter prison.

As criminologists considered these strategies during recent decades, many looked to the field of public health for inspiration and insight (Welsh 2005). At the same time, public health scholars began to regard violence as a public health issue and to develop strategies to prevent and reduce violence (Kellerman 1996). The two fields have increasingly converged on the need to prevent crime, with criminologists and public health scholars collaborating on any number of projects (Welsh, Braga, and Sullivan 2014).

Accordingly, this chapter outlines the relevance of the public health model for crime prevention and examines its potential as an effective and more cost-efficient alternative to the get-tough approach. This chapter also reviews the research methods used in criminology, criminal justice, public health, and related fields. This review is appropriate because research lies at the heart of crime

Chapter Outline

Learning Questions

1. What does the public health model emphasize?

2. How has the concept of harm reduction been applied to tobacco use?

3. What are the three levels of prevention in the field of public health?

4. What is the difference between an independent variable and a dependent variable?

(Continued)

(Continued)

5. Which research method offers the best potential for ruling out issues of causal order and spuriousness?

prevention. Most crime prevention efforts potentially make sense because they rest on theories of crime and criminal behavior (as summarized in Chapters 3 and 4) that have been empirically tested. The effectiveness of specific crime prevention efforts has also been empirically assessed. To appreciate the theoretical and practical basis for crime prevention efforts, then, it is important to be familiar with the research methodologies that point to their potential and with certain questions that commonly arise in the research enterprise.

THE PUBLIC HEALTH MODEL

Most readers of this book know someone who has or had cancer, and many readers know several such people. Perhaps these people are still alive, perhaps not. When their cancer was diagnosed, their physicians no doubt did everything possible to help them. Sometimes their efforts succeeded, but sometimes they did not succeed. Regardless of the outcome, we would all agree on the need for the best medical care possible to treat anyone with cancer. This is the standard model of medical care: to treat someone who develops cancer or other health problems.

If we all agree on the need for the best medical care possible, presumably we also all recognize that it is much better yet to prevent someone from getting cancer or another health problem in the first place. If we can prevent their health problem (let's continue to assume cancer), we save them the physical, emotional, and economic difficulties that their cancer will almost certainly cause; we save their friends and loved ones the emotional trauma of knowing someone who is seriously ill; and we save our society the health care expenses and lost wages associated with cancer cases and deaths. Certainly, some people will develop cancer no matter how many preventive measures they take individually (for example, eating a healthy diet and not smoking) and our society takes corporately (for example, via government efforts to reduce air pollution). Still, efforts that effectively prevent cancer nonetheless save much money and much physical and emotional distress in the long run. In short, it is far better to prevent people from getting cancer than to wait and treat them after they do become ill.

The need to prevent health problems (disease, illness, and injury) before they begin is the focus of the field of **public health**. According to the American Public Health Association (2018), "Public health promotes and protects the health of people and the communities where they live, learn, work and play. While a doctor treats people who are sick, those of us working in public health try to prevent people from getting sick or injured in the first place. We also promote wellness by encouraging healthy behaviors." Major public health efforts in the 20th century included the development of vaccinations for polio and other serious diseases, measures that improved motor-vehicle safety, the establishment of healthier workplaces, improvements in hygiene and nutrition for new mothers and babies, and reductions in the use of tobacco. These and other public health efforts have prevented uncountable diseases and illnesses and saved millions of lives in the United States and around the world.

Public health certainly recognizes the need to treat people who already have a health problem. Even if all these people are cured, however, there will always be more people becoming ill or injured and becoming new patients to replace the cured patients. Public health realizes it would be shortsighted to neglect the causes of disease, illness, and injury and to fail to do everything possible to address these causes.

In the field of public health, the causes of disease, illness, and injury include problems in the natural and physical environments, problems in the behavior of individuals, and problems in how individuals interact with one another. Not every health problem can be traced to these larger problems and, to return to our earlier example, certainly not every cancer. Still, many occurrences of disease, illness, and injury do indeed have their roots in these larger problems. Recognizing this fact, public health tries to determine the exact causes of specific health problems and then develop strategies—policies, programs, and practices—to eliminate the causes or, failing that, to at least weaken their impact.

Harm Reduction

Note that the last part of the previous sentence referred to either eliminating the causes of health problems or at least weakening their impact. Public health recognizes that some causes of health problems can be eliminated and in fact have been eliminated (or almost so). To cite just two examples of this success, the development of the smallpox vaccination in the 19th century led to the eventual elimination of smallpox, and the development of the polio vaccination in the 20th century likewise led to the eventual elimination of that disease, or almost so. Despite these successes, public health also recognizes that many causes of health problems cannot be eliminated, at least not in the foreseeable future. For example, although air pollution is a major health problem, we cannot simply wave a magic wand and make air pollution disappear.

For the many causes of health problems that cannot be eliminated easily or at all, public health recognizes the need to *limit* their negative impact. To say this another way, public health focuses on the need to reduce the harm from these causes. This major component of the public health approach is called **harm reduction**. This component reflects the recognition that because many causes of health problems cannot be eliminated, our society should at least strive to reduce the harm to individual and social health arising from them.

A good example of a harm reduction approach involves tobacco use (Pierce, White, and Emery 2012). Tobacco is a slow poison that eventually kills about one-third of all cigarette smokers and other regular tobacco users. When the dangers of tobacco use became known more than a half-century ago, the U.S. public health community realized it would be virtually impossible to make tobacco disappear. Too many people smoked cigarettes or used tobacco in other ways, tobacco was too entrenched in the popular culture, and tobacco companies had too much influence via their ability to spend huge sums of money on advertising and congressional lobbying.

Public health experts thus decided to use a harm reduction strategy involving such steps as public education on the dangers of tobacco use, the raising of cigarette taxes to make smoking more expensive, and the introduction of warning labels on cigarette packages. Many people still smoke, of course, with almost one in five American adults smoking cigarettes regularly. However, the proportion of smokers has dropped considerably from several decades ago, when more than two in five adults smoked regularly. Public health has thus helped greatly reduce the harm caused by tobacco use. Even if it has not eliminated this harm altogether, its harm reduction approach has nonetheless prevented many cases of lung cancer, heart disease, and other health problems arising from tobacco use and, as a result, saved countless lives.

Public Health and Crime Prevention

What is the relevance of this discussion for crime prevention? During the 1970s and especially the 1980s, public health experts turned their attention to violent crime. During the 1980s, homicides killed more than 20,000 Americans annually on average, the number of robberies was as high as 1.4 million annually, and the number of aggravated assaults was as high as 1.8 million annually. Against this frightening backdrop, public health researchers labeled violent crime a major health problem (Hemenway 2009). Their goal was to prevent violent crime before it occurred, rather than just "treating" the offenders who had already committed violence.

This approach led these researchers to examine the causes of violent crime and possible ways of addressing these causes. As noted earlier, criminologists also began to devote more attention to "evidence-based" crime prevention and launched new research to assess the crime-reduction effectiveness of various policies and practices. This book's discussion and advocacy of crime prevention strategies draws heavily on the research of public health scholars, criminologists, and other policy experts.

The Three Levels of Public Health and Crime Prevention

Public health researchers emphasize three levels of causation at which disease, illness, and injury may be prevented or at least have their harm reduced (Schneider 2017). These levels are called the *primary*, *secondary*, and *tertiary* levels. Reflecting these terms, public health researchers speak of *primary prevention*, *secondary prevention*, and *tertiary prevention*, or prevention at the primary level, the secondary level, and the tertiary level, respectively. Crime prevention research also focuses on ways to prevent or reduce crime at these levels. We now discuss these levels in greater detail.

Primary Prevention

In the field of public health, **primary prevention** refers to preventing health problems altogether by addressing features of the social, physical, and natural environments that help generate these problems. For example, air pollution is a major problem in the natural environment that causes much disease and death. Reducing air pollution would thus reduce disease and save lives. Inadequate sanitation (due to lack of bathrooms) is a major problem in the physical environment of low-income nations that also causes much disease and death. Improving sanitation to reduce disease and death is a major primary prevention focus of international agencies such as the World Health Organization. Turning to an example from the social environment, poverty contributes to many types of physical and mental illness (Cockerham 2013). Efforts that successfully reduce poverty would also be very likely to reduce the rate of physical and mental illness among the poor.

Reflecting this public health approach, primary prevention of crime involves efforts to address aspects of the social and physical environments contributing to criminal behavior and victimization. These roots, to be discussed further in Chapter 4, include poverty, joblessness, racial segregation, dilapidation in urban neighborhoods, and male socialization. More generally, primary crime prevention focuses on the social, cultural, and community causes of crime. This form of crime prevention recognizes that some people are more likely to commit crime because they live amid **criminogenic** (crime-causing) conditions in their social and physical environments. Accordingly, many primary prevention efforts focus on improving these conditions to prevent crime. Chapters 5, 6, and 7 discuss primary prevention of crime at much greater length.

Secondary Prevention

Secondary prevention in public health refers to preventing health problems by focusing on the many behaviors and practices that put people at greater risk for becoming ill or sustaining an injury. Our earlier discussion of public health efforts to reduce tobacco use involved an example of secondary prevention because these efforts focus on reducing a risky behavior—cigarette smoking, as well as other kinds of tobacco use. Another example of secondary prevention in public health involves vaccinations. Because low-income children are more likely than wealthier children to not get needed vaccinations, they are more likely to incur serious childhood diseases. Public health experts thus aim to increase the vaccination rates for these children through public education programs and other efforts. A third example of secondary prevention involves motor vehicle accidents. Many fewer people die in these accidents now than 50 years ago because public health experts and other advocates urged that safety features such as seat belts and air bags be installed in every vehicle. For this reason, the Centers for Disease Control and Prevention (1999) has called motor-vehicle safety a "20th century public health achievement."

Secondary prevention of crime similarly involves the behaviors, practices, and situations that put certain people at greater risk for committing crime or becoming victims of crime. Much secondary crime prevention research focuses on the experiences that put *children* at greater risk for growing up to commit delinquency and crime. Because children are involved, these experiences are called *developmental experiences* (or *developmental processes*), to use a term from psychology, and secondary crime prevention is often called *developmental crime prevention*. Chapters 8, 9, and 10 discuss secondary crime prevention, including developmental prevention, in more detail.

Tertiary Prevention

Tertiary means "third," and tertiary prevention is the third level of public health (and crime) prevention. To be more precise, **tertiary prevention** in public health refers to efforts to reduce the consequences of a health problem *after* it has begun. When you visit a physician's office or other health care facility for an illness or injury, the health care professional who treats you is engaging in tertiary prevention. Such prevention thus focuses on people who are already patients. The practice of medicine and the field of public health have certainly made enormous strides over the decades in treating health problems. Many lives are saved now that would have been lost just a decade or two ago, and patients fare better overall now than in earlier years. Tertiary prevention helps more patients now than when you were born and many, many more patients than when your parents or grandparents were born.

If patients are the focus of tertiary prevention in the practice of medicine and in much medical research, then criminals are the focus of tertiary prevention in the field of criminology and in the operation of the criminal justice system. Just as tertiary prevention for health problems focuses on the people (patients) who already have a health problem, tertiary prevention for crime focuses on the people (criminals) who already have a "crime problem." Put another way, tertiary prevention focuses on people who have already committed crimes.

Tertiary prevention is an important aim of the criminal justice system. As this chapter discussed earlier, arrest and imprisonment aim to deter potential offenders from committing crime, and imprisonment aims to keep convicted offenders from committing new crimes against the public while they remain behind bars. Much recent research on tertiary crime prevention involves changes in criminal justice practices and policies to more effectively prevent crime. Chapters 11, 12, and 13 discuss this research in greater detail.

STUDYING CRIME AND CRIME PREVENTION

As noted earlier, this book draws heavily from the research of public health scholars, criminologists, and other policy experts. Sound research is necessary to determine the causes of crime and to assess the actual or potential effectiveness of various crime prevention strategies. This section outlines the strengths and weaknesses of the major research methods that scholars use to study criminal behavior and crime prevention. As you learn about these strengths and weaknesses, you will be better able to assess for yourself the research studies discussed throughout this book.

Before turning to research methodology, we need to define a few terms. The first is *variable*. A **variable** is any factor that can vary from one person to another. Gender is a variable, and so are age, income, religiosity, political views, criminal involvement, and countless other factors. Although we have defined variables as differing from one person to another, variables can also be *ecological* in nature by differing from one geographic unit to another geographic unit: from one city to another city, from one county or state to another county or state, and from one nation to another nation. Crime rates vary among cities, counties, states, and nations, and so do other factors such as education level, gun ownership, and incarceration rates. All such factors are ecological variables.

An **independent variable** is any variable that may affect or influence another variable, called the **dependent variable**. If we find an association between gender and criminality—for example, men are more likely than women to commit homicide—gender is the *independent variable* and the likelihood of committing homicide is the *dependent variable*. The reason for these particular designations should be clear: Gender might very well affect the likelihood of committing homicide (for reasons that need not concern us now), while it is highly unlikely that an inclination to commit homicide can affect gender. As we shall soon see, however, when two variables are associated, it is not always so easy to determine which is the independent variable and which is the dependent variable.

With this terminological diversion out of the way, we now turn to a brief outline of the strengths and weaknesses of the major research methods in criminology and crime prevention.

Survey Research

Survey research is probably the most popular research method in criminology and other fields such as sociology and political science. Such research involves questionnaires administered to people over the phone (*telephone survey*), in person (*face-to-face survey*), by mail (*mailed survey*), or over the Internet (*Internet survey* or *Web survey*). The people who answer the questions on these questionnaires are called **respondents**.

In criminology, many studies analyze data from so-called **self-report surveys**, which ask respondents to indicate whether and how often they have committed various offenses during the past year or some other time frame. Most self-report surveys involve adolescents, although a growing number involve young adults. The surveys of adolescents typically ask about such matters as their relationship with their parents; their grades, school activities, and views about their schooling; and their involvement with any delinquent friends. The answers they give enable self-report surveys to provide important information on the various factors that lead to criminal behavior.

Surveys of crime victims are also important. The best known such survey is the National Crime Victimization Survey (NCVS), discussed in Chapter 1. The NCVS and other victim surveys tell us much about crime rates that the Uniform Crime Reports methodology leaves hidden. Because NCVS respondents are also asked about aspects of their criminal victimization, this and similar surveys also tell us much about where and how criminal victimization occurs and about its economic and social impact on victims.

Surveys have several strengths. One strength is that surveys can ask many questions to gather a good deal of information about their respondents. Another strength is that many surveys are given to random samples of the population of a city, state, or entire nation. This fact means that respondents' answers represent the answers of the population that the sample represents. The ability to *generalize* the respondents' answers to the population is a major strength of surveys that use random samples. A third strength of surveys is that the information they gather can easily be analyzed with statistical software. Surveys thus enable *quantitative analysis*, which is the most popular form of data analysis in criminological research today.

Surveys also have some weaknesses. One weakness is that a good deal of information they gather is rather shallow. For example, adolescents in a self-report survey may be asked a few questions to measure how well they get along with their parents, but these questions barely tap the full complexity of the relationship that adolescents have with their parents.

A second weakness is more important for this book's subject matter. Surveys are not the strongest research method for demonstrating *causation*: whether, when two variables are associated, the presumed independent variable is actually affecting the presumed dependent variable. This problem manifests in two ways, as we now discuss.

Causal Order

The first manifestation is when two variables are associated but, even so, it is not clear which variable is affecting which variable. In our earlier example of gender and the likelihood of committing homicide, there was no question that gender had to be the independent variable and the likelihood of committing homicide had to be the dependent variable. We could thus reasonably assume that gender was affecting homicide behavior, not the other way around. Similarly, if we find that age is associated with frequency of illegal drug use, it is clear that age might affect drug use and that drug use cannot affect age.

But there are many associations between variables in criminology and other fields where the causal order is less clear. This problem is called the **causal order problem**, or, to use a more common phrase, the *chicken or egg problem*. Whatever we call it, this problem is summarized in the familiar saying that "correlation does not mean causation." To illustrate this problem, suppose that we find an association in self-report data between quality of parental relationship and extent of juvenile delinquency: Respondents with worse relationships with their parents are more likely to be delinquent than are those with good relationships with their parents. It is very reasonable to assume here that quality of parental relationship affects the likelihood of delinquency, or, to say this somewhat differently, that quality of parental relationship is the independent variable and extent of delinquency is the dependent variable.

However, it is also possible for delinquency to affect the quality of parental relationship. For example, if an adolescent male commits delinquency for the first time and continues to do so, his parents will probably be very concerned about his new behavior and do their best to discipline him. Various arguments will occur, and relations between the adolescent and his parents will suffer. In short, delinquency has affected the quality of the parental relationship.

So if an analysis using survey data does find an association between the quality of parental relationship and delinquency, which variable is affecting which? Which variable is independent, and which is dependent? To compound the situation, it is also possible that both variables are affecting each other, in what is called a **reciprocal relationship**. For certain pairs of variables, then, causal order is at least somewhat unclear, and **cross-sectional surveys**—those that assess people at one point in time—cannot easily deal with the causal order problem for these sets of variables.

Partly for this reason, criminologists increasingly analyze data from **longitudinal surveys**, those that study the same people over time. For example, if adolescents who are less religious at age 12 are more likely to be drinking alcohol at age 15 (taking all other relevant variables into account), we can reasonably conclude that their early degree of religiosity somehow affected their later alcohol use, as it is impossible for their alcohol use at age 15 to have affected their religiosity at age 12. Here religiosity would be the independent variable and alcohol use the dependent variable. Causal order, then, is a less important problem in longitudinal surveys than in cross-sectional surveys.

Spuriousness

The second type of causation problem in survey research concerns *spuriousness*. **Spuriousness** exists when two variables are associated but only because a third variable, called an **antecedent variable**, is affecting each of the other two variables. For example, there is probably an association between ice cream sales and crime rates: When ice cream sales are higher, crime rates are higher. If we accept this association at first glance, we must think that eating more ice cream somehow causes more crime, perhaps because ice cream eaters get a "sugar high" and become violent. Of course, we could instead think there is a causal order problem with this interpretation and that it is actually crime rates that are prompting higher ice cream sales. Perhaps a rising crime rate makes people so anxious about crime that they pig out on ice cream to help deal with their anxiety!

As you probably realize, this ice cream–crime rate link is actually a *spurious*, or misleading, association, because we have not taken into account the effects of an important antecedent variable: outside temperature. When the weather is warm, ice cream sales are higher, and when the weather is warm, crime rates are also higher. These crime rates are higher *not* because of ice cream consumption but because of other factors, including the fact that people tend to interact more in warm weather, which provides more opportunities for violence to occur (Mares 2013). The initial ice cream–crime rate link becomes spurious when we take into account the effects of the warmness of the weather.

This was a rather silly example to clarify the concept of spuriousness, so let's return to the more realistic example for causal order that we discussed earlier: The worse the parental–adolescent relationship, the higher the delinquency rate. Although the parental relationship generally does affect the likelihood of delinquency, at least part of this association might be spurious because one or more antecedent variables are affecting both the parental relationship and delinquency. In this regard, consider family income as a possible antecedent variable. Without meaning to stereotype, low-income families are more likely because of the stress they experience to have strained relations between parents and adolescents (Conger, Conger, and Martin 2010). Partly because of this stress, but also for some other reasons to be discussed in Chapter 4, these adolescents are more likely to commit delinquency. Family income thus affects both the parental relationship and the likelihood of delinquency. If so, at least some of the initial association found between parental relationship and delinquency may be spurious.

Analyses of survey data typically test for spuriousness by statistically controlling for all possible antecedent variables. Because they do so, they can usually rule out the possibility of spuriousness when they find an association between two variables. However, some *unknown* antecedent variable or variables may still be accounting for this association. For this reason, possible spuriousness often cannot be completely ruled out.

An exception to this latest statement occurs when the independent variable cannot logically have an antecedent variable because nothing can affect the independent variable. A good example here involves age. If we find an association between age and crime, with younger adults more likely than older adults to commit crime, this association cannot be at all spurious, because no variable can affect age. To say this another way, no antecedent variable can exist for age. By the same token, no antecedent variables can exist for gender or race, to cite two other very common independent variables. For almost all other independent variables, however, antecedent variables and thus spuriousness remain a potential concern in survey research.

Qualitative Research

Qualitative research also studies people but in a very different manner from survey research. As the term *qualitative* implies, qualitative research typically does not involve the gathering and analysis of numerical data. Instead, it involves two other methods of gathering information: (1) observing people in the *field*, or in their natural settings (called *field research* or *ethnographic research*), and (2) interviewing individuals one-on-one at length about their views, behaviors, and/or perceptions regarding one or more topics.

Qualitative research is probably less common than survey research in studying the causes of crime, in part because criminals typically, and unsurprisingly, do not want criminologists to observe them or to interview them. Criminologists are also often reluctant to associate with known criminals in this way. Despite these problems, some wonderful criminological studies have been qualitative studies. Criminologists have interviewed active robbers and burglars, illegal drug users, and prison inmates, and they have also interviewed and observed gang members (Carbone-Lopez and Miller 2012; Watkins and Moule 2014). In other very important qualitative research, they have also interviewed crime victims and observed police and prosecutors carrying out their jobs (Campbell, Adams, and Wasco 2009; Weidner and Terrill 2005). These and other studies have contributed significantly to criminological understanding of crime and the criminal justice system. In particular, they provide important information on the causes and dynamics of criminal behavior that aids in the development of crime prevention strategies.

Having said that, we should also note that qualitative research lacks a significant strength of survey research: using a random sample. Because qualitative research typically does not involve a random sample, its results cannot necessarily be generalized beyond the particular group or individuals who are studied qualitatively. If a criminologist studies a gang in Los Angeles for 2 years, can we be certain that the conclusions from this study would automatically apply to any other gang in Los Angeles or to gangs in Denver, Chicago, Atlanta, or New York? Absent some strong reason to believe otherwise, the conclusions probably would generalize to these other gangs, but generalizability is a more salient problem in qualitative research than in survey research that uses random samples.

Experimental Research

Experiments are very common in psychology but less common in criminology and especially sociology. This is a shame, because an important strength of experiments, if they are conducted properly, is that they can almost certainly rule out the problems of causal order and spuriousness. Let's see why this is so.

In a typical experiment, as you might know, subjects are divided into an *experimental group* and a *control group*. Something (this something is called the *experimental condition*) happens to the experimental group that does not happen to the control group. Perhaps most significantly, subjects in the ideal experiment are *randomly* assigned to either the experimental group or the control group. This random assignment rules out the possibility that any differences found between the experimental group and control group *after* the experimental condition is applied could have stemmed from preexisting differences between the subjects before the experiment began. Another way of saying this is that random assignment rules out the possibility of spuriousness. Causal order is also not a problem in experiments, because the experimental condition (the equivalent of the independent variable) occurs *before* the outcome variable (the equivalent of the dependent variable) occurs. Experiments that meet these ideal methodological criteria are called *randomized experiments* or *randomized controlled experiments* (or *randomized trials* or *randomized controlled trials*). They are the "gold standard" of research methodology because neither spuriousness nor causal order is a concern when the data are analyzed.

However, it is often not very possible in the real world of criminological research to carry out randomized controlled experiments, in part because of concerns about public safety. Consider the following hypothetical study. We want to determine whether a 2-year prison term or a 4-year prison term more effectively reduces the rearrest rate for offenders convicted of aggravated assault. Ideally, we would randomly assign these offenders to serve either 2 years or 4 years in prison, with half the offenders serving 2 years and half serving 4 years. If we find a year after each group is released from prison that the 2-year group has a higher rearrest rate than the 4-year group, we can reasonably conclude (without knowing exactly why) that the 4-year term was more effective in reducing **recidivism** (repeat offending) than the 2-year term was, at least during that first year after release. If, on the other hand, we find that the rearrest rate was lower for the 2-year group than for the 4-year group, we can reasonably conclude that the 4-year term was less effective in reducing recidivism.

This would be a very interesting study, but in reality it would be difficult to carry out because legal officials, elected officials, and the public may balk at having half the offenders sentenced to only 2 years in prison. This concern for public safety may make this type of experiment impossible to consider in the first place. Despite this type of problem, an increasing number of crime prevention studies use randomized controlled experiments, with many of these studies focusing on aspects of policing. In drawing conclusions on the best strategies for crime prevention, this book places special emphasis on randomized controlled experiments involving policing, other aspects of crime and criminal justice, or policy interventions at the primary or secondary levels of prevention.

Although experiments can be a powerful research tool for the reasons just stated, they do have a weakness that should be kept in mind: Their results cannot necessarily be generalized to the larger population. As with qualitative research, this is because experiments do not rely on random samples. If a randomized controlled experiment involving police in Chicago shows that a certain new strategy reduces crime rates, can we be sure that this strategy would have the same effect in Philadelphia, Miami, Dallas, or

San Francisco? Unless there is some reason to believe otherwise, this strategy probably would have the same effect regardless of which city uses it (assuming it was implemented properly), but generalizability with experiments in criminological research is still an issue to keep in mind.

Evaluation Research

Evaluation research assesses the effectiveness of a policy or program. It usually does so by comparing outcomes before and after the implementation of a policy or program. In the study of crime prevention, recidivism is a typical outcome that evaluation research assesses. Suppose, for example, that a city establishes new drug treatment services for released prisoners on parole. It might then compare the recidivism rate for released prisoners in the city during the 3-year period before the new services were established with the recidivism rate during the 3-year period after the services were established. If the later recidivism rate is lower than the earlier recidivism rate, that would suggest that the new drug treatment services prevented future criminal behavior.

Although this conclusion might make sense, other factors also might have reduced the later recidivism rate. For example, if the economy improved around the time the drug treatment services were established or if policing strategies became more effective, those types of changes, rather than the drug treatment services, may explain the lower recidivism rate. In practice, it is often difficult in evaluation research to rule out alternative reasons for any outcome differences that are found.

As might be clear from the hypothetical example of drug treatment services, evaluation research resembles an experiment in that it often involves comparison of "before" and "after" outcomes. Some evaluation research involves an actual experiment. If so, this research design helps rule out alternative reasons for any outcome differences. Returning to our drug treatment example, suppose the city randomly assigned parolees to either receive the new drug treatment services or not receive them. These two groups' recidivism rates could then be compared. If the drug treatment group had a lower recidivism rate than the control group, that would suggest that drug treatment services helped reduce recidivism. Other unknown factors might still explain the outcome difference just described, but a conclusion that the drug treatment services "worked" would be reasonable in view of the use of random assignment.

CONCLUSION

The public health model offers a promising alternative to get-tough approaches for preventing and reducing crime. As with health problems, crime may be prevented at the primary, secondary, and tertiary levels. To assess the potential for crime prevention strategies, it is important to be familiar with the advantages and disadvantages of the research methodologies that social scientists use to study crime and crime prevention. Each of these methodologies has its strengths and weaknesses, but together they enable criminologists and public health scholars to better understand the causes of crime and ways to prevent and reduce it.

SUMMARY

1. Public health emphasizes addressing the causes of health problems. A public health approach to crime reduction therefore emphasizes addressing the causes of crime to reduce crime.

2. The three levels of public health prevention are the primary, secondary, and tertiary levels. These levels involve primary prevention, secondary prevention, and tertiary prevention, respectively.

3. Regarding health problems, primary prevention focuses on aspects of the social, physical, and natural environments that contribute to health problems, while secondary prevention focuses on the behaviors and practices that put certain people at greater risk for developing a health problem. Tertiary prevention refers to efforts to reduce the consequences of a health problem after it has begun. A public health approach to crime prevention involves all three levels of prevention.

4. Surveys, qualitative research, and experiments are the main research methodologies that scholars use to study crime and crime prevention. Each methodology has its strengths and weaknesses, but together they enable social scientists to gain much knowledge about the causes of crime and about the potential for various crime prevention strategies.

5. Two particular issues in assessing the results of social research, including research on crime prevention, are causal order and spuriousness. Randomized controlled experiments provide the best way of minimizing these issues, but survey research and qualitative research are still very helpful in understanding why crime occurs and in assessing the effectiveness of crime prevention efforts.

6. Evaluation research assesses the effectiveness of a program or policy. The possibility of alternative explanations sometimes makes it difficult to reach any strong conclusions from evaluation research.

KEY TERMS

antecedent variable 31
causal order problem 30
criminogenic 27
cross-sectional surveys 30
dependent variable 29
evaluation research 34
experiments 32
harm reduction 25

independent variable 29
longitudinal surveys 30
primary prevention 26
public health 24
qualitative research 32
recidivism 33
reciprocal relationship 30
respondents 29

secondary prevention 27
self-report surveys 29
spuriousness 31
survey research 29
tertiary prevention 27
variable 28

REFERENCES

American Public Health Association. 2018. "What Is Public Health?" Retrieved August 29, 2019 (https://www.apha.org/what-is-public-health).

Campbell, R., A. E. Adams, and S. M. Wasco. 2009. "Training Interviewers for Research on Sexual Violence: A Qualitative Study of Rape Survivors' Recommendations for Interview Practice." *Violence Against Women* 15(5): 595–617.

Carbone-Lopez, Kristin, and Jody Miller. 2012. "Precocious Role Entry as a Mediating Factor in Women's Methamphetamine Use: Implications for Life-Course and Pathways Research." *Criminology* 50(1):187–220. doi: 10.1111/j.1745-9125.2011.00248.x.

Centers for Disease Control and Prevention. 1999. "Achievements in Public Health, 1900–1999. Motor-Vehicle Safety: A 20th Century Public Health Achievement." *Morbidity and Mortality Weekly Report* 49(18):369–374.

Cockerham, William C. 2013. *Social Causes of Health and Disease*. Malden, MA: Polity Press.

Conger, Rand D., Katherine J. Conger, and Monica J. Martin. 2010. "Socioeconomic Status, Family Processes, and Individual Development." *Journal of Marriage and Family* 72(3):685–704.

Hemenway, David. 2009. *While We Were Sleeping: Success Stories in Injury and Violence Prevention*. Berkeley: University of California Press.

Kellerman, Arthur. 1996. *Understanding and Preventing Violence: A Public Health Perspective*. Washington, DC: Office of Justice Programs, National Institute of Justice.

Mares, Dennis. 2013. "Climate Change and Crime: Monthly Temperature and Precipitation Anomalies and Crime Rates in St. Louis, Mo 1990–2009." *Crime, Law and Social Change* 59: 185–208.

Pierce, John P., Victoria M. White, and Sherry L. Emery. 2012. "What Public Health Strategies Are Needed to Reduce Smoking Initiation." *Tobacco Control* 21: 258–264.

Schneider, Mary-Jane. 2017. *Introduction to Public Health*. Burlington, MA: Jones and Bartlett.

Watkins, Adam M., and Richard K. Moule, Jr. 2014. "Older, Wiser, and a Bit More Badass? Exploring Differences in Juvenile and Adult Gang Members' Gang-Related Attitudes and Behaviors." *Youth Violence & Juvenile Justice* 12: 121–136.

Weidner, Robert R., and William Terrill. 2005. "A Test of Turk's Theory of Norm Resistance Using Observational Data on Police-Suspect Encounters." *Journal of Research in Crime and Delinquency* 42: 84–109.

Welsh, Brandon C. 2005. "Public Health and the Prevention of Juvenile Criminal Violence." *Youth Violence and Juvenile Justice* 3(1):23–40.

Welsh, Brandon C., Anthony A. Braga, and Christopher J. Sullivan. 2014. "Serious Youth Violence and Innovative Prevention: On the Emerging Link Between Public Health and Criminology." *JQ: Justice Quarterly* 31(3):500–523. doi: 10.1080/07418825.2012.690441.

3

SETTING THE STAGE
The Individual Roots of Crime

As Chapter 1 discussed, the field of public health stresses the need to address the causes of disease, illness, and injury to prevent these health problems from arising in the first place. This approach has saved countless lives since the 19th century and prevented or reduced much suffering. The analogy to crime is clear: To prevent crime from occurring, we need to address the causes of crime through appropriate programs, policies, and practices. This strategy certainly sounds sensible, especially because it has worked so well for public health, but it is not the strategy the United States has followed for the past several decades. Instead the United States has followed its get-tough approach and relied on mass incarceration as its chief tool of crime control.

Because this strategy is flawed for the reasons Chapter 1 discussed, a public health approach is needed. For this approach to succeed, we must first know why crime occurs. Fortunately, criminologists have been working for the past century to provide this awareness. Their work has yielded a huge volume of theorizing and research on the causes of crime. To provide a foundation for the discussion of crime prevention strategies in later chapters, this chapter and the next chapter review what criminologists say about these causes.

Chapter Outline

- Preview of the Discussion
- Biological Factors Then and Now
  - Children's Cognitive and Neurological Development
  - Prenatal and Maternal Problems and Fetal Development
  - Genetics and Crime
- Psychological Factors: Mental Illness and Personality
  - Mental Illness
  - Personality Traits and Crime
- Cognitive Processes and Motivation: Rational Choice and Deterrence
  - Rational Choice Theory
  - Deterrence Theory
- Conclusion

Learning Questions

1. In explaining criminal behavior, what is meant by individual-level factors and environmental factors?

2. Do genetic explanations offer sound strategies for reducing crime? Why or why not?

(Continued)

37

(Continued)

3. What does toxic stress mean, and what are its implications for crime prevention?

4. Why does testosterone research not point to a conclusive cause-and-effect relationship between testosterone levels and criminal behavior?

5. What does research suggest about the relationship between mental illness and criminal behavior?

6. To what degree do criminal offenders think and act in the way rational choice and deterrence theories assume?

PREVIEW OF THE DISCUSSION

Many academic disciplines try to explain human behavior. These disciplines' perspectives differ in respects far beyond the scope of this book. One fundamental way they do differ, however, involves their answers to this question: To what degree do the causes of human behavior lie in the individual or, instead, in the external social and physical environments? At the risk of oversimplifying, the fields of biology, psychology, and economics tend to locate the causes of human behavior inside the individual, while sociology, anthropology, history, and political science tend to locate these causes outside the individual and in the social and/or physical environments. Because human behavior is incredibly complex, all these disciplines' perspectives are important, and it is fair to say that most and perhaps all human behaviors do have roots both inside and outside the individual. This is true of crime at least as much as it is true of other behaviors.

Accordingly, this chapter focuses on factors arising in the individual that make criminal behavior more or less likely, while Chapter 4 focuses on aspects of the social and physical environments that make criminal behavior and victimization more or less likely. The individual-level factors include certain biological and psychological traits and cognitive processes, while the environmental factors include certain characteristics of urban neighborhoods and the influence of families, peers, and schools. Although criminologists often disagree regarding which causes of crime are the most important and whether some supposed causes are really causes at all, their work does point to the many kinds of factors that help generate criminal behavior and criminal victimization. Knowledge of these factors is essential for the development of effective crime prevention strategies.

With this backdrop in mind, we now turn to explanations of crime that trace the roots of criminal behavior to factors residing in the individual. These factors are biological, psychological, and cognitive. To the extent these factors matter, they point the way to many potentially effective strategies for reducing crime. Table 3.1 summarizes the explanations and factors discussed in this chapter.

BIOLOGICAL FACTORS THEN AND NOW

During the Middle Ages, many people had religious explanations for criminal behavior: The devil was possessing the bodies of individuals who committed violence and other deviance, or God was punishing these individuals or testing their religious loyalty. After the Middle Ages ended, science slowly but surely displaced religion as the dominant mode for understanding social reality. Most relevant for our purposes, major advances in biology during the 18th century and especially the 19th century led to the rise of scientific medicine. With these advances, it was almost inevitable that biologists and

Table 3.1	Summarizing Individual-Level Explanations of Crime and Antisocial Behavior
Type of Explanation	**Specific Risk Factor or Explanation Discussed**
Biological	Human skull size or shape (antiquated explanation)
	Atavism (antiquated explanation)
	Adverse childhood experiences and toxic stress
	Inadequate childhood nutrition
	Prenatal and maternal problems
	Genetic anomalies
	Testosterone
Psychological	Mental illness
	Negative personality traits
Cognitive	Rational choice
	Deterrence

physicians would think that criminal behavior had biological roots, just as disease and illness had biological causes (Rafter, Posick, and Rocque 2016).

The most popular biological explanations of crime during this period concerned two sets of factors: (1) human skull size and shape, and (2) evolution. Regarding skull shape, German physician Franz Joseph Gall and other scientists claimed that certain parts of the brain would be larger if a person had certain personalities or behaviors. Scientists could discover these brain segments by feeling someone's skull and looking for bumps or swellings. A focus of their work was criminal behavior: Criminals supposedly had certain brain enlargements that could be discovered by inspecting their skulls, and these enlargements allegedly meant that someone had a criminal predisposition. This field of **phrenology**, as it was called, was rather popular during the first half of the 19th century before losing favor for lack of evidence.

In the second half of the 19th century, Charles Darwin's theory of evolution revolutionized scientific thinking and the intellectual world. Social scientists accordingly paid new attention to how human societies had changed since ancient times. A key scholar in the history of criminology, Italian physician Cesare Lombroso, attempted to explain criminal behavior in evolutionary terms. Specifically, he theorized that some violent criminals were born as *atavists*, or evolutionary accidents. Rather than resembling modern people, they resembled prehistoric people, with hairy bodies, long arms, and protruding skulls. Because they were primitive in nature and had primitive brains, they were less civilized than modern humans and thus more prone to criminal behavior. To test his theory, Lombroso took body measurements of male inmates in Italian prisons, and these measurements supposedly supported his theory of **atavism**. This theory, too, was quite popular for a time before falling out of favor for lack of evidence.

As explanations of crime, phrenology and atavism are now of interest only for historical reasons. Although their assumptions were quite wrong, they did help move the understanding of crime from religion to science, and history now credits them for this key achievement if not for their actual explanations.

Biological explanations of crime continued to be popular during the early 20th century. Harvard anthropologist Ernest A. Hooton and many other scholars thought that criminal behavior reflected and arose from biological inferiority. Because African Americans and immigrants during this period had higher rates of criminal behavior, Hooton and these other scientists assumed that these two groups of people were therefore biologically inferior to native white people. Many of these other scientists, including Hooton, urged that young women from African American and immigrant backgrounds be sterilized to prevent them from having crime-prone children.

Their views helped justify and therefore provoke the sterilization of thousands of young women in what is now called the **eugenics** movement, one of the most shameful episodes of American history. Although eugenics reached its zenith during the 1920s and 1930s, it fell into disgrace soon after because of the Nazi Holocaust, which involved the extermination of 6 million Jews and millions of other people whom the Nazis viewed as biologically inferior. Not surprisingly, biological explanations of crime fell out of favor for half a century before making a recent comeback thanks to advances in genetics, medical technology, and other biological areas (Rafter et al. 2016). We now turn to these contemporary biological explanations, which together compose the approach called **biosocial criminology** (Chen et al. 2016; Rocque and Posick 2017).

Children's Cognitive and Neurological Development

Childhood is an absolutely critical time in the life course. What happens in childhood has immediate and long-term effects, good or bad, on behavior and other life events. Proper development of children's brains, nervous systems, and other aspects of their biological functioning is essential for them to have happy lives during childhood and adolescence and productive lives during adulthood. Conversely, improper biological development can harm their health, affect their behavior, worsen their school performance, and have other damaging effects. For these reasons, scholars in many disciplines pay much attention to the numerous aspects of children's lives that promote or impair the many aspects of their biological functioning. This growing body of research is of the utmost importance for preventing crime and addressing many other social problems.

In this regard, brain imaging and other advances in medical technology have allowed scientists to study children's neurological and cognitive development as never before. Recent research finds that certain aspects of children's lives may impair their neurological and cognitive development and leave a permanent, negative impact. This impact is called the **long arm of childhood**. A key focus of this research is the chronic **toxic stress** that many children experience from stressors called adverse childhood experiences (ACEs) (DeSocio 2015; Monnat and Chandler 2015). ACEs include child abuse and neglect, family conflict and violence, neighborhood violence, and poverty. Toxic stress from these and other sources impairs children's neurological and cognitive development in ways that produce antisocial behavior during childhood, delinquent behavior during adolescence, and criminal behavior during adulthood. Because toxic stress is especially common among poor children, Chapter 5's discussion of poverty examines toxic stress further and outlines the biological mechanisms that account for its impact.

Another problem that can impair children's neurological and cognitive development is inadequate nutrition. This problem subjects children to a greater risk of many kinds of problems, including poor school performance, health issues, and, for our purposes, behavioral problems throughout the life course (Jackson 2016; Liu et al. 2004). Inadequate nutrition has these effects because infants and older children certainly need proper nourishment for normal brain development. In addition, inadequate nutrition is a significant stressor for children old enough to realize their nutrition is inadequate, and this stress can again impair their development for the reasons already discussed.

We have just seen that toxic stress and inadequate nutrition impair children's cognitive and neurological development in ways that may induce bad behavior during childhood and beyond. This causal sequence has important implications for crime prevention. If we can reduce the occurrence of ACEs in children's lives and minimize their impact when they do occur (for example, by providing children with nurturing parenting and other positive relationships that can help buffer the impact of toxic stress), we can reduce the likelihood of antisocial behavior, delinquency, and crime at the various stages of the life course (Rocque, Welsh, and Raine 2012; Thompson and Haskins 2014). Similarly, if we can improve the nutrition of children who lack an adequate diet, we can also reduce their likelihood of engaging in problematic behavior throughout the life course. Several of the crime strategies discussed in later chapters build on these fundamental insights. Here it is worth noting that most of the children who have the problems just described come from poor or low-income backgrounds. This means that social policies that might reduce poverty or at least alleviate its many effects hold good promise for reducing crime and delinquency, as Chapter 5 emphasizes.

Prenatal and Maternal Problems and Fetal Development

Neurological and cognitive development also occurs in the womb. Growing research finds that proper fetal development is essential for positive life outcomes during childhood and the later life course. Conversely, improper fetal development can lead to negative outcomes, including antisocial behavior during childhood and beyond (Tibbetts and Rivera 2015).

Several kinds of problems can impede proper fetal development. One such problem is maternal stress. Mothers may live in a highly stressful environment for several reasons: They may be poor, they may live in a crime-ridden neighborhood, or they may live with an abusive husband or partner. Whatever the reason, maternal stress impairs fetal development (Marques et al. 2015). As one nursing professor observes, "Maternal exposures to toxic stress during pregnancy impact the developing brain of the fetus, altering the architecture of brain circuits and regions responsible for executive functions and emotional/behavioral regulation. The pregnant mother and her fetus are a biological system. Fetal development actively adapts to the physical state and health of the mother" (DeSocio 2015:70). When a pregnant woman is highly stressed, her biological systems are adapted to favor her survival more than that of the fetus. The result is the "development of a fetal brain that is biologically wired for stress reactivity, impulsivity, and prolonged activation of survival mechanisms" (p. 70). Brain regions that govern attention spans, emotional regulation, learning, and problem solving are all affected. All these consequences increase the risk for a variety of problems, including antisocial behavior, during childhood and beyond.

Another problem impairing fetal development is maternal alcohol, tobacco, and/ or other recreational drug use. Many studies find that individuals whose mothers used recreational drugs during pregnancy are again at increased risk for various problems throughout the life course, including antisocial behavior during childhood and delinquency and crime in later life (David et al. 2014; McGloin, Pratt, and Piquero 2006).

A third problem involves maternal nutrition (Marques et al. 2015). Most pregnant women in the United States have adequate nutrition, but a small percentage do not: About 8% of babies are born with low birth weight, a problem that is usually the result of inadequate maternal nutrition due to poverty and lack of education. Inadequate maternal nutrition impairs fetal development for two reasons. First, fetuses certainly need proper in utero nourishment for their normal development. If a mother does not eat well, the fetus does not receive this nourishment. Second, lack of adequate nutrition is a stressor for pregnant women, and this stress can impair fetal development as just discussed. In this regard, inadequate nutrition has an *indirect* effect on fetal development.

This brief discussion of the importance of the prenatal period for behavior and other outcomes throughout the life course again suggests an important avenue for crime prevention, namely the need to improve the overall well-being of pregnant women. The pregnant women at greatest risk of the problems we have discussed tend to be rather young, to come from low-income backgrounds, and to lack the social support of a loving husband or partner, parents, and friends. Their children are at greater risk for childhood aggression, which is a strong predictor of later delinquent and criminal behavior, as well as other problems (Tremblay et al. 2004). For this reason, programs aimed at helping these women hold much potential for reducing delinquency and crime. Several of the crime strategies discussed in later chapters again build on this key insight.

Genetics and Crime

Scholars have long thought that some people might be more likely to commit crime because of their genetic makeup. Just as a tendency for heart disease, certain cancers, and other health problems might stem from a person's genetic makeup, this reasoning goes, so might a tendency to commit crime, especially violent crime. Just as someone might inherit a predisposition for a serious health problem, so might someone inherit a predisposition for violent behavior.

This general idea goes back to at least the 19th century, long before the discovery of DNA and the advent of modern genetics. An 1877 study by Richard Dugdale focused on a rural New York family named the Jukes, whose family tree exhibited a long line of prisoners. Dugdale concluded that this fact reflected a biologically inherited tendency to commit crime. A few decades later, Henry H. Goddard (1912) studied the descendants of a 1700s individual he called Martin Kallikak to protect the family's privacy. Kallikak, a Revolutionary War hero, had children with two different women. One of these women was his Quaker wife, and the other woman was a barmaid. Two different women bore Kallikak's children, leading to two different family lines. The descendants of the children by his Quaker wife were all generally economically successful and law-abiding, while the descendants of the one child, a son, he had with the barmaid often had criminal records and other negative outcomes. Goddard attributed the disparate outcomes of the two family lines to biological inheritance, in particular to the genetically produced "feeble-mindedness" (low intelligence) of the barmaid, her son, and their descendants.

Both these works attracted much attention after their publication and popularized the notion that criminal behavior and other problems could be inherited. However, many other factors could have explained these scholars' findings. For example, Kallikak's descendants through his wife were relatively wealthy, while the barmaid's descendants were poor. At the risk of stereotyping, it is also likely that effective parenting skills were lacking among the Jukes and among the barmaid and her descendants. Thus, many social factors could have well accounted for the fact that crime apparently "ran in the families" of the Jukes and the barmaid's son.

Twin Studies

To help rule out the influence of these social factors, contemporary scholars have examined sets of identical twins. Because identical twins are by definition identical genetically, they should exhibit similar behaviors (*concordant* behavior). Many studies find that when one twin has been delinquent, so generally has the other twin; conversely, when one twin has not been delinquent, neither generally has been the other twin. The higher levels of concordant behavior than of discordant behavior found in these studies suggest to these scholars that criminal behavior has a genetic basis (Raine 2013).

However, because identical twins spend much time together, have the same friends, and are alike in other social respects, the concordance that is found may reflect their very similar social backgrounds at least as much, and perhaps more than, their identical genetic makeup (Guo 2005). To help rule out this possibility, a few studies examine identical twins who were separated during infancy and raised in different households. Some but not all of these studies do find a high level of concordance. However, methodological problems, including the fact that many of these twins were actually raised in households in the same communities and spent much time with each other as they grew, again make it difficult to infer a genetic cause of crime from these studies (Burt and Simons 2015; Lewontin 2010).

Molecular Genetics

Because of these methodological problems, advances in molecular genetics offer a potentially useful means of assessing genetic causation of criminal behavior. DNA testing enables research to determine whether individuals have certain genes or gene variants. In conjunction with self-report surveys in which subjects provide DNA samples and also respond to questions about their criminal behavior, researchers can determine whether these genetic traits are associated with a greater likelihood of committing crime or with attributes such as impulsivity linked to criminal behavior (Boisvert et al. 2013). Researchers have so far identified several genetic traits linked to criminal and antisocial behavior (Beaver, Schwartz, and Gajos 2015; Ouellet-Morin et al. 2016). MAOA, a gene that regulates serotonin, has received perhaps the most attention. Serotonin is a neurotransmitter that tends to have a calming effect. People who have a variant form of MAOA tend to have lower levels of serotonin and higher rates of aggression and criminal behavior (Beaver et al. 2013).

These genetic findings are intriguing but do not readily lend themselves to crime prevention strategies. The idea of changing someone's genes to reduce their criminal behavior sounds like a frightening proposition from the world of science fiction. As in the field of medicine, drugs could be developed to modulate the effects of criminogenic genes, but this, too, sounds like a problematic policy. Ethical questions would also arise. For example, if an adolescent is found to have a genetic makeup linked to aggression, what should we do? Should law enforcement authorities pay more attention to him (assuming the adolescent is a male)? What would be the social consequences for this adolescent if it became known that he had a genetic propensity for violence? For these and other reasons, contemporary genetic research on criminality does not seem to offer many viable options for crime prevention strategies.

Testosterone

Testosterone, the so-called "male hormone," has also been implicated in aggressive and criminal behavior. Because males commit much more crime, especially violent crime, than females and also have much higher levels of testosterone, researchers for some time have thought that testosterone is at least partly responsible for the higher level of male aggression and violence. By the same token, males who have more testosterone should be more likely to be violent than those with less testosterone. Research finds this is indeed the case (Carré and Olmstead 2015).

However, the exact role that testosterone plays in male aggression remains unclear. The testosterone–aggression correlations found in research tend to be rather small (Carré and Olmstead 2015), suggesting that any effect of testosterone on aggression is also small. Perhaps more important, these correlations do not necessarily indicate that testosterone "causes" aggression. Recalling our discussion in Chapter 1 of causal order, it is also possible that aggression and the competition it involves produce higher testosterone levels (Carré and Olmstead 2015). Thus, although many researchers are convinced that higher levels of testosterone indeed produce more aggression, their case is far from proven.

Even if it could be established that testosterone levels do affect aggression, the relevance of this finding for crime prevention strategies would still remain unclear. That is because this finding would imply the need to reduce the testosterone levels of males who have been aggressive. This again sounds like a frightening proposition from the world of science fiction and would have serious biological and other effects for the males with the reduced testosterone. How aggressive or violent would a male have to be to receive testosterone-reduction treatment? How old? These and other questions indicate that research on testosterone and aggression/violence again does not offer viable options for crime prevention strategies.

A Final Word on Biology and Crime Prevention

Contemporary research on the biological bases of criminality represents an exciting path for criminologists and policymakers to consider (Rocque and Posick 2017). In this regard, these experts should pay special attention to the increasing research evidence of problems in the neuroendocrinological and cognitive development of infants, children, and adolescents. These problems contribute to negative outcomes, including a greater tendency for criminal behavior, throughout the life course. As our review has emphasized, because these problems arise from social factors such as poverty and household violence, crime prevention strategies that target these social factors hold much promise for reducing crime.

PSYCHOLOGICAL FACTORS: MENTAL ILLNESS AND PERSONALITY

Biological explanations of crime assume that certain individuals have biological risk factors that make them more likely to break the law. Psychological explanations of crime similarly assume that certain individuals have psychological traits or problems that predispose them to breaking the law (Bartol and Bartol 2017). Much contemporary work in psychology focuses on mental illness and personality traits.

Mental Illness

Many psychologists, psychiatrists, and members of the public believe that mental illness predisposes individuals to violent behavior. In a recent national survey, 46% of Americans agreed that "people with serious mental illness are, by far, more dangerous than the general population" (Barry et al. 2013:1080). In another national survey, 60% of respondents who were read a description of an individual with symptoms of schizophrenia said this person would be likely to be more violent toward other people. One-third of respondents reported the same response when read a description of someone with symptoms of depression (Pescosolido et al. 2010). In line with these views, almost half of Americans say that the "failure of the mental health system to identify individuals who are a danger to others" deserves "a great deal" of blame for mass shootings (Saad 2013).

Mental Illness and Prison and Jail Inmates

Supporting this public perception, research finds a shockingly high rate of mental health problems among prison and jail inmates (Kim, Becker-Cohen, and Serakos 2015;

Swanson 2015). For example, a nationwide U.S. Bureau of Justice Statistics inmate survey found that 56% of state prisoners, 45% of federal prisoners, and 64% of jail inmates had a mental health problem during the 12 months before being interviewed (James and Glaze 2006). These problems included major depression, mania, and psychotic disorder. Regional and local studies of prison and jail inmates also find significant numbers having serious mental illness. The exact prevalence of mental illness is difficult to determine because different studies define and measure mental illness differently (Sarteschi 2013). Still, a fair conclusion is that "individuals with mental illness are overrepresented in the US correctional system" (Kim et al. 2015).

Because so many prison and jail inmates appear to be mentally ill, perhaps public opinion is correct in linking criminal behavior to mental illness. However, many methodological and conceptual issues suggest that this particular public opinion is premature and mistaken.

First, recall from Chapter 1 that "correlation does not mean causation." Two variables may be related, but issues of *causal order* and *spuriousness* sometimes make it difficult to be certain that a purported independent variable is indeed affecting the dependent variable. In this regard, consider that incarceration damages the mental health of many inmates, according to much research on this subject (Krisberg, Marchionna, and Hartney 2015). To the extent this is true, at least some inmates' mental health problems may stem from their incarceration and thus developed or worsened long after they broke the law. It is also possible that one or more *antecedent* variables (see Chapter 1), such as poverty or childhood abuse, may have precipitated both their mental disorder and their criminal conduct. Both these possibilities make it difficult to conclude that inmates' mental health problems prompted the criminal behavior that led to their incarceration.

Second, recall also from Chapter 1 that the number of inmates represents only a very small fraction of all criminal offenders (the *funnel effect*). Because this is true, inmates cannot be considered a random sample of all offenders, and their rate of mental illness may not necessarily apply to the bulk of offenders who are not incarcerated. Perhaps any mental health problems that inmates had before their incarceration somehow made them more susceptible to being arrested than offenders without mental health problems. These considerations again suggest that the high rate of mental health problems among inmates does not necessarily indicate that these problems produced their criminal behavior.

A third issue is more conceptual and involves the widespread perception that many criminals *must* be mentally ill or at least have a psychological problem, for why else would they be committing violent and other serious crime? This reasonable question overlooks the fact that people can commit very harmful behavior without having any identifiable mental illnesses or other psychological problems. Experiments such as the famed *Milgram experiment* involving "teachers" administering what they thought was potentially lethal electric shock to "learners" strongly suggest various circumstances may induce very psychologically normal people to commit great harm (Milgram 1974). The Nazi Holocaust provides similar evidence, as the Nazi leaders and guards who exterminated millions of people were generally found later to be psychologically normal (Harding 2013; Zillmer et al. 1995). Wartime soldiers kill people—other soldiers—but they are not doing so because of some psychological problem. All these examples remind us that people can commit violence and other crime without necessarily being mentally ill or having another psychological problem.

Population-Based Evidence

All these issues mean that we cannot infer a mental illness→criminal behavior causal sequence from the rate of mental illness among prison and jail inmates. A better way of assessing this possible sequence is to perform a *population-based* (also called *prospective*) study in which subjects are studied and assessed for mental health problems before they commit any crime. As might be apparent, these subjects are typically adolescents or even younger children, although some prospective studies of adults also exist. After controlling for all relevant factors such as family income and parenting quality, if subjects with mental health problems are later more likely than those without these problems to commit crime, we can reasonably assume that their mental health problems contributed to their criminal behavior.

Studies like these, which typically focus on violent behavior, are rather uncommon but report mixed results (Elbogen and Johnson 2009). Many studies do find a slightly higher likelihood of violence among people diagnosed with schizophrenia and sometimes other mental disorders (Brennan, Mednick, and Hodgins 2000; Fazel et al. 2009). However, because these studies typically control for only a limited range of relevant factors, their findings do not necessarily demonstrate a mental illness→violence linkage. Moreover, other studies find no association between mental illness and violence, or they find a linkage only among individuals with substance abuse problems (Elbogen and Johnson 2009).

A recent nationwide longitudinal study of more than 34,000 adults interviewed in two waves (Time 1 and Time 2) several years apart reflected the complexity of these results (Elbogen and Johnson 2009). This study aimed to determine whether mentally ill adults at Time 1 were more likely to commit violence during the years until their Time 2 interviews. Controlling for a range of relevant factors, the study found that bipolar disorder, major depression, and schizophrenia by themselves did *not* predict this future violence. However, mental illness combined with substance abuse did predict future violence. Other factors in the backgrounds of mentally ill adults, such as poverty and a history of being abused, also predicted future violence. The study's authors concluded, "Because severe mental illness did not independently predict future violent behavior, these findings challenge perceptions that mental illness is a leading cause of violence in the general population" (Elbogen and Johnson 2009:152).

As this study's results suggested, mentally ill individuals may occasionally commit violence, but that does not necessarily mean that it was their mental illness that caused the violence. Instead, mentally ill individuals have many other problems that seem to explain whatever violence they do commit. A study of 143 Minneapolis, Minnesota, offenders with severe mental illness who committed 429 crimes supports this point (Peterson et al. 2014). This research found that mental illness was directly related to only 18% of these offenders' crimes. Doing a bit of math, this means that mental illness was *not* related to more than four-fifths of their crimes.

Other evidence finds that people with mental illness commit no more than 5% of all U.S. crimes and that they are less likely than mentally healthy people to commit gun crimes (Metzl and MacLeish 2015). Reviewing all the evidence, it is fair to say that mental illness plays only a very small role, if that, in criminal violence. As the lead author of the Minneapolis study commented, "When we hear about crimes committed by people with mental illness, they tend to be big headline-making crimes so they get stuck in people's heads. The vast majority of people with mental illness are not violent, not criminal and not dangerous" (American Psychological Association 2014). The authors of another study on mental disorder and criminal violence similarly wrote, "Most individuals with major mental disorders are not violent, and most violent individuals do not have a major mental disorder" (Brennan et al. 2000:499).

A Final Word on Mental Illness

We have just seen that mental illness accounts for only a small amount of criminal violence. This conclusion has an important implication for crime prevention strategies. If, as seems true, mental illness hardly matters for criminal violence, strategies that improve mental health services or otherwise help mentally ill individuals will reduce crime by only a small degree, if any. This does *not* mean these strategies should be abandoned, as improved mental health services are certainly essential for many reasons not related to criminal violence (Swanson et al. 2015). But it does mean that crime prevention strategies must focus on problems other than mental illness if they are to succeed.

Personality Traits and Crime

Many psychologists believe that certain negative personality traits contribute to antisocial behavior among young children, adolescents, and adults. Including coldness, impulsivity, irritability, and suspiciousness, these traits are often measured by administering personality *inventories* (questionnaire items such as "I do things without thinking") to subjects old enough to provide responses; parents provide responses for young children. For adolescents and adults, the antisocial behavior these traits are thought to produce often involves breaking the law by committing violent crime or property crime or by engaging in illegal drug use and excessive drinking (Bartol and Bartol 2017).

Early studies of this possible connection focused on incarcerated offenders (youths and adults) and compared their personality traits and behavior to those of nonoffenders. These studies found a greater prevalence of negative personality traits among the offenders than among the nonoffenders and concluded that these traits helped explain the law-breaking behavior that led the offenders to be incarcerated.

However, and recalling that correlation does not mean causation, methodological problems left this conclusion less than certain (Akers, Sellers, and Jennins 2017). For example, the worse personality traits of the offenders may have stemmed from their incarceration and/or from the offense that led to their incarceration. As well, many of these early studies did not take into account socioeconomic status and other factors that might have shown the correlation between personality traits and offending to be spurious. These problems led many scholars to conclude that personality traits mattered little or not at all for criminal behavior (Andrews and Wormith 1989).

Some recent research avoids these methodological problems by using longitudinal random samples of the population. As with the mental illness research discussed earlier in this chapter, people (often children or adolescents) are studied at Time 1 and then again at Time 2 one or more years later, and perhaps again in subsequent years. If a negative personality trait at Time 1 predicts antisocial behavior at Time 2 or a subsequent time while controlling for relevant factors, it is reasonable to conclude that the trait helped produce the antisocial behavior.

Research using this approach finds that negative personality traits do predict future antisocial behavior. Perhaps the most important studies that do so have followed young children as they age into adolescence and then into adulthood. These studies find that children with the "worst" personalities are more likely to commit delinquency during adolescence and then criminality and other problematic behavior, such as uncontrolled gambling, during adulthood (Slutske et al. 2012; Viding et al. 2011). This general finding has led an increasing number of criminologists to embrace the importance of negative personality traits for criminal behavior (Morizot 2015; Van Gelder and De Vries 2012).

For crime prevention, it is worth noting that these negative personality traits often begin in childhood. Some experts attribute these traits to genes and other innate biological factors, while other experts attribute these traits to inadequate parenting and to living in poverty and in disadvantaged neighborhoods. A complete discussion of these reasons is beyond the scope of this book, but these bases for personality problems do have important implications for crime prevention. We suggested earlier that genetic explanations do not readily lend themselves to crime prevention strategies but that social explanations do lend themselves to these strategies. To the extent that children's personality problems do stem from inadequate parenting, poverty, and disadvantaged neighborhoods, crime prevention strategies aimed at reducing these social problems should also reduce children's likelihood of engaging in antisocial behavior during childhood and delinquent and criminal behavior as they grow older.

COGNITIVE PROCESSES AND MOTIVATION: RATIONAL CHOICE AND DETERRENCE

How and why do potential offenders decide whether or not to commit a crime? Scholars have been interested in this question at least since the 1700s. That century marked the flourishing of the *Enlightenment*, or the *Age of Reason*, in which scientific reasoning began to replace the religious thinking that had dominated the Middle Ages. One assumption of Enlightenment philosophy was that people had free will to make rational decisions by deciding whether a potential behavior would produce more rewards or more pain, and then acting accordingly.

In line with this view, criminal justice reformers such as Italian economist Cesare Beccaria (1738–1794) and English philosopher Jeremy Bentham (1748–1832) assumed that potential offenders also calculated whether the possible rewards of their criminal activity outweighed the possible risks of arrest and punishment. If potential offenders decide the possible rewards outweigh the possible risks, they will commit crime; if they instead decide the potential risks outweigh the potential rewards, they will not commit crime. Beccaria and Bentham both thought the criminal justice system of their era was far harsher than it needed to be to keep these rational offenders from committing crime. Important essays by these two scholars led to significant reforms in the criminal justice systems of Italy and England.

Rational Choice Theory

Beccaria and Bentham's view that *rational* individuals commit crime is called the *classical perspective* in criminology. A significant contemporary explanation of crime, **rational choice theory (RCT)**, similarly argues that crime is a rational act committed by rational individuals who calculate whether the potential rewards of their planned criminal behavior outweigh the potential risks of arrest, punishment, or other negative outcomes (Clarke and Cornish 2001; Pogarsky, Roche, and Pickett 2018). This general view comes from the field of economics, which has long assumed that people are rational actors who seek to maximize their financial well-being by carefully considering the possible benefits and costs of their actions.

RCT does *not* address why (for example, to inflict revenge or to acquire money) someone decides to commit a crime in the first place, nor does it consider the underlying roots (for example, poverty or bad parenting) for someone's criminal behavior. Rather, it focuses on the **event decision**: the decision-making process that prompts someone to decide to commit or not to commit a specific crime in a specific location at a specific time. Such event decisions have several stages, including (1) planning to commit a crime, (2) choosing a target, (3) doing the crime, and (4) escaping from the scene of the crime.

RCT is the basis for the belief that potential offenders can be deterred from committing crime if they perceive that the risk of arrest and harsh punishment is too severe. As we discuss in the next section, however, many offenders do not take the time to consider the consequences of their actions or are unable because of alcohol and other drug use to consider these consequences. They thus do not act as rationally as RCT theory assumes. In general, RCT applies more to property criminals than to violent criminals, who often act emotionally without considering their chances of arrest and punishment (Lilly, Cullen, and Ball 2015).

Still, RCT has proven invaluable in highlighting the importance of *opportunity* and *situational* factors that may lead the many offenders who do plan their actions and consider the possible consequences to be more likely to commit a crime. Chapter 4 further discusses these factors. As we will see then, an understanding of opportunity and situational factors has important implications for crime prevention strategies. Because many offenders do act fairly rationally in many circumstances, RCT's general view on the rationality of offending is significant for crime prevention.

Deterrence Theory

Recall from Chapter 1 that *deterrence* refers to the idea that the threat of arrest and punishment reduces the crime rate because potential offenders do not want to risk being arrested, convicted, and incarcerated. Implicit in this concept is the further idea that potential offenders consider the possible consequences of their actions before deciding to commit a crime. Accordingly, an offshoot of RCT is **deterrence theory**, which assumes that deterrence occurs because potential offenders do carefully weigh their chances of getting arrested, convicted, and incarcerated before proceeding with a crime. If so, more certain arrest and more certain prison terms should deter them from committing crime.

Deterrence theory considers two types of deterrence. **General deterrence** refers to the situation that occurs when potential offenders in the general public decide not to commit crime because they fear arrest and punishment. **Specific deterrence** (also called *individual deterrence*) refers to the situation that occurs when convicted offenders who have already been legally punished, and in particular have been released from prison or jail, decide not to commit a new crime because they do not want to risk a new incarceration.

To continue with Chapter 1's discussion of mass incarceration, to the extent that this practice may have reduced the crime rate, this impact may reflect a general or specific deterrent effect. Because almost no one wants to go to prison, it might make sense to think that mass incarceration should have a strong deterrent effect. However, certain conceptual issues suggest that any deterrent effect of mass incarceration must be small at best. These issues suggest that potential offenders in fact do not think and act often enough in the ways assumed by RCT and deterrence theory for deterrence to have a large impact. This is because the threat of longer and more certain imprisonment does not appear to deter many potential offenders. We now turn to these issues

Conceptual Issues Regarding Deterrence

A first issue is that many and perhaps most criminals actually fail to carefully weigh their chances of getting arrested and imprisoned. Instead, they act impulsively (Apel and Nagin 2011). This is especially true of violent criminals, because violence tends to be a fairly emotional, spontaneous behavior. When people commit violence out of anger, jealousy, or another intense emotion, they are not taking the time to assess their chances of getting arrested and imprisoned.

In a second issue, many property offenders do plan their crimes, but they plan their offenses to minimize their risk of arrest (Tunnell 2006). Because they do not think they will be arrested and thus imprisoned, the prospect of incarceration does not deter them.

A third issue is that many prisoners—between one-third and one-half—report being under the influence of alcohol and/or other drugs at the time they committed their crime (Mumola and Karberg 2006). If so, these offenders would have been unlikely to think very coherently about their chances of getting arrested and imprisoned. Therefore, many criminals may not be capable of being deterred because they are drunk or high when they break the law.

Fourth, although criminologists might know how severe a prison term is for various crimes, potential criminals do not have this knowledge (Western 2006). Thus, severe prison sentences are unlikely to deter them.

Next, one reason potential incarceration is said to deter potential offenders is that they do not want to be known as convicted criminals. As mass incarceration took hold, however, incarceration in urban communities became so common that imprisonment was seen more as a rite of passage than as a stigma. To the extent this different perception developed, incarceration lost at least some of whatever small deterrent effect it might have had earlier (Kovandzic and Vieraitis 2006).

Finally, the specific deterrent effect of imprisonment—the idea that released offenders will be less likely to commit new crimes because they do not want to be reincarcerated—is highly questionable. Research shows that imprisonment generally and longer prison terms in particular tend overall to *increase* the risk of new crimes after inmates leave prison (Nagin, Cullen, and Jonson 2009). This criminogenic (crime-causing) effect occurs for reasons that Chapter 12 discusses. If incarceration does make many offenders worse, then it would be surprising if mass incarceration had a large deterrent effect on crime.

As with the incapacitation issues discussed in Chapter 1, all these issues for deterrence mean that any deterrent effect of mass incarceration should be relatively small. The research discussed in Chapter 1 on the actual impact of mass incarceration on the crime rate confirms this pessimistic appraisal. In this regard, addressing the opportunity and situational factors that increase the certainty of arrest may have a stronger deterrent impact on crime, as Chapters 4 and 7 discuss further.

CONCLUSION

To reduce crime, it is important to know why people commit criminal behavior. The fields of biology, psychology, and economics all offer insights that suggest to many criminologists that criminal behavior has its roots in individual-level factors. Several explanations of crime from these fields point to potentially effective crime-reduction strategies that later chapters will discuss. Although implementation of these strategies holds great potential for reducing crime, certain other explanations from these fields do not hold this potential.

SUMMARY

1. A public health approach to crime prevention emphasizes the need to address the causes of crime for crime prevention to be achieved.

2. Biological research has a long history in the study of criminology, but early biological research identified causes of crime that are now regarded as inaccurate.

3. Contemporary biological research focuses on such factors as genetics, testosterone, and toxic stress during childhood. This stress generates cognitive and neurological deficits that contribute to antisocial behavior and other problems during childhood, adolescence, and beyond.

4. To the extent these deficits matter for such behavioral problems, strategies that address the causes of toxic stress should help reduce crime.

5. Mental illness plays only a very small role in criminal behavior, but impulsivity and other negative personality traits play a larger role. Because these traits often begin during childhood and continue into adolescence, crime prevention strategies must focus on the factors contributing to these traits.

6. Rational choice theory depicts offenders as rational actors. Although many offenders do not act in the way this theory assumes, this theory still identifies several opportunity and situational factors that foster or prevent criminal behavior. Strategies that address these factors should help reduce crime.

KEY TERMS

atavism 40
biosocial criminology 40
deterrence theory 51
eugenics 40

event decision 50
general deterrence 51
long arm of childhood 40
phrenology 39

rational choice theory (RCT) 50
specific deterrence 51
toxic stress 40

REFERENCES

Akers, Ronald L., Christine S. Sellers, and Wesley G. Jennins. 2017. *Criminological Theories: Introduction, Evaluation, and Application*. New York, NY: Oxford University Press.

American Psychological Association. 2014. "Mental Illness Not Usually Linked to Crime, Research Finds." Retrieved September 2, 2019 (http://www.apa.org/news/press/releases/2014/04/mental-illness-crime.aspx).

Andrews, D. A., and J. Stephen Wormith. 1989. "Personality and Crime: Knowledge Destruction and Construction in Criminology." *Justice Quarterly* 6: 289–309.

Apel, Robert, and Daniel S. Nagin. 2011. "General Deterrence: A Review of Recent Evidence." Pp. 411–436 in *Crime and Public Policy*, edited by J. Q. Wilson and J. Petersilia. New York, NY: Oxford University Press.

Barry, Colleen L., Emma E. McGinty, Jon S. Vernick, and Daniel W. Webster. 2013. "After Newtown—Public Opinion on Gun Policy and Mental Illness." *New England Journal of Medicine* 368(12):1077–1081.

Bartol, Curt R., and Anne Bartol. 2017. *Criminal Behavior: A Psychological Approach*. New York, NY: Pearson.

Beaver, Kevin M., Joseph A. Schwartz, and Jamie M. Gajos. 2015. "A Review of the Genetic and Gene–Environment Interplay Contributors to Antisocial Phenotypes." Pp. 109–122 in *The Development of Criminal and Antisocial Behavior: Theory, Research and Practical Applications*, edited by J. Morizot and L. Kazemian. New York, NY: Springer.

Beaver, Kevin M., John Paul Wright, Brian B. Boutwell, J. C. Barnes, Matt DeLisi, and Michael G. Vaughn. 2013. "Exploring the Association Between the 2-Repeat Allele of the MAOA Gene Promoter Polymorphism and Psychopathic Personality Traits, Arrests, Incarceration, and Lifetime Antisocial Behavior." *Personality & Individual Differences* 54(2):164–168. doi: 10.1016/j.paid.2012.08.014.

Boisvert, Danielle, John Paul Wright, Valerie Knopik, and Jamie Vaske. 2013. "A Twin Study of Sex Differences in Self-Control." *Justice Quarterly* 30: 529–559.

Brennan, Patricia A., Sarnoff A. Mednick, and Sheilagh Hodgins. 2000. "Major Mental Disorders and Criminal Violence in a Danish Birth Cohort." *Archives of General Psychiatry* 57(5):494–500. doi: 10.1001/archpsyc.57.5.494.

Burt, Callie H., and Ronald L. Simons. 2015. "Heritability Studies in the Postgenomic Era: The Fatal Flaw Is Conceptual." *Criminology* 53(1):103–112. doi: 10.1111/1745-9125.12060.

Carré, Justin M., and N. A. Olmstead. 2015. "Social Neuroendocrinology of Human Aggression: Examining the Role of Competition-Induced Testosterone Dynamics." *Neuroscience* 286: 171–186. doi: 10.1016/j.neuroscience.2014 .11.029.

Chen, Frances R., Yu Gao, Andrea L. Glenn, Sharon Niv, Jill Portnoy, Robert Schug, Yaling Yang, and Adrian Raine. 2016. "Biosocial Bases of Antisocial and Criminal Behavior." Pp. 355–379 in *The Handbook of Criminological Theory*, edited by A. R. Piquero. Malden, MA: Wiley Blackwell.

Clarke, Ronald V., and Derek B. Cornish. 2001. "Rational Choice." Pp. 23–42 in *Explaining Criminals and Crime*, edited by R. Paternoster and R. Bachman. Los Angeles, CA: Roxbury.

David, Anna L., Andrew Holloway, Louise Thomasson, Argyro Syngelaki, Kypros Nicolaides, Roshni R. Patel, Brian Sommerlad, Amie Wilson, William Martin, and Lyn S. Chitty. 2014. "A Case-Control Study of Maternal Periconceptual and Pregnancy Recreational Drug Use and Fetal Malformation Using Hair Analysis." *PLOS One* 9(10):1–10. doi: 10.1371/journal.pone.0111038.

DeSocio, Janiece. 2015. "A Call to Action: Reducing Toxic Stress During Pregnancy and Early Childhood." *Journal of Child & Adolescent Psychiatric Nursing* 28(2):70–71. doi: 10.1111/ jcap.12106.

Dugdale, Richard. 1877. *The Jukes: A Study in Crime, Pauperism, Disease, and Heredity*. New York, NY: G. P. Putnam's Sons.

Elbogen, Eric B., and Sally C. Johnson. 2009. "The Intricate Link Between Violence and Mental Disorder: Results From the National Epidemiologic Survey on Alcohol and Related Conditions." *Archives of General Psychiatry* 66(2):152–161.

Fazel, Seena, Gautam Gulati, Louise Linsell, John R. Geddes, and Martin Grann. 2009. "Schizophrenia and Violence: Systematic Review and Meta-Analysis." *PLOS Medicine* 6(8). doi: 10.1371/journal.pmed.1000120.

Goddard, Henry H. 1912. *The Kallikak Family: A Study in the Heredity of Feeblemindedness*. New York, NY: Macmillan.

Guo, Guang. 2005. "Twin Studies: What Can They Tell Us About Nature and Nurture?" *Contexts* 4(3):43–47.

Harding, Thomas. 2013. "Inside the Nazi Mind at the Nuremberg Trials." *The Daily Beast*. September 7. Retrieved September 2, 2019 (http://www.thedailybeast.com/articles/2013/09/07/inside-the-nazi-mind-at-the-nuremberg-trials.html).

Jackson, Dylan B. 2016. "The Link Between Poor Quality Nutrition and Childhood Antisocial Behavior: A Genetically Informative Analysis." *Journal of Criminal Justice* 44: 13–20.

James, Doris J., and Lauren E. Glaze. 2006. *Mental Health Problems of Prison and Jail Inmates*. Washington, DC: Bureau of Justice Statistics, U.S. Department of Justice.

Kim, KiDeuk, Miriam Becker-Cohen, and Maria Serakos. 2015. *The Processing and Treatment of Mentally Ill Persons in the Criminal Justice System*. Washington, DC: Urban Institute.

Kovandzic, Tomislav V., and Lynne M. Vieraitis. 2006. "The Effect of County-Level Prison Population Growth on Crime Rates." *Criminology & Public Policy* 5: 213–244.

Krisberg, Barry A., Susan Marchionna, and Christopher J. Hartney. 2015. *American Corrections: Concepts and Controversies*. Thousand Oaks, CA: Sage.

Lewontin, R. C. 2010. *Biology as Ideology: The Doctrine of DNA*. Toronto, Canada: House of Anansi Press.

Lilly, J. Robert, Francis T. Cullen, and Richard A. Ball. 2015. *Criminological Theory: Context and Consequences*. Thousand Oaks, CA: Sage.

Liu, Jianghong, Adrian Raine, Peter H. Venables, and Sarnoff A. Mednick. 2004. "Malnutrition at Age 3 Years and Externalizing Behavior Problems at Ages 8, 11, and 17 Years." *American Journal of Psychiatry* 161(11):2005–2013.

Marques, Andrea Horvath, Anne-Lise Bjørke-Monsen, Antônio L. Teixeira, and Marni N. Silverman. 2015. "Maternal Stress, Nutrition and Physical Activity: Impact on Immune Function, CNS Development and Psychopathology." *Brain Research* 1617:28–46. doi: 10.1016/j.brainres.2014.10.051.

McGloin, Jean Marie, Travis C. Pratt, and Alex R. Piquero. 2006. "A Life-Course Analysis of the Criminogenic Effects of Maternal Cigarette Smoking During Pregnancy." *Journal of Research in Crime and Delinquency* 43: 412–426.

Metzl, Jonathan M., and Kenneth T. MacLeish. 2015. "Mental Illness, Mass Shootings, and the Politics of American Firearms." *American Journal of Public Health* 105(2):240–249.

Milgram, Stanley. 1974. *Obedience to Authority*. New York, NY: Harper and Row.

Monnat, Shannon M., and Raeven Faye Chandler. 2015. "Long-Term Physical Health Consequences of Adverse Childhood Experiences." *The Sociological Quarterly*. doi: 10.1111/tsq.12107.

Morizot, Julien. 2015. "The Contribution of Temperament and Personality Traits to Criminal and Antisocial Behavior and Desistance." Pp. 137–166 in *The Development of Criminal and Antisocial Behavior: Theory, Research and Practical Applications*, edited by J. Morizot and L. Kazemian. New York, NY: Springer.

Mumola, Christopher J., and Jennifer C. Karberg. 2006. *Drug Use and Dependence, State and Federal Prisoners, 2004*. Washington, DC: Bureau of Justice Statistics, U.S. Department of Justice.

Nagin, Daniel S., Francis T. Cullen, and Cheryl Lero Jonson. 2009. "Imprisonment and Reoffending." *Crime and Justice: A Review of Research* 38: 115–200.

Ouellet-Morin, Isabelle, Sylvana M. Côté, Frank Vitaro, Martine Hébert, René Carbonneau, Éric Lacourse, Gustavo Turecki, and Richard E. Tremblay. 2016. "Effects of the MAOA Gene and Levels of Exposure to Violence on Antisocial Outcomes." *British Journal of Psychiatry* 208(1):42–48.

Pescosolido, Bernice A., Jack K. Martin, J. Scott Long, Tait R. Medina, Jo C. Phelan, and Bruce G. Link. 2010. "'A Disease Like Any Other'? A Decade of Change in Public Reactions to Schizophrenia, Depression, and Alcohol Dependence." *American Journal of Psychiatry* 167(11):1321–1330.

Peterson, Jillian, Patrick Kennealy, Jennifer Skeem, Beth Bray, and Andrea Zvonkovic. 2014. "How Often and How Consistently Do Symptoms Directly Precede Criminal Behavior Among Offenders With Mental Illness?" *Law and Human Behavior* 38(5):439–449.

Pogarsky, Greg, Sean Patrick Roche, and Justin T. Pickett. 2018. "Offender Decision-Making in Criminology: Contributions From Behavioral Economics." *Annual Review of Criminology* 1: 379–400.

Rafter, Nicole, Chad Posick, and Michael Rocque. 2016. *The Criminal Brain: Understanding Biological Theories of Crime*. New York: New York University Press.

Raine, Adrian. 2013. *The Anatomy of Violence: The Biological Roots of Crime*. New York, NY: Pantheon.

Rocque, Michael, and Chad Posick. 2017. "Paradigm Shift or Normal Science? The Future of (Biosocial) Criminology." *Theoretical Criminology* 21(3):288–303. doi: 10.1177/1362480617707949.

Rocque, Michael, Brandon C. Welsh, and Adrian Raine. 2012. "Biosocial Criminology and Modern Crime Prevention." *Journal of Criminal Justice* 40(4):306–312.

Saad, Lydia. 2013. "Americans Fault Mental Health System Most for Gun Violence." Retrieved September 2, 2019 (http://www.gallup.com/poll/164507/americans-fault-mental-health-system-gun-violence.aspx).

Sarteschi, Christine M. 2013. "Mentally Ill Offenders Involved With the U.S. Criminal Justice System: A Synthesis." *SAGE Open* July–September: 1–11. doi: 10.1177/2158244013497029.

Slutske, Wendy S., Terrie E. Moffitt, Richie Poulton, and Avshalom Caspi. 2012. "Undercontrolled Temperament at Age 3 Predicts Disordered Gambling at Age 32: A Longitudinal Study of a Complete Birth Cohort." *Psychological Science (Sage Publications Inc.)* 23(5):510–516. doi: 10.1177/0956797611429708.

Swanson, Ana. 2015. "A Shocking Number of Mentally Ill Americans End Up in Prison Instead of Treatment." *Washington Post*. April 30. Retrieved September 2, 2019 (http://www.washingtonpost.com/news/wonkblog/wp/2015/04/30/a-shocking-number-of-mentally-ill-americans-end-up-in-prisons-instead-of-psychiatric-hospitals/).

Swanson, Jeffrey W., E. Elizabeth McGinty, Seena Fazel, and Vickie M. Mays. 2015. "Mental Illness and Reduction of Gun Violence and Suicide: Bringing Epidemiologic Research to Policy." *Annals of Epidemiology* 25: 366–376.

Thompson, Ross A., and Ron Haskins. 2014. *Early Stress Gets Under the Skin: Promising Initiatives to Help Children Facing Chronic Adversity.* Princeton, NJ: The Future of Children, Princeton University.

Tibbetts, Stephen G., and Jose Rivera. 2015. "Prenatal and Perinatal Factors in the Development of Persistent Criminality." Pp. 167–180 in *The Development of Criminal and Antisocial Behavior: Theory, Research and Practical Applications*, edited by J. Morizot and L. Kazemian. New York: Springer.

Tremblay, Richard E., Daniel S. Nagin, Jean R. Séguin, Mark Zoccolillo, Philip D. Zelazo, Michel Boivin, Daniel Pérusse, and Christa Japel. 2004. "Physical Aggression During Early Childhood: Trajectories and Predictors." *Pediatrics* 114(1):e43–e50.

Tunnell, Kenneth D. 2006. *Living Off Crime.* Lanham, MD: Rowman & Littlefield.

Van Gelder, Jean-Louis, and Reinout E. De Vries. 2012. "Traits and States: Integrating Personality and Affect Into a Model of Criminal Decision Making." *Criminology* 50(3):637–671. doi: 10.1111/j.1745-9125.2012.00276.x.

Viding, Essi, Michel Boivin, Nathalie M. G. Fontaine, Eamon J. P. McCrory, and Terrie E. Moffitt. 2011. "Predictors and Outcomes of Joint Trajectories of Callous-Unemotional Traits and Conduct Problems in Childhood." *Journal of Abnormal Psychology* 120(3):730–742. doi: 10.1037/a0022620.

Western, Bruce. 2006. *Punishment and Inequality in America.* New York, NY: Russell Sage Foundation.

Zillmer, Eric A., Molly Harrower, Barry A. Ritzler, and Robert P. Archer. 1995. *The Quest for the Nazi Personality: A Psychological Investigation of Nazi War Criminals.* Hillsdale, NJ: Lawrence Erlbaum.

4

SETTING THE STAGE
The Environmental Roots of Crime

Chapter Outline

Learning Questions

1. What are the social characteristics of disadvantaged neighborhoods?

2. How does routine activities theory help us understand why crime and victimization occur?

This chapter complements the previous chapter by examining the roots of crime in the social and physical environments. These causes fall into several categories of factors as summarized in Table 4.1: community and situational, the family, peer influences, and schools and schooling. We will see that explanations focusing on these roots have many significant implications for crime prevention strategies. The chapter ends with discussions of the sociodemographic correlates of criminal behavior and the need for multifaceted crime prevention.

COMMUNITY AND SITUATIONAL FACTORS

One of criminology's most important insights is that the social and physical characteristics of locations matter mightily for their levels of crime and victimization. This is true regardless of the personal qualities and personalities of the people living in these locations. Another way of saying this is that "kinds of places" may matter more than "kinds of people" for crime and victimization rates (Stark 1987). Good people living in "bad" locations may be drawn into crime and delinquency; not-so-good people living in "good" locations may be less able and/or willing to commit crime and delinquency.

3. Why does good family functioning help prevent delinquency and crime?

4. How does the relationship between schooling and delinquency sometimes become a vicious circle?

An analogy for traffic accidents may help explain this key criminological insight. Suppose you are a good driver: You obey all traffic laws and are attentive behind the wheel. You approach an intersection that is widely known as a dangerous one. It is busy with traffic, and it has bad sight lines when drivers are turning into and out of it. As you enter the intersection, a bad sight line causes you

Table 4.1 Summarizing the Environmental Roots of Crime

Category of Factors	Specific Risk Factors for Crime and Antisocial Behavior
Community	High unemployment
	High poverty level
	Weak institutional resources
	Low collective efficacy
	High levels of stress
Situational	Lack of adequate street lighting
	Warmer weather
	High residential density
	Presence of bars and taverns
	Handguns
Families	One-parent households
	Multiple transitions
	Early motherhood
	Family conflict
	Nonuse of authoritative discipline
	Child abuse and neglect
	Parental substance abuse
Peers	Delinquent friends and acquaintances
Schools	Poor school performance
	Negative attitudes about school
	Crowded classrooms
	Fewer instructional resources
	Larger student populations
	Overly strict rules and harsh punishment

to fail to see another car turning in front of you, and you scrape their car in a minor collision. Although you are indeed a good driver, you are involved in an accident because of *where* you are driving. If good drivers are more likely to have accidents in bad locations, the opposite is also true: Bad drivers are less likely to cause accidents if they are fortunate enough to drive in good locations, those with little traffic and good sight lines. These considerations suggest that location characteristics may affect the extent to which drivers cause accidents. By the same token, location characteristics may also affect the extent to which people commit and/or become victims of crime and delinquency.

Two sets of factors affect whether locations are apt to have higher or lower crime and victimization rates. **Community factors** involve certain social aspects of neighborhoods that motivate persons (especially adolescents and young adults, who have higher crime rates than older people) to break the law or, instead, to obey it. **Situational factors** involve certain physical aspects of neighborhoods and elements of social interaction that help foster criminal behavior and victimization or, conversely, inhibit criminal behavior and victimization. We examine each set of factors in turn.

Community Factors

The idea that neighborhoods' social aspects shape their crime and victimization rates goes back to the early days of criminology. Writing about a century ago, social scientists at the University of Chicago emphasized that some neighborhoods have higher crime rates because of their **social disorganization** (Shaw and McKay 1942). These were neighborhoods with high rates of residential instability (many people moving in and out), high divorce rates, run-down housing, and deep poverty. Amid such conditions, informal social control mechanisms are weaker, and family, religion, and other social institutions in particular are able to exercise less control over people's behavior. As a result, deviant values are better able to compete with conventional values, and youths are drawn into delinquency.

Drawing on this theoretical tradition, contemporary criminology confirms that certain types of neighborhoods indeed tend to have higher crime and victimization rates (Friedson and Sharkey 2015; McNulty, Bellair, and Watts 2013; Sampson 2013). These are neighborhoods characterized by *community disadvantage* (also called *neighborhood disadvantage*): high unemployment rates, high poverty rates, and high rates of single-parent households and dilapidated housing. These neighborhoods tend not to have the strong institutional resources (e.g., schools, childcare, employment, neighborhood associations) that are so important for good behavior by children and adolescents and for other positive outcomes (Elliott, Dupéré, and Leventhal 2015). These neighborhoods also tend to have low levels of *collective efficacy* (community supervision of adolescents and a general "watching out" for signs of potential offenders and criminality). Finally, they also tend to have high levels of stress that affect parents' ability to raise their children well. As child scholar Margaret C. Elliott and colleagues (2015:256) observe, "Parents in disadvantaged neighborhoods, where disorder, crime, and subpar institutions are part of daily life, live under more stressful conditions than parents in more advantaged neighborhoods. Stressful neighborhood conditions take a toll on parents' health and well-being and compromise effective parenting."

These factors all foster higher crime and victimization rates in disadvantaged neighborhoods. In a vicious cycle, the higher rate of violence in these neighborhoods exposes their children and adolescents to this violence, and witnessing this violence increases these youths' rates of violent crime and other delinquency (Fix and Burkhart 2015; Nofziger and Kurtz 2005).

All these problems in urban neighborhoods are thought to generate alienation and despair that further help explain their higher rates of crime. A related effect is a heightened need for *respect* to help compensate for the lack of respect urban residents feel. This need for respect in turn leads to a *code of the street*, to use sociologist Elijah Anderson's (1999) notable term, that involves heightened sensitivity to insults and a willingness to commit physical violence to command respect. Many scholars feel that this code of the street also helps explain the higher violence rates of many urban neighborhoods (McNeeley and Wilcox 2015; Moule et al. 2015).

If we could somehow clone an infant and then have one clone grow up in the kinds of urban neighborhoods just described, and another clone grow up in a much more wealthy and otherwise advantaged neighborhood, which clone would be more likely to commit crime by age 18 or 21? You probably answered the clone in the disadvantaged neighborhood. If so, you recognize that some neighborhoods have higher crime rates because they are "bad" neighborhoods, just as some intersections have higher accident rates because they are dangerous intersections. Just as we can lower accident rates if we can make an intersection less dangerous, so, perhaps, can we lower crime rates if we can improve the conditions that typify disadvantaged neighborhoods. This possibility is often neglected in popular debates over why individuals commit crime and in discussions of how best to reduce crime. The crime prevention strategies discussed in Chapters 5 and 6 build on the framework suggested by theory and research on community factors and crime.

Situational Factors

From a crime prevention standpoint, some of the most exciting work in criminology concerns the factors that promote or discourage the opportunity for crime and victimization to occur (Wilcox and Cullen 2018). As Chapter 3 noted, rational choice theory states that potential offenders weigh the possible benefits and costs of their actions before deciding to break the law. This theory has led criminology to pay attention to the cognitive processes that lead offenders to decide to commit a crime or not to commit a crime. Criminologists have thus studied the various factors that create the opportunity for victimization to occur without an offender fearing arrest or other risks. These so-called situational factors are features of the immediate location, such as the amount of street lighting, that may lead offenders contemplating a crime to decide to go ahead and commit it or to refrain from doing so.

In this regard, a key advance in criminological thinking was **routine activities theory** (with the unfortunate acronym RAT), first advanced four decades ago and still popular today (Cohen and Felson 1979; Felson and Eckert 2016). Viewing crime as a matter of plain practicality, RAT reasons that for a crime to occur, it takes at least two to tangle, so to speak: a potential offender and a potential victim. These two parties must be in the same place at the same time for a crime to occur. Even if they are in the same place at the same time, a crime will likely *not* occur if the offender perceives too much risk, for example, if police or witnesses are nearby. Given this understanding of the practicality of crime, RAT reasons that crime is more likely when the three factors just described occur at the same time: (1) *motivated offenders*, (2) *attractive targets* or victims (people, stores, etc.), and (3) *an absence of guardianship* (police, witnesses, etc.). If you have ever known someone who became a crime victim because he or she was in the wrong place at the wrong time, RAT should make sense to you.

RAT's understanding of the practicality of crime helps explain variations and changes in crime rates. For example, crime is typically higher in the summer than in the winter (Tompson and Bowers 2013). Violent crime is higher because people spend more time with other people in the summer, creating the opportunity for violence; property crime is higher because people leave their houses more often in the summer, creating the opportunity for burglary. RAT also helps explain why some kinds of people are more likely to commit crime and/or become crime victims. For example, young people have higher crime and victimization rates than older people because they spend much more time away from home. While away from home, they have more opportunity both to break the law and to become crime victims. By the same token, adolescents who are uninvolved in school activities and come home to an empty house also have higher crime and delinquency rates because they spend more time with friends and have more unsupervised time on their hands (Augustyn and McGloin 2013).

RAT's understanding of the practicality of crime also helps explain why some areas will almost automatically have higher crime rates than other areas. In sociologist Rodney Stark's (1987) words, these higher-crime areas are more likely to be "deviant places" because of how they are arranged. For example, in neighborhoods with high residential density—many people living near one another—more social interaction generally occurs simply because it is easier for it to occur. Young people, the age group with the highest crime rate, are more easily able to find each other and spend time with each other, and so they do. As RAT would predict, these dynamics create opportunities for people to commit crime and for other people to become victims of crime. The neighborhoods just described are typically urban neighborhoods. By contrast, in the suburbs and especially rural areas, people live farther apart and social interaction is less possible. This in turn means that there are fewer opportunities for crime and victimization to occur. Urban areas thus have more street crime than suburban and especially rural areas because of dynamics reflecting RAT's understanding of the practicality of crime and victimization.

As might be clear from our discussion of RAT, people's lifestyles affect their chances of both committing crime and becoming crime victims. For example, people who spend much of their time away from home and in bars are more likely than those who stay at home to become crime victims. The importance of people's lifestyles for crime and victimization is the key thesis of **lifestyle theory**, which was developed at about the same time as RAT and is closely related to it; many scholars consider the two theories to be equivalents (Marcum 2010). A key similarity between the two theories is that both assume that "the habits, lifestyles, and behavioral patterns of potential crime victims enhance their contact with offenders and thereby increase the chances that crimes will occur" (Miethe and Meier 1990:244).

To the degree that crime and victimization are the practical matters depicted by these two theories, efforts that address the situational factors that expose potential victims to potential offenders and lead the offenders to perceive a low risk of arrest or other risks should help reduce crime. For example, brighter and more abundant street lighting may reduce robberies and assaults because potential offenders know their acts will be more visible. Public surveillance cameras may have the same effect for the same reason. This understanding forms the basis for situational crime prevention (discussed in Chapter 7), which involves efforts in specific locations that try to "reduce exposure to motivated offenders, decrease target suitability, and increase capable guardianship" (Marcum 2010:54; Smith and Clarke 2012).

Before we leave situational factors, it is worth discussing two additional risk factors for crime that are part of many people's lifestyles. These factors are (1) alcohol and illegal drugs, and (2) handguns and other firearms; we discuss them in that order.

Alcohol and Illegal Drugs

Many prison and jail inmates report being under the influence of alcohol and/or other drugs at the time they commit the crime that leads to their arrest and subsequent incarceration (see Chapter 1). Self-report studies find that people who use illegal drugs are also more likely to commit other crimes. These facts suggest that alcohol and illegal drug use may play a significant role in criminal offending because of their biochemical effects. To the extent this is true, efforts that somehow reduce the amount of drinking and illegal drug use may also reduce criminal behavior.

To gauge how much crime reduction might be achieved in this manner, we must first know the degree to which alcohol use and illegal drug use do, in fact, contribute to criminal behavior. Let's first address the issue of illegal drugs. Although many offenders use illegal drugs, that does not necessarily mean that their drug use produced their criminal behavior. Perhaps they would have committed their crimes anyway. Again keeping in mind that correlation does not mean causation, any correlation between illegal drug use and crime might be spurious if one or more antecedent variables prompt both drug use and criminal behavior. In a causal order issue, perhaps committing crime leads to illegal drug use because someone is associating with offenders using illegal drugs. All these possibilities mean that we cannot necessarily infer an illegal drug use→criminal behavior causal sequence from a correlation between illegal drug use and criminality.

Criminologists have sought to determine the exact role that illegal drugs play in criminal behavior. A fair conclusion from studies of juvenile offenders and young adults is that much of the illegal drug use/criminality correlation is indeed spurious once factors producing both drug use and criminality are taken into account (Faupel, Horowitz, and Weaver 2013). There is also evidence that delinquency is more likely to precede illegal drug use than the reverse (Menard, Mihalic, and Huizinga 2001). Despite what we might read or hear in the popular and news media, the biochemical effects of illegal drugs only rarely cause people to go berserk and commit violence; some illegal drugs such as opiates and marijuana even reduce violence (Boyum, Caulkins, and Kleiman 2011). Findings like these lead criminologists to conclude that illegal drug use plays only a small role, if any, in producing crime because of drugs' biochemical effects (Walker 2015). To the extent this is true, reducing illegal drug use would have only a small crime-reduction effect at best.

Illegal drug users do commit crimes like robbery to support their drug habit, and illegal drug traffickers do commit violence against police and other drug traffickers to protect their business. The legal war on drugs has failed to stem illegal drug use and trafficking (Robinson and Scherlen 2014). If other types of efforts could somehow reduce illegal drug use and therefore reduce illegal drug trafficking, the types of crimes just described would likely decline. Many of the crime prevention strategies discussed in this book may also help reduce illegal drug use, because street crime and illegal drug use often have similar roots. However, the long history of drug use warrants skepticism about the potential effectiveness of any such efforts (Goode 2015). For this reason, some observers advocate legalizing or decriminalizing most or all drugs to reduce the problems created by the war against drugs, including the violence committed by illegal drug traffickers (Allen 2011; Law Enforcement Against Prohibition 2015).

One drug does seem to consistently produce violent behavior because of its biochemical and social effects: alcohol. Researchers think alcohol plays an important role in interpersonal violence, including domestic violence and gun violence, and refer to "the strong causal nature of the relationship between alcohol and violence" (Parker and McCaffree 2013:5; Wintemute 2015). As recent reviews summarize the evidence, "the relation between alcohol and violence has been well documented in many studies" (Parker et al. 2011:506), and "indeed, of all psychoactive substances, alcohol is the only one that has been shown in behavioral experiments to commonly (not inevitably) increase aggression" (Boyum et al. 2011:371).

Neighborhoods with greater numbers of bars and other drinking establishments per capita tend to have higher crime rates even when other causal factors are considered (Parker and McCaffree 2013). This effect results from alcohol's biochemical effects, but it also results from two dynamics reflecting RAT's and lifestyle theory's understanding of crime. First, bars and other drinking settings attract large numbers of people, whose interaction then creates greater opportunities for violence. Second, people who have been drinking and become less able to exercise caution also become more attractive targets for robbers and other criminals. These dynamics suggest that efforts involving drinking establishments, including limiting their number or the hours they are open, can reduce interpersonal violence and other crime (Parker and McCaffree 2013).

Handguns and Other Firearms

The topic of gun ownership and gun control continues to be one of the most controversial social issues in the United States, and with good reason. Americans own some 300 million firearms, including about 100 million handguns, and about 43% of U.S. households possess at least one firearm (Leshner et al. 2013). This rate of gun ownership is the highest by far among the world's democracies. Firearms kill more than 32,000 Americans each year and injure more than 67,000 other Americans. About two-thirds of firearm deaths are suicides, and one-third are homicides or accidental shootings (Fowler et al. 2015). Many firearm victims are youths under age 18, for whom firearms are the second-leading cause of death (Hemenway and Webster 2015). Firearm injuries and deaths cost the nation almost $50 billion annually in medical expenses and lost wages. The combination of firearm ownership and excessive alcohol use is especially deadly, as excessive drinking is implicated in many fatal and nonfatal shootings (Wintemute 2015).

Three kinds of evidence underline firearms' role in homicides. First, households with guns are more likely than households without guns to have a household member murdered, typically by a family member or friend; this relationship holds true even when relevant factors such as age, sex, race, alcohol and illegal drug use, and domestic violence history are controlled (Kellerman et al. 1993). Second, states with higher firearm ownership rates have higher homicide rates involving firearms but do not have higher homicide rates involving other weapons (Miller, Hemenway, and Azrael 2007). Third, the United States has a much higher homicide rate than other democracies, even though its rate of aggravated assault and other serious violence is only about average (Zimring and Hawkins 1997).

Many people own firearms to protect themselves against home invasion, robbery, and other crimes. Some firearm owners report using their guns to prevent such crimes (defensive gun use, or DGU). If DGU were very common and helped prevent these crimes, perhaps this benefit would outweigh the harm caused by the great number of firearm homicides and suicides. However, survey evidence indicates that DGU is rather rare. As analyzed by David Hemenway and Sara J. Solnick (2015), National Crime Victimization Survey victims report using a gun (threatening or actually shooting a perpetrator) in only about 1% of relevant (i.e., the victim was present at the time of the crime) crime incidents. Victims who used a gun were *not* less likely to be injured than victims who did not use a gun. These findings suggest that firearms actually prevent relatively few crimes and led the authors to conclude, "The NCVS data provide little evidence that self-defense gun use reduces the likelihood of victim injury during a crime" (Hemenway and Solnick 2015:27). Any beneficial effects that DGU may sometimes have appear to be outweighed by the deaths and injuries firearms cause, as a recent National Academy of Sciences report speculated (Leshner et al. 2013).

Given the involvement of firearms in homicides, nonfatal shootings, and robberies and other gun crimes, significant reductions in firearm ownership and availability should reduce these problems. However, firearm access is very difficult to reduce because firearms are so ingrained in the American culture, because the National Rifle Association (NRA) has been a very effective lobbying organization, and because the U.S. Supreme Court has ruled that the Second Amendment upholds the right to private firearm ownership. Despite these circumstances, certain measures involving firearm access and firearm technology show promise of reducing gun availability and improving gun safety in ways consistent with the Second Amendment. For example, efforts to restrict firearm access by people with alcohol abuse histories may be able to reduce gun violence (Wintemute 2015). Although the present political climate may make it very difficult to implement this and other firearm-related measures, they still should be part of a larger strategy of crime prevention. Accordingly, Chapter 7 discusses these measures at greater length.

FAMILIES, FRIENDS, AND SCHOOLS

When Americans hear that teenagers commit serious crime or other delinquency, they are apt to blame the teenagers' family upbringing more than any other factor. In national polling evidence, Americans named "lack of strong families" as the most significant cause of juvenile delinquency (Soler 2001). Many criminologists would agree with this assessment. Others would cite the importance of peer influences on adolescents' behavior, and some would point to the importance of schools and schooling for delinquency. All these factors do matter because all these aspects of young people's lives—family, friends, and schools—shape children's and adolescents' behavior and attitudes in so many ways that can last well into adulthood. As we shall see in later chapters, many crime prevention strategies focus on improving aspects of family life, peer relationships, and schooling. This section reviews what is known about how families, friends, and schools contribute to antisocial behavior and delinquency, and about certain aspects of their dynamics that may protect youths from engaging in delinquency.

Family Structure, Family Functioning, and Parenting

The family does matter greatly for antisocial behavior and delinquency, and thus for adult criminality (Farrington 2011). As a recent review noted, "Theoretical models and empirical research have consistently linked aspects of the family environment to the early emergence of conduct problems in childhood and serious delinquent behaviors during adolescence" (Pardini, Waller, and Hawes 2015:201). Many theories of criminality trace its origins to various aspects of the family situations that children and adolescents experience. Because the family is so important for children's behavior, many crime prevention strategies focus on various aspects of family life, as Chapter 8 will discuss.

In thinking about how family life promotes or inhibits antisocial behavior and delinquency, criminologists consider many aspects of what families are all about. It is helpful to divide most of these aspects into two broad categories: *family structure* and *family functioning*. **Family structure** refers to how the family is organized: whether one parent or two parents are living in a household, whether the biological parents are divorced, whether a stepparent or cohabiting partner is living in the household, how many children a family has, and so forth. **Family functioning** (also called *family interaction*) refers to the quality of the social interaction among family members: how well they get along, how much conflict there is, how warm the parent–child relationship is, how well the parent(s) are raising the child, and so forth.

Family Structure

The most studied aspect of family structure and antisocial behavior and delinquency is whether a child's household is headed by two biological parents (*intact household*) or instead by only one biological parent (*single-parent household*), usually the mother. A child may live in a single-parent household for several reasons: (1) the biological parents divorced or separated; (2) the biological parents never married and one parent, usually the father, does not live with the family; or (3) far more rarely, one of the biological parents died.

Much research compares the behavior of children in one-parent households with children in two-parent households. Some research also examines the behavior of children in other arrangements. For example, the mother (assuming the single parent is the mother) may have remarried after a divorce or the father's death, or she may have married for the first time to someone who is not the father. In addition, the mother may be in a cohabiting relationship with someone who is not the father. (In plain English, the mother is living with her partner.) Whatever the arrangement, the behavior of the children being studied is again compared with the behavior of children in two-parent households. The best studies in all this research use random samples of children from the national or more local population, with some studies looking at children over time in a longitudinal investigation.

With that bit of methodological explanation out of the way, what does all this research show? Let's first consider the research comparing children in one-parent households with children in two-parent households. Do the former children behave worse than the latter children during childhood and adolescence? The answer is a resounding *yes*. Many studies find that children in one-parent households are more likely than children in two-parent households to have behavioral problems during childhood, to commit delinquency during adolescence, and to commit crime as young adults (Pardini et al. 2015).

Several reasons are thought to explain this difference (Amato 2010; Apel and Kaukinen 2008). First, one parent simply may not be able to do as good a job parenting as two parents, and single parents may often have poor parenting skills. Second, when a divorce has occurred, children may behave worse because of the divorce's emotional impact. Third, because the single parent is usually the mother, children's behavioral problems in single-parent households may reflect the absence of a father figure.

Although children of single parents do tend to behave worse, this relationship and the supposed reasons for it come with an important qualification. Children in single-parent households may behave worse not because of their number of parents per se but because single-parent households are typically low-income households. This is because unmarried parents, and especially unmarried mothers, are much more likely than married parents to come from low-income backgrounds (McLanahan 2009). It may be single-parent households' poverty and corresponding neighborhood conditions, not the presence of only one parent, that produce their children's behavioral problems. To help understand this point, imagine that a high-income physician, attorney, or banker, or even a lower paid but highly educated professor, is a single mother. Despite having only one parent, this mother's children will nonetheless grow up with many advantages and likely go to college and have successful careers and family lives. It is difficult to believe that children in these circumstances will become serious delinquents, even though they live with only their mother.

To investigate the impact of having a single parent versus the impact of the economic situation typifying single-parent households, it is necessary to control for family income and related variables (for example, neighborhood conditions) so that single-parent households are in effect being compared with two-parent households with identical incomes. In some such research, the criminogenic effect of having a single parent disappears or greatly diminishes (Rankin and Kern 1994). It is never easy to be a single parent, but the behavioral problems of children in single-parent households may stem more from their households' financial and related circumstances than from the presence of only one parent (McLanahan and Sandefur 1995).

Research also compares children in two-parent households with children whose mother is living with a partner or has remarried. This research shows that children in the latter circumstances tend to behave worse, both during childhood and during adolescence, than children in intact households (Apel and Kaukinen 2008; Pardini et al. 2015). Related to this point, children tend to behave worse if their mother has multiple relationships: living with one partner for several months, then living with another partner, and so forth. As a recent review summarized this point, "Adolescents who experience changes in family structure as parents begin and end romantic unions are more likely than adolescents in stable family structures to engage in aggressive, antisocial, or delinquent behavior" (Fomby and Sennott 2013:197). Children with these changes go through *multiple transitions* by having to live with a new adult and sometimes by having to physically move to another dwelling unit and another town or city. These transitions are emotionally and practically taxing for many children, in part because of the conflict that led their mother's relationship with a partner to dissolve, and thus produce behavioral problems.

Here again, though, the importance of income must be kept in mind. Single mothers tend to come from low-income backgrounds and then tend to live with or marry partners from low-income backgrounds. The resulting household income is still low. If a single mother married a physician, attorney, or other wealthy or fairly wealthy spouse and then lived in a swanky neighborhood, it is unlikely that her children's behavior would worsen in the long run after an initial adjustment period. Of course, because single mothers do tend to be low-income, they are very unlikely to marry wealthy, well-educated spouses. Still, the point remains that the economic context of children's family transitions must be kept in mind when these transitions produce behavioral and other problems among children.

Before we leave family structure, it is worth commenting on early motherhood. Much research shows that single mothers not only come from low-income backgrounds but also tend to have had their first child before age 20, that is, while still a teenager. Children of these very young mothers are at much greater risk for a variety of behavioral, cognitive, emotional, and health problems (Pardini et al. 2015; Pogarsky, Lizotte, and Thornberry 2003).

These problems stem from several factors. First, many young mothers, because of their age, are still immature and lack good parenting skills. Second, most of these mothers come from low-income backgrounds, and their poverty and related conditions (including the neighborhoods in which they must live because of their poverty) help contribute to their children's problems. Third, these mothers are more likely than older mothers to have substance abuse and emotional problems. Fourth, they are more likely to lack the strong social support networks that parents often need to be good parents. All these reasons point to the need for crime prevention strategies to pay special attention to families headed by young, low-income mothers. Chapter 8 examines these strategies further.

Family Functioning and Parenting

How well a family functions is very important for its children's behavior and may be more important than family structure in this regard. Many of the family-oriented crime prevention strategies discussed in Chapter 8 build on this fundamental fact and on the abundant research demonstrating this importance.

This research examines several dimensions of family functioning, including (1) the nature and quality of family interaction, (2) the quality of parental discipline and supervision of children, (3) the presence or absence of child abuse and neglect, and (4) parental substance abuse. All these dimensions matter greatly for children's behavior and other outcomes, and children and adolescents in the "bad" kind of family situation along these dimensions are much more likely to misbehave than children in the "good" kind of family situation (Farrington 2011; Pardini et al. 2015). This is true for antisocial behavior during childhood, delinquency during adolescence, and criminality during young adulthood. We discuss each of these dimensions in turn.

Nature and Quality of Family Interaction

Travis Hirschi's (1969) acclaimed **social bonding theory** emphasized the importance of strong attachments to parents (and also schools and teachers) for reducing the chances of delinquency. Adolescents with strong bonds to their parents (assuming their parents are law-abiding!) are less likely to break the law because they value their parents' perceptions, because they feel it morally right to abide by their parents' wishes, and because they do not want to disappoint their parents by misbehaving. Conversely, when they have weak bonds to their parents, they feel freer to disregard their parents' norms and instructions and may even wish to "get back at" their parents by disobeying their rules.

Another acclaimed criminological theory developed by Hirschi also emphasizes the importance of how well parents raise their children. This is **self-control theory**, which argues that individuals with low self-control are more likely to be impulsive, to violate social norms, and to misbehave during childhood and commit delinquency during adolescence (Gottfredson and Hirschi 1990). Low self-control develops from low-quality parenting during childhood and can persist throughout the life course (Botchkovar et al. 2015; Meldrum, Young, and Lehmann 2015).

The strong parent–child bonds and high-quality parenting that are so important for preventing delinquency are most likely to exist and flourish when parents have a good, loving relationship with each other and with their children, with little or no conflict. Conversely, when the household is filled with interpersonal conflict, family harmony suffers and attachments weaken. Children in such households are at much greater risk for antisocial behavior and delinquency for this reason, and also because of the emotional impact of the conflict.

An overwhelming amount of research confirms this fundamental insight from social bonding theory. Children living in households with higher levels of family conflict and lacking warm, strong bonds to their parents are much more likely than children in harmonious families with strong parental bonds to misbehave during childhood and to commit delinquency as teenagers. As a recent review summarizes the evidence, "Families characterized by high levels of inter-parental conflict, particularly the tendency to engage in arguments that involve verbal and physical aggression, tend to have children who engage in early conduct problems and chronic forms of delinquency.... High levels of parental warmth and shared parent-child activities are associated with fewer conduct problems during early childhood and adolescence" (Pardini et al. 2015:204–205, 207). This evidence holds important implications for crime prevention strategies, as Chapter 8 will discuss.

Parental Discipline and Supervision of Children

Here again, a large amount of research confirms the importance of the nature and quality of child discipline and other parenting practices for child and adolescent behavior. Parents who practice *authoritative discipline* (also called *firm but fair discipline*) are more likely than parents who practice other types of discipline (*authoritarian, erratic,* or *lax*) to have better-behaved children and adolescents. In authoritative discipline, the parents set clear but fair rules for their children's behavior at an early age and apply these rules consistently but with little or no spanking. As their names imply, *authoritarian discipline* involves harsh discipline characterized by frequent spanking, *erratic discipline* involves discipline that can be reasonable one day and overly harsh the next day, and *lax discipline* is overly permissive and permits offspring to do many things without fear of parental sanctions. Compared with authoritative discipline, all three of these other discipline styles produce more child and adolescent misbehavior (Pardini et al. 2015).

Despite the old saying "Spare the rod and spoil the child," frequent spanking and other harsh discipline do produce more misbehavior (MacKenzie et al. 2015). This effect occurs because children experiencing this harsh discipline have lower attachment to their parents, are more likely to misbehave if they think they will not get caught, and are more likely to believe that interpersonal violence (which is what spanking involves) helps solve interpersonal disputes.

An important aspect of parenting during adolescence involves *parental supervision* (monitoring and regulating) of teenagers' activities. Effective supervision is often difficult because teenagers spend a lot of time with their friends, especially when at least one friend acquires a driver's license. Still, a large number of studies find that effective supervision does help reduce delinquency and other behavioral problems, while ineffective supervision helps increase the potential for these problems (Hoeve et al. 2009).

The evidence on parental discipline and supervision again holds significant implications for crime prevention strategies. As Pardini et al. (2015:205) comment, "The role of parenting practices in the development of delinquent behavior is of particular importance for 'theory-driven' prevention and intervention efforts involving parent-training programs." Chapter 8 again discusses strategies aimed at improving parenting practices.

Child Abuse and Neglect

One particular parental practice deserves special mention, and that is abuse (physical and/or sexual) and/or neglect of children. Regarding delinquency and other misbehavior, abuse is more often studied than neglect. Abundant research demonstrates that abused and neglected children are much more likely than well-treated children to have behavior problems during childhood and to engage in delinquency/crime and substance use during adolescence and beyond (Dalsklev et al. 2019; Kerig and Becker 2015; Widom et al. 2013). This consequence stems from the emotional impact of abuse and neglect and from the greatly weakened parent–child bond that abuse and neglect produce. Efforts that can reduce child abuse and neglect certainly help children in the short run but can also help them in the long run. These efforts are essential in and of themselves, but they also hold promise for reducing delinquency and crime.

Parental Substance Use

Many parents unfortunately drink too much and/or misuse other drugs, both legal and illegal. These parents harm the health, safety, and behavioral, cognitive, and emotional development of their children. Many studies show that parental substance abuse produces a greater likelihood of childhood antisocial behavior and adolescent delinquency and substance use (Lander, Howsare, and Byrne 2013; Park and Schepp 2015). This effect reflects the poorer parenting practices of parents who misuse alcohol and other drugs, the weaker parent–child bond that results, the emotional impact of the substance use, the greater family conflict that often occurs, and the greater amount of child abuse and neglect committed by substance-using parents. Once again, efforts to reduce parental substance abuse are important in and of themselves for many reasons, and one of these reasons is that they, too, hold promise for reducing delinquent and criminal behavior.

Peer Influences

Friendships are incredibly important for most teenagers. During this stage of the life course, friends and acquaintances influence many of our attitudes and behaviors, for better or for worse. Most teenagers want their peers to like them and to hang out with them. For this reason, they tend to conform to their peers' expectations for their behavior and to share their views on matters big and small.

Perhaps not surprisingly, then, one of criminology's most important sets of explanations for delinquency concerns the impact of friends and acquaintances. These **social learning explanations** stress that adolescents are more or less likely to commit delinquency depending on the types of friends they have (Akers, Sellers, and Jennins 2017). Teenagers with delinquent friends are more likely to commit delinquency; teenagers with law-abiding friends are less likely to commit delinquency. Specific social learning explanations emphasize this or that reason for why friends have these effects, but the differences among these explanations need not concern us now.

Generally, however, delinquent friends are thought to affect the potential for delinquency because they affect the values that other teenagers hold and the behavior they perform. Conformity to these values and behaviors is rewarding because it helps win and maintain the friendships that teenagers cherish so much. Because such conformity is rewarding, teens are more likely to commit delinquency if their friends are doing the same. Conversely, if they indicate any dislike for joining their friends in illegal behavior, they risk ridicule and exclusion from their friends' other activities.

Much research confirms that the consequence of these dynamics is a greater likelihood of delinquency, drinking and other drug use, and other problematic behavior. According to a recent review, deviant peer affiliation (DPA), as involvement with delinquent peers is often called, "has been shown to be one of the strongest predictors of delinquent behavior in children and adolescents" (Vitaro, Brendgen, and Lacourse 2015:221). Criminologist Mark Warr (2002:40) adds, "No characteristic of individuals known to criminologists is a better predictor of criminal behavior than the number of delinquent friends an individual has. The strong correlations between delinquent behavior and delinquent friends has been documented in scores of studies from the 1950s up to the present day."

However, questions persist as to whether the DPA→delinquency relationship is truly causal in the way that social learning explanations assume (Miller, Shutt, and Barnes 2010). In a causal order question, delinquency may in fact contribute to DPA. If a teenager is already delinquent or inclined to begin committing delinquent acts, he or she may seek out peers with the same delinquent interests. The DPA→delinquency relationship may also be spurious: poverty, low-quality parenting, and other factors may make teens more likely both to have delinquent friends and to commit delinquency. Longitudinal and other research finds that the strength of the DPA→delinquency relationship diminishes when all these possibilities are considered. Still, most studies conclude and most criminologists agree that DPA does, in fact, tend to increase delinquent behavior.

To the extent this is true, DPA helps us understand why certain kinds of teens (in terms of their social backgrounds) are more likely to be delinquent. For example, males are more likely than females to be delinquent, and one reason for this gender difference is that boys are more likely than girls to have delinquent peers. Similarly, African American and Latino youths are more likely to commit serious delinquency, and one reason for this racial/ethnic difference is that African American and Latino youths are also more likely to have delinquent peers (Haynie and Payne 2006). In a related interesting finding, adolescents who are dating someone who commits delinquency or other "deviant" behavior are more likely themselves to become delinquent from this romantic relationship (Seffrin et al. 2009).

The influence of peers on delinquency underscores the need for parents to provide adequate supervision of their teenaged children (Farrington 2011). Parenting of teenagers is never easy, but parents who provide such supervision can limit the time their children spend with "bad" kids and thus limit the influence that delinquent peers may have on their children.

The research on peer influences and delinquency has complex implications for crime prevention strategies. Social service agencies and the government cannot simply decide which friends any teenager should be allowed to have and not to have. Thus, crime prevention strategies cannot easily and directly reduce delinquent peer influences. However, strategies can help parents become better supervisors of their teens' activities and friendships, and strategies can address other causes of delinquency and crime. If these latter efforts succeed and crime and delinquency decline in a particular neighborhood, peer influences become less negative because fewer adolescents are breaking the law. This consequence can mean that a good "domino effect" may occur, whereby teens become less likely to influence each other to commit delinquency because crime prevention strategies focusing on causes other than peer influences have proven effective.

Schools and Schooling

Peers play a significant role in adolescents' lives, but so do their schools. Teens spend many of their waking hours in school during the academic year and some of their waking hours doing homework and/or engaging in sports and other extracurricular activities. The importance of schools and schooling for adolescents led criminologists long ago to become interested in the effects of educational factors on delinquency.

Albert K. Cohen (1955) was one of the first scholars to emphasize the importance of schooling for delinquency. Cohen reasoned that adolescents who do poorly in school will become frustrated by their school failure. To compensate for their frustration, they will spend more time with delinquent friends, from whom they will learn certain values, such as selfishness and maliciousness, that will make it more likely they will break the law. As they commit delinquency with these friends, they will gain new status and respect that reduces their frustration from their school failure, and their self-esteem will also improve.

Hirschi's social bonding theory, discussed earlier, also emphasized the importance of schools and schooling for delinquency, but with different reasoning. To review, Hirschi thought that strong attachments to, and involvement with, conventional social instructions help reduce delinquency. Because schools are a key social institution for adolescents, Hirschi reasoned that strong bonds to one's school and teachers should help reduce delinquency, and weak bonds of these types should raise the potential for delinquency.

Stimulated by the theoretical work of Cohen and Hirschi, much research examines the relationship between delinquency and various aspects of schooling (Hirschfield 2018; Payne and Welch 2015). This research finds that students are less likely to be delinquent if they like their schools and teachers, if they value the importance of their education, if they get good grades, and if they are active in school-related extracurricular activities. Conversely, students are more likely to be delinquent if they dislike their schools, dismiss the value of their education, get poor grades, and are less active in school activities. Research also finds that disciplining students by suspending or expelling them makes them more likely to commit delinquency and crime (Hirschfield 2018).

Here again there are possibilities of causal order and spuriousness. In a causal order problem, perhaps the schooling→delinquency relationship exists because adolescents who become delinquent lose interest in their education and in school affairs. In a spuriousness problem, perhaps factors such as poverty and parental relationships affect schooling variables and also delinquency. Research that considers these possibilities finds that the strength of the schooling→delinquency relationship does diminish because of some spuriousness and because delinquency does affect schooling factors. Still, a fair conclusion is that schooling success on all the dimensions mentioned earlier still seems to reduce the chances of delinquency, while schooling failure seems to raise the potential for delinquency.

Structural aspects of children's schools also influence their likelihood of delinquency. In particular, delinquency and other problematic behavior are more common in schools with more crowded classrooms, with fewer instructional resources, and with larger student populations (Payne and Welch 2015). In these types of schools, academic performance suffers, and children's bonds to their teachers and commitment to their learning become weaker. Drawing on the earlier discussion, these latter problems help produce delinquency.

The nature of school discipline also matters for the rate of delinquency. Here the research findings are similar to those for parental discipline. Schools that practice authoritative discipline by having firm but fair rules and appropriate but not overly punitive discipline tend to have lower rates of delinquency; schools with overly strict rules and harsh punishments such as the frequent use of suspension and expulsion tend to have higher rates of delinquency. The students receiving these harsh punishments become more likely to commit delinquency because of the harsh punishments, the opposite effect from what school officials intend and expect. Two reasons for this criminogenic effect are that these students perform more poorly in school because of the harsh punishments and develop more negative attitudes about their school and schooling (Payne and Welch 2015).

Although most research on schooling and behavior focuses on secondary schools, some research does consider the impact of higher education on offending in young adulthood and beyond. The findings of this research are clear: Young people in college are less likely than those not in college to commit crime during this period of their lives (Payne and Welch 2015). The interpretation of these findings is less clear because of possible causal order and spuriousness issues. People who are already offenders may be less likely to go to college (causal order), and various antecedent variables (such as family income) may affect both the likelihood of attending college and of committing crime (spuriousness). Still, studies that take these possibilities into account conclude that college attendance does in fact reduce the likelihood of criminal behavior (Ford and Schroeder 2011).

This crime-reduction effect is thought to occur for several reasons. Attending college (1) reduces the time and opportunity to commit crime; (2) limits contact with deviant peers; (3) enhances cognitive abilities and certain personality traits (such as self-esteem and lower impulsivity) that help reduce antisocial tendencies; (4) enhances employment prospects that help keep young adults out of trouble; and (5) increases the likelihood of marriage, which reduces criminality outside the home. This crime-reduction effect holds true for young adults generally but is especially strong for young adults who were the most delinquent during adolescence (Ford and Schroeder 2011).

The vast body of research on schools, schooling, and delinquency and crime again has key implications for crime reduction strategies. If the nation could improve its secondary schools and the quality of the education they provide, many benefits would ensue, and one of these benefits should be reduction of delinquency and other problematic behavior. Education critics have pointed to many U.S. schools, especially those in urban areas, as bleak, alienating places where little learning occurs (Kozol 1991, 2005). If these schools could be significantly improved on many levels, one of the side benefits would very likely be reduced delinquency and crime. Similarly, if more young people were able to attend college, criminal behavior during young adulthood and beyond should decline. Chapter 9 explores school-related crime prevention further.

SOCIODEMOGRAPHIC CORRELATES OF CRIME

The many reasons for crime and delinquency discussed in this chapter and in Chapter 3 help explain why four fundamental sociodemographic variables predict criminality. These variables are *age*, *gender*, *social class*, and *race/ethnicity*. These correlates in turn have implications for crime prevention.

Age

Young people, those in roughly the 15-to-30 age range, commit more than their fair share of street crime. Another way of saying this is that they commit a *disproportionate* amount of crime. This age–crime relationship is one of the clearest, strongest, and least controversial findings in the criminological literature. People ages 15 to 30 compose only about one-fifth of the U.S. population, but they account for about half of all arrests (Federal Bureau of Investigation 2018). If young people had crime rates no higher than older age groups, the United States would have much less crime, and the need for effective crime prevention would be at least somewhat less urgent.

Many reasons help explain why young people have higher crime rates. First, and in no particular order, an increasing amount of biological research finds that brains do not become fully mature until about age 25. Before this age, the areas of the brain responsible for reasoning ability and other cognitive functions are not fully developed for most young people. Researchers think this fact makes them more likely to engage in crime and other antisocial behavior (Bonnie and Scott 2013; Steinberg and Chein 2015). Second, friends and other peers play a very important role in the lives of most adolescents and young adults. To the extent that peer influences matter for delinquency and crime, young people are more likely than older people to be affected by these influences. Third, young people are more likely than older people to lack stakes in conformity, such as marriage and employment, as cited earlier in this chapter. This fact leaves them freer in many ways to break the law.

If young people do commit more than their fair share of crime, crime prevention strategies would benefit from focusing on the 15-to-30 age group, as well as on the many childhood influences discussed earlier in this chapter that help set the stage for crime by this age group. You will see in later chapters of this book that many crime prevention efforts, including many of the most promising, are in fact aimed at children, teenagers, and young adults.

Gender

Gender is another variable on which there is little criminological disagreement: Males are far more likely than females to commit violent and property crime. Males are about half of the population but account for about four-fifths of violent crime arrests and two-thirds of property crime arrests (Federal Bureau of Investigation 2018).

Although there is little disagreement on this gender difference, there is more disagreement on *why* this difference exists (Chesney-Lind and Shelden 2014; Sapolsky 2012). Biologically oriented criminologists and other scholars trace it to factors such as testosterone and evolutionary needs that favored strong, aggressive men. Sociologically oriented criminologists trace it to gendered socialization that promotes male aggressiveness, boys' weaker attachments to their parents and schooling, and boys' greater opportunities to commit crime and higher numbers of delinquent peers.

Although a detailed discussion of this disagreement within criminology is beyond the scope of this book, it is worth noting that our society cannot do anything about testosterone and evolution, but perhaps it can do something about male socialization patterns and other aspects of males' lives that promote their criminality. As you will see in later chapters of this book, many current crime prevention strategies focus on young boys, teenage boys, and adult men. More generally, the large gender difference in criminality points to the need for crime prevention strategies to focus more on males than on females. Our society should be concerned about female offenders, but if male rates of crime and delinquency were as low as female rates, the United States would have much less crime, and effective crime prevention would certainly be less urgent, however still helpful.

Social Class

There is a rather surprising amount of disagreement within criminology over the relationship between social class and crime/delinquency. Although most people arrested for street crime come from low-income backgrounds and are certainly not college-educated, some criminologists say that their arrests reflect social class bias by the police more than actual social class differences in criminality. Relying on self-report survey evidence indicating little or no social class differences in delinquency, some criminologists even label the presumed social class/criminality link a "myth" (Tittle, Villemez, and Smith 1978). Other criminologists say that low-income youths are indeed more likely to engage in youth violence and other serious delinquency (Bjerk 2007). This debate led one sociologist to caustically note that "social scientists somehow still knew better than to stroll the streets at night in certain parts of town or even to park there" and that they also "knew that the parts of town that scared them were not upper-income neighborhoods" (Stark 1987:894).

While acknowledging that some social class bias might exist, most criminologists would probably agree that low-income individuals are indeed more likely to commit street crime. These criminologists would quickly add that higher-income individuals are much more likely to commit many types of white-collar crime. The poor certainly have no monopoly on crime, as social class affects what kinds of crime people commit.

If lower social class status does indeed prompt higher rates of street crime, why does this happen? Chapter 5 examines this issue in greater detail, but several currents discussed earlier in the present chapter help provide some answers. Children living in poverty and low-income settings suffer various cognitive and neurological deficits, and they are more likely to experience low-quality parenting. They are also more likely during childhood and adolescence to live in socially and economically disadvantaged higher-crime neighborhoods and to come under the influence of delinquent peers. Poverty and its related conditions are also said to foster anger, frustration, and economic need that in turn promote criminal behavior (Sampson and Wilson 1995). The psychological reactions just cited are thought to reflect the poor's feeling of **relative deprivation** as they compare their situation to the situations of those who are better off (Peterson and Krivo 2009).

Because low-income people do appear to commit most street crime, it is essential that crime prevention strategies focus on reducing poverty and also address the many reasons that account for the poverty and crime connection. Many of the crime prevention strategies examined in later chapters have precisely this focus.

Race and Ethnicity

One of the most controversial criminological issues involves the relationship between race/ethnicity and criminal behavior (Peterson 2012). Most of this controversy concerns African Americans. Arrest statistics suggest that African Americans commit more crime than members of other races. Although African Americans compose about 13% to 14% of the population, they account for more than one-third of violent crime arrests and almost one-third of property crime arrests. Within violent crime, they account for about half of all homicide arrests and more than half of robbery arrests (Federal Bureau of Investigation 2018). Do these arrest statistics reflect police racial bias, or do they reflect real racial differences in offending? While acknowledging racial bias in arrests, most criminologists conclude that African Americans do, in fact, commit serious street crime at higher rates than other races (Barkan 2018; Gabbidon and Greene 2016; Walker, Spohn, and DeLone 2018).

The important question to answer is why this racial difference exists. Here criminologists flatly reject as racist and unfounded any explanations suggesting that African Americans are biologically inferior. These explanations were popular many decades ago but have long been abandoned by the scholarly community. Instead, criminologists point to the conditions in which African Americans live as fostering their higher rates of offending (Barkan and Rocque 2018; Gabbidon and Greene 2016; Peterson 2012).

Compared with whites, African Americans are much more likely to be poor and to live in the disadvantaged neighborhoods discussed earlier in this chapter. These conditions foster frustration and anger and impede good parenting skills. As two criminologists have written, "African Americans and other minorities exhibit higher rates of violence than do whites because they are more likely to reside in community contexts with high levels of poverty, unemployment, family disruption, and residential instability. . . . If whites were embedded in similar structural contexts, they would exhibit comparable rates of violence" (McNulty and Bellair 2003:5).

A related factor is simply that African Americans are more likely than whites to live in dense urban areas (Stark 1987). As this chapter discussed earlier, these areas have higher crime and victimization rates, regardless of who lives in them, for reasons explained by routine activities theory; again, if more whites lived in these same areas, their crime rates would be higher. A final reason for the higher rate of African American offending is racial discrimination, which heightens the anger and frustration that help generate criminal behavior (Simons and Burt 2011; Unnever and Gabbidon 2011). All these reasons help explain why Latinos and Native Americans also tend to have higher rates of criminality than non-Latino whites (Painter-Davis 2012; Phillips 2002).

Racial and ethnic differences in offending alert us to the need for crime prevention to focus on the reasons for these differences. Prevention efforts that effectively address the many reasons for crime discussed in this chapter would especially benefit African Americans and other people of color, who are all much more likely than non-Latino whites to experience criminogenic conditions. Successful efforts in this regard would reduce the racial difference in street crime that now exists.

Before we leave the issue of race and ethnicity, it is important to comment on a related topic—immigration and crime. During the past decade, Americans have heard from politicians, law enforcement personnel, and other parties that recent immigrants to the United States pose a significant danger of violent crime and other lawbreaking (Kight 2019). Despite these alarmist cries, much criminological research finds that immigrants do not have higher crime rates than native-born Americans and may even have lower crime rates (Adelman et al. 2017; Ousey and Kubrin 2018). The research evidence simply does not support the belief that immigrants cause more crime, and any such assertions regarding immigrants and crime are not grounded in reality.

THE NEED FOR MULTIFACETED CRIME PREVENTION

The many causes of crime and delinquency discussed in this chapter point to the need for multifaceted crime prevention. Crime prevention strategies focusing on only one cause of crime can have only a limited impact because they leave other causes of crime unaddressed. Two theoretical perspectives in criminology, *general strain theory* and *life-course criminology*, especially underscore this point.

General Strain Theory

As developed by Robert Agnew (1992, 2007), **general strain theory (GST)** emphasizes that many people suffer strain from difficult circumstances such as lack of money, arguments with parents, poor grades, being bullied, or perceptions of other mistreatment. Whatever its source, strain may produce stress, frustration, and emotions like anger and unhappiness. These outcomes in turn may prompt individuals (especially adolescents and young adults) to commit violence or to steal money or valuables as a way of reducing their frustration or of taking revenge on people they feel have wronged them.

Several of the factors identified earlier in this chapter as underlying crime and delinquency may be interpreted through a GST framework (Agnew 2007). For example, one reason why poor parenting fosters antisocial behavior is that the children subjected to poor parenting feel various kinds of strains from their negative home situation. One reason poverty fosters antisocial behavior is that it involves many kinds of strains that create frustration, anger, and other negative emotions. If strain occurs for many reasons and is also a common aspect of many of the underlying causes of crime and delinquency, crime prevention must address the many sources of strain to achieve its maximal impact.

Life-Course Criminology

A second theoretical perspective suggests even more strongly the need for multi-faceted crime prevention. This theoretical perspective is called **life-course criminology**. There are actually many life-course theories, but they all emphasize the need to study the *trajectory* of problematic behavior throughout the life course: the beginning of antisocial behavior during childhood, its fruition as delinquency during adolescence and crime during young adulthood, and its waning (for most offenders) after young adulthood (Carlsson and Sarnecki 2016; Farrington and Ttofi 2015). A related empha-sis is that what happens during childhood can have effects throughout the life course. Life-course criminology reflects exciting lines of thought from the fields of biology, psychology, and sociology, and points to the development of, and desistance from, crime and delinquency as reflecting multiple reasons and contexts.

Life-course criminology's framework reminds us that many aspects of the life course interact to help create antisocial behavior and that for some individuals, these aspects can become a vicious cycle. As an example, consider that children enter school (kindergarten and first grade) with different backgrounds and characteristics. Some children are well behaved and very prepared for school, while others begin school already beset by behav-ioral and other problems. These problems impair their ability to do well in school, and this school failure in turn worsens their behavioral and other problems.

Once these problems worsen, school failure becomes even more likely, which may then worsen their behavioral problems, and so on. As this cycle continues into high school, the potential for delinquency and then adulthood crime heightens, as described earlier in this chapter. According to criminologists Allison Payne and Kelly Welch (2015:238), "Children who are already displaying antisocial behavior at home enter schools with a limited behavioral repertoire for interacting with teachers and other stu-dents. These students are then more difficult to handle in the classroom, which increases the likelihood of poor academic performance, poor attachment to teachers, lower school commitment, and rejection by conventional peers. . . . Ultimately, this entire process greatly increases the likelihood of persistent antisocial behavior."

This dynamic points to the need for multifaceted crime prevention strategies that address the multiple causes of antisocial behavior during childhood and at later stages of the life course. Staying with the schooling example, our schools could become the best in the world and thus achieve some delinquency and crime reduction, but this achievement would be less than optimal unless family problems, economic problems, and other criminogenic factors were also addressed. Because delinquency and crime do have multiple causes, crime prevention strategies that address only one or two of these causes will be less effective than strategies that focus on most or all of these causes.

So far we have been focusing on addressing the causes of crime, delinquency, and more general antisocial behavior. Another virtue of life-course criminology is its emphasis on the *protective* factors promoting *desistance* from crime (Kazemian 2015; Rocque and Slivken 2019). Although most adult offenders were juvenile delinquents, most delinquents do not continue to commit crime during adulthood. This fact leads criminologists to consider the factors that help most delinquents *not* continue their pattern of offending as they grow older. Many of these factors, such as caring parents and teachers, are the converse of the factors promoting antisocial behavior, but life-course criminology's emphasis on desistance still suggests the need for crime prevention strategies to aim at enhancing desistance factors.

For example, life-course criminology identifies employment and marriage as two particular *turning points* that help some youthful offenders begin desisting from criminality (Laub, Sampson, and Sweeten 2006). This effect occurs for at least two reasons. First, and recalling RAT, employment and marriage both reduce the time and opportunity to get into legal trouble. Second, employment and marriage strengthen an individual's social bonds to society and therefore the individual's stakes in conformity. People who realize that breaking the law may lead to their being fired and to their spouse becoming angry are that much less likely to break the law.

Although these reasons might sound compelling, not all research finds that employment and marriage do, in fact, produce desistance (Kazemian 2015). Leaving aside the mixed results of the research for now, if employment and marriage do help offenders desist from crime, social policies that promote full employment and strengthen families (such as economic aid to low-income families and subsidized childcare) should help reduce criminal behavior. These and similar policies are especially important for helping formerly incarcerated people desist from criminal behavior (see Chapter 13). Policies that promote other protective factors should also help offenders desist from crime.

CONCLUSION

Many factors explain why some people are more likely than others to commit crime. For crime to be reduced to the greatest degree possible, crime prevention strategies must address these factors. Recent biological and personality research suggests the need to focus on many types of problems during childhood that impair children's cognitive and neurological development. Research on community factors suggests the need to focus on the structural and social aspects of urban neighborhoods that help generate criminality. Research on families, peers, and schools points to additional factors for crime prevention to address. Crime prevention strategies will succeed only to the extent that they are able to address the many causes of crime and delinquency throughout the life course.

SUMMARY

1. Crime tends to be higher in disadvantaged communities characterized by high poverty, residential instability, and other problems. To reduce crime most effectively, crime prevention must focus on all these problems.

2. Routine activities theory emphasizes the practicality of crime. This emphasis provides an important rationale for the potential of situational crime prevention.

3. Alcohol and firearms contribute to violent crime. Certain types of strategies discussed later in this book may reduce the harm caused by alcohol and firearms while recognizing the legality of alcohol and the constitutional right to own firearms.

4. Families, peers, and schools shape children and adolescents in profound ways. Poor parenting, deviant peers, and low-quality schools and schooling all contribute to delinquency and antisocial behavior and set the stage for adult criminality.

KEY TERMS

community factors 60

family functioning 66

family structure 66

general strain theory (GST) 78

life-course criminology 79

lifestyle theory 62

relative deprivation 77

routine activities theory 62

self-control theory 69

situational factors 60

social bonding theory 69

social disorganization 60

social learning explanations 71

REFERENCES

Adelman, Robert, Lesley Williams Reid, Gail Markle, Saskia Weiss, and Charles Jaret. 2017. "Urban Crime Rates and the Changing Face of Immigration: Evidence Across Four Decades." *Journal of Ethnicity in Criminal Justice* 15(1):52–77. doi: 10.1080/15377938.2016.1261057.

Agnew, Robert. 1992. "Foundation for a General Strain Theory of Crime and Delinquency." *Criminology* 30(1):47–87.

Agnew, Robert. 2007. *Pressured Into Crime: An Overview of General Strain Theory*. New York, NY: Oxford University Press.

Akers, Ronald L., Christine S. Sellers, and Wesley G. Jennins. 2017. *Criminological Theories: Introduction, Evaluation, and Application*. New York, NY: Oxford University Press.

Allen, MacKenzie. 2011. "Why This Cop Asked the President About Legalizing Drugs."

The Huffington Post. February 23. Retrieved September 5, 2019 (http://www.huffingtonpost.com/mackenzie-allen/why-this-cop-asked-the-pr_b_827338.html).

Amato, Paul R. 2010. "Research on Divorce: Continuing Trends and New Developments." *Journal of Marriage and the Family* 72: 650–666.

Anderson, Elijah. 1999. *Code of the Street: Decency, Violence, and the Moral Life of the Inner City.* New York, NY: W. W. Norton.

Apel, Robert, and Catherine Kaukinen. 2008. "On the Relationship Between Family Structure and Antisocial Behavior: Parental Cohabitation and Blended Households." *Criminology* 46(1):35–70.

Augustyn, Megan Bears, and Jean Marie McGloin. 2013. "The Risk of Informal Socializing With Peers: Considering Gender Differences Across Predatory Delinquency and Substance Use." *JQ: Justice Quarterly* 30(1):117–143. doi: 10.1080/07418825.2011.597417.

Barkan, Steven E. 2018. *Race, Crime, and Justice: The Continuing American Dilemma.* New York, NY: Oxford University Press.

Barkan, Steven E., and Michael Rocque. 2018. "Socioeconomic Status and Racism as Fundamental Causes of Street Criminality." *Critical Criminology* 26(2):211–231.

Bjerk, David. 2007. "Measuring the Relationship Between Youth Criminal Participation and Household Economic Resources." *Journal of Quantitative Criminology* 23: 23–39.

Bonnie, Richard J., and Elizabeth S. Scott. 2013. "The Teenage Brain: Adolescent Brain Research and the Law." *Current Directions in Psychological Science* 22: 158–161.

Botchkovar, Ekaterina, Ineke Haen Marshall, Michael Rocque, and Chad Posick. 2015. "The Importance of Parenting in the Development of Self-Control in Boys and Girls: Results From a Multinational Study of Youth." *Journal of Criminal Justice* 43: 133–141.

Boyum, David A., Jonathan P. Caulkins, and Mark A. R. Kleiman. 2011. "Drugs, Crime, and Public Policy." Pp. 368–410 in *Crime and Public Policy,* edited by J. Q. Wilson and J. Petersilia. New York, NY: Oxford University Press.

Carlsson, Christoffer, and Jerzy Sarnecki. 2016. *An Introduction to Life-Course Criminology.* Thousand Oaks, CA: Sage.

Chesney-Lind, Meda, and Randall G. Shelden. 2014. *Girls, Delinquency, and Juvenile Justice.* Malden, MA: Wiley-Blackwell.

Cohen, Albert K. 1955. *Delinquent Boys: The Culture of the Gang.* New York, NY: Free Press.

Cohen, Lawrence E., and Marcus Felson. 1979. "Social Change and Crime Rate Trends: A Routine Activity Approach." *American Sociological Review* 44: 588–607.

Dalsklev, Madeleine, Twylia Cunningham, Martin Dempster, and Donncha Hanna. 2019. "Childhood Physical and Sexual Abuse as a Predictor of Reoffending: A Systematic Review." *Trauma, Violence, & Abuse.* https://doi.org/10.1177%2F1524838019869082.

Elliott, Margaret C., Veronique Dupéré, and Tama Leventhal. 2015. "Neighborhood Context and the Development of Criminal and Antisocial Behavior." Pp. 253–265 in *The Development of Criminal and Antisocial Behavior: Theory, Research and Practical Applications,* edited by J. Morizot and L. Kazemian. New York, NY: Springer.

Farrington, David P. 2011. "Families and Crime." Pp. 130–157 in *Crime and Public Policy,* edited by J. Q. Wilson and J. Petersilia. New York, NY: Oxford University Press.

Farrington, David P., and Maria M. Ttofi. 2015. "Developmental and Life-Course Theories of Offending." Pp. 19–38 in *The Development of Criminal and Antisocial Behavior: Theory, Research and Practical Applications*, edited by J. Morizot and L. Kazemian. New York, NY: Springer.

Faupel, Charles E., Alan M. Horowitz, and Greg S. Weaver. 2013. *The Sociology of American Drug Use*, 3rd ed. New York, NY: Oxford University Press.

Federal Bureau of Investigation. 2018. *Crime in the United States, 2017.* Washington, DC: Author.

Felson, Marcus, and Mary Eckert. 2016. *Crime and Everyday Life.* Thousand Oaks, CA: Sage.

Fix, Rebecca L., and Barry R. Burkhart. 2015. "Relationships Between Family and Community Factors on Delinquency and Violence Among African American Adolescents: A Critical Review." *Race and Justice* 5(4): 378–404.

Fomby, Paula, and Christie A. Sennott. 2013. "Family Structure Instability and Mobility: The Consequences for Adolescents' Problem Behavior." *Social Science Research* 42(1):186–201. doi: 10.1016/j.ssresearch.2012.08.016.

Ford, Jason A., and Ryan D. Schroeder. 2011. "Higher Education and Criminal Offending Over the Life Course." *Sociological Spectrum* 31(1):32–58. doi: http://dx.doi.org/10.1080/02732173.2011.525695.

Fowler, Katherine A., Linda L. Dahlberg, Tadesse Haileyesus, and Joseph L. Annest. 2015. "Firearm Injuries in the United States." *Preventive Medicine* 79(October):5–14.

Friedson, Michael, and Patrick Sharkey. 2015. "Violence and Neighborhood Disadvantage After the Crime Decline." *Annals of the American Academy of Political & Social Science* 660(1): 341–358. doi: 10.1177/0002716215579825.

Gabbidon, Shaun L., and Helen Taylor Greene. 2016. *Race and Crime.* Thousand Oaks, CA: Sage.

Goode, Erich. 2015. *Drugs in American Society.* New York, NY: McGraw-Hill.

Gottfredson, Michael, and Travis Hirschi. 1990. *A General Theory of Crime.* Stanford, CA: Stanford University Press.

Haynie, Dana L., and Danielle C. Payne. 2006. "Race, Friendship Networks, and Violent Delinquency." *Criminology* 44: 775–805.

Hemenway, David, and Sara J. Solnick. 2015. "The Epidemiology of Self-Defense Gun Use: Evidence From the National Crime Victimization Surveys 2007–2011." *Preventive Medicine* 79(October):22–27.

Hemenway, David, and Daniel W. Webster. 2015. "Guest Editorial: Increasing Knowledge for the Prevention of Firearm Violence." *Preventive Medicine* 79(October):3–4.

Hirschfield, Paul J. 2018. "Schools and Crime." *Annual Review of Criminology* 1: 149–169.

Hirschi, Travis. 1969. *Causes of Delinquency.* Berkeley: University of California Press.

Hoeve, Machteld, Judith Semon Dubas, Veroni I. Eichelsheim, Peter H. van der Laan, Wilma Smeenk, and Jan R. M. Gerris. 2009. "The Relationship Between Parenting and Delinquency: A Meta-Analysis." *Journal of Abnormal Child Psychology* 37(6):749–775. doi: 10.1007/s10802-009-9310-8.

Kazemian, Lila. 2015. "Desistance From Crime and Antisocial Behavior." Pp. 295–312 in *The Development of Criminal and Antisocial Behavior: Theory, Research and Practical Applications*, edited by J. Morizot and L. Kazemian. New York, NY: Springer.

Kellerman, Arthur L., Frederick P. Rivara, Norman B. Rushforth, Joyce G. Banton, Donald T. Reay, Jerry T. Francisco, Ana B. Locci, Janice Prodzinski, Bela B. Hackman, and Grant Somes. 1993. "Gun Ownership as a Risk Factor for Homicide in the Home." *New England Journal of Medicine* 329: 1084–1092.

Kerig, Patricia K., and Stephen P. Becker. 2015. "Early Abuse and Neglect as Risk Factors for the Development of Criminal and Antisocial Behavior." Pp. 181–199 in *The Development of Criminal and Antisocial Behavior: Theory, Research and Practical Applications*, edited by L. K. Julien Morizot. New York, NY: Springer.

Kight, Stef W. 2019. "Reality Check: Trump's Claims on Immigrants and Crime." *Axios.com*. January 9. Retrieved September 5, 2019 (https://www.axios.com/immigration-crime-border-trump-national-address-facts-6d752931-1a2b-40b2-a9e8-a912853b81ca.html).

Kozol, Jonathan. 1991. *Savage Inequalities: Children in America's Schools*. New York, NY: Crown.

Kozol, Jonathan. 2005. *The Shame of the Nation: The Restoration of Apartheid Schooling in America*. New York, NY: Crown.

Lander, Laura, Janie Howsare, and Marilyn Byrne. 2013. "The Impact of Substance Use Disorders on Families and Children: From Theory to Practice." *Social Work in Public Health* 28: 194–205.

Laub, John H., Robert J. Sampson, and Gary A. Sweeten. 2006. "Assessing Sampson and Laub's Life-Course Theory of Crime." Pp. 313–333 in *Taking Stock: The Status of Criminological Theory, Vol. 15, Advances in Criminological Theory*, edited by F. T. Cullen. New Brunswick, NJ: Transaction.

Law Enforcement Against Prohibition. 2015. "Why Legalize Drugs?" Retrieved September 5, 2019 (http://www.leap.cc/about/why-legalize-drugs/).

Leshner, Alan I., Bruce M. Altevogt, Arlene F. Lee, Margaret A. McCoy, and Patrick W. Kelley. 2013. *Priorities for Research to Reduce the Threat of Firearm-Related Violence*. Washington, DC: National Academies Press.

MacKenzie, Michael, Eric Nicklas, Jeanne Brooks-Gunn, and Jane Waldfogel. 2015. "Spanking and Children's Externalizing Behavior Across the First Decade of Life: Evidence for Transactional Processes." *Journal of Youth & Adolescence* 44(3):658–669. doi: 10.1007/s10964-014-0114-y.

Marcum, Catherine D. 2010. "Routine Activity Theory: An Assessment of a Classical Theory." Pp. 43–55 in *Criminological Theory: Readings and Retrospectives*, edited by H. Copes and V. Topalli. New York, NY: McGraw-Hill.

McLanahan, Sara. 2009. "Fragile Families and the Reproduction of Poverty." *Annals of the American Academy of Political and Social Science* 621: 111–131.

McLanahan, Sara, and Gary Sandefur. 1995. *Growing Up With a Single Parent: What Hurts, What Helps*. Cambridge, MA: Harvard University Press.

McNeeley, Susan, and Pamela Wilcox. 2015. "Street Codes, Routine Activities, Neighbourhood Context and Victimization." *British Journal of Criminology* 55(5):921–943. doi: 10.1093/bjc/azu116.

McNulty, Thomas L., and Paul E. Bellair. 2003. "Explaining Racial and Ethnic Differences in Adolescent Violence: Structural Disadvantage, Family Well-Being, and Social Capital." *Justice Quarterly* 20: 1–31.

McNulty, Thomas L., Paul E. Bellair, and Stephen J. Watts. 2013. "Neighborhood Disadvantage and Verbal Ability as Explanations of the Black–White Difference in Adolescent Violence: Toward an Integrated Model." *Crime & Delinquency* 59(1):140–160. doi: 10.1177/0011128712461472.

Meldrum, Ryan C., Jacob T. N. Young, and Peter S. Lehmann. 2015. "Parental Low Self-Control, Parental Socialization, Young Adult Low Self-Control, and Offending: A Retrospective Study." *Criminal Justice and Behavior* 42(11):1183–1199.

Menard, Scott, Sharon Mihalic, and David Huizinga. 2001. "Drugs and Crime Revisited." *Justice Quarterly* 18: 269–299.

Miethe, Terance D., and Robert F. Meier. 1990. "Opportunity, Choice, and Criminal Victimization: A Test of a Theoretical Model." *Journal of Research in Crime and Delinquency* 27(3):243–266.

Miller, J. Mitchell, J. Eagle Shutt, and J. C. Barnes. 2010. "Learning Theory: From Seminal Statements to Hybridization." In *Criminological Theory: Readings and Retrospectives*, edited by H. Copes and V. Topalli. New York, NY: McGraw-Hill.

Miller, Matthew, David Hemenway, and Deborah Azrael. 2007. "State-Level Homicide Victimization Rates in the US in Relation to Survey Measures of Household Firearm Ownership, 2001–2003." *Social Science and Medicine* 64: 656–664.

Moule, Richard K., Callie H. Burt, Eric A. Stewart, and Ronald L. Simons. 2015. "Developmental Trajectories of Individuals' Code of the Street Beliefs Through Emerging Adulthood." *Journal of Research in Crime & Delinquency* 52(3):342–372. doi: 10.1177/0022427814565904.

Nofziger, Stacey, and Don Kurtz. 2005. "Violent Lives: A Lifestyle Model Linking Exposure to Violence to Juvenile Violent Offending." *Journal of Research in Crime and Delinquency* 42:3–26.

Ousey, Graham C., and Chris E. Kubrin. 2018. "Immigration and Crime: Assessing a Contentious Issue." *Annual Review of Criminology* 1: 63–84.

Painter-Davis, Noah. 2012. "Structural Disadvantage and American Indian Homicide and Robbery Offending." *Homicide Studies* 16(3):219–237. doi: 10.1177/1088767912441471.

Pardini, Dustin A., Rebecca Waller, and Samuel W. Hawes. 2015. "Familial Influences on the Development of Serious Conduct Problems and Delinquency." Pp. 201–220 in *The Development of Criminal and Antisocial Behavior: Theory, Research and Practical Applications*, edited by J. Morizot and L. Kazemian. New York, NY: Springer.

Park, Sihyun, and Karen Schepp. 2015. "A Systematic Review of Research on Children of Alcoholics: Their Inherent Resilience and Vulnerability." *Journal of Child & Family Studies* 24(5):1222–1231. doi: 10.1007/s10826-014-9930-7.

Parker, Robert Nash, and Kevin J. McCaffree. 2013. *Alcohol and Violence: The Nature of the Relationship and the Promise of Prevention.* New York, NY: Lexington Books.

Parker, Robert N., Kirk R. Williams, Kevin J. McCaffree, Emily K. Acensio, Angela Browne,

Kevin J. Strom, and Kelle Barrick. 2011. "Alcohol Availability and Youth Homicide in the 91 Largest US Cities, 1984–2006." *Drug & Alcohol Review* 30(5):505–514. doi: 10.1111/j.1465-3362.2011.00336.x.

Payne, Allison Ann, and Kelly Welch. 2015. "How School and Education Impact the Development of Criminal and Antisocial Behavior." Pp. 237–251 in *The Development of Criminal and Antisocial Behavior: Theory, Research and Practical Applications*, edited by J. Morizot and L. Kazemian. New York, NY: Springer.

Peterson, Ruth D. 2012. "The Central Place of Race in Crime and Justice: The American Society of Criminology's 2011 Sutherland Address." *Criminology* 50(2):303–328. doi: 10.1111/j.1745-9125.2012.00271.x.

Peterson, Ruth D., and Lauren J. Krivo. 2009. "Segregated Spatial Locations, Race-Ethnic Composition, and Neighborhood Violent Crime." *Annals of the American Academy of Political and Social Science* 623: 93–107.

Phillips, Julie A. 2002. "White, Black, and Latino Homicide Rates: Why the Difference?" *Social Problems* 49: 349–374.

Pogarsky, Greg, Alan J. Lizotte, and Terence P. Thornberry. 2003. "The Delinquency of Children Born to Young Mothers: Results From the Rocheser Youth Development Study." *Criminology* 41: 1249–1286.

Rankin, Joseph H., and Roger Kern. 1994. "Parental Attachments and Delinquency." *Criminology* 32: 495–515.

Robinson, Matthew B., and Renee G. Scherlen. 2014. *Lies, Damned Lies, and Drug War Statistics: A Critical Analysis of Claims Made by the Office of National Drug Control Policy*. Albany: State University of New York Press.

Rocque, Michael, and Lisa Slivken. 2019. "Desistance From Crime: Past to Present." Pp. 377–394 in *Handbook on Crime and Deviance*, edited by M. D. Krohn, N. Hendrix, G. P. Hall, and A. J. Lizotte. Cham, Switzerland: Springer.

Sampson, Robert J. 2013. *Great American City: Chicago and the Enduring Neighborhood Effect*. Chicago, IL: University of Chicago Press.

Sampson, Robert J., and William Julius Wilson. 1995. "Toward a Theory of Race, Crime, and Urban Inequality." Pp. 37–54 in *Crime and Inequality*, edited by J. Hagan and R. D. Peterson. Stanford, CA: Stanford University Press.

Sapolsky, Robert M. 2012. *The Trouble With Testosterone: And Other Essays on the Biology of the Human Predicament*, Reprint edition. New York, NY: Scribner.

Seffrin, Patrick M., Peggy C. Giordano, Wendy D. Manning, and Monica A. Longmore. 2009. "The Influence of Dating Relationships on Friendship Networks, Identity Development, and Delinquency." *Justice Quarterly* 26(2): 238–267. doi: 10.1080/07418820802245052.

Shaw, Clifford R., and Henry D. McKay. 1942. *Juvenile Delinquency and Urban Areas*. Chicago, IL: University of Chicago Press.

Simons, Ronald L., and Callie Harbin Burt. 2011. "Learning to Be Bad: Adverse Social Conditions, Social Schemas, and Crime." *Criminology* 49(2):553–598. doi: 10.1111/j.1745-9125.2011.00231.x.

Smith, Martha J., and Ronald V. Clarke. 2012. "Situational Crime Prevention: Classifying Techniques Using 'Good Enough' Theory." Pp. 291–315 in *The Oxford Handbook of Crime Prevention*, edited by B. C. Welsh and

D. P. Farrington. New York, NY: Oxford University Press.

Soler, Mark. 2001. *Public Opinion on Youth, Crime and Race: A Guide for Advocates*. Washington, DC: Youth Law Center.

Stark, Rodney. 1987. "Deviant Places: A Theory of the Ecology of Crime." *Criminology* 25: 893–911.

Steinberg, Laurence, and Jason M. Chein. 2015. "Multiple Accounts of Adolescent Impulsivity." *PNAS* 112(29):8807–8808.

Tittle, Charles R., Wayne J. Villemez, and Douglas A. Smith. 1978. "The Myth of Social Class and Criminality: An Empirical Assessment of the Empirical Evidence." *American Sociological Review* 43: 643–656.

Tompson, Lisa, and Kate Bowers. 2013. "A Stab in the Dark? A Research Note on Temporal Patterns of Street Robbery." *Journal of Research in Crime and Delinquency* 50(4):616–631. doi: 10.1177/0022427812469114.

Unnever, James D., and Shaun L. Gabbidon. 2011. *A Theory of African American Offending: Race, Racism, and Crime*. New York, NY: Routledge.

Vitaro, Frank, Mara Brendgen, and Eric Lacourse. 2015. "Peers and Delinquency: A Genetically Informed, Developmentally Sensitive Perspective." Pp. 221–236 in *The Development of Criminal and Antisocial Behavior: Theory, Research and Practical Applications*, edited by J. Morizot

and L. Kazemian. Cham, Switzerland: Springer International.

Walker, Samuel. 2015. *Sense and Nonsense About Crime, Drugs, and Communities*. Stamford, CT: Cengage Learning.

Walker, Samuel, Cassia Spohn, and Miriam DeLone. 2018. *The Color of Justice: Race, Ethnicity, and Crime in America*. Belmont, CA: Wadsworth.

Warr, Mark. 2002. *Companions in Crime: The Social Aspects of Criminal Conduct*. New York, NY: Cambridge University Press.

Widom, Cathy Spatz, Sally Czaja, Helen W. Wilson, Maureen Allwood, and Preeti Chauhan. 2013. "Do the Long Term Consequences of Neglect Differ for Children of Different Races and Ethnic Backgrounds?" *Child Maltreatment* 18(1):42–55. doi: 10.1177/1077559512460728.

Wilcox, Pamela, and Francis T. Cullen. 2018. "Situational Opportunity Theories of Crime." *Annual Review of Criminology* 1: 123–148.

Wintemute, Garen J. 2015. "Alcohol Misuse, Firearm Violence Perpetration, and Public Policy in the United States." *Preventive Medicine* 79: 15–21.

Zimring, Franklin E., and Gordon Hawkins. 1997. *Crime Is Not the Problem: Lethal Violence in America*. New York, NY: Oxford University Press.

PART II

PRIMARY CRIME PREVENTION
Focus on the Social and Physical Environments

5

ECONOMIC AND EMPLOYMENT STRATEGIES

Suppose you asked your friends how they think we should prevent crime. Would they first think of reducing poverty and unemployment? Or, more likely, would they instead mention strategies involving the police, prisons and jails, criminal courts, and other aspects of the criminal justice system? Criminal justice strategies are absolutely essential for crime prevention and are treated extensively later in this book. However, as this book's first few chapters emphasized, crime prevention must also focus on the many aspects of people's lives that foster criminal behavior in the first place. Our discussion here of economic and employment strategies is the first of three chapters to focus on primary prevention—that is, on efforts to address aspects of the social and physical environments that create the potential for criminal behavior.

Many of these efforts are in fact key features of the social policies of wealthy democracies around the world (Canada, the many Western European nations, and Australia and New Zealand). In contrast, the United States has implemented these strategies only fitfully (Russell 2018). The federal government funds some programs and policies related to these strategies, but not nearly at the level funded by the national governments of other wealthy democracies. Some states fund their own programs and policies, but many states do so only meagerly. The poor record of the United States overall in addressing problems in the social and physical environments is unfortunate for this fundamental reason: Implementing strategies to address these problems will not only reduce

Chapter Outline

Learning Questions

1. What percentage of Americans and how many Americans live in official poverty?

2. What are any three reasons that help explain why poverty contributes to criminal behavior?

(Continued)

(Continued)

3. What are any three factors that help explain why employment status should be related to criminal behavior?

4. What are any three strategies that should help reduce poverty and/or promote stable employment.

crime but also improve the lives of millions of Americans in many other ways.

To help you think about the issues addressed in this chapter, let's do a thought experiment that is admittedly fanciful. Suppose for some foolish reason you wanted to create a society that would be guaranteed to have a high crime rate. What kind of society would this be? You might well respond by saying your society would have a high rate of poverty and a high rate of unemployment, among other problems. For reasons discussed in Chapter 4 and examined further in this chapter, your society would almost certainly end up with a high crime rate because of its poverty and unemployment (or, to be more precise, a higher crime rate than a society with low rates of poverty and unemployment). This consequence would occur regardless of the race or ethnicity of the people who populate your society, and it would continue to occur from one generation to the next generation as your society grew older.

In many ways, the society with much poverty and unemployment that we have just described is the United States. Our high rate of poverty and high rates of unemployment among certain population groups help guarantee that we will have more crime than if these rates were much lower. Much social scientific evidence supports this statement (Currie 2013). Much evidence also points to successful strategies for reducing poverty and reducing unemployment, if only the federal, state, and local governments and the American public were willing to fund and implement these strategies. We now expand on these points by discussing poverty and crime before turning to employment and crime. These related discussions will highlight the need for strategies to reduce poverty and unemployment, which our final section will discuss.

POVERTY AND CRIME

Before discussing the relationship between poverty and crime, and strategies to reduce poverty, it will be helpful to first sketch the nature and extent of U.S. poverty.

Poverty in the United States: An Overview

It is surprisingly difficult to define poverty and therefore to measure its extent. When the federal government first started measuring poverty in the early 1960s, it drew on a study that found the average American family spending about one-third of its cash income on food. Using this figure, the government determined what a family must spend annually for a minimally nutritious diet (depending on the size and composition of the family) and then multiplied this amount by a factor of three to yield the income a family needs to feed itself. The government designated as officially poor all families whose income fell short of this calculated income.

This definition and measurement of **poverty** remains the government's benchmark for official poverty more than a half century later and is adjusted annually for inflation. Critics of this benchmark come from all sides of the political spectrum and point to at least three deficiencies in the measurement of poverty. First, the "three times a minimal food budget" benchmark ignores the fact that American families pay much more than in the early 1960s for energy costs, childcare, health care, housing, transportation, and other needs. Second, the benchmark does not take into account tax benefits and other types of non-cash income. Third, the benchmark ignores regional differences in the cost of living and especially in housing costs. A family whose income enables its members to live somewhat comfortably in a small town in the Midwest or South would not be able to make ends meet in many cities and suburbs elsewhere. Although the U.S. Census Bureau has incorporated the first and second criticisms into its relatively new Supplemental Poverty Measure, the official poverty benchmark remains the "three times a minimal food budget" standard. The following discussion reflects this official definition and measurement of poverty.

In 2018, the latest year for which data were available at the time of this writing, the U.S. poverty threshold for a non-farm family of four with two children under age 18 was $25,465. Recalling that this threshold is adjusted for a family's size and composition, the official poverty rate in 2018 was 11.8%, meaning that 11.8% of Americans lived below the poverty threshold determined by the federal government's official definition of poverty. This percentage translates to 38.1 million people (Semega et al. 2019).

The official poverty rate differs dramatically by race and ethnicity: It was only 8.1% in 2018 for non-Latino whites, but it was 20.8% for African Americans, 17.6% for Latinos, and 10.1% for Asians. African Americans and Latinos are more than twice as likely as non-Latino whites to live in poverty.

Child Poverty

The poverty rates for children under age 18 are higher than those just listed for all people. In 2018, 16.2% of children under age 18 lived in (official) poverty. This percentage translates to 11.9 million poor children. The **child poverty** rate again differs dramatically by race and ethnicity. For children under age 18, the poverty rate in 2018 for non-Latino whites was only 8.9%, but it was 29.5% for African Americans, 23.7% for Latinos, and 11.3% for Asians. African American and Latino children are thus much more likely than non-Latino white children to live in poverty, a fact that has significant implications for crime and crime prevention.

Near Poverty

Several additional facts about official poverty are worth noting. First, many people live in **near poverty**. This means they are above the government's poverty threshold but still have trouble making ends meet. Many experts think that families and individuals need incomes twice as high as the poverty threshold for their family size and composition to meet their basic needs. These experts thus favor using a *twice-poverty* rate (incomes up to twice as high as the poverty threshold) to measure "true" poverty. Families with incomes under the twice-poverty rate are referred to as *low-income families*; they consist of families who are either poor (under the poverty threshold) or near poor (between the poverty threshold and twice the poverty threshold).

Using this standard, 28.9% of all Americans were low-income in 2018 because they lived in official poverty or near poverty. This percentage translates to 93.6 million people (Semega et al. 2019). About 37.3% of children under age 18, or about 27 million children overall, live in low-income families. This percentage again varies dramatically by race and ethnicity. Whereas 28% of non-Latino white children live in low-income families, 61% of African American children, 59% of Latino children, and 60% of Native American children live in low-income families (2016 data; Koball and Jiang 2018). As these figures indicate, almost two-thirds of children of color live in families that either cannot make ends meet or are struggling to make ends meet. This situation again has significant implications for crime and crime prevention.

Episodic Poverty

The second additional fact about poverty is closely related to near poverty. This fact concerns the concept of **episodic poverty**: the idea that families and individuals slip into and out of official poverty. If a family earns just $1 above the poverty threshold for its size and composition, it is not officially poor, even though it is just as poor for all intents and purposes. Because income can vary month by month, families can be officially poor one month and not officially poor (though still in near poverty) the next month. The Census Bureau defines episodic poverty as being (officially) poor for at least two consecutive months. During the 2009–2012 period for the latest available data, the episodic poverty rate was 34.5%, meaning that slightly more than one-third of Americans lived in poverty for at least two consecutive months during this time (U.S. Census Bureau 2016). Race and ethnicity again exhibit a large difference: The episodic poverty rate for non-Latino whites was 27.9%, whereas for African Americans it was 49.4% and for Latinos it was 53.1%.

Concentrated Poverty and Poverty Areas

The third fact concerns *concentrated poverty*. The Census Bureau uses the term **concentrated poverty** to refer to census tracts with poverty rates above 20%. Other definitions of concentrated poverty use a 40% poverty threshold (Jargowsky 2015). However concentrated poverty is defined, census tracts or neighborhoods that have concentrated poverty are called **poverty areas**. Concentrated poverty has very harmful effects on the people and families who live in these areas (Sharkey 2013; Whitehead 2018). It is difficult to be a poor family living in a non-poor area, but such an area is likely to have many kinds of resources to help its poor families. It is far worse to be a poor family living in a poverty area, because poverty areas' concentrated poverty ensures that these areas have few resources and are also likely to exhibit many kinds of social problems beyond poverty. These problems affect not only the poor people who live in a poverty area but also the near poor and any non-poor people who live there.

Race/Ethnicity and Concentrated Poverty

About one-fourth of all Americans live in poverty areas, and more than half of all poor Americans live in poverty areas (Bishaw 2014). Because poor areas have many kinds of problems, including higher crime and victimization rates, racial and ethnic differences in living amid concentrated poverty are very revealing. Fewer than 17% of all non-Latino whites live in poverty areas, but about 50% of African Americans, 48% of Native Americans, and 44% of Latinos live in these areas. If we just examine where poor Americans live, about 45% of poor non-Latino whites live in poverty areas, compared with 72% of poor African Americans, 66% of poor Native Americans, and 66% of poor Latinos. Whether they are poor or not poor, people of color are far more likely than non-Latino whites to live in poverty areas and thus to experience all the problems arising from living amid concentrated poverty. This situation again has significant implications for crime and crime prevention.

Poverty in the World's Wealthy Democracies

A final fact about poverty concerns differences in poverty rates among the world's wealthy democracies. To compare these rates, international agencies commonly cite the proportion of a nation's population with household incomes below half of the nation's median household income. This proportion is called a nation's **relative poverty** rate. The United States holds the dubious honor of having the highest relative poverty rate of the world's wealthy democracies. For the most recent data (2017 or latest year available), the U.S. relative poverty rate was 17.8%. By contrast, Canada's relative poverty rate was 14.2%, the United Kingdom's rate was 11.1%, France's rate was 8.1%, and Denmark's was only 5.5% (OECD 2018). The U.S. relative poverty rate is significantly higher than any other democracy's rate and more than three times greater than some democracies' rates.

Perhaps even worse, the U.S. child poverty rate is also much higher than almost any other wealthy democracy's rate. The UNICEF Office of Research (2017) reports that the U.S. relative child poverty rate (which UNICEF defines as below 60% of median household income) is 29.4%, second only to Spain's among the wealthy democracies. By contrast, Canada's relative child poverty rate is 22.2%. Democracies with even lower rates include the United Kingdom, 19.7%; France, 17.7%; Germany, 15.1%; and Norway, 10.2%.

Beyond the Numbers

You have just read a lot of poverty-related numbers, and these numbers tell a disturbing tale. This tale is that the United States has the highest poverty rate among the world's wealthy democracies; an alarming number of Americans, and especially children, live in poverty or near poverty; and people of color are especially likely to live in low-income situations and amid concentrated poverty. As we have said several times, all these circumstances have significant implications for crime and crime prevention in the United States. These implications will become clearer as we now discuss the fundamental connection between poverty and crime.

How Poverty Contributes to Criminal Behavior

Low-income people dominate arrests, convictions, and incarcerations for violent and property crime and for many other offenses. Some of this overrepresentation in legal punishment might reflect social class bias against low-income persons by criminal justice professionals. However, most criminologists believe that poor and low-income people are indeed more likely than wealthier people to commit conventional crime (violent and property crime) despite any such bias (Barkan 2018; Graif 2015). Although this poverty→conventional crime connection seems beyond dispute, it is important to keep in mind that most poor people still do *not* commit conventional crime, and that wealthy people commit white-collar crime. With this caution in mind, why are low-income individuals indeed more likely to commit conventional crime? Drawing from various currents in criminology and other disciplines, several reasons appear to explain this relationship between social class and conventional criminality (Barkan and Rocque 2018). To better appreciate these reasons, readers should review the explanations for crime discussed in Chapters 3 and 4 before reading further.

Toxic Stress

A first reason is the stress of living in poverty. Children's brains develop rapidly from the moment they are born, but toxic stress from adverse childhood experiences, or ACEs, can affect how their brains develop (see Chapter 3). To quote the title of a report by the National Scientific Council on the Developing Child (NSCDC 2014), "Excessive stress disrupts the architecture of the developing brain." ACEs and toxic stress are much more common among poor and low-income children than among children in wealthier families. For this reason, a growing body of research finds that poverty "gets under the skin" by causing toxic stress (Hinojosa et al. 2019; Thompson and Haskins 2014).

This stress results from the many problems associated with living in poverty. Poor families are more likely to live in run-down, crowded conditions and in areas with higher rates of violence. They have trouble paying their bills and have higher rates of illness. Domestic violence and child abuse and neglect in such families are more common, as are changes in family structure due to divorce or other changes, as when a single mother begins to live with or leaves a cohabiting partner. Because toxic stress from these and other sources impairs poor children's cognitive and neurological development, it worsens their behavior during childhood, adolescence, and beyond. This consequence occurs because toxic stress has both a direct effect and an indirect effect on children's behavior.

The *direct* effect occurs through two related pathways (NSCDC 2014). First, toxic stress tends to increase neural connections in the areas of the brain governing anxiety, fear, and impulsivity—all traits that promote antisocial behavior. At the same time, toxic stress also decreases neural connections in the brain regions governing behavioral control, planning, and reasoning—all traits that help prevent antisocial behavior. All these consequences of toxic stress for the brain's development mean that the stressed children will be more likely to commit antisocial behavior during childhood, and delinquency and crime as they grow older.

Second, toxic stress alters children's neuroendocrinological expression. In particular, it causes them to produce high levels of stress hormones such as adrenaline and cortisol. These high levels reduce children's capacity to respond appropriately to stress during and beyond childhood in ways that can produce antisocial and criminal behavior. Because of their high levels of stress hormones, stressed children "become hypervigilant to signs of danger and, when threatened, respond quickly and with strong emotion in self-defense" (Thompson and Haskins 2014:3). In general, these children have more difficulty controlling their emotions and impulses. These effects mean that children are more likely to respond aggressively when insulted, threatened, frightened, or otherwise experiencing a situation they find uncomfortable.

As the NSCDC (2014:2) summarizes the two neural and hormonal pathways just described,

> Toxic stress . . . can affect developing brain circuits and hormonal systems in a way that leads to poorly controlled stress response systems that will be overly reactive or slow to shut down when faced with threats throughout the lifespan. As a result, children may feel threatened by or respond impulsively to situations where no real threat exists, such as seeing anger or hostility in a facial expression that is actually neutral, or they may remain excessively anxious long after a threat has passed.

The *indirect* effect of toxic stress on children's behavior occurs as follows: Because toxic stress impairs normal cognitive and neurological development, it worsens children's school performance and ability to maintain positive social relationships (Hinojosa et al. 2019). Problems in school tend to produce and/or aggravate behavioral problems (see Chapter 4). School-related problems also make it less likely that children will graduate high school and find gainful employment even if they do graduate. As we discuss later in this chapter, lack of gainful employment contributes to criminality during adulthood. Turning to social relationships, children who cannot hold positive relationships have more difficulty relating to their parents and teachers and more difficulty holding on to friendships with well-behaved children during childhood and law-abiding teenagers during adolescence (van Goozen 2015). These problems again generate worse behavior. Toxic stress thus indirectly worsens children's behavior because it first worsens their school performance and weakens their social relationships.

Whether its effects are direct or indirect, then, toxic stress prompts low-income children to be more likely to engage in antisocial behavior during childhood, and delinquency (violent and property offenses) and substance abuse during adolescence and young adulthood. The stress of living in poverty is thus one reason why low-income individuals are more likely to commit delinquency and crime.

Inadequate Nutrition

Inadequate nutrition is a second factor that puts low-income persons at greater risk for committing conventional crime. In a groundbreaking investigation, several researchers studied 1,559 children from age 3 through age 17; the children lived on an island off the coast of Africa (Liu et al. 2004). At age 3, more than one-fifth of these children showed evidence of malnutrition. The researchers found that these malnourished children were more likely than the well-nourished children to be aggressive or hyperactive at ages 8 and 11, and more likely to exhibit conduct disorder at age 17.

Although this study involved African children with fairly severe malnutrition, other research suggests that inadequate nutrition also generates misbehavior in wealthy nations such as the United States. In particular, deficits in iron, magnesium, zinc, vitamin B6, omega-3 fatty acids (found in fish and fish oil supplements), and certain other nutrients are associated with a greater likelihood of aggression and other behavior problems during childhood, adolescence, and young adulthood (Jackson 2016; Liu, Zhao, and Reyes 2015). Most evidence of this inadequate nutrition→antisocial behavior link comes from correlational studies, which are not as convincing as randomized controlled experiments (see Chapter 2). But some experimental evidence does indicate that nutritional improvements and supplements reduce behavioral problems; this evidence strongly implies that inadequate nutrition helped generate these problems in the first place (Mousain-Bosc et al. 2006; Zaalberg et al. 2010). Much of the nutrition research concerns children, and this research finds a causal process as follows: (1) Inadequate nutrition impairs neuropsychological functioning, and (2) this impairment in turn produces hyperactivity and aggressive behavior. As a recent review stated, "In short, research suggests that poor nutrition during childhood seems to predispose children to higher levels of aggression and related antisocial behaviors" (Jackson 2016:13). These higher levels may last into adolescence and beyond.

If poor nutrition in childhood has these consequences, it is important to note that childhood nutrition problems are more often found in low-income families (Cabieses, Pickett, and Wilkinson 2016). This situation occurs partly because low-income families are less able to afford a healthy diet that includes such items as fresh fruits and vegetables, fish, and organic foods, and instead are more likely to have diets that lack the nutrients listed earlier and are deficient in other ways as well (e.g., featuring high levels of saturated fat and sodium). Because low-income children are thus more likely to experience poor nutrition, they are also more likely to commit antisocial behavior.

Maternal Nutrition

If children's poor nutrition produces aggression and other antisocial behavior, so does poor maternal nutrition, that is, poor nutrition during pregnancy. Inadequate nourishment during this period may impair fetal cognitive and neurological development in ways that carry into childhood and beyond, and this impairment may again produce antisocial behavior that may last into adolescence and beyond (Marques et al. 2015; Tibbetts and Rivera 2015). Because low-income mothers are more likely to experience poor maternal nutrition, this fact again helps explain why poverty contributes to conventional crime.

Maternal Stress and Drug Use

Two other problems during pregnancy may also impair fetal development, with the consequences for eventual antisocial behavior just discussed. These problems are maternal stress and drug use (including alcohol use), both of which low-income mothers are again more likely to experience. Low-income mothers experience more stress because of their poverty and because they are more likely than wealthier pregnant women to have an abusive partner (Jasinski 2004). They are also more likely to consume alcohol during pregnancy and to use tobacco and other recreational drugs (McGloin, Pratt, and Piquero 2006). These twin problems again impair fetal development and raise the risk of eventual antisocial behavior.

Parenting and Other Family Functioning

Chapter 4 discussed the importance of family functioning, including proper parenting, for the onset of children's and adolescents' antisocial behavior. To review, families that are marked by conflict and/or child abuse and neglect, and that fail to discipline and supervise children in the ways recommended by child and family experts, are more likely to produce children with higher levels of antisocial behavior and other problems.

The relevance of this tendency is this: Although it might sound like a stereotype, low-income families are more likely than wealthier families to exhibit the problems just listed that help produce antisocial children (Bornstein and Bradley 2012). Low-income families are also more likely to have mothers who go through multiple transitions by having a series of romantic partners (Fomby and Sennott 2013). These transitions also help produce aggressive and antisocial behavior by these mothers' children.

Negative Peer Influences

Negative peer influences are an important source of delinquent behavior. Low-income adolescents are more likely than their wealthier counterparts to have friends and acquaintances who have committed serious delinquency. Their associations with these delinquent peers help explain their own higher rates of conventional criminality (Fergusson and Horwood 1999).

Schools

Delinquency and other problematic behavior are found more often in schools that have severely crowded classrooms and are underfunded (see Chapter 4). These problems weaken students' school performance and weaken their bonds to their teachers and schools. In turn, their behavior suffers. These types of schools are found more often in low-income neighborhoods and are more likely to have greater proportions of students from low-income families (Banerjee 2016; Kozol 1991). The poor quality of schools and schooling, then, helps explain why low-income students are more likely to develop problematic behaviors.

Anger and Other States of Mind

Criminological work highlights the role played by various emotions and social-psychological states in decisions to commit criminal behavior (Agnew 2007; Webber 2007). These states of mind include anger, frustration, feelings of being deprived compared with other groups (*relative deprivation*), alienation, and unhappiness. This work also emphasizes that low-income persons are more likely because of their economic problems to experience these criminogenic states of mind (Agnew et al. 2008; Bernard 1990). These states of mind, then, are yet another factor that helps account for the poverty–conventional crime link.

Low Self-Control

Children, adolescents, and older persons with low self-control are impulsive and more likely to engage in crime and other antisocial behavior (see Chapter 4) (Gottfredson and Hirschi 1990). Low self-control stems from inadequate parenting and living in a socially disorganized neighborhood, and perhaps also from neuropsychological problems (Boutwell and Beaver 2010; Gibson et al. 2010). Because these sources of low self-control are more often found in low-income families, people from low-income backgrounds are more likely to exhibit low self-control (Hostinar et al. 2015). The greater likelihood of low self-control among low-income persons thus helps explain the poverty–crime relationship.

Weak Social Bonds

Hirschi's social bonding theory attributes higher rates of delinquency to weak social bonds arising from family and school issues (Chapter 4). Because these issues are more often found among low-income families and in schools in low-income areas, low-income adolescents have weaker social bonds than wealthier adolescents. These weaker bonds help explain why they are more likely to engage in delinquency during adolescence and crime during adulthood (Hay et al. 2006).

Environmental Toxins

A growing amount of research finds that prenatal and childhood exposure to lead and other environmental toxins such as methylmercury promotes violence and other antisocial behavior (Posick, Lasko, and Tremblay 2018; Sampson and Winter 2018). Low-income families and individuals are more likely to suffer this type of exposure because they are more likely to live in communities and housing contaminated by these toxins (Muller, Sampson, and Winter 2018). Their greater exposure to environmental toxins thus is an additional factor that helps explain why poverty contributes to criminal behavior.

Neighborhood Conditions

In addition to living in toxin-contaminated communities and housing, low-income families are also more likely to live in neighborhoods that have certain features contributing to higher crime rates by their residents. As Chapter 4 explained, these are neighborhoods with higher levels of social disorganization and disadvantage, which means that they have higher levels of such phenomena as poverty, single-parent households, and dilapidated housing. These problems weaken their institutional resources, such as schools and neighborhood associations, that are important for the social control of the behavior of children and other neighborhood residents, and they also weaken the neighborhoods' levels of collective efficacy. Because low-income families are more likely to live in areas with these criminogenic (crime-causing) features, their children are more likely to grow up to be adolescents who commit more serious offenses, and their adolescents are more likely to grow into adults who continue to commit crime.

Another criminogenic feature of these neighborhoods is a greater presence of bars and taverns. Consistent with routine activities theory, these establishments create greater opportunities for people to commit crime and to become victims of crime (Pridemore and Grubesic 2013). The presence of these establishments in low-income neighborhoods is yet another reason for the poverty–conventional crime connection.

Some intriguing evidence on the importance of neighborhood disadvantage for violent crime comes from two experiments that relocated low-income families to higher-income neighborhoods. Both these experiments found encouraging if not entirely consistent evidence that crime declines when neighborhood conditions improve.

Moving to Opportunity One of these experiments, Moving to Opportunity (MTO), began in the early 1990s and involved 4,600 low-income families in public housing projects in Baltimore, Boston, Chicago, Los Angeles, and New York City. All the families volunteered to participate in the experiment, which was undertaken by the U.S. Department of Housing and Urban Development. At the outset of the experiment, the volunteer families were randomly assigned to one of three groups: (1) *the experimental group*, which received a housing voucher to move to a low-poverty neighborhood; (2) *the traditional voucher group*, which received a housing voucher for housing of their choice, including public housing or low-poverty neighborhood housing; and (3) *the control group*, which did not receive any housing vouchers. Researchers have since studied the children of these families and have been particularly interested in whether the children in the experimental group whose families moved to low-poverty areas ended up with better behaviors and other outcomes (such as good health) than their counterparts in the control group. Because some time has gone by since MTO began, researchers have been able to study the MTO children into their young adulthood (Kling, Ludwig, and Katz 2005; Sciandra et al. 2013).

Their research has yielded several findings: (1) For males, arrests for violent crime were about one-third lower for those in the experimental group than for those in the control group during the first 4 years after random assignment.

(2) There was no difference in the arrest rates for these two groups after this time. (3) Somewhat surprisingly, experimental-group males were more likely than control-group males to be arrested for property crime during the first few years after random assignment. (4) Arrests for both violent crime and property crime were lower after random assignment for experimental-group females than for control-group females.

Despite findings (2) and (3), the results of the MTO experiment are encouraging overall, as findings (1) and (4) do suggest that low-poverty residence reduces criminality to some extent. This reduction was especially notable because all the experimental-group youths spent the formative years of their childhoods in low-income areas and thus had been subject to the criminogenic effects of their neighborhoods as described earlier in this chapter.

Chicago Housing Authority A similar experiment began in Chicago in 1997, when the Chicago Housing Authority randomly selected low-income families to receive housing vouchers to enable them to move from their low-income neighborhoods to higher-income neighborhoods (Ludwig and Burdick-Will 2012). During the next 8 years, violent-crime arrests were significantly lower for boys in families that received vouchers than for boys in families that did not receive vouchers; no such difference was found for girls or for property-crime or drug-crime arrests for either sex. Violent-crime arrests were also lower for the household heads—almost all of them women—ages 18 to 30 whose families received vouchers than for their counterparts whose families did not receive vouchers.

The results of the MTO and Chicago experiments "suggest that living in a more disadvantaged neighborhood increases an individual's risk of involvement with violent criminal behavior" (Ludwig and Burdick-Will 2012:202). If so, policy efforts that improve neighborhoods' economic and other conditions should reduce violent crime. Economic-based efforts to reduce crime should focus not only on the economic circumstances of individual families but also on the circumstances of the neighborhoods in which they live. Chapter 6 will discuss efforts to address the conditions of disadvantaged neighborhoods to help produce lower crime rates.

Racial Differences in Conventional Criminality

Chapter 4 observed that racial differences in conventional criminality stem from the different life circumstances in which the different races live. As that chapter mentioned, two of these life circumstances are poverty and residence in disadvantaged neighborhoods. Simply put, African Americans and, to a lesser extent, Latinos are much, much more likely than non-Latino whites to be very poor and to live in severely disadvantaged neighborhoods (Sampson, Wilson, and Katz 2018). To the extent this is true, the many reasons for the poverty–conventional crime link we have discussed help mightily to explain racial differences in conventional criminality. If so, efforts that successfully reduce poverty and improve disadvantaged neighborhoods should reduce not only conventional crime but also racial differences in such crime.

EMPLOYMENT AND CRIME

We have just examined a host of reasons that help explain why "there is little question that growing up in extreme poverty exerts powerful pressures toward crime" (Currie 2013:126). **Employment** (the condition of holding a paid job) status is closely related to poverty. **Unemployment** (the condition of looking for work but not being able to find a job) can cause severe financial problems, plunge families into poverty or near poverty, and make poor families even poorer. Just as episodic poverty exists, with families moving into and out of poverty during a period of months, so does episodic unemployment: Someone can be employed one month, unemployed the next, employed for two more months, then unemployed, and so on. This fact means that many people may experience unemployment at least once during their lifetimes. To illustrate from the 2018 General Social Survey (GSS)—a national random sample of Americans 18 years of age or older—31.0% of respondents ages 35 to 65 said they had been unemployed for at least 1 month during the previous 10 years. Given the importance of work for so many Americans and the frequency of unemployment, this section examines the relationship between employment and crime.

Employment and Unemployment in the United States: An Overview

Millions of Americans make up the **civilian labor force**, which consists of all civilians 16 years of age or older who hold a paid job or are looking for work. In October 2018, 162.6 million people were in the labor force. Of this number, 96.3% were employed full- or part-time, and 3.7% were unemployed. This percentage amounted to 6.1 million unemployed Americans. People who have given up seeking work out of frustration over not finding a job are not considered as being in the labor force and thus do not count among the ranks of the unemployed. For this reason, many economists think that the **underemployment** rate (consisting of people who are unemployed, those who work part-time but wish to work full time, and those who have stopped looking for work because they cannot find a job) yields a more accurate picture of actual employment problems in the United States than the unemployment rate does (Sherman 2018). In October 2018, this underemployment rate was 7.4%—exactly twice as high as the unemployment rate and amounting to more than 12 million people (Bureau of Labor Statistics 2018a).

It is important to note how much the unemployment rate varies by social class. We can see this by using educational attainment as a proxy for social class. In 2017, when the average annual unemployment rate was 4.4%, this rate varied by educational attainment (see Table 5.1).

As these numbers indicate, the unemployment rate is higher for people with less educational attainment, and in fact it is more than three times higher for people without a high school degree than for those with an advanced degree.

Table 5.1	Educational Attainment and Average Annual Unemployment Rate, 2017	
Less than a high school degree:		6.5%
High school degree:		4.6%
Some college:		3.8%
Bachelor's degree:		2.5%
Advanced degree:		2.0%

Source: Bureau of Labor Statistics (2018b).

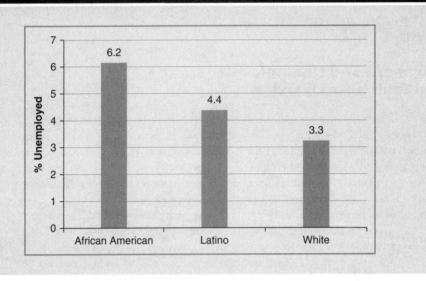

Figure 5.1   Race, Ethnicity, and Unemployment, October 2018 (% unempolyed)

It is important to note that the unemployment rate varies by race and ethnicity. In October 2018, the national unemployment rate was 3.7%. This figure broken down by race and ethnicity in Figure 5.1 illustrates the racial and ethnic difference in unemployment (Bureau of Labor Statistics 2018b).

African Americans were almost twice as likely as whites to be unemployed in October 2018, while Latinos were also more likely than whites to be unemployed. Assuming from the October 2018 figures mentioned earlier that underemployment is twice as high as unemployment, roughly 12.4% of African Americans and 8.8% of Latinos were underemployed in that month, compared with only 6.6% of whites.

GSS data on unemployment for at least a month during the previous 10 years also show strong racial and ethnic differences. As Figure 5.2 illustrates, African Americans

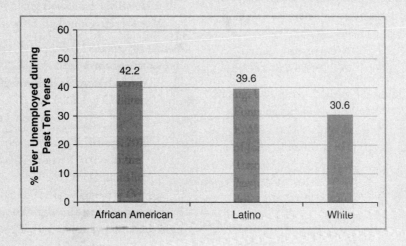

Figure 5.2 Race, Ethnicity, and Unemployment during Past Ten Years, 2016–2018 General Social Survey, Ages 35-36 (% unemployed)

were much more likely than whites to have been unemployed during this period, while Latinos were also more likely to have been unemployed.

The percentages reported in Figure 5.1 were for all people age 16 or older. Because young people, and especially young males, disproportionately commit crime (Ulmer and Steffensmeier 2015), it is instructive to examine unemployment rates for young males. In the third quarter of 2018, when the average national unemployment rate was 3.9%, the rate for males ages 18 to 19 was 14.0%. This figure was again much higher for African Americans and Latinos than for whites, with more than one-fifth of African American males in this age group being unemployed (see Figure 5.3). During the "great recession" of the late 2000s, more than one-third of black males ages 16 to 19 who were seeking work were unemployed (Cawthorne 2009).

To the extent that unemployment and underemployment might contribute to conventional criminality, the social class and racial/ethnic differences just shown for unemployment might help explain social class and racial/ethnic differences in criminality. With this possibility in mind, we now turn to the evidence on employment status and conventional criminality.

The Potential Relevance of Employment Status for Conventional Crime

There is ample reason to believe that employment status (being employed or unemployed/underemployed) should be related to conventional criminality (Andresen 2015). Consider these factors:

- Because employed older teens and adults have more income than the unemployed, they are less likely to be poor and thus less apt to experience the

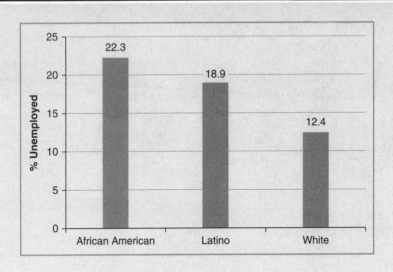

many problems discussed in the previous section that contribute to higher crime rates among the poor.

- The employed also "keep busy" being employed, yielding them less opportunity to hang out with any deviant peers they may have. Consistent with opportunity theories of crime (Wilcox and Cullen 2018), they should thus be less apt to get into legal trouble.

- Employment has long been thought to give individuals a sense that they have a purpose in life, greater feelings of self-worth and self-esteem, the perception that they are contributing members of society, and a lower feeling of alienation (Cohn 1978; Orth, Maes, and Schmitt 2015); all these social-psychological states in turn may help reduce any inclination to commit crime (Mier and Ladny 2018). Conversely, unemployed people may suffer lower self-worth and self-esteem, and greater feelings of alienation and depression (Zuelke et al. 2018); these feelings may help drive them to commit crime (Anderson, Cesur, and Tekin 2015).

- Stable employment provides income and the social-psychological benefits just listed that all help create well-functioning families. Conversely, unemployment increases family stress and impairs family functioning. These problems may worsen children's and adolescents' behavior in both the short-term and long-term (Farrington 2011). Unemployment in a family should thus increase the chances that the family's children may commit antisocial behavior, including crime, during adolescence and beyond. As criminologist Elliott

Currie (2013:136–137) puts it, "The state of the labor market affects children long before they are old enough to participate in it because it influences— often profoundly—the quality of their family life and the character of the communities in which they will grow up."

- Finally, and as Currie's statement just indicated, mass joblessness may damage the character of whole communities. It can lead to despair and reduce marriage rates (because people cannot afford to marry and a jobless person is not seen as an ideal potential spouse), and it may foster drug trafficking and other illegal activities that sound appealing amid chronic unemployment. For these and other reasons, mass joblessness may promote higher rates of violent and property crime at the community level (Currie 2013).

To many criminologists, these factors all point to the potential relevance of employment status for criminal behavior and in particular to the need to enhance employment opportunities to reduce crime. As Currie (1985:263) wrote three decades ago, "A commitment to full and decent employment remains the keystone of any successful anticrime policy." Calling youth joblessness a "cauldron of idleness, resentment, disconnection, and despair," Currie (2013:226) added more recently that "job creation [is] a critically important part of any enduring and progressive attack on violence in America. It is difficult to see an acceptable way out of the current paradox of endemic violence and overgrown prisons as long as staggeringly high levels of youth joblessness are permitted to persist."

Research on Employment Status and Crime

Much research confirms the importance of employment status for crime rates and, on a related topic, children's behavior and other aspects of their well-being. Starting with the latter topic, one long-standing line of research finds that unemployment and loss of income worsen the quality of parenting, which in turn impairs children's development and behavior (Conger et al. 1994; McLoyd et al. 1994). Long-standing research also connects unemployment (and/or underemployment) at both the individual and community levels with higher rates of conventional crime (Allan and Steffensmeier 1989; Andresen 2012; Apel and Horney 2017; Elliott 1994; Sampson and Laub 1993).

Despite these bodies of research, other research does not always find the expected link between unemployment and crime, and higher rates of unemployment do not always produce higher crime rates (Cantor and Land 1985; Kapuscinski, Braithwaite, and Chapman 1998). Still other research finds a link between unemployment and property crime but not between unemployment and violent crime (Raphael and Winter-Ebmer 2001).

Certain methodological differences beyond the scope of this discussion help account for these inconsistent findings. But one reason for the absence of the expected link in some studies between unemployment and crime reflects the concept of guardianship as highlighted in routine activities theory (see Chapter 4) (Andresen 2012). In this way of thinking, when unemployment rates are high, people spend more time at home rather than going out to bars, restaurants, or theaters, or going on vacation, simply because they have less money. Because they spend more time at home, guardianship against property crime such as burglary is higher: Because their homes are occupied rather than empty, burglars will be less likely to try to enter. By the same token, robbery is less likely to occur if people are home rather than out on the streets, and so are bar fights and other violence. As bad as unemployment is, then, it may ironically help keep people safer from crime by reducing the opportunities for crime and thus crime rates themselves.

Despite the inconsistent findings, the bulk of the research does find that stable employment reduces criminal behavior and that unemployment and/or underemployment increases such behavior (Apel and Horney 2017). To the extent this is true, social policy efforts that promote stable employment and reduce unemployment and underemployment offer much promise for reducing criminal behavior. We discuss these efforts in the next section.

REDUCING POVERTY AND PROMOTING STABLE EMPLOYMENT

As noted earlier, other wealthy democracies have much lower rates of poverty and near poverty than the United States does. A major reason for this situation is that these nations provide their low-income citizens much more social and financial support than is provided in the United States, which helps lift their citizens out of poverty and helps them in many other ways. In contrast, the United States' commitment to capitalism leads it to prefer that the free market determine how people end up in life. As James W. Russell (2018:171) observes regarding Western Europe, "The reason why Western European countries have significantly less income inequality and poverty is precisely that their governments are more willing to alter market outcomes. They collect relatively more taxes and use them more aggressively to finance social programs that do more to close the gaps. Reducing those gaps in turn has beneficial effects that ripple through the society and lessen the gravity of a range of other social problems."

Examples of the supports provided in Western European nations include generous income transfers, free or heavily subsidized childcare, free or heavily subsidized medical care, and job training programs (Russell 2018; Waldfogel 2010). Western European nations provide paid unemployment benefits that average 18 months, whereas the United States provides only 6 months. Western European nations provide an average of 30 weeks of paid maternity leave, and in some nations more than 1 year, whereas the United States provides no such leave under federal law (Ingraham 2018). They also provide many more weeks of paid sick leave than does the United States, which has no national sick leave policy (Dishman 2016). Some European nations provide a *universal child allowance* in the form of cash payments for each child a family has; this allowance is meant both to help families meet the many expenses that children incur and to help parents decide to have children in an era when birth rates have dropped below population-replacement levels (Matthews 2016). For example, Germany's program, called *Kindergeld*, provides more than $200 monthly for each child (Luyken 2017). In these and other ways, other wealthy democracies reduce their nations' poverty levels and help their low-income families to a far greater extent than does the United States.

The United States does have some national social welfare programs, of course. Among the largest are Temporary Assistance for Needy Families (TANF), the Supplemental Nutrition Assistance Program (SNAP), and Medicaid and other public health insurance. These programs help greatly to relieve the many hardships facing America's low-income families (McKernan, Ratcliffe, and Iceland 2018). Despite this help, comparisons with other wealthy democracies remind us that the United States still lags far behind its peer nations in its efforts to assist low-income citizens. Much more can and should be done.

Many scholars, think tanks, and social reform organizations have proposed social policies and programs for the United States to follow to reduce its high poverty level and to increase employment prospects for the many Americans with low incomes and low educational attainment. Although these programs have not gained political and public approval (because otherwise we would already have them), in general they merely bring the United States into line with other wealthy democracies. The list of policies and programs in the next section draws on the abundant literature concerning these efforts; details of these strategies beyond our space limitations here may be found in this literature (Berger, Cancian, and Magnuson 2018; Children's Defense Fund 2015; Currie 2013; Iceland 2013; McNicholas, Sanders, and Shierholz 2018; Mishel 2015).

Note that these strategies focus directly on reducing poverty and promoting stable employment. Many other crime prevention strategies focus on the many problems that low-income families and individuals face because of their socioeconomic status. For example, Chapter 8's discussion of family efforts and Chapter 9's discussion of school-related efforts focus largely on efforts involving low-income families and schools in low-income areas, respectively. To recall Chapter 2's discussion of the public health model, these efforts involve secondary prevention, whereas the list in the next section of strategies to reduce poverty and promote stable employment involves primary prevention.

Strategies to Reduce Poverty and Promote Stable Employment

1. Increase the Earned Income Tax Credit for working families or provide a universal child allowance to families with children under age 18.

2. Raise the minimum wage everywhere to at least $12 per hour. The federal minimum wage was $7.25/hour in late 2018, although some states and cities mandate a higher minimum wage than that. In 1968, the federal minimum wage was $1.60/hour. Adjusted for inflation, that wage would have been $11.59 in late 2018. Doing a bit of math, the federal minimum wage is thus 37% lower than it should be if it had only kept up with inflation. The minimum wage has also not kept up with the nation's increase in productivity. In 2015, the Children's Defense Fund (CDF 2015) estimated that raising the federal minimum wage to just $10/hour would still lift 900,000 people, including 400,000 children, out of poverty.

3. Increase childcare subsidies to help enable working parents to pay for childcare and to increase their working hours if so desired.

4. Establish publicly funded or subsidized jobs programs for unemployed or underemployed workers.

5. Increase SNAP benefits, which average only about $1.40 per person per meal and still leave about half of families receiving SNAP benefits facing food insecurity.

6. Expand housing subsidies for low-income families.

7. Better enforce laws that protect workers' efforts to form and join unions.

8. Establish a national sick-day standard to ensure that all workers receive sick pay.

9. Establish laws that protect all workers, not just those in unions, from being fired without just cause.

According to the CDF (2015), the first six strategies (but not including a universal child allowance) would lift more than 6 million children out of poverty and reduce the number of poor children by 60%. They would also benefit more than 30 million other children who live above official poverty but who still live in low-income families. The policies would also reduce the number of poor working-age adults by about one-fourth.

These strategies would cost an estimated $77 billion annually, the CDF (2015) estimates, certainly not a small figure. In the long run, however, they would more than pay for themselves, as the CDF estimates that child poverty costs the nation an estimated $500 billion annually in lost productivity, worse health, and, yes, increased crime. Moreover, the $77 billion annual cost of these strategies represents less than 1% of the nation's gross domestic product (GDP) and is lower than the more than $100 billion the nation spent every year between 2001 and 2015 (when the CDF estimates were published) on the wars in Iraq and Afghanistan. According to the CDF, the $77 billion cost would be paid for by any one of the following: closing corporate tax loopholes; eliminating the many tax breaks that very wealthy families and individuals enjoy; or reducing military spending, which many experts think is higher than it needs to be to keep the nation and world safe (Preble 2017; Stein 2018; Williams 2013).

As we hope our discussion has made clear, it is very possible for the United States to greatly reduce its level of poverty through strategies that have proven to be successful in other wealthy democracies. These nations have lower rates of poverty and near poverty than the United States precisely because they have economic and employment programs and policies to help their low-income citizens. Between 1999 and 2004, Great Britain lowered its child poverty rate by half through a concerted, multifaceted national effort that involved several of the general strategies we have presented (Waldfogel 2010). As the old saying goes, where there's a will, there's a way. If the United States had the will to reduce poverty and enhance employment, it could do so. Many benefits would result, including significant crime prevention.

CONCLUSION

Poverty, near poverty, and lack of stable employment contribute mightily to involvement in conventional crime. It is no accident that people who commit serious conventional crime stem disproportionately from the ranks of the poor and near poor. Many reasons help explain the fundamental link between low socioeconomic status and lack of stable employment, and conventional criminality. Reducing poverty and promoting stable employment thus rank as important priorities for any primary prevention effort to reduce crime. The United States has the resources to implement measures to achieve these priorities, which other wealthy democracies emphasize much more than the United States does. If this nation had the desire and will to implement these measures, it could reduce crime substantially.

SUMMARY

1. The official poverty rate in 2018 was 11.8%, with 38.1 million Americans living in poverty. Many additional families and individuals live in near poverty or experience episodic poverty. The poverty rate varies greatly by race and ethnicity, with African Americans and Latinos having noticeably higher poverty rates.

2. The U.S. rates of poverty and child poverty are much higher than those of other wealthy democracies, which have many more social supports to help their low-income citizens.

3. Many reasons help explain why poverty contributes to involvement in conventional crime. These reasons include toxic stress experienced by children; inadequate maternal and childhood nutrition; inadequate parenting; negative school conditions; and negative community conditions.

4. Unemployment and underemployment may also contribute for several reasons to involvement in conventional crime. Among other reasons, these problems increase poverty and near poverty, reduce people's self-esteem and increase their alienation, and weaken family functioning.

5. Efforts that successfully reduce poverty and promote stable employment should help prevent conventional criminality. Implementation of these efforts would bring the United States in line with other wealthy democracies. These efforts include greater income transfers to low-income families, raising the minimum wage, establishing publicly funded jobs programs, expanding housing subsidies, and protecting workers' rights to form and join unions.

KEY TERMS

child poverty 93
civilian labor force 103
concentrated poverty 94
employment 103

episodic poverty 94
near poverty 93
poverty 93
poverty areas 94

relative poverty 95
underemployment 103
unemployment 103

REFERENCES

Agnew, Robert. 2007. *Pressured Into Crime: An Overview of General Strain Theory.* New York, NY: Oxford University Press.

Agnew, Robert, Shelley Keith Matthews, Jacob Bucher, Adria N. Welcher, and Corey Keyes. 2008. "Socioeconomic Status, Economic Problems, and Delinquency." *Youth & Society* 40(2):159–181.

Allan, Emilie, and Darrel Steffensmeier. 1989. "Youth, Unemployment, and Property Crime: Differential Effects of Job Availability and Job Quality on Juvenile and Young Adult Arrest Rates." *American Sociological Review* 54: 107–123.

Anderson, D. Mark, Resul Cesur, and Erdal Tekin. 2015. "Youth Depression and Future Criminal Behavior." *Economic Inquiry* 53(1):294–317. doi: 10.1111/ecin.12145.

Andresen, Martin A. 2012. "Unemployment and Crime: A Neighborhood Level Panel Data Approach." *Social Science Research* 41(6):1615–1628. doi: 10.1016/j.ssresearch.2012.07.003.

Andresen, Martin A. 2015. "Unemployment, GDP, and Crime: The Importance of Multiple Measurements of the Economy." *Canadian Journal of Criminology & Criminal Justice* 57(1):35–58. doi: 10.3138/CJCCJ.2013.E37.

Apel, Robert, and Julie Horney. 2017. "How and Why Does Work Matter? Employment Conditions, Routine Activities, and Crime Among Adult Male Offenders." *Criminology* 55(2):307–343. doi: 10.1111/1745-9125.12134.

Banerjee, Pallavi Amitava. 2016. "A Systematic Review of Factors Linked to Poor Academic Performance of Disadvantaged Students in Science and Maths in Schools." *Cogent Education* 3(1). https://www.tandfonline.com/doi/full/10.1080/2331186X.2016.1178441.

Barkan, Steven E. 2018. *Criminology: A Sociological Understanding.* Upper Saddle River, NJ: Pearson.

Barkan, Steven E., and Michael Rocque. 2018. "Socioeconomic Status and Racism as Fundamental Causes of Street Criminality." *Critical Criminology* 26(2):211–231.

Berger, Lawrence M., Maria Cancian, and Katherine Magnuson. 2018. "Anti-Poverty Policy Innovations: New Proposals for Addressing Poverty in the United States." *RSF: The Russell Sage Foundation Journal of the Social Sciences* 4(2):1–19.

Bernard, Thomas J. 1990. "Angry Aggression Among the 'Truly Disadvantaged.'" *Criminology* 28: 73–96.

Bishaw, Alemayehu. 2014. *Changes in Areas With Concentrated Poverty: 2000–2010. U.S. Census*

Bureau. American Community Survey Reports ACS-27. Washington, DC: U.S. Government Printing Office.

Bornstein, Marc H., and Robert H. Bradley, eds. 2012. *Socioeconomic Status, Parenting, and Child Development.* New York, NY: Psychology Press.

Boutwell, Brian B., and Kevin M. Beaver. 2010. "The Intergenerational Transmission of Low Self-Control." *Journal of Research in Crime & Delinquency* 47: 174–209.

Bureau of Labor Statistics. 2018a. "Economic News Release." November 2. Retreived September 9, 2019 (https://www.bls.gov/news.release/empsit .t15.htm).

Bureau of Labor Statistics. 2018b. *2018 Employment and Earnings Online* Washington, DC: Bureau of Labor Statistics, U.S. Department of Labor. Retrieved September 9, 2019 (https://www.bls .gov/opub/ee/2018/cps/annual.htm#empstat).

Cabieses, Baltica, Kate E. Pickett, and Richard G. Wilkinson. 2016. "The Impact of Socioeconomic Inequality on Children's Health and Well-Being." Pp. 244–265 in *The Oxford Handbook of Economics and Human Biology*, edited by J. Komlols and I. R. Kelley. New York, NY: Oxford University Press.

Cantor, David, and Kenneth C. Land. 1985. "Unemployment and Crime Rates in the Post-World War II United States: A Theoretical and Empirical Analysis." *American Sociological Review* 50: 317–332.

Cawthorne, Alexandra. 2009. "Weathering the Storm: Black Men in the Recession." Americanprogress .org. April 15. Retrieved September 9, 2019 (https://www.americanprogress.org/issues/ economy/reports/2009/04/15/5906/weathering- the-storm-black-men-in-the-recession/).

Children's Defense Fund. 2015. *Ending Child Poverty Now.* Washington, DC: Author.

Cohn, Richard M. 1978. "The Effect of Employment Status Change on Self-Attitudes." *Social Psychology* 41(2):81–93.

Conger, Rand D., Xiaojia Ge Jr., Glen H. Elder, Frederick O. Lorenz, and Ronald L. Simons. 1994. "Economic Stress, Coercive Family Process, and Developmental Problems of Adolescents." *Child Development* 65(2):541–561.

Currie, Elliott. 1985. *Confronting Crime: An American Challenge.* New York, NY: Pantheon Books.

Currie, Elliott. 2013. *Crime and Punishment in America.* New York, NY: Metropolitan Books.

Dishman, Lydia. 2016. "How U.S. Employee Benefits Compare to Europe's." Fastcompany .com. February 17. Retrieved September 9, 2019 (https://www.fastcompany.com/3056830/how- the-us-employee-benefits-compare-to-europe).

Elliott, Delbert S. 1994. "Serious Violent Offenders: Onset, Developmental Course, and Termination—the American Society of Criminology 1993 Presidential Address." *Criminology* 32(1):1–21.

Farrington, David P. 2011. "Families and Crime." Pp. 130–157 in *Crime and Public Policy*, edited by J. Q. Wilson and J. Petersilia. New York, NY: Oxford University Press.

Fergusson, David M., and L. John Horwood. 1999. "Prospective Childhood Predictors of Deviant Peer Affiliations in Adolescence." *Journal of Child Psychology and Psychiatry* 40(4):581–592.

Fomby, Paula, and Christie A. Sennott. 2013. "Family Structure Instability and Mobility: The Consequences for Adolescents' Problem Behavior." *Social Science Research* 42(1):186–201. doi: 10.1016/j.ssresearch.2012.08.016.

Gibson, Chris L., Christopher J. Sullivan, Shayne Jones, and Alex R. Piquero. 2010. "'Does

It Take a Village?' Assessing Neighborhood Influences on Children's Self-Control." *Journal of Research in Crime and Delinquency* 47(1):31–62.

Gottfredson, Michael, and Travis Hirschi. 1990. *A General Theory of Crime*. Stanford, CA: Stanford University Press.

Graif, Corina. 2015. "Delinquency and Gender Moderation in the Moving to Opportunity Intervention: The Role of Extended Neighborhoods." *Criminology* 53(3):366–398. doi: 10.1111/1745-9125.12078.

Hay, Carter, Edward N. Fortson, Dusten R. Hollist, Irshad Altheimer, and Lonnie M. Schaible. 2006. "The Impact of Community Disadvantage on the Relationship Between the Family and Juvenile Crime." *Journal of Research in Crime and Delinquency* 43: 326–356.

Hinojosa, Melanie Sberna, Ramon Hinojosa, Melissa Bright, and Jenny Nguyen. 2019. "Adverse Childhood Experiences and Grade Retention in a National Sample of Us Children." *Sociological Inquiry* 89(3):401–426.

Hostinar, Camelia E., Kharah M. Ross, Edith Chen, and Gregory E. Miller. 2015. "Modeling the Association Between Lifecourse Socioeconomic Disadvantage and Systemic Inflammation in Healthy Adults: The Role of Self-Control." *Health Psychology* 34(6):580–590. doi: 10.1037/hea0000130.

Iceland, John. 2013. *Poverty in America: A Handbook*. Berkeley: University of California Press.

Ingraham, Christopher. 2018. "The World's Richest Countries Guarantee Mothers More Than a Year of Paid Maternity Leave. The U.S. Guarantees Them Nothing." *Washington Post*. February 5. Retrieved September 9, 2019 (https://www.washingtonpost.com/news/wonk/wp/2018/02/05/the-worlds-richest-countries-guarantee-mothers-more-than-a-year-of-paid-maternity-leave-the-u-s-guarantees-them-nothing/? utm_term=.47d31967d203).

Jackson, Dylan B. 2016. "The Link Between Poor Quality Nutrition and Childhood Antisocial Behavior: A Genetically Informative Analysis." *Journal of Criminal Justice* 44: 13–20.

Jargowsky, Paul A. 2015. *Architecture of Segregation: Civil Unrest, the Concentration of Poverty, and Public Policy*. New York, NY: The Century Foundation.

Jasinski, Jana L. 2004. "Pregnancy and Domestic Violence: A Review of the Literature." *Trauma, Violence, & Abuse* 5(1):47–64.

Kapuscinski, C. A., J. Braithwaite, and B. Chapman. 1998. "Unemployment and Crime: Toward Resolving the Paradox." *Journal of Quantitative Criminology* 14(3):215–243.

Kling, Jeffrey R., Jens Ludwig, and Lawrence F. Katz. 2005. "Neighborhood Effects on Crime for Female and Male Youth: Evidence From a Randomized Housing Voucher Experiment." *Quarterly Journal of Economics* 120(1):87–130.

Koball, Heather, and Yang Jiang. 2018. *Basic Facts About Low-Income Children: Children Under 18 Years, 2016*. New York, NY: National Center for Children in Poverty, Mailman School of Public Health, Columbia University.

Kozol, Jonathan. 1991. *Savage Inequalities: Children in America's Schools*. New York, NY: Crown.

Liu, Jianghong, Adrian Raine, Peter H. Venables, and Sarnoff A. Mednick. 2004. "Malnutrition at Age 3 Years and Externalizing Behavior Problems at Ages 8, 11, and 17 Years." *American Journal of Psychiatry* 161(11):2005–2013.

Liu, Jianghong, Sophie R. Zhao, and Teresa Reyes. 2015. "Neurological and Epigenetic

Implications of Nutritional Deficiencies on Psychopathology: Conceptualization and Review of Evidence." *International Journal of Molecular Sciences* 16(8):18129–18148.

Ludwig, Jens, and Julia Burdick-Will. 2012. "Poverty Deconcentration and the Prevention of Crime." Pp. 189–206 in *The Oxford Handbook of Crime Prevention*, edited by D. F. Farrington and B. C. Welsh. New York, NY: Oxford University Press.

Luyken, Jörg. 2017. "This Is How Much You Get Paid for Having Kids in Germany." *The Local*. July 4. Retrieved September 9, 2019 (https://www.thelocal.de/20170704/this-is-how-much-you-get-paid-for-having-kids-in-germany).

Marques, Andrea Horvath, Anne-Lise Bjørke-Monsen, Antônio L. Teixeira, and Marni N. Silverman. 2015. "Maternal Stress, Nutrition and Physical Activity: Impact on Immune Function, CNS Development and Psychopathology." *Brain Research* 1617: 28–46. doi: 10.1016/j.brainres.2014.10.051.

Matthews, Dylan. 2016. "Sweden Pays Parents for Having Kids—and It Reaps Huge Benefits. Why Doesn't the U.S.?" Vox.com. May 23. Retrieved September 9, 2019 (https://www.vox.com/2016/5/23/11440638/child-benefit-child-allowance).

McGloin, Jean Marie, Travis C. Pratt, and Alex R. Piquero. 2006. "A Life-Course Analysis of the Criminogenic Effects of Maternal Cigarette Smoking During Pregnancy." *Journal of Research in Crime and Delinquency* 43: 412–426.

McKernan, Signe-Mary, Caroline Ratcliffe, and John Iceland. 2018. *Policy Efforts to Reduce Material Hardship for Low-Income Families*. Washington, DC: Urban Institute.

McLoyd, Vonnie C., Toby Epstein Jayaratne, Rosario Ceballo, and Julio Borquez. 1994. "Unemployment and Work Interruption Among African American Single Mothers: Effects on Parenting and Adolescent Socioemotional Functioning." *Child Development* 62(2):562–589.

McNicholas, Celine, Samantha Sanders, and Heidi Shierholz. 2018. *First Day Fairness: An Agenda to Build Worker Power and Ensure Job Quality*. Washington, DC: Economic Policy Institute.

Mier, Carrie, and Roshni T. Ladny. 2018. "Does Self-Esteem Negatively Impact Crime and Delinquency? A Meta-Analytic Review of 25 Years of Evidence." *Deviant Behavior* 39(8) 1006–1022. doi: 10.1080/01639625.2017.1395667.

Mishel, Lawrence. 2015. "Here's How to Achieve Full Employment." *The American Prospect*. February 6. Retrieved September 9, 2019 (http://prospect.org/article/heres-how-achieve-full-employment).

Mousain-Bosc, M., M. Roche, A. Polge, D. Pradal-Prat, J. Rapin, and J. P. Bali. 2006. "Improvement of Neurobehavioral Disorders in Children Supplemented With Magnesium-Vitamin B6." *Magnesium Research* 19: 46–52.

Muller, Christopher, Robert J. Sampson, and Alix S. Winter. 2018. "Environmental Inequality: The Social Causes and Consequences of Lead Exposure." *Annual Review of Sociology* 44: 263–282. doi: 10.1146/annurev-soc-073117-041222.

National Scientific Council on the Developing Child. 2014. "Excessive Stress Disrupts the Architecture of the Developing Brain." Retrieved September 9, 2019 (https://developingchild.harvard.edu/wp-content/

uploads/2005/05/Stress_Disrupts_
Architecture_Developing_Brain-1.pdf).

OECD. 2018. "Poverty Rate." Retrieved September 9, 2019 (https://data.oecd.org/inequality/poverty-rate.htm).

Orth, Ulrich, Jürgen Maes, and Manfred Schmitt. 2015. "Self-Esteem Development Across the Life Span: A Longitudinal Study With a Large Sample From Germany." *Developmental Psychology* 51(2):248–259. doi: 10.1037/a003848110.1037/a0038481.supp (Supplemental).

Posick, Chad, Emily Lasko, and Richard E. Tremblay. 2018. "On the Need for a Biopsychosocial Victimology: A Foundational Model for Focusing Violence Prevention on Women and Children." *Victims & Offenders*. https://doi.org/10.1080/15564886.2018.1506852.

Preble, Christopher. 2017. "The Right Way to Cut Wasteful Defense Spending." *Politico*. January 18. Retrieved September 9, 2019 (https://www.politico.com/agenda/story/2017/01/the-right-way-to-cut-wasteful-defense-spending-000282).

Pridemore, William Alex, and Tony H. Grubesic. 2013. "Alcohol Outlets and Community Levels of Interpersonal Violence: Spatial Density, Outlet Type, and Seriousness of Assault." *Journal of Research in Crime & Delinquency* 50(1):132–159. doi: 10.1177/0022427810397952.

Raphael, Steven, and Rudolph Winter-Ebmer. 2001. "Identifying the Effect of Unemployment on Crime." *Journal of Law and Economics* 44: 259–283.

Russell, James W. 2018. *Double Standard: Social Policy in Europe and the United States*. Lanham, MD: Rowman & Littlefield.

Sampson, Robert J., and John H. Laub. 1993. *Crime in the Making: Pathways and Turning Points Through Life*. Cambridge, MA: Harvard University Press.

Sampson, Robert J., William Julius Wilson, and Hanna Katz. 2018. "Reassessing 'Toward a Theory of Race, Crime, and Urban Inequality': Enduring and New Challenges in 21st Century America." *Du Bois Review: Social Science Research on Race* 15(1):13–34.

Sampson, Robert J., and Alix S. Winter. 2018. "Poisoned Development: Assessing Childhood Lead Exposure as a Cause of Crime in a Birth Cohort Followed Through Adolescence." *Criminology* 58(2):269–301.

Sciandra, Matthew, Lisa Sanbonmatsu, Greg J. Duncan, Lisa A. Gennetian, Lawrence F. Katz, Ronald C. Kessler, Jeffrey R. Kling, and Jens Ludwig. 2013. "Long-Term Effects of the Moving to Opportunity Residential Mobility Experiment on Crime and Delinquency." *Journal of Experimental Criminology* 9(4):451–489. doi: 10.1007/s11292-013-9189-9.

Semega, Jessica, Melissa Kollar, John Creamer, and Abinash Mohanty. 2019. *Income and Poverty in the United States: 2018*. Current Population Reports, P60-266. Washington, DC: U.S. Government Printing Office.

Sharkey, Patrick. 2013. *Stuck in Place: Urban Neighborhoods and the End of Progress Toward Racial Equality*. Chicago, IL: University of Chicago Press.

Sherman, Erik. 2018. "Underemployment Takes an Outsized Toll on the Economy, According to a New Study." *Forbes*. September 25. Retrieved September 9, 2019 (https://www.forbes.com/sites/eriksherman/2018/09/25/underemployment-takes-an-outsized-toll-

on-the-economy-according-to-a-new-
study/#7e790bc4234e).

Stein, Jeff. 2018. "What America Could Do With
European Levels of Military Spending."
Washington Post. July 12. Retrieved September
9, 2019 (https://www.washingtonpost.com/
business/2018/07/12/what-america-could-
do-with-european-levels-military-spending/?
utm_term=.d65a7f8bb2c8).

Thompson, Ross A., and Ron Haskins. 2014. *Early
Stress Gets Under the Skin: Promising Initiatives
to Help Children Facing Chronic Adversity*.
Princeton, NJ: The Future of Children,
Princeton University.

Tibbetts, Stephen G., and Jose Rivera. 2015.
"Prenatal and Perinatal Factors in the
Development of Persistent Criminality."
Pp. 167–180 in *The Development of
Criminal and Antisocial Behavior: Theory,
Research and Practical Applications*, edited by
J. Morizot and L. Kazemian. New York, NY:
Springer.

Ulmer, Jeffery T., and Darrell Steffensmeier. 2015.
"The Age and Crime Relationship: Social
Variation, Social Explanations." Pp. 377–396
in *The Nurture Versus Biosocial Debate in
Criminology*, edited by K. M. Beaver, J. C.
Barnes, and B. B. Boutwell. Thousand Oaks,
CA: Sage.

UNICEF Office of Research. 2017. *Building the
Future: Children and the Sustainable Development
Goals in Rich Countries*. Innocenti, Florence,
Italy: Author.

U.S. Census Bureau. 2016. "Dynamics of Economic
Well-Being: Poverty, 2009–2012." Retrieved
September 9, 2019 (https://www.census.gov/
data/tables/time-series/demo/income-poverty/
poverty-dynamics-09-12.html).

van Goozen, Stephanie H. M. 2015. "The
Role of Early Emotion Impairments in the
Development of Persistent Antisocial Behavior."
Child Development Perspectives 9(4):206–210.

Waldfogel, Jane. 2010. *Britain's War on Poverty*. New
York, NY: Russell Sage Foundation.

Webber, Craig. 2007. "Reevaluating Relative
Deprivation Theory." *Theoretical Criminology*
11: 97–120.

Whitehead, Ellen M. 2018. "'Be My Guest':
The Link Between Concentrated Poverty,
Race, and Family-Level Support." *Journal
of Family Issues* 39(12):3225–3247. doi:
10.1177/0192513X18776449.

Wilcox, Pamela, and Francis T. Cullen. 2018.
"Situational Opportunity Theories of Crime."
Annual Review of Criminology 1: 123–148.

Williams, Cindy. 2013. *Making Defense Affordable*.
Washington, DC: Brookings Institution.

Zaalberg, A. P., Henk Nijman, Erik Bulten,
Luwe Stroosma, and Cees van der Staak.
2010. "Effects of Nutritional Supplements
on Aggression, Rule-Breaking, and
Psychopathology Among Young Adult
Prisoners." *Aggressive Behavior* 36(2):117–126.
doi: 10.1002/ab.20335.

Zuelke, Andrea E., Tobias Luck, Matthias L.
Schroeter, A. Veronica Witte, Andreas Hinz,
Christoph Engel, Cornelia Enzenbach,
Silke Zachariae, Markus Loeffler, Joachim
Thiery, Arno Villringer, and Steffi G.
Riedel-Heller. 2018. "The Association Between
Unemployment and Depression: Results From
the Population-Based Life-Adult-Study."
Journal of Affective Disorders 235: 399–406. doi:
10.1016/j.jad.2018.04.073.

6

COMMUNITY AND NEIGHBORHOOD APPROACHES

Chapter Outline

All of us live in some form of a community. We live in neighborhoods, belong to sports teams, go to colleges, and work in offices. Our lives are interconnected in countless, often invisible ways. To some degree, we choose the groups we belong to. Even so, these groups and communities influence us in terms of the way we think and behave.

There is an age-old adage that "it takes a village to raise a child." According to some, this saying comes from an African proverb. It was used to great effect by Hillary Clinton when she was the First Lady of the United States (and later become the inspiration for one of her book titles). The saying implies that, contrary to some perspectives, the job of ensuring children are safe and develop in healthy ways is not just the domain of parents but of entire communities. The idea that communities can help make us safe is the subject of this chapter.

Community crime prevention involves strategies and programs designed to reduce risk factors for criminal behavior in neighborhoods and communities. They range from neighborhood watch–style efforts to community-based drug treatment programs. To be effective, these strategies and programs must address risk factors that lie in the community's social structure. It is thus important to understand which community characteristics increase the risk of criminal behavior on the part of a community's residents.

1. What is the history of community-based approaches to crime prevention?

2. Why is neighborhood disorder thought to contribute to criminal behavior?

3. How might community bonds or social ties be strengthened?

4. Which physical features of a community help prevent crime?

5. What community programs can help reduce substance abuse?

COMMUNITY RISK FACTORS FOR CRIME

Community characteristics have long featured prominently in theories of crime. Even the Italian criminal anthropologist Cesare Lombroso, famous for his "born criminal" biological perspective more than a century ago, suggested that community factors increase crime. For example, Lombroso (1911:53) wrote that "congestion of population by itself gives an irresistible impulse toward crime and immorality." Lombroso was referring to what we today call **population density**, or the concentration of people in locally defined areas. How might a high population density lead to crime? Although Lombroso was not clear on this point, he did speculate that the bringing together of a high number of criminal-minded people would have dangerous effects. Later generations of criminologists highlighted population density as a key community risk factor for crime. For example, and as Chapter 4 discussed, population density increases social interaction, which in turn increases the opportunities for crime and victimization to occur.

Social Disorganization

Social scientists Clifford Shaw and Henry D. McKay (1969) developed a very influential community-based theory of crime about a century ago. Their **social disorganization theory** argued that crime rates remained high in certain areas because of three related factors: poverty, population turnover, and a heterogeneous ethnic makeup. Shaw and McKay used mapping techniques to show that these risk factors correlated with crime and disorder rates in Chicago, no matter which group largely occupied the high-crime areas. These factors were thought to increase crime because they reduce the ability of a community to garner resources and come together to control the behavior of its residents. Ethnic heterogeneity, for example, decreased the closeness of neighbors and made for weaker ties that could be leveraged to accomplish community goals.

Shaw and McKay's theory is historically important, but their presentation of the theory was vague and sometimes included crime as an indicator of social disorganization. If crime is part of a "cause" of crime, the theory is said to be circular or non-falsifiable—crime, of course, will *always* predict crime! However, more recent studies of social disorganization theory have measured social disorganization separately from crime and show it predicts crime rates much like Shaw and McKay thought (Kubrin and Weitzer 2003; Sampson and Groves 1989). In the 1970s, theorists also began to view social disorganization theory as a macro perspective emphasizing the importance of social control (Kornhauser 1978). In this way of thinking, when a community is socially disorganized, it is unable to effectively control its residents' behavior. As such, social disorganization can be thought of as the inability of the community to realize its shared values.

Disorder

Disorder is another characteristic of communities with high crime rates. Disorder refers to indicators of disarray, socially disruptive behaviors, and physical deterioration in particular areas. This term is attributed to Wesley Skogan (2012), who applied it to what one theory had referred to as "broken windows." **Broken windows theory** is the view that signs of deterioration in a community signal to its members that no one cares about the space and that no one is protecting or taking ownership of it. As such, disorder encourages serious misbehavior and crime. The authors of broken windows theory put it this way:

> We suggest that "untended" behavior also leads to the breakdown of community controls. . . . A piece of property is abandoned, weeds grow up, a window is smashed. Adults stop scolding rowdy children; the children, emboldened, become rowdier. Families move out, unattached adults move in. Teenagers gather in front of the corner store. The merchant asks them to move; they refuse. Fights occur. Litter accumulates. People start drinking in front of the grocery; in time, an inebriate slumps to the sidewalk and is allowed to sleep it off. Pedestrians are approached by panhandlers. (Wilson and Kelling 1982)

Disorder can be measured by such things as signs of vandalism, broken-down buildings (and broken windows), graffiti, trash, and public drunkenness. Research indicates that disorder is common in underresourced urban communities with high crime rates. Whether disorder *causes* crime, however, has not been definitively concluded. Some researchers have shown that rather than disorder, **collective efficacy** leads to crime in disordered communities (Sampson and Raudenbush 2001).

Collective Efficacy

Collective efficacy is in some ways the offspring of social disorganization theory. Think about your home life. Do you know your neighbors? Do they feel empowered to intervene when they see wrongdoing? When one of your authors was a young boy, his retired next-door neighbors would peek through their home's windows and let his parents know anytime he was up to mischief. At the time, he found this frustrating; looking back, it is a clear example of collective efficacy at work. Collective efficacy relates back to the idea that a community has shared goals and values, and certain factors help them achieve those goals and values. Mutual trust and common expectations of neighborly involvement, including the idea that neighbors will step in when they see trouble, are two factors that make up collective efficacy and help a community prevent crime and achieve other goals, including lower crime (Sampson 2013; Sampson, Raudenbush, and Earls 1997).

Lack of Resources

Lack of resources like jobs and social welfare safety nets is another community factor linked to crime. Some criminological research shows that in places that are disadvantaged economically, an urban underclass can develop with cultural features (such as "tolerance for crime") conducive to violence (Sampson and Wilson 1995:50). Places without legitimate job opportunities may also encourage young people to turn to illegal, "underground" markets such as drug trafficking. Structural and political factors have led to certain areas having a concentration of disadvantage, which compounds these problems.

The Physical Environment

You may have noticed that most of the risk factors or theories we have discussed so far in this chapter have to do with social organization and social relationships. But the broken windows and disorder theories hint at another set of community or neighborhood characteristics that are important for encouraging or discouraging crime: the physical environment in an area. Disorder theories assume that signs of physical decline increase crime rates, while other theories suggest that aspects of the built environment may shape opportunities for crime. These theories draw on the work of Jane Jacobs (1961) and Oscar Newman (1972). Jacobs wrote about how the physical design of places may facilitate crime. For example, neighborhoods with shared spaces (places that multiple families utilize and feel some degree of attachment to) and visible pathways are easier to guard against unwanted behavior. Newman wrote of "defensible space," arguing that communities can be physically organized in such a way that encourages "ownership" over areas so that people act as guardians against crime. If places were privately owned rather than public, those who owned them would see to it that they were protected (for an overview, see Felson and Eckert 2016). When people feel ownership of an area, they are likely to protect it and guard against outside intrusions. This informal social surveillance may deter would-be offenders.

Research shows that factors such as bad sight lines from houses to streets and lack of shared spaces are linked to the commission of as well as fear of crime (Schweitzer, Kim, and Mackin 1999). There is a whole subfield of criminology, called, appropriately enough, **environmental criminology**, that seeks to show how aspects of the built community affect crime patterns (Brantingham and Brantingham 1981).

Table 6.1 summarizes the theories we have just discussed that emphasize various community risk factors for crime. Although they focus on different community factors, ultimately they are saying that aspects of communities may contribute to higher crime rates. To the extent this is true, crime prevention efforts addressing these criminogenic aspects should help prevent crime.

EARLY COMMUNITY CRIME PREVENTION APPROACHES

In some ways, the earliest forms of law enforcement in the United States were shining examples of community crime prevention approaches. In colonial America, the "brotherly watch" existed as an informal system in which townsfolk depended on one another

Table 6.1 Theories of Community Risk Factors for Crime

Theory	Main Argument	Theorists
Social disorganization	Crime rates increase in areas with high poverty, population turnover, and ethnic diversity.	Clifford Shaw Henry D. McKay Bob Bursik
Broken windows	Incivilities and disorder in areas lead to high crime rates.	George Kelling James Q. Wilson
Concentrated disadvantage	Areas with a severe lack of resources develop cultural responses conducive to crime.	William J. Wilson Elijah Anderson
Collective efficacy	Crime increases in communities without shared trust and expectations of intervening.	Robert J. Sampson
Environmental criminology	Aspects of the built environment structure criminal opportunities.	Paul Brantingham Patricia Brantingham C. Ray Jeffrey

to make sure no funny business occurred. The church was also an important institution helping mediate disputes and issues of wrongdoing. Finally, more formal night-watch systems emerged in which citizens would take turns keeping an eye out for nefarious behavior (Walker 1998).

The Chicago Area Project

As discussed earlier, social disorganization theory emerged a century ago as an explanation of crime. The Chicago theorists who developed this theory were not content to sit in their armchairs pontificating about the causes of crime but actually wanted to do something about it. Clifford Shaw worked with youngsters who had found themselves on the wrong side of the law. He also was instrumental in developing the **Chicago Area Project (CAP)**, a first-of-its-kind community crime prevention approach.

CAP involved creating strong role models for youth in local areas and creating locally driven organizations (Kobrin 1959). The people who lived in the area would be primarily responsible for running the program, thereby giving them buy-in and ownership. This program was based on the idea that when people view a program as legitimate, they are much more likely to become involved with it and try to benefit from it. Established in 1932, CAP attempted to develop some degree of social organization in communities. Youth were given opportunities to be in recreation clubs, and groups were organized to advocate for community improvement. Counseling was also a prominent feature of CAP.

Was CAP effective? We do not really know. Kobrin's (1959) assessment of CAP's first 25 years was vague on the effect the program had on delinquency, but it did suggest that CAP demonstrated how social organization can benefit disorganized areas. Later assessments also did not show much in the way of delinquency prevention (Hope 1995).

Mobilization for Youth

Another historically well-known example of a community prevention program was called **Mobilization for Youth (MFY)**. This program was a part of President Lyndon B. Johnson's war on poverty of the 1960s, in which federally funded approaches to improve disadvantaged areas proliferated. In terms of preventing delinquency, programs aimed at reducing poverty drew on *anomie or strain theories*, which argued that crime resulted from an inability to obtain needs legitimately. In fact, one of the main influences on MFY was Lloyd Ohlin, who, along with Richard Cloward, had developed a version of anomie theory in 1960 (Berger and Berger 1985).

MFY was a "comprehensive community-based prevention" program (Berger and Berger 1985:138) that was implemented on the Lower East Side of Manhattan, costing $12.9 million (Fox 2009), equal to some $100 million today. It included several layers, such as job training, improving education systems, creating social groups in local communities, and providing family assistance. The program, and indeed the entire war-on-poverty approach, was critiqued for several reasons and came into conflict with local governments, eventually withering away from its early ambitious foundation (Hope 1995). It does not appear that its effects on crime were examined rigorously, however.

CONTEMPORARY COMMUNITY CRIME PREVENTION APPROACHES

Although the effectiveness of these early approaches in reducing crime was not clear, several types of community-based crime prevention efforts have highlighted the contemporary era. In some ways community crime prevention may be more challenging today, as communities become more diverse and anonymous in the postmodern era. We now discuss the most notable such efforts.

Approaches Focused on Poverty and Resources

Reducing poverty or increasing community resources remains a key part of crime prevention in community settings. If, as we have seen, poverty or lack of resources is linked to antisocial behavior, then providing needed resources should theoretically reduce crime. However, as sociologists Patrick Sharkey, Max Besbris, and Michael Friedson (2017) have shown, poverty at the individual level may not be directly related to crime but rather is associated with other risk factors that are the "real" causes of criminal behavior. On the community level, this relationship is even more complex. Crime, they write, is not the result of a simple aggregation of people with inclinations to crime, but instead is the result of complex community-level factors.

Sharkey et al. discuss a federal crime prevention program called **Moving to Opportunity (MTO)** to show how there is not a simply "more poverty = more crime" community relationship. In this program, people in low-income areas in several cities were randomly assigned, with their consent, to be given housing vouchers and other aid to move out of their impoverished neighborhoods into other neighborhoods with more resources. The experimental design of this program made it a "natural experiment" for assessing whether moving out of a poverty-stricken area can lead to reduced criminal behavior and other positive outcomes. However, the overall impact on crime for the youths in MTO seems to have been minimal; certain moves led to decreases in violence, but other moves led to increases in violence (Sharkey and Sampson 2010).

Sharkey has recently written on the importance of community investment to reduce crime. Rather than building up the criminal justice system, having more police and more people behind bars, he argues that

> in recent years, rigorous evaluations of several types of community-oriented programs have shown that summer jobs programs and initiatives to clean up abandoned lots have had tremendous success in reducing violent crime. In Chicago, youth who were randomly assigned to take part in a program called Becoming a Man, which combined after-school sports programs and cognitive behavioral therapy, were half as likely as those who did not take part to be arrested for a violent crime. (Sharkey 2018a)

Sharkey (2018b) has specifically examined the effect of the crime decline in America on communities. As mentioned in Chapter 1, violent crime across the United States has decreased substantially since the early 1990s. He says that when cities became safer, people with more resources moved back into low-income areas, "thus reducing the concentration of poverty in urban America." But interestingly, by inviting people back into the city, the crime decline may have actually made those cities safer. Cities were no longer places of disorder and abandonment but places of ownership. Cities, he found, have come back alive. In his recent book, *Uneasy Peace: The Great Crime Decline, the Renewal of City Life, and the Next War on Violence* (Sharkey 2018c), he found that community nonprofit organizations had a large effect on community crime. For example, he wrote: "In a given city with 100,000 people, we found that every new organization formed to confront violence and build stronger neighborhoods led to about a 1% drop in violent crime and murder" (p. 53).

The crime decline since the 1990s has thus apparently had a positive impact on communities. What about intentional efforts to organize communities against crime? Rosenbaum (1988:354) discussed several types of what he called the "social problems approach to community crime prevention," finding that overall there was "little *hard* evidence" pointing to their ability to reduce crime. A more recent evaluation of neighborhood youth programs in Chicago concluded that, similarly, the programs did not seem to have a direct effect on crime overall. However, the programs may have an indirect effect on crime by influencing risk factors such as self-control (Zimmerman, Welsh, and Posick 2015).

Providing Resources

In general, then, it appears that efforts to instill organization in communities have not worked, both in the historical and present-day context. A more promising approach may be to provide resources in disadvantaged areas or to people from those areas. For example, youth job programs have been shown to reduce violence in communities (Heller 2014). Job Corps, a program that helps youth from risky areas receive training to be more marketable, reduces crime among participants (Schochet, Burghardt, and McConnell 2008). A program in Boston, Massachusetts, to offer employment to juveniles reduced crime by 35% for violent crimes and 57% for property crimes (Modestino 2017). This program was evaluated with a **randomized clinical trial**, which is often used in medicine, when a group of individuals is assigned randomly to either receive the "treatment" or to a control group. Because of randomization, the causal effect of the treatment can be identified more easily.

However, job programs for adults, particularly those operated by the criminal justice system, have a somewhat less optimistic record. A **meta-analysis**, which is an attempt to synthesize the results of numerous studies into one overall outcome, sought to examine the state of the literature on employment programs after incarceration for adults and older adolescents. Meta-analyses combine several studies into an average **effect size**, which is a standardized metric for the strength of association between two variables. For example, an effect size of .50 in this context would mean that the studies in the meta-analysis showed an overall medium effect on crime. This study (Visher, Winterfield, and Coggeshall 2006) found no effect, but it argued there were too few high-quality studies in the literature to be conclusive. Bushway and Reuter (2001:211) speculate that "offenders are too deeply entrenched in crime, or the criminal justice system is not an effective delivery system for these types of programs."

Approaches Focused on Disorder

While the early community crime prevention approaches sought to help improve the social organization of local areas, crime prevention strategies began in the 1990s to focus on physical and social disorder. One such strategy is **broken windows policing**, also called *order maintenance policing*. In this type of policing, based on broken windows theory, law enforcement widen their nets to control not just serious criminal behavior but public order issues such as turnstile jumping (when someone in a subway does not pay for their fare), public urination, and acts of vandalism. These strategies are controversial because they often target the underprivileged, and their effects on crime are not clear.

One randomized study in Massachusetts used crime **hot spots** (areas of concentrated criminal activity) as the unit of analysis. Thirty-four hot spots were randomly assigned to either disorder policing or policing as usual. What did disorder policing look like? The officers paid attention to the cleanliness of the area, they fixed streetlights and installed surveillance cameras, and they ensured building codes were followed. After a year of this experiment, the researchers looked at whether calls for service (an indicator of crime) as well as disorder differed between the two groups of hot spots. They found that both crime and disorder declined in the disorder-policing hot spots (Braga and Bond 2008).

However, disorder or broken windows policing is not always associated with better outcomes. One study found that broken windows policing actually *increased* fear of crime in neighborhoods (Hinkle and Weisburd 2008). A recent systematic review and meta-analysis of 30 studies (Braga, Welsh, and Schnell 2015) found that disorder/broken windows policing tactics do reduce crime to some degree. But programs classified as "community problem-solving" approaches were more effective than so-called "aggressive order maintenance" approaches (which did not reduce crime at all). So policing disorder can work, but it must be done, seemingly, with the cooperation of the community and not done *to* the community. Sharkey (2018c) argues that this less aggressive form of policing has taken over in recent years, as policing tactics have come to rely on the neighborhood to control itself more.

With respect to informal approaches, one study in the Netherlands examined the effect of "social caretakers," who were assigned to public housing units to provide supervision and upkeep. The program consisted of deploying 150 caretakers to 300 housing units in the Netherlands. The social caretaker's job included "more emphasis on patrolling the estate in order to deter vandalism and crime, and to maintain contact with the residents" (Hesseling 1992:2). The study of this program found that both disorder and crime declined overall (Hope 1995).

A problem still exists with respect to the main arguments from broken windows and disorder theories. Does disorder *lead* to crime, or is it just one manifestation of a high-crime area? One study found that residents cannot distinguish between indicators of disorder and indicators of crime (Gau and Pratt 2008). Another study, mentioned above, found that disorder was only indirectly related to crime: Disorder reduced collective efficacy, and this reduction led to more crime (Sampson and Raudenbush 2001).

Recall that collective efficacy is about whether neighbors trust one another and are willing to intervene when they see behavior that violates community norms. A large body of research has shown that collective efficacy is related to community crime levels (Mazerolle, Wickes, and McBroom 2010). Local organizations play a role in collective efficacy as they contribute to its trust and cohesion (Sampson, Morenoff, and Earls 1999). Interestingly, one study found that the rate of community prevention programs in particular areas did not predict crime once collective efficacy was taken into account (Mazerolle et al. 2010). This study thus reinforced the importance of enhancing collective efficacy for effective crime prevention.

Can the police increase collective efficacy? Interestingly, there is a line of research that is tied to the concept of **legitimacy**. In policing literature, legitimacy means that the citizens feel the police are justified in having power over them. It also increases trust, a key element of collective efficacy. Legal cynicism, the inverse of trust and legitimacy, is linked to lower collective efficacy in neighborhoods (Kirk and Matsuda 2011). Some have argued that police should engage in "collective-efficacy policing," where police in high-crime areas identify problems, gather community stakeholders to engage in the work of crime reduction, and then report their findings (Weisburd, Davis, and Gill 2015). The research that does exist, however, casts doubt on whether police can influence collective efficacy among residents (Kochel 2012; Weisburd, Hinkle, and Famega 2010). This may not be surprising, because collective efficacy relies more on relationships and values among citizens and neighbors, something a police agency may have trouble influencing.

Collective efficacy, though, does seem to be related to trust in the police: In areas with higher levels of collective efficacy, there is more trust in the police (Nix et al. 2015). This may be yet another reason why collective efficacy reduces crime, as it influences not only informal but formal layers of social control. It appears that collective efficacy can improve police effectiveness, but police may not be able to influence collective efficacy.

Work, Sports, and Recreation Programs

Several interesting theories try to explain crime by young people. Research tells us that unsupervised socializing—that is, when youth are engaged in activities either alone or with their peers that are unstructured and out in the public—often leads to trouble (Osgood and Anderson 2004). If so, then engaging youth in their free time may be an effective way to reduce crime. This idea is related to the adage that "idle hands are the devil's workshop." Providing support for this adage, some scholars speculate that video games, rather than increasing crime, actually reduce it because they occupy people in their living rooms; they are less likely to be outside, where they can misbehave (Markey, Markey, and French 2015). One intriguing possibility (as yet untested as far as we know) from this line of reasoning is that the explosion of home video game consoles (e.g., Nintendo, Sega) in homes in the mid- to late 1980s contributed to the crime decline that began in America (and other nations) in the early 1990s. The rise of cell phone technology and social media may have further contributed to the safety of streets by keeping youths inside and away from trouble.

Work and recreation have a long history in the crime prevention world. At the same time, they are rather controversial. In the Maryland Report on "what works" to reduce crime, Sherman (1997:3–26) wrote, "The hypothesis that recreation can prevent crime has become one of the most acrimonious in the history of crime policy." About a century ago, wilderness or forestry programs were established for juveniles who had gotten into trouble. One well-known program was the California Youth Authority camp, which opened its doors in 1931. The camps were used for labor projects with the idea that delinquent youths would gain valuable structure in their lives and be able to contribute to society in useful ways. Recreation was part of the experience in the camps, as was individualized counseling (Breed 1953). However, research on this program failed to find any degree of effectiveness in reducing delinquency and other behavioral problems (Shireman et al. 1972).

More recent **wilderness programs** have fared better than the early forestry camps, which were really vocation/work-oriented. Wilderness challenge programs are more concerned with having a group of at-risk youths come together to complete tasks in the woods. In addition to "building confidence," Wilson and Lipsey (2000:1) describe the logic of the programs this way: "By solving challenging problems in situations that require positive group interaction and cooperation, participants are expected to learn prosocial interpersonal skills that will transfer to situations outside the program." A meta-analysis of 28 studies of wilderness programs found that they reduced *recidivism* (repeat offending) by 29% (Wilson and Lipsey 2000). Despite this positive appraisal, more recent research has indicated the need for more rigorous research on these programs (Clem, Prost, and Thyer 2015).

In addition to work and recreation, sports have been leveraged for crime prevention purposes. For example, in the 1990s there was a push in particular cities to organize sports programs for youths, with the idea that it would keep them out of trouble. One such program, **Midnight Basketball**, began in Maryland but gained traction in Chicago (Hartmann 2016; Hartmann and Depro 2006). The idea was to have a league that played late at night, when youths are at risk for engaging in or being exposed to criminal activity. While this makes sense, it is not clear what impact these programs have had on crime. One study looked at crime rates in places with midnight basketball and places without such leagues. The results indicated that cities with midnight basketball leagues experienced greater crime drops over time (from 1985 to 2001) than those without midnight basketball leagues. This finding held even after accounting for demographic factors that may have differed between the two groups (Hartmann and Depro 2006). However, there was no statistically significant effect for violent crimes. Hartmann and Depro (2006:192) conclude that there is some evidence that these programs can work, but there is also "a great deal of public and scholarly skepticism."

The use of sports programs and sports leagues may not be a panacea, however. Criminologist Travis Hirschi, the famed criminologist who is credited with two popular criminological theories (see Chapter 4), initially assumed that mere "involvement" in prosocial activities would reduce crime. His analyses found that involvement was not that important, and he concluded that "delinquency requires very little time: the most delinquent boys in the sample may not have devoted more than a few hours in the course of a year to the acts that define them as delinquent. Since this is so, it might be necessary to account for almost all the time available to the boys in the sample to find differences in conventional involvements that account for delinquent activity" (Hirschi 1969/2002:190). A 2000 report by the Australian Institute of Criminology echoed these sentiments 30 years after Hirschi published his book, finding that "sport and physical activity were important, but not sufficient, components of a broader strategy" (Cameron and MacDougall 2000:5).

Neighborhood Watch Programs

Interestingly, one of the earliest forms of community crime prevention is still in use. When one of your authors was growing up, his neighborhood participated in a neighborhood watch program. Every few streets had a sign with a menacing-looking villain crossed out and the phrase "If I don't call the police my neighbor will." This was a clear warning to would-be criminals that the neighborhood was being policed by citizens who were constantly on alert.

On some level, neighborhood watch programs may cause you to scoff. Are people really watching, or is this the equivalent of putting a home security sign out in front of your home but not actually purchasing the security kit? After all, in the neighborhood your author grew up in, he never heard a word about meetings or how to sign up for the watch. In fact, a recent film called *The Watch* (2012) poked fun at the idea, with members of the neighborhood watch acting foolish and not taking their role seriously. More gravely, around the time the film was released, a member of a neighborhood watch, George Zimmerman, killed a young black male, Trayvon Martin, sparking protests and outcries against the allowance of use of force for relatively untrained citizens (Gau and Jordan 2015).

What does the research say? One systematic review, published by the Campbell Collaboration (campbellcollaboration.org), which houses systematic reviews and meta-analyses on all manner of crime control interventions, found that neighborhood watches are generally effective. Overall, crime decreased 26% in the neighborhood watch areas compared with the control areas (Bennett, Holloway, and Farrington 2008). Although this was a valuable finding, none of the 19 studies included in the review were published after 1994. That noted, more recent evidence does continue to suggest that neighborhood watch programs reduce crime (Greene et al. 2014).

Preventing Crime Through Environmental Design

Community efforts to reduce crime have also focused on the physical environment. One strategy, called **crime prevention through environmental design (CPTED**, pronounced sep-ted), emerged in the 1970s in response to Jacobs's and Newman's work on defensible space, discussed above. CPTED is the idea that communities can change the way their neighborhoods are structured to reduce opportunities for crime. Certain aspects of the physical environment—low-lit back alleys, abandoned lots, and the like—make it easier for would-be offenders to commit crime. C. R. Jeffrey, a biosocial criminologist, is credited with coining the phrase CPTED, but it has come to be associated with environmental criminology (Cozens 2008). Table 6.2 illustrates the main components of CPTED.

In their book *Crime and Everyday Life*, Marcus Felson and Mary Eckert (2016) discuss several CPTED approaches. They argue that "natural" strategies are more effective than formal ones. For example, two aspects of place are (1) the activities that occur there and (2) when those activities occur. If activities occur when people are around to help deter potential offenders, crime will be less likely to occur. Reflecting this insight, Felson (2006) recommends scheduling activities in such a way that there are more people around to act as guardians against crime. Felson also discusses the "Crowe-Zahm mixing principle," which is to place unsafe activities in risky areas and safe activities in safe areas (Felson 2006). They suggested that "safe locations are often found next to high-activity areas or are associated with organized functions such as an administration office or some type of concession stand or sales booth" (Crowe and Zahm 1994:26). A safe activity is one that inherently involves other people who can provide guardianship—eyes and ears.

Table 6.2 Components of CPTED

Component	Definition
Natural observation	Designing spaces so the public can view activities, minimizing the ability of would-be offenders to go undetected
Natural access control	Having control over entryways and access points and minimizing access to nonpublic areas
Spatial division	Making clear the lines between private and public spaces and encouraging ownership over particular areas so they may be defended
Taking care of spaces	Keeping up and maintaining spaces to ensure they remain defensible

Source: Created using information from National Crime Prevention Council (2009).

The research on environmental criminology and environmental design suggests that to reduce crime, the focus should be on particular streets and locations rather than on the overall community (Taylor and Gottfredson 1986). It makes more sense for a specific neighborhood to organize itself or to take steps to change the physical environment in ways that encourage prosocial behaviors and discourage antisocial behaviors than for a community-wide effort to do so.

Although the research results on CPTED strategies are somewhat mixed, these strategies do seem promising overall (Cozens, Saville, and Hillier 2005). To illustrate, putting up more streetlights increases the ability of residents to guard or provide surveillance of the local area. Because dark alleys and streets allow potential offenders to sneak up to and away from a target, brightly lit areas may deter them from considering the attack in the first place. The evidence on additional street lighting does point to a crime prevention effect (Farrington and Welsh 2002). Another effective CPTED strategy appears to be the use of **closed-circuit television (CCTV) cameras,** which are widely used in Great Britain. CCTV cameras in that nation are placed in strategic locations not only to help identify offenders after the fact but also as a deterrent for those who may be considering such behavior. A meta-analysis by Welsh and Farrington (2004) found that CCTV cameras reduced crime by 27%.

Physical environment approaches are not only about changing the layout of neighborhoods to increase sight lines and the ability to observe potential offenders. Some approaches also involve increasing ownership of particular areas and changing the social organization of those areas in ways that discourage criminal activity. This is what separates these approaches from purely situational crime prevention techniques, to be discussed in the next chapter. With the concept of defensible space, the social is as important as the physical. The physical facilitates the defense of space, but it is the people who must do the defending. It is therefore an informal approach.

In an illustration of this idea, Merry (1981) described the difference between low-rise and high-rise slab buildings. In the low-rise buildings, fewer families share the space. This fact allows them to know one another, to know when a stranger is present, and to feel some degree of ownership over the place. In contrast, many people live in high-rise buildings, which also feature so few common areas that interaction is rare and brief. People in these buildings thus do not get to know each other well, and no sense of "neighborliness" develops. They are also less likely to know when strangers are present. Thus, there is less likely to be any degree of defending their space, making crime more likely.

Merry's (1981) research found that despite studying an area that seemed to be designed for defense—"The buildings are low. Four-story row houses with piggyback maisonette apartments (two stories each) cluster around small courtyards. Access to the upper apartments through an exterior stairwell provides a minimum of interior public space. A short corridor links the two upper apartments at the top landing of the stairwell" (p. 403)—there was a large amount of crime. In part this was because of subtle physical aspects that made observation difficult, but also a recognition that neighbors did not know each other and would not have each other's backs. When interventions did happen (20 times in her study), they tended to occur where people lived and socialized. Even people she interviewed who were admitted robbers said they paid attention to the physical features of the environment and were more likely to victimize others in places where there would be a smaller chance of observation and intervention.

COMMUNITY CRIME PREVENTION AND SUBSTANCE ABUSE

Some important community crime prevention strategies aim at reducing substance use and abuse. There is, criminologists have long known, a strong connection between substance use and criminal behavior (Jennings et al. 2015). Yet this connection is not a simple one. It is not true that all those who use drugs also commit crime or that crimes are committed because people are under the influence of substances. As the National Council on Alcoholism and Drug Dependence (2015) points out, it is unclear if people who have risk factors for crime also have risk factors for drug use, or if drug use is causally connected to crime. The link between alcohol and crime, particularly violence, seems more straightforward, as some studies have suggested that upwards of 41% of those convicted of violent crimes were under the influence of alcohol at the time of the offense (Greenfeld and Henneberg 2001).

While alcohol has long been a cultural mainstay in the United States, recently there has been a rising concern over opioid addiction. Some outlets have taken to calling it an "epidemic," due to the rapid increase in use and overdoses occurring daily (Mitchell 2018). In fact, recent epidemiological research suggests that the average life expectancy for whites is on the decline in America, in no small part due to opioids (Stein 2017).

Given the connection between substance addiction and crime, it would make sense that drug treatment programs have an effect on crime. What programs seem to work to reduce substance use? One popular strategy in the 1980s and 1990s called **Drug Abuse Resistance Education (D.A.R.E.)** does *not* work. On the face of it, providing education to children in schools regarding the dangers of drugs, which D.A.R.E. does, should reduce drug use. Yet there is a near complete consensus among scientists that D.A.R.E. does not reduce drug use substantially (Ennett et al. 1994; West and O'Neal 2004). Programs in schools to prevent alcohol use show similarly unimpressive results (Strøm et al. 2014).

So what seems to work? In the community context, a program developed by J. David Hawkins and Richard F. Catalano in the early 1990s called **Communities That Care (CTC)** seems to have promise. CTC is an approach to community prevention that focuses on leveraging resources and evidence-based strategies to reduce problem behavior. There are five phases of CTC (Hawkins, Catalano, and Kuklinski 2014):

1. Examining what issues need to be addressed

2. Determining who should take on leadership

3. Determining which groups should be involved

4. Determining which risk factors should be addressed

5. Evaluating the results of the program

Research has shown that CTC reduces crime and substance use (Hawkins et al. 2008, 2014) but seems to have more effect on preventing people from using substances in the first place than on decreasing current use.

The 1997 report on "what works" to reduce crime (Sherman et al. 1997), cited earlier, found that other community approaches seem to reduce youth substance use. For example, community-based mentoring was found to reduce drug abuse (see also Grossman and Tierney 1998). **Big Brothers Big Sisters** is one such program that matches at-risk youths with mentors. The mentor can serve as a source of support and as a role model for the youth. The Sherman et al. (1997) report concluded that these programs have demonstrated effectiveness in reducing substance use but not crime. However, a more recent review of mentoring programs found reductions in criminal behavior (Tolan et al. 2013). Mentoring programs, then, show strong promise of reducing both substance abuse and crime.

Does reducing substance use also reduce crime? One study in England that examined outcomes for patients across 54 different programs found a reduction in criminal convictions compared with before they were enrolled (Gossop et al. 2005). This study included both residential programs (meaning the patients are housed within the program) and community programs. While the residential programs saw a larger decrease in convictions in Year 1, by Year 5 the community programs had reduced convictions slightly more.

With respect to the use of opiates, one community-based strategy to reduce such behavior is called **methadone maintenance**. These programs provide an alternative, controlled substance (methadone) to wean people addicted to drugs like heroin. Some research has found that enrollment in such programs reduces criminal behavior (Bali et al. 1988; Parker and Kirby 1996). While the research on methadone maintenance suffers from methodological problems, one study used a before-and-after design to show that patients' crime involvement decreases after treatment (Lind et al. 2005). A Campbell Collaboration review found that heroin maintenance has a larger effect on crime compared with methadone maintenance and that Naltrexone (which is a drug that blocks the pleasurable feelings derived from opiates to promote reduced use) works better than treatment without maintenance components (Egli et al. 2011).

There is not much research on the crime-reducing effects of alcohol addiction treatment. Well-known programs such as Alcoholics Anonymous and the Minnesota Model take place within the community but do not have a conclusive body of evidence supporting their efficacy. It is unclear, therefore, whether they would have an effect on criminal behavior, but there is reason to doubt such a view if they do not actually reduce substance use.

In sum, drug and alcohol treatment seems to work, not only to reduce addiction but also criminal behavior that may be connected to such substances. However, school-based approaches such as D.A.R.E. show little or no evidence of effectiveness.

DIFFICULTIES WITH COMMUNITY CRIME PREVENTION

It is all well and good to discuss what works in community crime prevention, but actually implementing these approaches is another matter. As mentioned previously, as the population grows and diversifies, it may become more difficult to find strategies to which all groups buy in and contribute. Social disorganization, according to some authors (Kornhauser 1978), is the failure of a community to realize its shared goals and desires. If a community is diverse or not close-knit, there may be few shared goals. In addition, to the extent that a community is poor or in disarray, it will have difficulty organizing—disorder, recall, is linked to higher crime rates (Hope 1995).

Hope (1995) also discussed differences among community approaches across socioeconomic status. In more wealthy areas, rather than community members working together to address problems, he argued that "social order in affluent suburban communities may be maintained by its opposite, a strategy of social avoidance" (p. 67). Not knowing neighbors, though, may raise suspicion of people who mean and pose no harm. In 2018, several stories hit social media of white individuals (often women) calling the police on African Americans simply going about their business, swimming, or selling water (Jerkins 2018).

Finally, as we noted previously, community prevention efforts often require resources such as time and money. These may be in short supply in the communities that need them the most. Thus, crime prevention in communities may require the involvement of the government—an approach that (at least in the mid-20th century) does not have the best track record. Community crime prevention strategies face challenges that need to be addressed for them to be successful.

CONCLUSION

The history of community and neighborhood crime prevention approaches is complex. On the one hand, there have been many examples of strategies that did not seem to work to reduce crime. In fact, in their 1998 report on what works, Sherman and colleagues wrote that "by the criteria used in this report, there are no community-based programs of 'proven effectiveness' by scientific standards to show with reasonable certainty that they 'work' in certain kinds of settings." Yet these authors were convinced that the types of approaches discussed in this chapter were promising, and the more recent research discussed in this chapter supports their conviction.

This chapter has reviewed what seems to work and what does not regarding community prevention and crime. In general, job programs for youths (but not adults), physical environment and disorder strategies, and drug treatment seem able to reduce crime in communities. Attempts to "organize" communities do not seem to have much effectiveness. In general, it appears that "natural" approaches or those taking place in smaller units (neighborhoods) are more effective than approaches coming from the top or government-sponsored strategies.

SUMMARY

1. Communities and neighborhoods vary in their level of criminal activity. Risk factors include disorganization, disorder, poverty, and a lack of trust/cohesion among residents.

2. Historical approaches to organize communities or provide resources did not seem to reduce crime.

3. Modern approaches, including youth summer job programs and investment in community organizations, are more promising.

4. Broken windows and disorder have mostly been addressed by police, with some evidence of effectiveness.

5. Youth recreation/sports strategies show mixed results. Some may reduce crime while others may not, but the reasons for these inconsistent results are unclear.

6. Neighborhood watch programs have been shown to reduce crime, most likely via deterring would-be offenders.

7. Physical environment strategies (e.g., CCTV cameras and street lighting) can reduce crime.

8. Substance use treatment programs in the community can reduce addiction and consequently criminal behavior. For youths, mentoring approaches seem most effective.

KEY TERMS

Big Brothers Big Sisters 132
broken windows policing 125
broken windows theory 120
Chicago Area Project (CAP) 122
closed-circuit television (CCTV)
   cameras 130
collective efficacy 120
Communities That Care
   (CTC) 132
community crime
   prevention 118

crime prevention through
   environmental design
   (CPTED) 129
disorder 120
Drug Abuse Resistance
   Education (D.A.R.E.) 132
effect size 125
environmental criminology 121
hot spots 125
legitimacy 126
meta-analysis 125

methadone maintenance 132
Midnight Basketball 128
Mobilization for Youth
   (MFY) 123
Moving to Opportunity
   (MTO) 124
population density 119
randomized clinical trial 125
social disorganization theory 119
wilderness programs 127

REFERENCES

Bali, J. Corty, H. Bond, C. Myers, and
   A. Tommasello. 1988. "The Reduction of
   Intravenous Heroin Use, Non-Opiate Abuse
   and Crime During Methadone Maintenance
   Treatment: Further Findings." *NIDA Research
   Monograph* 81: 224–230.

Bennett, Trevor, Katy Holloway, and David
   Farrington. 2008. "The Effectiveness of
   Neighborhood Watch." *Campbell Systematic
   Reviews* 18: 1–48.

Berger, Ronald J., and Cherylynne E. Berger. 1985.
   "Community Organization Approaches to the
   Prevention of Juvenile Delinquency." *Journal of
   Sociology & Social Welfare* 12(1):129–153.

Braga, Anthony A., and Brenda J. Bond. 2008.
   "Policing Crime and Disorder Hot Spots:
   A Randomized Controlled Trial." *Criminology*
   46(3):577–607.

Braga, Anthony A., Brandon C. Welsh, and
   Cory Schnell. 2015. "Can Policing Disorder
   Reduce Crime? A Systematic Review and
   Meta-Analysis." *Journal of Research in Crime and
   Delinquency* 52(4):567–588.

Brantingham, Paul J., and Patricia L. Brantingham,
   eds. 1981. *Environmental Criminology*. Beverly
   Hills, CA: Sage.

Breed, Allen F. 1953. "California Youth Authority
   Forestry Camp Program." *Federal Probation* 17:
   37–43.

Bushway, Shawn, and Peter Reuter. 2001. "Labor
   Markets and Crime." Pp. 191–224 in *Crime and
   Public Policy*, 2nd ed., edited by James Q. Wilson
   and Joan Petersilia. New York, NY: Oxford
   University Press.

Cameron, Margaret, and Colin James MacDougall.
   2000. *Crime Prevention Through Sport and*

Physical Activity, Vol. 165. Canberra: Australian Institute of Criminology.

Clem, Jamie M., Stephanie Grace Prost, and Bruce A. Thyer. 2015. "Does Wilderness Therapy Reduce Recidivism in Delinquent Adolescents? A Narrative Review." *Journal of Adolescent and Family Health* 7(1):1–19.

Cozens, Paul. 2008. "Crime Prevention Through Environmental Design." Pp. 153–177 in *Environmental Criminology and Crime Analysis*, edited by Richard Wortley and Lorraine Mazerolle. New York, NY: Routledge.

Cozens, Paul Michael, Greg Saville, and David Hillier. 2005. "Crime Prevention Through Environmental Design (CPTED): A Review and Modern Bibliography." *Property Management* 23(5):328–356.

Crowe, Timothy D., and Diane L. Zahm. 1994. "Crime Prevention Though Environmental Design." *Land Development Magazine*. Fall. National Association of Home Builders.

Egli, Nicole, Miriam Pina, Pernille Skovbo Christensen, Marcelo Aebi, and Martin Killias. 2011. *Effects of Drug Substitution Programs on Offending Among Drug-Addicts*. Oslo, Norway: Campbell Systematic Reviews.

Ennett, Susan T., Nancy S. Tobler, Christopher L. Ringwalt, and Robert L. Flewelling. 1994. "How Effective Is Drug Abuse Resistance Education? A Meta-Analysis of Project DARE Outcome Evaluations." *American Journal of Public Health* 84(9):1394–1401.

Farrington, David P., and Brandon C. Welsh. 2002. "Improved Street Lighting and Crime Prevention." *Justice Quarterly* 19(2):313–342.

Felson, Marcus. 2006. *Crime and Nature*. Thousand Oaks, CA: Sage.

Felson, Marcus, and Mary A. Eckert. 2016. *Crime and Everyday Life*, 5th ed. Thousand Oaks, CA: Sage.

Fox, Margalit. 2009. "Lloyd E. Ohlin, Expert on Crime and Punishment, Is Dead at 90." *New York Times*. January 3.

Gau, Jacinta M., and Kareem L. Jordan. 2015. "Profiling Trayvon: Young Black Males, Suspicion, and Surveillance." Pp. 7–22 in *Deadly Injustice: Trayvon Martin, Race, and the Criminal Justice System*, edited by D. Johnson, P. Y. Warren, and A. Farrell. New York: New York University Press.

Gau, Jacinta M., and Travis C. Pratt. 2008. "Broken Windows or Window Dressing? Citizens' (In)Ability to Tell the Difference Between Disorder and Crime." *Criminology & Public Policy* 7(2):163–194.

Gossop, Michael, Katia Trakada, Duncan Stewart, and John Witton. 2005. "Reductions in Criminal Convictions After Addiction Treatment: 5-Year Follow-Up." *Drug & Alcohol Dependence* 79(3):295–302.

Greene, Shannon, John Österholm, Yiqian Fan, and Joe Stone. 2014. *The Effect of Neighborhood Watch Programs on Neighborhood Crime in Medford Oregon*. Eugene: Sustainable Crime Initiative, University of Oregon.

Greenfeld, Lawrence A., and Maureen Henneberg. 2001. "Victim and Offender Self-Reports of Alcohol Involvement in Crime." *Alcohol Research & Health* 25(1):20–31.

Grossman, Jean Baldwin, and Joseph P. Tierney. 1998. "Does Mentoring Work? An Impact Study of the Big Brothers Big Sisters Program." *Evaluation Review* 22(3):403–426.

Hartmann, Douglas. 2016. *Midnight Basketball: Race, Sports, and Neoliberal Social Policy*. Chicago, IL: University of Chicago Press.

Hartmann, Douglas, and Brooks Depro. 2006. "Rethinking Sports-Based Community Crime Prevention: A Preliminary Analysis of the Relationship Between Midnight Basketball and Urban Crime Rates." *Journal of Sport and Social Issues* 30(2):180–196.

Hawkins, J. David, Eric C. Brown, Sabrina Oesterle, Michael W. Arthur, Robert D. Abbott, and Richard F. Catalano. 2008. "Early Effects of Communities That Care on Targeted Risks and Initiation of Delinquent Behavior and Substance Use." *Journal of Adolescent Health* 43(1):15–22.

Hawkins, J. David, Richard F. Catalano, and Margaret R. Kuklinski. 2014. "Communities That Care." Pp. 393–408 in *Encyclopedia of Criminology and Criminal Justice*, edited by Gerben Brunsma and David Weisburd. New York, NY: Springer.

Heller, Sara B. 2014. "Summer Jobs Reduce Violence Among Disadvantaged Youth." *Science* 346(6214):1219–1223.

Hesseling, R. B. P. 1992. "Social Caretakers and Preventing Crime on Public Housing Estates." In *Dutch Penal Law and Policy 06, 05-1992*. The Hague, Netherlands: Ministry of Justice, Research and Documentation Center.

Hinkle, Joshua C., and David Weisburd. 2008. "The Irony of Broken Windows Policing: A Micro-Place Study of the Relationship Between Disorder, Focused Police Crackdowns and Fear of Crime." *Journal of Criminal Justice* 36(6):503–512.

Hirschi, Travis. 1969/2002. *Causes of Delinquency*. Berkeley: University of California Press.

Hope, Tim. 1995. "Community Crime Prevention." *Crime and Justice* 19: 21–89.

Jacobs, Jane. 1961. *The Death and Life of American Cities*. New York, NY: Vintage.

Jennings, Wesley G., Alex R. Piquero, Michael Rocque, and David P. Farrington. 2015. "The Effects of Binge and Problem Drinking on Problem Behavior and Adjustment Over the Life Course: Findings From the Cambridge Study in Delinquent Development." *Journal of Criminal Justice* 43(6):453–463.

Jerkins, Morgan. 2018. "Why White Women Keep Calling the Cops on Black People." *Rolling Stone*. July 17. Retrieved September 11, 2019 (https://www.rollingstone.com/politics/politics-features/why-white-women-keep-calling-the-cops-on-black-people-699512/).

Kirk, David S., and Mauri Matsuda. 2011. "Legal Cynicism, Collective Efficacy, and the Ecology of Arrest." *Criminology* 49(2):443–472.

Kobrin, Solomon. 1959. "The Chicago Area Project—A 25-Year Assessment." *Annals of the American Academy of Political and Social Science* 322(1):19–29.

Kochel, Tammy Rinchart. 2012. "Can Police Legitimacy Promote Collective Efficacy?" *Justice Quarterly* 29(3):384–419.

Kornhauser, Ruth Rosner. 1978. *Social Sources of Delinquency: An Appraisal of Analytic Models*. Chicago, IL: University of Chicago Press.

Kubrin, Charis E., and Ronald Weitzer. 2003. "New Directions in Social Disorganization Theory." *Journal of Research in Crime and Delinquency* 40(4):374–402.

Lind, Bronwyn, Shuling Chen, Don Weatherburn, and Richard Mattick. 2005. "The Effectiveness of Methadone Maintenance Treatment in Controlling Crime: An Australian Aggregate-Level Analysis." *British Journal of Criminology* 45(2):201–211.

Lombroso, Cesare. 1911. *Crime, Its Causes and Remedies*. Boston, MA: Little, Brown.

Markey, Patrick M., Charlotte N. Markey, and Juliana E. French. 2015. "Violent Video Games and Real-World Violence: Rhetoric Versus Data." *Psychology of Popular Media Culture* 4(4):277–295.

Mazerolle, Lorraine, Rebecca Wickes, and James McBroom. 2010. "Community Variations in Violence: The Role of Social Ties and Collective Efficacy in Comparative Context." *Journal of Research in Crime and Delinquency* 47(1):3–30.

Merry, Sally E. 1981. "Defensible Space Undefended: Social Factors in Crime Control Through Environmental Design." *Urban Affairs Quarterly* 16(4):397–422.

Mitchell, Jerry. 2018. "With 175 Americans Dying a Day, What Are the Solutions to the Opioid Epidemic." *USA Today*. January 29. Retrieved September 11, 2019 (https://www.usatoday.com/story/news/nation-now/2018/01/29/175-americans-dying-day-what-solutions-opioid-epidemic/1074336001/).

Modestino, Alicia Sasser. 2017. *How Can Summer Jobs Reduce Crime Among Youth? An Evaluation of the Boston Summer Youth Employment Program*. Brookings. Retrieved September 11, 2019 (https://www.brookings.edu/research/how-can-summer-jobs-reduce-crime-among-youth/).

National Council on Alcoholism and Drug Dependence. 2015. "Alcohol, Drugs and Crime." https://www.ncadd.org/about-addiction/alcohol-drugs-and-crime

National Crime Prevention Council. 2009. *Best Practices for Using Crime Prevention Through Environmental Design in Weed and Seed Sites*. Arlington, VA: Author. Retrieved September 11, 2019 (https://www.ncpc.org/wp-content/uploads/2017/11/NCPC_BestPracticesCPTED.pdf).

Newman, Oscar. 1972. *Defensible Space*. New York, NY: MacMillan.

Nix, Justin, Scott E. Wolfe, Jeff Rojek, and Robert J. Kaminski. 2015. "Trust in the Police: The Influence of Procedural Justice and Perceived Collective Efficacy." *Crime & Delinquency* 61(4):610–640.

Osgood, D. Wayne, and Amy L. Anderson. 2004. "Unstructured Socializing and Rates of Delinquency." *Criminology* 42(3):519–550.

Parker, Howard J., and Perpetua Kirby. 1996. *Methadone Maintenance and Crime Reduction on Merseyside*. London, UK: Home Office, Police Research Group.

Rosenbaum, Dennis P. 1988. "Community Crime Prevention: A Review and Synthesis of the Literature." *Justice Quarterly* 5(3):323–395.

Sampson, Robert J. 2013. "The Place of Context: A Theory and Strategy for Criminology's Hard Problems." *Criminology* 51(1):1–31.

Sampson, Robert J., and W. Byron Groves. 1989. "Community Structure and Crime: Testing Social-Disorganization Theory." *American Journal of Sociology* 94(4):774–802.

Sampson, Robert J., Jeffrey D. Morenoff, and Felton Earls. 1999. "Beyond Social Capital: Spatial Dynamics of Collective Efficacy for Children." *American Sociological Review* 64(5):633–660.

Sampson, Robert J., and Stephen W. Raudenbush. 2001. *Disorder in Urban Neighborhoods: Does It Lead to Crime*. Washington, DC: U.S. Department of Justice, Office of Justice Programs, National Institute of Justice.

Sampson, Robert J., Stephen W. Raudenbush, and Felton Earls. 1997. "Neighborhoods and Violent Crime: A Multilevel Study of Collective Efficacy." *Science* 277(5328):918–924.

Sampson, Robert J., and William Julius Wilson. 1995. "Toward a Theory of Race, Crime, and Urban Inequality." Pp. 37–56 in *Crime and Inequality*, edited by John Hagan and Ruth D. Peterson. Stanford, CA: Stanford University Press

Schochet, Peter Z., John Burghardt, and Sheena McConnell. 2008. "Does Job Corps Work? Impact Findings From the National Job Corps Study." *American Economic Review* 98(5):1864–1886.

Schweitzer, John H., June Woo Kim, and Juliette R. Mackin. 1999. "The Impact of the Built Environment on Crime and Fear of Crime in Urban Neighborhoods." *Journal of Urban Technology* 6(3):59–73.

Sharkey, Patrick. 2018a. "Community Investment, Not Punishment, Is the Key to Reducing Violence." *Los Angeles Times*. January 25. Retrieved September 11, 2019 (http://www.latimes.com/opinion/op-ed/la-oe-sharkey-violence-community-investment-20180125-story.html).

Sharkey, Patrick. 2018b. "Two Lessons of the Urban Crime Decline." *New York Times*. January 13. Retrieved September 11, 2019 (https://www.nytimes.com/2018/01/13/opinion/sunday/two-lessons-of-the-urban-crime-decline.html).

Sharkey, Patrick. 2018c. *Uneasy Peace: The Great Crime Decline, the Renewal of City Life, and the Next War on Violence*. New York, NY: Norton.

Sharkey, Patrick, Max Besbris, and Michael Friedson. 2017. "Poverty and Crime." Pp. 623–636

in *The Oxford Handbook of the Social Science of Poverty*, edited by David Brady and Linda M. Burton. New York, NY: Oxford.

Sharkey, Patrick, and Robert J. Sampson. 2010. "Destination Effects: Residential Mobility and Trajectories of Adolescent Violence in a Stratified Metropolis." *Criminology* 48(3):639–681.

Shaw, Clifford R., and Henry D. McKay. 1969. *Juvenile Delinquency and Urban Areas*, Revised edition. Chicago, IL: University of Chicago Press.

Sherman, Lawrence W. 1997. "Communities and Crime Prevention." In *Preventing Crime: What Works, What Doesn't, What's Promising: A Report to the United States Congress Prepared for the National Institute of Justice*, edited by Lawrence W. Sherman, Denise C. Gottfredson, Doris L. MacKenzie, John Eck, Peter Reuter, and Shawn Bushway. Washington, DC: U.S. Department of Justice, Office of Justice Programs, National Institute of Justice.

Sherman, Lawrence W., Denise C. Gottfredson, Doris L. MacKenzie, John Eck, Peter Reuter, and Shawn Bushway. 1997. *Preventing Crime: What Works, What Doesn't, What's Promising: A Report to the United States Congress Prepared for the National Institute of Justice*. Washington, DC: U.S. Department of Justice, Office of Justice Programs, National Institute of Justice.

Shireman, Charles H., Katharine Baird Mann, Charles Larsen, and Thomas Young. 1972. "Findings From Experiments in Treatment in the Correctional Institution." *Social Service Review* 46(1):38–59.

Skogan, Wesley G. 2012. "Disorder and Crime." Pp. 173–188 in *The Oxford Handbook of Crime*

Prevention, edited by Brandon C. Welsh and David P. Farrington. New York, NY: Oxford University Press.

Stein, Rob. 2017. "Life Expectancy Drops Again as Opioid Deaths Surge in U.S." NPR. December 21. Retrieved September 11, 2019 (https://www.npr.org/sections/health-shots/2017/12/21/572080314/life-expectancy-drops-again-as-opioid-deaths-surge-in-u-s).

Strøm, Henriette Kyrrestad, Frode Adolfsen, Sturla Fossum, Sabine Kaiser, and Monica Martinussen. 2014. "Effectiveness of School-Based Preventive Interventions on Adolescent Alcohol Use: A Meta-Analysis of Randomized Controlled Trials." *Substance Abuse Treatment, Prevention, and Policy* 9(1):48.

Taylor, Ralph B., and Stephen Gottfredson. 1986. "Environmental Design, Crime, and Prevention: An Examination of Community Dynamics." *Crime and Justice* 8: 387–416.

Tolan, Patrick, David Henry, Michael Schoeny, Arin Bass, Peter Lovegrove, and Emily Nichols. 2013. *Mentoring Interventions to Affect Juvenile Delinquency and Associated Problems: A Systematic Review.* Oslo, Norway: Campbell Systematic Reviews.

Visher, Christy A., Laura Winterfield, and Mark B. Coggeshall. 2006. *Systematic Review of Non-Custodial Employment Programs: Impact on Recidivism Rates of Ex-Offenders.* Oslo, Norway: Campbell Systematic Reviews.

Walker, Samuel. 1998. *Popular Justice: A History of American Criminal Justice*, 2nd ed. New York, NY: Oxford University Press.

Weisburd, David, Michael Davis, and Charlotte Gill. 2015. "Increasing Collective Efficacy and Social Capital at Crime Hot Spots: New Crime Control Tools for Police." *Policing: A Journal of Policy and Practice* 9(3):265–274.

Weisburd, David, Joshua C. Hinkle, and Christine Famega. 2010. *Legitimacy, Fear and Collective Efficacy in Crime Hot Spots: Assessing the Impacts of Broken Windows Policing Strategies on Citizen Attitudes.* Washington, DC: U.S. Department of Justice, National Institute of Justice.

Welsh, Brandon C., and David P. Farrington. 2004. "Evidence-Based Crime Prevention: The Effectiveness of CCTV." *Crime Prevention and Community Safety* 6(2):21–33.

West, Steven L., and Keri K. O'Neal. 2004. "Project DARE Outcome Effectiveness Revisited." *American Journal of Public Health* 94(6):1027–1029.

Wilson, James Q., and George Kelling. 1982. "Broken Windows." *Atlantic Monthly*. March. Retrieved September 11, 2019 (https://www.theatlantic.com/magazine/archive/1982/03/broken-windows/304465/).

Wilson, Sandra Jo, and Mark W. Lipsey. 2000. "Wilderness Challenge Programs for Delinquent Youth: A Meta-Analysis of Outcome Evaluations." *Evaluation and Program Planning* 23(1):1–12.

Zimmerman, Gregory M., Brandon C. Welsh, and Chad Posick. 2015. "Investigating the Role of Neighborhood Youth Organizations in Preventing Adolescent Violent Offending: Evidence From Chicago." *Journal of Quantitative Criminology* 31(4):565–593.

7

SITUATIONAL CRIME PREVENTION

Much of criminological thought is devoted to understanding the motivations of offenders. Why did they decide to engage in such deviance? What could have happened to them that led to such an act? What makes "them" different from "us"? The focus, perhaps not surprisingly, is on the offender. Research that seeks to identify what it is about offenders that differentiates them from non-offenders falls into the school of thought called **positivism**. This school of thought, associated with the sociologist August Comte, when applied to criminology attempted to quantitatively assess differences between criminals and noncriminals. These differences could be biological or sociological (or both) (Rocque and Paternoster 2012).

But this was not the first school of thought in criminology. The **classical school** was based on the premise that everyone is a potential criminal because everyone makes decisions based on cost and benefit. When the equation tips in favor of crime, most often, people engage in it. The classical school was replaced by the positive school for decades. Then in the 1970s, skepticism about the usefulness of positivism brought the classical school back full circle. This **neoclassical school** developed in part as a response to the positive school's failure to identify the things that make people criminal in ways that can be effectively targeted by rehabilitation programs. Some even argued that "root causes" of crime, like poverty, could not be adequately addressed via policy (Wilson 1975).

Chapter Outline

- Situational Crime Prevention: Background
- Theoretical Background: Routine Activities and Rational Choice Theory
- Situational Crime Prevention: The Basics
- Situational Crime Prevention: Evidence
  - Dosage
  - Unique Settings
- Situational Crime Prevention: Critiques
  - Does Crime Just Move Around the Corner?
  - Are Offenders Rational?
  - Big Brother
- Preventing Gun Violence
- Conclusion

Learning Questions

1. What are the theoretical roots of situational crime prevention?

2. What are some differences between situational approaches and more traditional, positivistic approaches?

(Continued)

(Continued)

3. What are the five types of situational crime prevention strategies?

4. What is target hardening?

5. What are some concerns with situational crime prevention?

Criminological theory, as will be discussed further in subsequent sections, also began to turn away from positivistic approaches. First, in 1979, Lawrence Cohen and Marcus Felson published "Social Change and Crime Rate Trends: A Routine Activity Approach." This paper set the stage for what has come to be known as routine activities theory in criminology. Routine activities theory (which has one of the more fun acronyms in criminological theory, RAT) takes the offender for granted and instead focuses on what enables or facilitates criminal acts. There are three elements that must come together in time and space for a crime to happen, according to RAT: (1) motivated offender, (2) lack of capable guardians, and (3) a suitable target. This is the formula for crime. Disrupting any of the elements is enough to stop a crime from taking place.

Around the same time, Ronald Clarke and Derek Cornish were developing what would become rational choice theory in criminology. Rational choice theory (RCT for short) is the offspring of the classical school, focusing on the decisions made by would-be offenders (see Chapter 3). Why did the burglar choose that particular house? What factors went into the decision? Their book, *The Reasoning Criminal* (Cornish and Clarke 1986), has become a classic in the field.

Both RAT and RCT were similar in that there was very little, if any, attention paid to what was "wrong" with criminals and how we should address those deficiencies. Instead, the theories suggested that there are informal tactics that can reduce crime by reducing opportunities. Those tactics, often referred to as **situational crime prevention (SCP)**, are the subject of this chapter. SCP is a host of strategies meant to increase guardianship and decrease the attractiveness of potential targets. The latter simply means that some approaches seek to make it more difficult to attack someone or steal something.

SITUATIONAL CRIME PREVENTION: BACKGROUND

The concept of SCP is disarmingly simple. In fact, there is a very good chance that before reading this chapter, you engaged in some form of SCP. Did you lock your dorm room door? Do you have a lock-screen code for your cell phone? Did you need to use a keycard to get into a building on campus? These are all forms of security that fall within the scope of SCP and have a certain logic. Why did you lock your room or house when you left? Because you wanted to place some sort of impediment in the path of a would-be burglar. The lock screen? To frustrate anyone thinking they might swipe your phone and easily access all its games and apps.

In that sense, SCP is not a new or highly sophisticated approach. It is not difficult to think of historical examples, far before the advent of SCP as a criminological field of study. For example, in the Middle Ages, drawbridges and moats were commonly used to protect castles from invasion. Banks, where in the past large sums of money were stored, have historically been notorious for their SCP measures, from highly intricate bank vaults to iron bars protecting tellers from potential attack. Just recently in Maine, after the speed limit was raised on the interstate to 70 mph, experts noted an increase in accidents. The speed limit was therefore decreased, and very soon after, accidents were reduced (McGuire 2018).

Early criminological work also mentioned the importance of opportunity as a way to prevent crime. For example, while Charles Goring's (1913:373) *The English Convict* was primarily a statistical analysis of the biological correlates of crime, in the conclusion, he mentioned that one way to reduce crime would be to "modify opportunity for crime by segregation and supervision of the unfit." Four years later, Enrico Ferri (1917), in *Criminal Sociology*, wrote about several strategies that would today be considered forms of SCP. He described the switch from paper to metal coins, which makes it more difficult to produce fake currency. Ferri then wrote that "the construction of houses and wide streets, the extension of street illumination, the suppression of ghettos and other sordid quarters, the establishment of night refuges, are better for the prevention of burglaries, robberies, assaults, and the receiving of stolen goods, than all the agents of public safety" (p. 260).

The most recent antecedent of SCP is crime prevention through environmental design (CPTED) strategies, discussed in the previous chapter. This work was based on literature that argued the physical environment could be designed in such a way that made it more defensible against predators.

Today, SCP is associated with the work of Ronald Clarke above all others. He was a researcher for Great Britain's Home Office in the 1970s and 1980s and began to see that programs meant to rehabilitate offenders did not seem to work. This was part of a shift in criminology from the positive school and its perspective that to treat offenders and therefore "fix them," all one had to do was find out what was wrong with them. When evaluation research began to find that there was little actual evidence that these treatment programs had an effect on crime, it seemed important to explore other methods of reducing crime.

One problem with these **dispositional theories** of crime (Clarke 1980:136) was that they assumed criminals are different from noncriminals. But as he argued, "the bulk of crime . . . is committed by people who would not ordinarily be thought of as criminal at all" (p. 137). Not only that, but earlier in his career he had found that among delinquent youths, the ones who engaged in antisocial behavior (in this case, those who ran away from their training schools, which was called "absconding") were not different from the ones who stayed put. At the same time, among the 88 schools he was studying, some had high rates of running away and others had low rates. This led to the insight that it was not the predisposition that could explain this but something about the physical environment (Clarke and Felson 2011).

In the late 1970s and early 1980s, the SCP approach became formalized. One of the first publications to use this term was Clarke's 1980 article in the *British Journal of*

Criminology. In that piece, he laid the foundation for SCP, illustrating how the strategy analyzes crime by focusing on the decisions made by the offender, paying attention to the differences among types of crime and the context in which crimes occur. In terms of prevention tactics, in that article he specified two primary approaches: (1) reducing the opportunity for crimes to occur and (2) increasing the chances of a potential criminal being caught. As an example of reducing opportunities, Clarke described the effective strategy of exchanging aluminum coin holders with steel ones in public telephone booths. This made it more difficult for thieves to access the coins. Another example is a law mandating the use of helmets for motorcyclists. He noted that this was not supposed to be a crime prevention method but it ended up reducing motorcycle thefts because criminals would be unlikely to have a helmet readily on hand should they be tempted to steal a motorcycle. In terms of increasing the odds of being caught, Clarke argued that rather than relying on private citizens to protect their domiciles, employees can be placed in strategic locations to reduce crime. As an example, door attendants in apartment buildings and parking lot attendants can have a significant impact on crime.

It is notable that most of the strategies discussed in the SCP literature are informal means of crime prevention. That is, they do not rely on the criminal justice system. Part of the reasoning for this was that at the same time criminology was coming to view offender rehabilitation approaches with skepticism, so too were researchers beginning to conclude that the police had little impact on crime (Farrell and Tilley 2012). Treatment did not work, and police could not watch every corner of every street all day and night (Clarke 1980).

THEORETICAL BACKGROUND: ROUTINE ACTIVITIES AND RATIONAL CHOICE THEORY

The theoretical foundation for SCP, as mentioned previously, is RAT and RCT (Clarke 1997), as well as utilitarianism, which underlies both theories (see Table 7.1). **Utilitarianism** is a philosophical approach that views human beings as self-interested, seeking courses of action that maximize pleasure and reduce pain. RAT and RCT do not see anything special about criminals that makes them worthy of research, because they are utilitarian, just like everyone else. They are simply people making rational decisions, and they have perceived the benefits of criminal action to outweigh the costs. One aspect that both theories have in common is the idea that people will engage in crime when it is relatively easy to do, the benefits appear high, and the chances of being caught are low.

RAT emerged in 1979 when Cohen and Felson sought to explain why, during the 1960s when the United States was experiencing economic prosperity, crime skyrocketed. Traditional criminological theories, which relied on individual or group deficits to explain crime, did not seem as relevant to this trend (nor, they argued, did economic changes in general seem to be able to explain changes in predatory crime over time).

Table 7.1 Theoretical Underpinnings of Situational Crime Prevention

Theory	Main Arguments	Theorists
Routine activities theory	Crime results when three factors converge in time and space: 1. Suitable target 2. Lack of capable guardian 3. Motivated offender	Lawrence Cohen Marcus Felson
Rational choice theory	Acts of crime involve decisions to become involved in criminal activity and to engage in particular crimes. Those decisions should be analyzed to determine how to reduce crime.	Derek Cornish Ronald Clarke
Utilitarianism	People act in ways that maximize pleasure and reduce pain; social morality is guided by actions that provide for the most pleasure and least pain.	Jeremy Bentham John Locke

By examining how crime fits into the patterns and structure of everyday life, Cohen and Felson felt that new insights could be gleaned about how crime happens and, relatedly, how it can be prevented. They were clear in their work that what factors made a person a potential offender were not of concern to them—there will always be people willing, if the circumstances are right, to take advantage of others. Spending time trying to figure out those factors did not seem logical from a policy standpoint.

The RAT elements of a motivated offender, lack of capable guardian, and suitable target are the ingredients for crime. Cohen and Felson (1979) used their perspective to analyze crime trends in the United States, finding expected relationships, such as an increase in burglary with more people having routine activities outside of the home. In a clever analysis, Cohen and Felson also showed that during the time crime was increasing, the weight of electronic goods such as televisions was decreasing, making them more "suitable" targets. Large, heavy televisions may look ungainly but are difficult to covertly carry out of someone's home. Disrupting any of the three ingredients for crime, they wrote, would be sufficient to stop a crime from taking place. This argument had clear implications for crime prevention. Making televisions bigger or bolting them to a wall, for example, should reduce theft.

RCT also helps illuminate the SCP perspective, though it was fully developed subsequent to SCP (Freilich 2015). In other words, RCT is a way of explaining why SCP works. The logic behind the rational choice perspective was found in the classical school as well, whose adherents viewed criminals as normal people who were driven by self-interest to increase their lot (Freilich 2015). RCT argues that instead of classifying offenders versus non-offenders, theoretical focus should be on crime events and attention should be paid to how different kinds of crimes are committed. Clarke and Cornish (1985) described four types of decisions burglars make, from the first decision to engage in such an act to the decision to attack a particular dwelling to the decision to keep continuing to commit crimes to the eventual decision to quit crime (called desistance). Each of these four decision types includes several contributing factors.

So both RAT and RCT are differentiated from other theories of crime by a focus on how crimes are executed. What are the factors that allowed a person to be successful in burglarizing a house? Why did they choose House A rather than House B? What was the method of burglary? Why is crime concentrated at a particular location and time of day or night? These elements can then be used to make it more difficult to commit a crime. That is the essence of SCP.

This is not to say that other criminological theories have ignored similar concepts as those that make up the basis of SCP. Interestingly, one of the more popular "dispositional" theories of crime is Michael Gottfredson and Travis Hirschi's (1990) self-control theory, which relies on the concept of opportunity to explain crime. To them, people with low self-control will commit crimes when there is opportunity to do so; thus, they see merit in prevention techniques that focus on reducing opportunity, since their view is that self-control levels cannot be appreciably changed after childhood. While SCP proponent Ron Clarke has been firm that "dispositional" theories do not translate into useful crime prevention policies, early on, Hirschi argued that his social control theory was compatible with RCT (Hirschi 1986). Hirschi's social control theory makes the case that individuals are less likely to engage in criminal conduct to the extent that they are meaningfully bonded to society; in other words, those with strong relationships with their parents or teachers, those who believe in the moral validity of the law, will see much less benefit to crime than others. Hirschi suggested that according to social control theory, people are rational actors, and part of what they consider in calculating the costs of crime is social bonds. In addition, Ronald Akers (1990), who is known for his social learning theory of crime, argued that rational choices are influenced by previous learning and are part of reinforcement. In other words, if someone commits a crime and is not punished (and benefits from the crime), that is part of the learning process that makes it more likely that person will engage in crime in the future. It is therefore possible that dispositional or sociological theories and SCP are not as at odds as they initially seemed (see also Nagin and Paternoster 1993).

In recent years, some effort has been dedicated toward understanding SCP as a theoretical approach in its own right. RAT and RCT certainly inform SCP, but SCP is also somewhat unique in its focus on, for example, utilitarianism. As mentioned, utilitarianism is the idea that people behave in ways that maximize their own pleasure and minimize their own discomfort. Society should support actions that bring about the largest amount of pleasure and avoid those that bring pain (Brogan 1959). SCP helps do just that (Newman 1997). SCP as a theoretical approach thus has things to say about motivation of offenders and the importance of situations or context in encouraging or discouraging crime.

SITUATIONAL CRIME PREVENTION: THE BASICS

SCP is, at its core, about reducing **opportunity** to commit crimes. What is opportunity? Opportunity in the criminal context can be thought of as circumstances that allow for undetected and successful criminal conduct. Opportunities are also heightened when a particular criminal act becomes attractive—that is, when the benefits appear to outweigh the costs. So SCP attempts to reduce the benefits and increase the costs of crime. Because each type of crime is unique—SCP views residential burglary as distinct from industrial burglary—opportunities will differ across crimes, and prevention strategies must as well. The techniques that are encompassed by SCP have grown considerably since its inception.

Today, there are 25 strategies that fall under five types of prevention (see Table 7.2). The five types of prevention are as follows: (1) Increase the effort needed to successfully complete a criminal act; (2) increase the risks associated with the commission of a crime; (3) reduce the rewards associated with particular crimes; (4) inhibit provocations or motivating factors; and (5) eliminate possible excuses for crime. Under each of these five types of prevention are five distinct techniques. For example, with respect to increasing effort, one technique is to use "target hardening" approaches. Target hardening approaches focus on making particular targets for crime more difficult to attack. An example would be a steering wheel lock on a vehicle, which would make it more difficult for a thief to drive away. With respect to eliminating excuses, example techniques include posting signs (no trespassing) and making rules for conduct explicit.

One way that SCP has been illustrated is through case studies. Particular organizations or groups will make changes to their immediate environment and assess whether crime was reduced. Clarke (1997) gathered 25 of these case studies, including one describing changes to convenience stores to reduce robbery. After reviewing pertinent studies, the authors found that the number of employees, the way cash is protected, and the location of entryways in the business itself influence the probability of crime (Hunter and Jeffery 1997).

A detailed example of an SCP technique in action may help illuminate how and why the theory is effective. One specific type of SCP is to increase the risks associated with particular acts. Drug use is a type of antisocial behavior that, as we saw in the previous chapter, can be addressed effectively after initiation, in the form of rehabilitation and treatment. But are there situational strategies that may work to prevent such behavior? One study included 36 high schools where some were assigned **random drug testing** earlier than others. These drug tests were not optional for the students but only applied to those who engaged in sports or other extracurricular activities. Parents provided permission for their children to be tested. While the intention of the program as stated is to determine which students need substance use treatment and to deter others from using, this method seems to fit within the "increasing risk" of use approach of SCP. Athletes would know that their school was performing random drug tests and this knowledge may result in a decrease in such use to avoid getting caught. The findings indicated that there was a 6% decrease in drug use in the random-drug-testing schools (16% vs. 22%

Table 7.2   Twenty-Five Techniques of Situational Crime Prevention (With Examples)

Increase Effort	Increase Risk	Remove Excuses	Remove Provocations	Decrease Rewards
1. Harden targets (locks, passwords)	6. Increase guardianship (walk in groups)	11. Create rules (behavioral codes)	16. Reduce strains (quick lines and polite interactions between servers and guests)	21. Hide targets (unmarked bank vehicles, hidden parking lots)
2. Control access to buildings (keys, cards)	7. Improve natural surveillance (street lighting)	12. Post rules (parking, loitering)	17. Reduce chances of disputes (separate practice fields for schools)	22. Remove targets (car radios, park in garage)
3. Observe exits (receptionist, sign-out lists)	8. Reduce anonymity (increase identification, dress codes)	13. Activate conscience (reminders that speed should be reduced, customs agreements)	18. Reduce emotional antagonizing (control violent media, behavior of fans at sports events)	23. Mark property (identification, labels)
4. Deflect would-be offenders (barriers to entry)	9. Use place managers (CCTV cameras, encourage people to take ownership of places)	14. Facilitate compliance (public trash cans, access to libraries)	19. Control peer influence ("just say no" campaigns)	24. Disrupt markets (ensure sellers have licenses)
5. Control crime tools (lock guns, disable stolen cell phones)	10. Improve formal surveillance (alarms)	15. Control substances (limit sales of alcohol in events, use breathalyzers)	20. Discourage imitation (control access to media, immediately clean graffiti)	25. Reduce benefits (speed bumps, cleaning vandalism)

Source: Center for Problem-Oriented Policing (http://www.popcenter.org/25techniques/).

admitted using substances). Interestingly, the researchers found no "spillover" effects, meaning that non-eligible students (e.g., those not in extracurricular activities) did not reduce their drug use (James-Burdumy et al. 2010).

One of your authors was pleased to know that his satellite radio company employed a form of SCP that would fall under several of the 25 techniques listed above. Upon moving to Maryland for graduate studies, the author found that his car had been broken into and his beloved satellite radio console was stolen. This console could have been stolen for personal use or for resale. The author then called the satellite radio company and reported the theft, whereupon the company informed him that they would switch off the console so it would not operate in the future. This is a form of target hardening but also a crime control tool and a reduction in the benefit of crime. It should be noted that this is not uncommon; certain techniques do overlap and seek to reduce crime in several ways.

Finally, scholars have offered a recent example of technology reducing opportunity for violence, focusing on cellular phones. The crime drop of the 1990s and 2000s has continued to baffle researchers and policymakers alike; crime, particularly violent crime, fell precipitously for a variety of reasons. One that had not been considered, however, is the adoption of cell phone technology. Researchers argued that cell phones disrupted traditional drug "turf wars" that had led to enormous violence in cities during the 1980s and early 1990s (Edlund and Machado 2019). The researchers suggested that before cell phones, drug transactions took place out in the open, which made the parties vulnerable to being seen and attacked, often in remote locations. "The move away from turf-based dealing reduced violence principally through its effects on gangs, we propose. Simply put, as the turf lost its value, so did the turf war" (Edlund and Machado 2019:2). Others had made this connection, but argued that cell phones allow people to report crimes more efficiently, which could have reduced crime (Orrick and Piquero 2015). Both of these studies used data on cell phone adoption and crime to show a negative relationship between the two. However, it should be noted that any factor that increased in the 1990s/2000s (such as video game console adoption, personal computers, etc.) will be negatively related to crime, which declined during this period. Demonstrating a causal relationship is much more difficult (Madrigal 2019).

SITUATIONAL CRIME PREVENTION: EVIDENCE

As we have seen, SCP rests on several assumptions about the nature of criminals and specific types of criminal acts. If offenders are motivated or driven by "dispositional" factors, as much of criminological thinking of the 20th century suggested, then simply making crime harder in particular places will likely not have much of an overall effect. There is a growing body of work that demonstrates SCP reduces crime.

There are numerous case studies that examine specific types of crime prevention. These case studies often are used to illustrate how SCP works. In Clarke's (1997) book on crime prevention case studies, the first chapter, written by Barry Webb, reviews the effectiveness of using steering column locks on reducing motor vehicle theft. Steering locks should be familiar to most who have driven a car. If you have ever moved your steering wheel back and forth while the vehicle is turned off, it will become stuck or locked in place. The only way to unlock it is to insert the ignition key. Webb reviewed changes in motor vehicle theft after changes in regulations requiring such locks. He found that, for example, in Germany, after legislation was passed in the early 1960s, motor vehicle theft did, in fact, decrease. However, such thefts then steeply increased in the 1970s. Without stringent controls for other changes taking place in the early 1960s and 1970s, however, it is rather difficult to attribute the movement of motor vehicle theft to the steering column locks.

Another method of determining effectiveness is to review existing studies in a systematic review or meta-analysis. The study by Guerette and Bowers (2009:1348), mentioned previously, indicated that the vast majority of studies (84%) showed success "where the decrease in the action area outweighed that in the control area."

In another paper, Bowers and Guerette (2014) reviewed evaluations of SCP. They argued that SCP strategies are difficult to evaluate from an academic standpoint. SCP is an environmental approach and does not involve assigning people to a well-defined treatment after which effects can be examined. In addition, SCP is not something that generally gets implemented and then removed. It is an ongoing "process" that often involves multiple efforts (Bowers and Guerette 2014:1319). Yet the research that has been conducted thus far points to a positive overall effect of SCP. They reported that according to one study, about 75% of studies indicated SCP works. SCP also seems more effective than hot-spot policing. While these are promising results, the authors point out that the vast majority of studies are not randomized trials (only 3% were), so it is hard to rule out alternative explanations for the findings.

Bowers and Guerette (2014) drew on the work of Guerette (2009), who had compiled more than 200 assessments of SCP approaches. As mentioned, in this study he found that 75% of evaluations indicated a drop in crime associated with SCP techniques. They also reported on a study that examined the same data set and found that SCP strategies that were located in public places fared the worst overall. In other words, SCP in private places—businesses or homes—may be the most effective. In terms of specific types of interventions, crime prevention through environmental design (CPTED), mixed techniques, and access control were the most effective.

Another meta-analysis focused specifically on one type of SCP: making it more difficult to gain entry into particular areas. Aiden Sidebottom and colleagues (2018) found 43 studies that examined the effect of "alley gating," or putting up a gate to prevent or impede access to paths or streets. Six of those studies used a rigorous enough design to be included in the meta-analysis. Sidebottom and colleagues found that gating alleys is an effective (moderately so) approach to preventing crime (here, burglary). According to the authors, gated entryways can reduce crime by "increasing the effort" needed for would-be offenders to commit a crime, by increasing guardianship or feelings of ownership over an area, or by removing excuses. A person hopping a fence to get to a street would have a difficult time convincing a resident they belong there.

Does enacting SCP help save money? Crime is costly, after all, requiring funds to pay for law enforcement, court costs, and corrections. But it also takes a toll on work productivity and health care. So if SCP reduces crime, it stands to reason it may have a financial benefit. In **cost-benefit analyses**, researchers attempt to calculate all the costs of a particular intervention and weigh it against the benefits in terms of money saved. In one such study, researchers examined 13 evaluations and found that 8 showed benefits greater than costs. One evaluation of the "Safer Cities Program" in the United Kingdom, which among other things helped "harden" targets of crime (e.g., alarm systems, rigorous locks), relied on costs of burglary for its assessment. Burglary costs were set at £1,100. If a burglary was averted, then the "benefit" would be this figure.

The estimate of the cost of prevention was between £300 and £900. These figures resulted in an average cost-benefit ratio of 1.83 (Welsh and Farrington 1999). What this means is that for every 1 pound spent, the program produced a benefit of 1.83 pounds.

Dosage

One question that should be considered in assessing the effectiveness of crime prevention strategies is how much is enough. In medicine, the notion of proper dosages for particular afflictions is well-known. Some researchers have taken this approach to the area of crime prevention, arguing that some strategies may appear ineffective or even counterproductive because they are not intense enough. In a recent study, Linning and Eck (2018) argued that low-dosage crime prevention interventions may do harm. As an illustration, they use the approach of placing a street vendor in a particular location to provide guardianship. If there is only one vendor, though, would-be offenders may see that not as a guardian but as a suitable target. More vendors (a higher dose) may actually reduce crime. They label this phenomenon "weak intervention backfire."

Unique Settings

For the most part, SCP approaches have been undertaken in public spaces or private domains such as the home. Some work has explored SCP in other locations, such as schools. SCP is certainly not foreign to schools, as educational institutions have long undertaken measures to prevent mischief (consider the "hall monitor" as a guardian). One study looked at various types of SCP in schools (metal detectors, closed campus during lunch, cameras, etc.) (O'Neill and McGloin 2007). In terms of property crime, locking doors, closing for lunch, and the number of times students move between classrooms during the day were all related to offending. Locking doors produced less crime, while schools where the students stayed on campus during lunch and those that had more classroom changes experienced more crime. For violent crime, none of the SCP tactics had an effect except that more classroom changes during the day were associated with more violent crime. Interestingly, more recent work shows that some SCP tactics, like metal detectors, may make students feel less safe (Bachman, Randolph, and Brown 2011; Gastic 2011; Hankin, Hertz, and Simon 2011). One study did find that metal detectors reduced crime, but overall, SCP tactics did not reduce victimization (Tillyer, Fisher, and Wilcox 2011). That few SCP tactics seemed to have an effect in schools is interesting and may point to schools being a unique setting requiring different approaches. In the aftermath of school shootings, pundits are often found arguing for greater security in schools despite the evidence that this is seemingly ineffective.

Another arena in which SCP techniques have been trialed recently is cyberspace. Without much reference to the literature, many online vendors and products use forms of SCP. We all know about password rules that require a certain number of letters along with "special characters," like @ or #. These are examples of target hardening. How many of us have received a phone call from our bank informing us of a "suspicious charge"? This is an example of guardianship meant to prevent fraud. One researcher suggested that SCP could help prevent **cyberstalking**, which is when someone follows and harasses another online. Reyns (2010) argued that reducing exposure online (e.g., not posting personal information) and blocking contact by perpetrators could prevent cyberstalking. He also suggested having "online security guards" to monitor interactions (Reyns 2010:112; see also Hinduja and Kooi 2013). To date, there appear to be very few, if any, evaluations of these approaches.

SITUATIONAL CRIME PREVENTION: CRITIQUES

Does Crime Just Move Around the Corner?[1]

As should be clear by now, SCP cuts against much of the criminological grain. It suggests that "disposition" and individual differences—the heart and soul of most criminological theorizing—are not an effective or efficient use of time if we are serious about reducing crime. So it should not be surprising that it has come under attack from some quarters.

First, an early concern was that if SCP and other situational/context-related approaches are simply making it more difficult or less attractive to commit crime in Place A, motivated offenders will simply "move around the corner," to Place B. After all, SCP does not try to reduce individual risk factors or even address the reasons why particular people may resort to crime. Thus, it makes logical sense that SCP will reduce crime only where it is implemented, and the overall level of crime will not decrease. This idea is called **displacement**. Displacement can be defined as "the relocation of crime from one place, time, target, offense, tactic or offender as the result of some crime prevention initiative" (Guerette 2009:36).

Displacement has been examined quite extensively. SCP proponents argue that displacement would only be an issue if it were true that offenders are "different" and driven to crime (Clarke 1995, 1997). If offenders do not have unique dispositions, then reducing crime opportunities should not result in displacement. As Clarke (1995:122) argued, "Very few offenders are so driven by a need or desire that they have to maintain a certain level of offending whatever the cost." While there is some evidence of displacement in early studies, there are numerous examples of SCP tactics that did not seem to result in crime being moved to another location. For example, the motorcycle helmet law, discussed previously, which resulted in a decrease in motorcycle thefts, was not associated with displacement (Clarke 1995).

While SCP may theoretically result in crime increasing in nearby areas, another possibility is that those nearby areas benefit from the strategies. This is called **diffusion of benefits** and occurs when areas surrounding places where SCP approaches have been implemented experience a decrease in crime, despite not engaging in any form of SCP. This concept is defined by Clarke and Weisburd (1994:169) as "the spread of the beneficial influence of an intervention beyond the places which are directly targeted,

---

[1]A clever title of a study conducted by David Weisburd and colleagues (2006).

the individuals who are the subject of control, the crimes which are the focus of intervention or the time periods in which an intervention is brought." Clarke (1995) showed that several studies have found diffusion of benefits, though the study authors sometimes refer to it in different ways, such as the "halo effect," "free rider effect," and "bonus effect."

Why might diffusion of benefits occur? After all, if SCP is about making specific types of crimes harder in particular places and those strategies are not implemented elsewhere, what would stop people from committing crime elsewhere? Clarke and Weisburd (1994) provided two possibilities. First, individuals may be deterred from committing crime in nearby areas because they are unaware of where the SCP strategies have been implemented. If CCTV cameras (see Chapter 6) have been publicized in particular areas, it may be unclear to offenders where such cameras are or are not placed. Clarke and Weisburd (1994) discuss one such study that indicated crime on buses declined overall via the use of CCTV cameras, even though they were put in only two buses.

Another reason for diffusion of benefits is that the effort to commit crime has been increased by virtue of SCP. For example, moving elsewhere to commit a crime requires effort. Therefore, SCP may promote crime declines in nearby areas via "discouraging" crime in one area (Clarke and Weisburd 1994).

Thus, there are theoretical and empirical reasons to think that SCP does not just move crime around, but there is also research showing that it may. What does the balance of research show? In a systematic review, Guerette and Bowers (2009) looked at more than 100 studies with 574 observations assessing SCP techniques. Their analysis found that diffusion of benefits and displacement both happened but at roughly the same rate (26% of evaluations evidenced displacement; 27% evidenced diffusion). They then looked at 13 studies that they were able to glean enough information from to compare diffusion and displacement directly. Overall, the reduction in crime induced by the SCP techniques outweighed the displacement such that overall crime decreased.

Are Offenders Rational?

One particular cornerstone of SCP is the assumption that offenders (as well as most people) are "rational." What does that mean? The adherents of RCT have used several terms, such as "limited" or "bounded" rationality, to articulate that they do not believe offenders are stopping and calculating costs and benefits using algebraic equations before they decide to offend. Clarke (1995:98) wrote that rationality here implies "crime is purposive behavior designed to meet the offender's commonplace needs . . . and that meeting these needs involves the making of (sometimes quite rudimentary) decisions and choices, constrained as these are by limits of time and ability and the availability of relevant information."

For certain types of crimes, there is reason to doubt that rationality plays much of a role. In an interesting study, De Haan and Vos (2003) suggested that RCT accounts do not mesh well with the portrayal of criminals. They focused on street robbery and showed that many offenders are impulsive, expressive, and feel guilty after the act. These factors, they argued, imply that offenders are not calculating and making a decision but acting on the spur of the moment or driven by expressive, not instrumental, factors. As one subject in their study said:

> You have different thoughts when you're robbing someone; then you don't remind yourself to run away. You remind yourself instead just to get him. . . . Not that you immediately want to stab him, but when he resists, you just see red. . . . And then you just start stabbing. (De Haan and Vos 2003:47)

Specifically regarding SCP, Keith Hayward (2007:233) has written that as an approach to deal with crime, it "lacks reflexivity." While SCP seems appropriate to handle instrumental crimes, or crimes for which a clear goal is the driving force, it may not apply to other types of crimes. Not all crimes are undertaken with the intention of benefiting the offender. The man who slugs his pal in the bar after a row, for example, is not necessarily benefiting from this behavior but acting on impulse or emotion. As Hayward (2007:237) noted, "While undeniably useful as a means of reducing certain forms of 'shallow end' or 'volume' crime, the situational/RC approach may be a less effective tool against the chaotic, violent or so-called 'expressive crimes' that cause most public distress and community disharmony."

In addition, individuals themselves may vary in their rationality, either due to personal or contextual differences. As we saw in the previous chapter, alcohol and other substances are implicated in a large portion of crimes. It is doubtful that individuals under the influence of substances are as rational as others or whether the same situational cues would influence such would-be offenders (Exum 2002). Additionally, other arousal states (e.g., sexual arousal) may influence decision-making (Ariely and Loewenstein 2006) and the effectiveness of SCP tactics. In one experiment, George Loewenstein, Daniel Nagin, and Ray Paternoster (1997) compared men who were sexually aroused and men who were not on attitudes toward sexual aggression. Aroused men (who were shown sexually explicit material) indicated more than non-aroused men that they would use aggressive tactics on a date. This finding held even controlling for perceived costs and benefits of such action. Loewenstein and his colleagues called for the integration of "cool" and "hot" states in RCT analyses. In other words, we make decisions either way but they differ when we are aroused compared with when we are not.

Big Brother

A final criticism of SCP approaches is that it promotes the normalization of surveillance and governmental intrusion in our lives. This type of critique is certainly relevant to CCTV strategies, which expand governmental surveillance in public spaces (Von Hirsch 2000). Big Brother, the fictional governmental arm in George Orwell's *1984*, is representative of governmental overreach. SCP techniques may also create a "'fortress society' in which citizens scuttle from one protected environment to another in perpetual fear and suspicion of their fellows" (Clarke 1983:250).

Proponents of SCP argue that there is little to fear from such tactics. As Clarke (1983) argued, SCP approaches are not always intrusive. They can be as benign as posting speed limit signs or increasing street lighting. Clarke and Bowers (2017) suggested that most fears of technology are overreactions and in democracies we have little to worry about in terms of governmental intrusion. In addition, they argued, in a democracy we are "willing to endure inconvenience and small infringements of liberty when these protect" us (p. 110).

PREVENTING GUN VIOLENCE

Chapter 4 documented the involvement of handguns in violent crime. Taking into account homicides and suicides, the United States leads the world's democracies by a very wide margin in rates of gun deaths (Santhanam 2018). If we could wave a magic wand and eliminate all handguns, America's homicide rate would drop significantly because handguns are so lethal. Given the use of handguns in many robberies, the robbery rate would likely drop as well, as would the suicide rate (if we may include a noncriminal behavior). But because magic wands do not exist in reality, handguns are not about to disappear in the United States. Millions of Americans own them, and the U.S. Supreme Court has declared that the Second Amendment protects their private ownership.

What, then, can be done to reduce gun violence? The best approach here seems to be one of *harm reduction*. As Chapter 2 discussed, this type of approach in essence tries to make the best of a bad situation by limiting the harm that a particular social problem may cause. Accordingly, public health researchers, criminologists, and other scholars have advanced several proposals to reduce gun violence that are consistent with the Second Amendment and that rely on theory and research evidence. All these proposals aim in various ways to drive down intentional and accidental shootings and the use of guns in so much crime. A fuller discussion of these proposals may be found in these scholars' writings (e.g., Braga and Weisburd 2015; Cook 2018; Cook and Goss 2014; Hemenway 2017; Webster and Vernick 2013). Their many proposals include the following:

- Establish a universal background check system that requires a background for anyone wishing to purchase a firearm

- Require firearm owners to report the loss or theft of a firearm within a specified number of days

- Require training and licensing for anyone who wishes to own a handgun, as is done now for anyone who wishes to drive a motor vehicle

- Deny the right to own a firearm to anyone with a history of domestic violence or of other violent crime, to anyone under a restraining order, or to anyone with a history of alcohol or other drug abuse

- Require anyone purchasing or owning a handgun to be at least 21 years old

- Require new handguns to be personalized as "smart" guns by the use of modern technologies (such as fingerprint technology) that limit their use to their single lawful owner

If fully funded and implemented, these and other measures would very likely reduce deaths and injuries from gun violence and the use of guns in violent crime. At the same time, they would allow law-abiding people to purchase new handguns and to keep any handguns they now own. The handgun issue is highly controversial, of course, and the measures just listed are not likely to win approval at the federal level anytime soon. But if they can be passed and implemented sometime in the future, many fewer Americans will be killed and injured from handgun violence.

CONCLUSION

Situational crime prevention has been on the criminological scene for more than three decades now. It is a novel approach to preventing crime that shuns traditional criminology research by ignoring offenders and what does or does not make them different from non-offenders. SCP focuses on the immediate environment and context, and seeks to reduce opportunities for offending. Approaches are numerous but include such things as increased street lighting, locked gates, and strategic placement of guardians who can watch over particular areas.

While SCP has come under attack for a variety of issues, including the notion that it may just "move crime around the corner," the evidence suggests that in general it is an effective way to reduce crime. Displacement does seem to occur, but so, too, does diffusion of benefits. The net result is often a decrease in crime. We should point out, though, that while there are many case studies (see Clarke 1997) illustrating innovative, creative, and seemingly effective SCP techniques, the meta-analyses and systematic reviews are limited by the relatively small number of randomized trials of SCP.

SCP traditionally has been implemented and tested in residential, public, and commercial locations. Other contexts may not be as suitable for these approaches. School-based SCP does not appear to be effective in reducing either property crime or violent crime, and in fact may actually increase fear of such crime. SCP may be useful in the prevention of cybercrime, but so far there is a lack of research testing such methods.

SUMMARY

1. Situational crime prevention is a set of strategies linked to the classical or neoclassical school of criminology.

2. Situational crime prevention does not view traits or dispositions of offenders as important in reducing crime.

3. Techniques falling under the situational crime prevention approach include steps to increase the effort, increase the risks, reduce the rewards, remove excuses, and reduce provocations associated with crime.

4. Some criticisms of situational crime prevention include the notion that not all offenders are rational; crime may be displaced elsewhere; and situational crime prevention produces an impersonal, distrustful society.

5. The evidence suggests that situational crime prevention does reduce crime with minimal displacement. Diffusion of benefits also indicates that situational crime prevention may reduce crime in places where such techniques are not put in place.

6. The evidence is less clear on whether situational crime prevention works in particular contexts, such as schools and in cyberspace.

7. Several proposals from scholars in various fields aim to reduce intentional and accidental gun shootings and the use of guns in much crime.

KEY TERMS

classical school 141
cost-benefit analyses   150
cyberstalking 152
diffusion of benefits 152
displacement 152

dispositional theories 143
neoclassical school 141
opportunity 147
positivism 141
random drug testing 147

situational crime prevention
  (SCP) 142
utilitarianism 144

REFERENCES

Akers, Ronald L. 1990. "Rational Choice, Deterrence, and Social Learning Theory in Criminology: The Path Not Taken." *Journal of Criminal Law & Criminology* 81(3):653–676.

Ariely, Dan, and George Loewenstein. 2006. "The Heat of the Moment: The Effect of Sexual Arousal on Sexual Decision Making." *Journal of Behavioral Decision Making* 19(2):87–98.

Bachman, Ronet, Antonia Randolph, and Bethany L. Brown. 2011. "Predicting Perceptions of Fear at School and Going to and From School for African American and White Students: The Effects of School Security Measures." *Youth & Society* 43(2):705–726.

Bowers, Kate J., and Rob T. Guerette. 2014. "Effectiveness of Situational Crime Prevention." Pp. 1318–1329 in *Encyclopedia of Criminology and Criminal Justice*, edited by Gerben Bruinsma and David Weisburd. New York: Springer.

Braga, Anthony A., and David L. Weisburd. 2015. "Focused Deterrence and the Prevention of Violent Gun Injuries: Practice, Theoretical Principles, and Scientific Evidence." *Annual Review of Public Health* 36: 55–68.

Brogan, A. P. 1959. "John Locke and Utilitarianism." *Ethics* 69(2):79–93.

Clarke, Ronald V. G. 1980. "Situational Crime Prevention: Theory and Practice." *British Journal of Criminology* 20(2):136–147.

Clarke, Ronald V. 1983. "Situational Crime Prevention: Its Theoretical Basis and Practical Scope." *Crime and Justice* 4: 225–256.

Clarke, Ronald V. 1995. "Situational Crime Prevention." *Crime and Justice* 19: 91–150.

Clarke, Ronald V. 1997. "Situational Crime Prevention." *Successful Case Studies*, 2nd ed. New York, NY: Harrow and Heston.

Clarke, Ronald V., and Kate Bowers. 2017. "Seven Misconceptions of Situational Crime Prevention." Pp. 109–142 in *Handbook of Crime Prevention and Community Safety*, 2nd ed., edited by Nick Tilley and Aiden Sidebottom. New York, NY: Routledge.

Clarke, Ronald V., and Derek B. Cornish. 1985. "Modeling Offenders' Decisions: A Framework for Research and Policy." *Crime and Justice* 6: 147–185.

Clarke, Ronald V., and Marcus Felson. 2011. "The Origins of the Routine Activity Approach." Pp. 245–260 in *The Origins of American Criminology*, edited by Francis T. Cullen, Cheryl Lero Jonson, Andrew J. Myer, and Freda Adler. New York, NY: Transaction.

Clarke, Ronald V., and David Weisburd. 1994. "Diffusion of Crime Control Benefits: Observations on the Reverse of Displacement." *Crime Prevention Studies* 2: 165–184.

Cohen, L. E., & Felson, M. 1979. "Social Change and Crime Rate Trends: A Routine Activity Approach." *American Sociological Review* 44(4):588–608.

Cook, Philip J. 2018. "Expanding the Public Health Approach to Gun Violence Prevention." *Annals of Internal Medicine* 169(10):723–724.

Cook, Philip J., and Kristin A. Goss. 2014. *The Gun Debate: What Everyone Needs to Know*. New York, NY: Oxford University Press.

Cornish, Derek, and Ronald V. Clarke. 1986. *The Reasoning Criminal*. New York, NY: Springer-Verlag.

De Haan, Willem, and Jaco Vos. 2003. "A Crying Shame: The Over-Rationalized Conception of Man in the Rational Choice Perspective." *Theoretical Criminology* 7(1):29–54.

Edlund, Lena, and Cecilia Machado. 2019. "It's the Phone, Stupid: Mobiles and Murder." NBER Working Paper Series. Retrieved September 14, 2019 (http://www.nber.org/papers/w25883).

Exum, M. Lyn. 2002. "The Application and Robustness of the Rational Choice Perspective in the Study of Intoxicated and Angry Intentions to Aggress." *Criminology* 40(4):933–966.

Farrell, Graham, and Nick Tilley. 2012. "Introduction: Ronald V. Clarke–the Quiet Revolutionary." Pp. 1-10 in Nick Tilley and Graham Farrell (eds.), The Reasoning Criminologist. Essays in Honour of Ronald V. Clarke. New York, NY: Routledge.

Ferri, Enrico. 1917. *Criminal Sociology*. Boston, MA: Little, Brown.

Freilich, Joshua D. 2015. "Beccaria and Situational Crime Prevention." *Criminal Justice Review* 40(2):131–150.

Gastic, Billie. 2011. "Metal Detectors and Feeling Safe at School." *Education and Urban Society* 43(4):486–498.

Goring, Charles. 1913. *The English Convict: A Statistical Study*. London, UK: Darling and Son.

Gottfredson, Michael R., and Travis Hirschi. 1990. *A General Theory of Crime*. Stanford, CA: Stanford University Press.

Guerette, Rob T. 2009. "The Pull, Push and Expansion of Situational Crime Prevention Evaluation: An Appraisal of Thirty-Seven

Years of Research." *Evaluating Crime Reduction Initiatives Crime Prevention Studies* 24: 29–58.

Guerette, Rob T., and Kate J. Bowers. 2009. "Assessing the Extent of Crime Displacement and Diffusion of Benefits: A Review of Situational Crime Prevention Evaluations." *Criminology* 47(4):1331–1368.

Hankin, Abigail, Marci Hertz, and Thomas Simon. 2011. "Impacts of Metal Detector Use in Schools: Insights From 15 Years of Research." *Journal of School Health* 81(2):100–106.

Hayward, Keith. 2007. "Situational Crime Prevention and Its Discontents: Rational Choice Theory Versus the 'Culture of Now.'" *Social Policy & Administration* 41(3):232–250.

Hemenway, David. 2017. "Reducing Firearm Violence." *Crime and Justice* 46: 201–230.

Hinduja, Sameer, and Brandon Kooi. 2013. "Curtailing Cyber and Information Security Vulnerabilities Through Situational Crime Prevention." *Security Journal* 26(4):383–402.

Hirschi, Travis. 1986. "On the Compatibility of Rational Choice and Social Control Theories of Crime." Pp. 105–118 in *The Reasoning Criminal: Rational Choice Perspectives on Offending*. New York, NY: Springer-Verlag.

Hunter, Ronald D., and C. Ray Jeffery. 1997. "Preventing Convenience Store Robbery Through Environmental Design." Pp. 191–199 in *Situational Crime Prevention: Successful Case Studies*, 2nd ed., edited by Ronald V. Clarke. New York, NY: Guilderland.

James-Burdumy, Susanne, Brian Goesling, John Deke, and Eric Einspruch. 2010. "The Effectiveness of Mandatory-Random Student Drug Testing." NCEE 2010-4025. National Center for Education Evaluation and Regional Assistance.

Linning, Shannon J., and John E. Eck. 2018. "Weak Intervention Backfire and Criminal Hormesis: Why Some Otherwise Effective Crime Prevention Interventions Can Fail at Low Doses." *British Journal of Criminology* 58(2):309–31.

Loewenstein, George, Daniel Nagin, and Raymond Paternoster. 1997. "The Effect of Sexual Arousal on Expectations of Sexual Forcefulness." *Journal of Research in Crime and Delinquency* 34(4):443–473.

Madrigal, Alexis C. 2019. "The Collapsing Crime Rates of the '90s Might Have Been Driven by Cellphones." *The Atlantic*. May 30. Retrieved September 14, 2019 (https://www.theatlantic .com/technology/archive/2019/05/how-mobile-phones-could-have-changed-the-drug-game/590503/).

McGuire, Peter. 2018. "Crashes Fall on I-295 After Speed Limit Decrease." *Portland Press Herald*. Retrieved February 27, 2018 (https://www .pressherald.com/2018/02/11/crashes-fall-on-i-295-after-speed-limit-decrease/).

Nagin, Daniel S., and Raymond Paternoster. 1993. "Enduring Individual Differences and Rational Choice Theories of Crime." *Law and Society Review* 27(3):467–496.

Newman, Graeme. 1997. "Introduction: Towards a Theory of Situational Crime Prevention." Pp. 1–23 in *Rational Choice and Situational Crime Prevention: Theoretical Foundations*, edited by Graeme Newman, Ronald V. Clarke, and Shlomo Shoham. New York, NY: Routledge.

O'Neill, Lauren, and Jean Marie McGloin. 2007. "Considering the Efficacy of Situational Crime Prevention in Schools." *Journal of Criminal Justice* 35(5):511–523.

Orrick, Erin A., and Alex R. Piquero. 2015. "Were Cell Phones Associated With Lower Crime in the 1990s and 2000s?" *Journal of Crime and Justice* 38(2):222–234.

Reyns, Bradford W. 2010. "A Situational Crime Prevention Approach to Cyberstalking Victimization: Preventive Tactics for Internet Users and Online Place Managers." *Crime Prevention and Community Safety* 12(2):99–118.

Rocque, Michael, and Ray Paternoster. 2012. "Positive Criminology and Positive Theories of Crime." Pp. 605–607 in *The Encyclopedia of American Law and Criminal Justice*, Rev. ed., Vol. II, edited by D. Schultz. New York, NY: Facts on File.

Santhanam, Laura. 2018. "There's a New Global Ranking of Gun Deaths. Here's Where the U.S. Stands." *PBS Newshour*. August 28. Retrieved September 14, 2019 (https://www .pbs.org/newshour/health/theres-a-new- global-ranking-of-gun-deaths-heres-where- the-u-s-stands).

Sidebottom, Aiden, Lisa Tompson, Amy Thornton, Karen Bullock, Nick Tilley, Kate Bowers, and Shane D. Johnson. 2018. "Gating Alleys to Reduce Crime: A Meta-Analysis and Realist Synthesis." *Justice Quarterly* 35(1):55–86.

Tillyer, Marie Skubak, Bonnie S. Fisher, and Pamela Wilcox. 2011. "The Effects of School Crime Prevention on Students' Violent Victimization, Risk Perception, and Fear of Crime: A Multilevel Opportunity Perspective." *Justice Quarterly* 28(2):249–277.

Von Hirsch, Andrew. 2000. "The Ethics of Public Television Surveillance." Pp. 59–76 in *Ethical and Social Perspectives on Situational Crime Prevention*, edited by Andrew von Hirsch, David Garland, and Alison Wakefield. Oxford, UK: Hart.

Webster, Daniel W., and Jon S. Vernick, eds. 2013. *Reducing Gun Violence in America: Informing Policy With Evidence and Analysis*. Baltimore, MD: Johns Hopkins University Press.

Weisburd, David, Laura A. Wyckoff, Justin Ready, John E. Eck, Joshua C. Hinkle, and Frank Gajewski. 2006. "Does Crime Just Move Around the Corner? A Controlled Study of Spatial Displacement and Diffusion of Crime Control Benefits." *Criminology* 44(3):549–592.

Welsh, Brandon C., and David P. Farrington. 1999. "Value for Money? A Review of the Costs and Benefits of Situational Crime Prevention." *British Journal of Criminology* 39(3):345–368.

Wilson, James. 1975. *Thinking About Crime*. New York, NY: Basic Books.

PART III

SECONDARY CRIME PREVENTION

Focus on Families, Schools, and Peers

8

PARENTS, CHILDREN, AND FAMILIES

In early 2018, a young man who was noted as troubled by neighbors and acquaintances took an Uber to Marjory Stoneman Douglas High School in Parkland, Florida. At 2:19 pm he walked into Building 12 armed with an AR-15 assault-style rifle. Three minutes later, the fire alarm had been set off and a call made to 911 in response to shots fired. At the end of the day, he had killed 17 people, including several students (Hennessy-Fiske 2018). In the aftermath of the event, the dialogue followed a recognizable pattern, with certain groups arguing for greater gun control and others arguing for greater gun protections, such as arming teachers (Reilly 2018).

However, as is often the case when a young person does something terrible, people began to wonder what the parents of the shooter had done (or not done) to create such a "monster." One teacher in Florida put all the blame on the parents. In a long Facebook post, which was shared more than 700,000 times, she wrote:

> I grew up with guns. Everyone knows that. But you know what? My parents NEVER supported any bad behavior from me. I was terrified of doing something bad at school, as I would have not had a life until I corrected the problem and straightened my ass out. My parents invaded my life. They knew where I was ALL the time. They made me have a curfew. They made me wake them up when I got home. They made me respect

Learning Questions

1. How does parenting prevent crime?

2. What parenting approaches are most associated with healthy child development?

3. Does parenting matter, or is it all genes?

4. What parenting programs have been shown to reduce child antisocial behavior?

5. What early childhood programs have been shown to reduce child antisocial behavior?

6. Can we prevent family violence?

their rules. They had full control of their house, and at any time could and would go through every inch of my bedroom, backpack, pockets, anything! Parents: it's time to STEP UP![1]

To some, then, there is a simple, clear link between youth misbehavior and parenting. If parents do their job, supervise, support, and provide for their children, they will not act out in ways that end tragically. Others argued that blaming parents is "hogwash" (Moyer 2018). Harsher parenting, they claimed, leads to negative outcomes overall.

Parenting is a sensitive and personal topic in our culture. We all have some experience with it, whether as parents ourselves or growing up with caregivers, and most of us have strong opinions on what is right and wrong. What is the best way to discipline children? What can we do to improve their academic outcomes? Are there types of activities for kids that promote healthy development? These are all important questions that have a bearing on crime prevention.

Not surprisingly, understanding what role the family plays in the criminal behavior of children is complex, with much conflicting information contributing to the debate. Yet there are several findings that appear robust enough to suggest that the family does influence child outcomes and that programs exist that have prevented youth antisocial behavior. In this chapter, we review first the literature on parenting and child behavior, including criminological theories that focus on parenting. Next, we present evidence on parenting programs meant to improve the ways parents interact with their children. In the third section of the chapter, we review crime prevention efforts aimed at children, excluding programs that take place in schools (which will be covered in Chapter 9). We conclude the chapter with a discussion of family violence and approaches to prevent it.

PARENTING AND CHILD OUTCOMES

Historical View

The idea that parents are responsible for their children's behavior is probably as old as society itself. According to the Bible, "He that spareth the rod hateth his own

[1] https://www.facebook.com/kellygraley/posts/10156224702772958

son but he that loveth him correcteth him betimes/Withhold not correction from a child: for if thou strike him with the rod, he shall not die. Thou shalt beat him with the rod, and deliver his soul from hell" (Proverbs 13:24). The implication is clear—firm, principled discipline saves children; spoiling them leads to trouble. Philosophers such as Jean-Jacques Rousseau also had strong opinions on how parents should treat children for optimal outcomes (see Rousseau 1762/1889). For example, in *Emile*, Rousseau made the case that parents should ensure their children are self-sufficient. In addition to this general advice, he had more specific thoughts: swaddling infants and heating bath water were unnecessary.

In early America, the sole responsibility for child welfare rested with parents. In fact, the first iterations of the juvenile justice system gave the government authority to decide outcomes for children on the basis of **parens patriae**, or the idea that the state could act in place of the parents (Mendiola-Washington and Emeka 2014). The authority of parents was absolute; in colonial America, children could be put to death for the crime of hitting their own parents (Walker 1998)!

Child psychologists began to enter the fray in the early 20th century, describing child development and producing texts meant to guide parents toward appropriate methods. One of the most popular was written by Dr. Benjamin Spock in 1946, called *The Common Sense of Baby and Child Care*. The book sold more than 50 million copies and revolutionized ideas about parenting, overturning advice popular at the time that parents should not be overly affectionate and needed to be very rigid with children (Hidalgo 2011). In that book, Spock touched on parental discipline and argued that "the ones who get into the most trouble are suffering from lack of affection rather than from lack of punishment" (Spock 1966:323). Yet he disagreed that "whenever anything goes wrong it's the parents' fault" (p. 324).

With respect to scholarly theories on parenting and child outcomes, the concept of **attachment** emerged in the early 20th century. John Bowlby and Mary Ainsworth argued that without close connection to mothers in early life, children will not develop in a healthy manner. Reportedly, Bowlby decided to study attachment in children partly due to meeting "a very isolated, remote, affectionless teenager who had been expelled from his previous school for theft and had had no stable mother figure" (Bretherton 1992:759). For these psychologists, a strong connection to the mother was key to normal growth.

In the criminological arena, parenting has been a staple of numerous theories, from Edwin Sutherland's **differential association theory** to Travis Hirschi's **social control theory**. Sutherland's theory, one of the first individual-level sociological theories of crime, argued that youth are led to delinquency by whoever they associate with—in other words, their peers. He recognized that "the family is potentially a most effective agency of control" but (at that time) "there is no real science of child rearing" (Sutherland 1939:153). While there did not seem to be a perfect correlation between home life and delinquency, Sutherland wrote that research had noted several important conditions that showed up in delinquents' homes, such as delinquent family members, use of alcohol, crowded homes, parental strictness, and poverty.

Travis Hirschi's social control theory was more specifically premised on the relationships between parents and children. To Hirschi, children who have a strong connection to their parents—who want to be like them and care about what they think—are less likely to engage in delinquency (Hirschi 1969). Hirschi's concept of social bonds extended to more than just parents, including teachers and prosocial activities. His theory stipulated that these strong connections to prosocial aspects of society would act as restraints against antisocial behavior. Importantly, he argued that attachments to parents would be effective even if parents were not physically with their children, referring to this as "virtual supervision" (Hirschi 1969:88).

What Do We Know About Parenting Styles?

The research on parenting often points to three distinct styles, each with varying outcomes (Baumrind 1971). To understand these styles, let's imagine a young boy named Jimmy. Let's further imagine that Jimmy is a rambunctious 4-year-old who likes to push his parents' buttons but does not engage in abnormal levels of antisocial behavior. When he wants a toy, he may bop his sibling on the head or throw a tantrum. One day he didn't like what his parents made for dinner, so he threw his plate in the air, smearing delicious smoked paprika and olive oil all over the nice clean walls.

His parents may react to Jimmy in one of three ways. First, his parents may be what is called **lax**, or permissive. Lax or permissive parenting involves a sort of laissez-faire attitude, permissiveness, and a lack of attention to children. In other words, here, Jimmy's parents let him get away with his behavior, maybe chuckling at how much of a "rascal" he is but leaving him well enough alone. Another way Jimmy's parents may react is to come down hard on him, punishing him severely for missteps and not doing much in the way of explaining why they are doing what they are doing. "Because I said so" may be a familiar refrain for Jimmy in this scenario. This second parenting style is called **authoritarian**. This parenting style may be thought of as rigid, strict, and disciplinarian. Rules are set in stone and punishments are nonnegotiable. This is a parenting style akin to a dictatorship governing approach. Jimmy would be lucky if his parents reacted in a different way. Maybe they watch him closely, tell him that what he's doing is wrong, and explain why. They also let him feel he has a say in the process. This democratic approach is called **authoritative** parenting. Parents who use this style are firm but fair. Authoritative parenting seems to be the style related to the best outcomes in school (Spera 2005) and delinquency (Baumrind 1991; Hoeve et al. 2008, 2011).

Hoeve and colleagues (2009) reviewed parenting styles and suggested they can be broken down into two dimensions: support and control (see Table 8.1). Authoritarian styles are low in support but high in control; lax is high in support but low in control; authoritative is high in both control and support. A final style can be added: **neglectful**, which is low in support and low in control. In a meta-analysis of 161 studies, the researchers found that several types of parenting styles had a statistically significant but small effect on delinquency, including supportive parenting (reduced delinquency), neglectful parenting (increased delinquency), authoritative control (decreased delinquency), and authoritarian control (increased delinquency). They were not able to fully analyze the effect of the three styles discussed above because there were not enough studies examining them.

Table 8.1 Parenting Styles

Style	Description	Support	Control
Neglectful	Parenting style in which parents do not pay much attention to children	Low	Low
Authoritarian	Parenting style that is rigid and harsh	Low	High
Lax/permissive	Parenting style that is considered laissez-faire. Children are allowed to "get away with it."	High	Low
Authoritative	Parenting style that is firm but fair	High	High

Source: Created using data from Baumrind (1971); Hoeve et al. 2009.

Why Might Parenting Not Matter?

Despite parenting being the focus of several criminological theories and countless advice books, not all researchers believe that parenting is important in child outcomes. There are some who believe that much of the research over the past hundred or so years that shows different types of parenting affect cognitive development, economic status, and behavior has been overstated. Much of the research that exists is observational in nature, which means parents (or children) are asked about parenting styles and child outcomes, and a correlation is calculated. This type of study cannot establish causality. It could be that parents who practice supportive and high-control styles also transmit other benefits (genetically) to their children and this is the reason for the correlation.

Research that uses what are called **twin studies** is able to determine whether environmental factors are important over and above genetic ones. How? One way is by looking at the behavioral similarity of identical (monozygotic) versus nonidentical (dizygotic) twins. Identical twins share 100% of their genes, while nonidentical or fraternal twins share 50%. This information allows researchers to generate estimates of how much variation in outcomes is due to the environment and to genes. This work has tended to show that parenting is not as influential once genes are taken into account (see Boutwell 2015; Harris 2011; Neiderhiser et al. 1999; Wright et al. 2008). These studies have found that parts of the environment do matter, but it's more about who your friends are and what you do outside the home.

It seems pretty noncontroversial to suggest that genetic factors are at least partially related to how and why parents do what they do *and* how children turn out. But do parenting practices not matter at all if genes are taken into account? There is evidence that genetics do not explain much maternal attachment to infants (Bokhorst et al. 2003) and that parenting does matter above and beyond genes in influencing child behavior (Burt et al. 2007). It is also important to point out that the twin studies mentioned above do not typically measure or observe parenting practices but assume that they are the same for each child in a family. This is called the **equal environments assumption**. While there is evidence that this assumption holds in particular situations (Derks, Dolan, and Boomsma 2006), a meta-analysis found both consistency and variability in parenting using genetic designs (Avinun and Knafo 2014).

In sum, new biosocial work is correct in pointing out the flaws of previous observational research. Genes account for a large amount of variance in child outcomes, and parents do not have all-mighty power to shape children like blocks of clay. Yet the weight of the evidence seems to suggest that parents do matter. In what follows, we review crime prevention programs focusing on parents and families. These programs may not magically change sinners to saints, but many have been evaluated using randomized clinical trials (in which genetic factors are effectively controlled) and demonstrated nontrivial effects on behavior.

PARENTING PROGRAMS AND CRIME PREVENTION

Can parenting prevent crime? Decades of sociological research suggests parenting matters, but this conclusion has been challenged of late by biosocial work. Perhaps the best way to arrive at an answer is to examine the experimental literature on the topic. Now, clearly we cannot randomly assign children to parents, nor would it be ethical to assign children to receive warm or harsh or neglectful parenting. But we can develop programs to help improve parenting skills and see if that improves child outcomes.

Programs addressing parent and family dynamics are often characterized as **developmental crime prevention**, as they seek to promote healthy development of young children to improve behavior (Tremblay and Craig 1995). In Sherman and colleagues' (1997) report on what works in crime prevention, the authors discussed different types of family-based programs. Programs can be **universal**, in which all families are eligible and provided services. **Targeted** programs focus only on certain families or groups, considered at risk for antisocial behavior. As they argue, "Almost all family-based crime prevention is currently offered on a focused basis. Absent an indicated reason to intervene in family life, American government generally leaves families alone" (p. 4-4).

The evidence from experimental and **quasi-experimental** (research designs that are not randomized but have some form of control group) studies does suggest parenting can prevent child antisocial behavior. In this section, we will review some of the more effective programs studied. Our selection of programs is not comprehensive, nor does it imply these are the *most* effective. They are simply used for illustration purposes.

Triple P: Positive Parenting Program

Triple P: Positive Parenting Program originated in Australia and includes several components or levels. The first is an informational campaign to educate parents about useful parenting approaches. The second involves pairing parents with health care providers to receive advice. The third level focuses on parents who have children with identified behavioral issues, and provides training for those parents. The fourth level is a group-based parenting program, directed at parents with serious child behavior issues. The final level is geared toward families whose parenting problems can be traced to specific factors (marriage problems, etc.) (Sanders 1999).

Triple P seeks to enhance parenting skills in several areas, including "observational skills," "parent-child relationship enhancement skills," "encouraging desirable behavior," "teaching new skills and behaviors," "managing misbehavior," "preventing problems in high-risk situations," "self-regulation skills," "mood management and coping skills," and "partner support and communication skills" (Sanders, Markie-Dadds, and Turner 2003:6). All these skills are intended to help parents be caring but firm and healthy when raising their children. These skills should then translate to healthy development of the children themselves.

Triple P has been subject to numerous evaluations since the late 1970s, including several randomized clinical trials. One meta-analysis of studies looking at Level 4 of the program found that Triple P had very strong results with a large effect size on average (d = .88) (de Graaf et al. 2008). Another meta-analysis a year earlier found similar large effects for all forms of Triple P, but a small effect size was found for media Triple P (Thomas and Zimmer-Gembeck 2007). A meta-analysis that included all Triple P studies found smaller effect sizes of the program and interestingly found that the effects were stronger if the parents were the ones reporting their children's behavior (Nowak and Heinrichs 2008).

Two more recent reviews found similar efficacy but with some caveats. Wilson and colleagues (2012) cautioned that there could be selection bias in many of the Triple P studies and long-term effects are still unknown. The most recent meta-analysis included more than 100 studies (over half of which were randomized trials) and included several outcomes such as changes in child behavior and parenting practices. The highest effect sizes were found for changing parenting practices, but moderate (d = .47) effects were found for child behavior. This study also found that randomized trials produced higher effect sizes for child outcomes (Sanders et al. 2014).

Incredible Years

Another program directed at parents is called Incredible Years. The program is intended for young children at risk for conduct disorder. The target age for youth in the program is 0 to 13. Incredible Years tries to give parents the tools to help their children learn and show them which approaches to discipline are most effective. For example, the program seeks to help parents move toward "decreasing harsh discipline and increasing positive strategies such as ignoring, logical consequences, redirecting, monitoring, and problem solving" (Webster-Stratton and Reid 2010:195). Parts of the Incredible Years program have been around since 1980 (Webster-Stratton and Reid 2003). The program includes three subprograms: one for children, one for parents, and one for teachers.

The parenting intervention in Incredible Years is called BASIC and initially began as a video program. Advice and illustrations of appropriate strategies were provided for different age groups. Later on, the developers created a new program called ADVANCE that seeks to help parents in everyday communication and with anger and self-control. The program has up to 12 sessions (Webster-Stratton and Reid 2011).

The Incredible Years program has been tested numerous times since its inception. One study (Scott et al. 2001) assessed the video parenting program in group format. One hundred and forty-one kids were assigned to the parenting program or a wait-list group (meaning they did not get the program initially). This is not a primary prevention study, as the children in both groups were already showing evidence of antisocial behavior. But the treatment group experienced a large decline in such behavior and the control group did not. Positive parenting interactions improved in the experimental group.

Once again, the best way to summarize a body of research is to combine well-done studies to determine overall effects. The effect sizes from one meta-analysis (Menting, de Castro, and Matthys 2013) showed that the parenting program does reduce child problem behavior. However the effects were smaller than for Triple P (.27). Interestingly, the meta-analysis found that the program worked better for kids with worse problems.

Nurse–Family Partnership

One of the more well-known parenting programs was developed by David Olds in the 1970s (Goodman 2006). Unlike other programs, this one begins before children are even born, targeting pregnant women who are at risk (e.g., single, in poverty). As implied in the title, the program involves nurses offering assistance to mothers. These nurses make home visits to mothers, counseling them on everything from the role of appropriate nutrition to advice on not smoking while pregnant. Home visits continue from pregnancy to the point at which the child turns 2 (Olds 2006).

The Nurse–Family Partnership (NFP) has been evaluated numerous times across different locations. In the first randomized trial testing the NFP program, women who were poor, in their teens, or not married were recruited. Visits took place during pregnancy. The results indicated that the children in the experimental group were less likely to be born early and were heavier when born (low birth weight is a correlate of later problem behavior) and more manageable (Olds et al. 1986). Other trials examined outcomes for children and found that those who received the NFP experienced fewer hospital visits for injuries.

Longer-term follow-ups have revealed remarkable effects of the program on the children's behavior. For example, when the children were age 15, they had less involvement in the criminal justice system and antisocial behavior than the control group (Olds 2006). At the 19-year follow-up, the youth from the families receiving the program had incurred fewer arrests compared with the control group youth (Eckenrode et al. 2010). Interestingly, these results held for girls rather than boys. For boys, there was no difference in arrests or convictions.

One study examined the current use of the NFP in the community and projected effects by year 2031. That study suggested that 500 infant deaths, 42,000 child abuse events, 4,700 abortions, and 90,000 juvenile crimes would be prevented by the program. Altogether, the program was estimated to possibly save society $1.4 billion (Miller 2015).

There are several other types of parenting programs used to reduce or prevent problem behavior in youth. Meta-analyses and systematic reviews of these programs demonstrate that behavioral parent training reduces child misbehavior at least in the short-term (Lundahl, Risser, and Lovejoy 2006; Piquero et al. 2009, 2016; Serketich and Dumas 1996). Research on parenting programs shows variation in effectiveness, however. One study (Reyno and McGrath 2006) sought to examine what factors influence whether a program will be successful or not. They found that low family income and the degree of problem behavior of the child had moderate effects on program effectiveness.

A popular criminological theory that we have mentioned in different parts of this book is Gottfredson and Hirschi's (1990) self-control theory. That theory proposes that self-control or self-regulation is the primary cause of individual-level offending. Self-control is instilled by parents, according to the theory, in early childhood. Can parents improve self-control? One randomized controlled study of the Strong African American Families Program found that improved parenting led to increased child self-control (Brody et al. 2005). Another program, called *Hitkashrut* (Hebrew for *attachment*), sought to improve "co-parenting" for young children (ages 3–5). A randomized trial of the program, with children at risk for conduct issues (one group receiving the program, another receiving "minimal intervention"), found it to be effective in improving child self-control, with a medium effect size (.47) (Somech and Elizur 2012).

In sum, the best evidence suggests that parenting does matter and can significantly impact child outcomes, from behavior to self-control. Not all family programs are directed at the parents, however. Certain programs seek to work with children who are at risk for behavioral issues or have already demonstrated some level of antisocial behavior. These child-centered programs are the subject of the next section.

EARLY CHILDHOOD AND FAMILY PROGRAMS

Child-centered programs seek to provide assistance to the children themselves, rather than assisting only parents. These programs often provide counseling, therapy, or education directly to the youth. Some programs take place within the community and some in school or residential settings. School-based crime prevention will not be covered here, as it is the focus of the next chapter. Some of the family programs target parents and seek to help support them in their efforts to raise their children. Below, we describe several programs in depth. Again, the selection of these programs does not imply they are more or less effective than others; they are simply used for illustration of how such programs work.

Yale Child Welfare Research Program

One program that sought to provide assistance to families in need is the Yale Child Welfare Research Program. The program was implemented in the 1960s and 1970s by Sally Provence and Audrey Naylor (specifically 1967–1972; Rescorla and Zigler 1981). While parenting was one aspect of the program, it sought to provide conditions in which parents would be able to be more effective as child-rearers. As the program developers noted, "Child care advice was rarely given gratuitously unless there was no other way to solve a problem" (Rescorla et al. 1979). Families involved were assigned a team that consisted of educators and health care specialists. The program had four parts: (1) home visits, (2) pediatric treatment, (3) evaluation of development, and (4) day care/school. Rescorla and colleagues' found that the program improved child cognitive outcomes (this study was a small sample, matched control design, however). A later follow-up at 10 years showed that the control group children were poorer behaved, with, for example, more court appearances than the intervention group (Zigler, Taussig, and Black 1992).

Syracuse University Family Development Research Program

Another family-based program that provided assistance to low-income families was called the Syracuse University Family Development Research Program. This program was developed by Ronald Lally and colleagues, and implemented in the late 1960s through the mid-1970s (Besharov et al. 2011). Again, parenting advice was part of the program, but it also provided help with child education. The "children's center" was a part of the program that focused specifically on helping youth develop in a healthy manner. The children's center worked with infants, babies, and children (18–60 months). Healthy cognitive development was promoted by the caregivers (Lally et al. 1987).

Results of the Syracuse program were generally favorable, demonstrating positive effects on child cognitive development (e.g., intelligence) and behavior. In addition, the program showed some effect on delinquency, with 6% of the treatment youth compared with 22% of the control-group youth incurring probation sentences (Tremblay and Craig 1995).

The Social Development Model

Another well-known child-centered program is called the social development model. Created by J. David Hawkins and colleagues and first trialed in Seattle, Washington, the program focuses on all important domains of a child's life (family, school, peers, community, etc.). The program began in Seattle in 1981 and included four different groups, one a full intervention group, one a parent-training-only group, one a late intervention group, and a control group. The program began when students were in first grade. When students were in fifth grade (around age 10), more schools were added and the four conditions were implemented. The fifth-grade students were then followed to age 21. The program included teacher and parent training as well as child behavioral management training.

The results of the age 21 follow-up showed strong effects on positive functioning at school or work and somewhat weaker effects on crime and drug/alcohol use. For example, there was no difference between the full intervention and control group in whether or not the subject committed a crime in the past year, but the control group was more likely to have committed a high variety of crimes and to have sold drugs (Hawkins et al. 2005).

Functional Family Therapy

Functional Family Therapy (FFT) is a designated **blueprints** program by the Blueprints for Healthy Youth Development group. This group, which is located at the Center for the Study and Prevention of Violence at the University of Colorado, makes lists of programs (as well as information about them and evidence supporting their efficacy) for researchers and practitioners. Blueprints model programs are those that have demonstrated success in reducing crime in at least two high-quality research designs and whose effects last at least a year. Promising programs must have clear intervention targets, at least one randomized trial or two quasi-experimental trials, and convincing evidence of effectiveness (blueprintsprograms.com).

FFT is used for older youths (adolescents) who are at risk for delinquency or who have committed delinquency. The goal of the program, which is about 30 hours in duration, is to improve functioning and communication in families. Therapy is provided by highly educated therapists who have caseloads of 10 to 12 families. Treatment is tailored to the needs of the family and youth (http://www.blueprintsprograms.com/factsheet/functional-family-therapy-fft).

FFT is a model blueprint program. It has a strong body of evidence supporting its effectiveness. The Blueprints website lists studies done in Utah, Ohio, Washington State, Sweden, and New Mexico, all demonstrating strong effects on crime and substance use (though the latter may not hold long-term) (Filges, Andersen, and Jørgensen 2015). One study looked at youths referred to probation in Washington State who were given FFT or probation at random. They then determined whether the FFT group was more likely to recidivate, or reoffend, after a year. They found that recidivism rates were identical across the two groups (22%). However, they found that not all therapists were equally faithful to the model. Therapists presented cases to supervisors, who then rated them in terms of how faithful to the FFT model they were. Those who had "high adherence" to the model had better outcomes (14.5% of their cases recidivated). Interestingly, for those youths who received FFT, if adherence was low, their outcomes were *worse* than for those who did not receive the program (Sexton and Turner 2010).

Another blueprint model program is called Multisystemic Therapy (MST). MST is somewhat similar to FFT in the population of youth. The focus is a bit different, though. Whereas FFT focuses mainly on family communication and functioning, MST targets the youth's environment outside of the home as well (including peer relationships). Parents are recruited to help keep a close eye on the youth's peer relationships and extracurricular activities (Huey et al. 2000). MST also lasts longer than FFT, with therapy provided for up to 5 months (http://www.blueprintsprograms.com/factsheet/multisystemic-therapy-mst). According to the Blueprints website, MST is a "model plus" program, which means it also has a rigorous evaluation by a team not connected to the program developers. The program also has shown long-term effects; one study found that siblings of individuals receiving MST had fewer arrests after 25 years (Wagner et al. 2014). However, one Campbell Collaboration Systematic Review (Littell, Forsythe, and Popa 2005) found that MST compared to other interventions was not more effective in reducing arrests or convictions.

There are also approaches to treatment that, rather than belonging to specific programs, describe therapeutic strategies that can be incorporated into the programs. One particular type of therapy appears to have promise in reducing antisocial behavior with youths (and adults) (Landenberger and Lipsey 2005). This type is called **cognitive behavioral therapy (CBT)**, which seeks to teach people how to recognize negative thinking patterns that lead to poor behavioral choices, identifying the link between the two.

A meta-analysis of CBT with youths showed it to be effective (medium effect size) in reducing anger (Sukhodolsky, Kassinove, and Gorman 2004), which is an emotional state implicated in some theories of crime (Agnew 1992). Another study examined three types of treatments for antisocial juveniles (age 7–13). One group received "problem-solving skills training." Children were taught how to think about possible solutions to problems and how other people respond to their actions. The second group received "problem-solving skills training with in vivo practice," which was similar to the first but also included practice activities outside of the therapy sessions. The third group received "relationship therapy," which entailed a therapist developing a close bond with the youth. Both problem-solving groups were more effective in reducing antisocial behavior than the relationship therapy (Kazdin et al. 1989).

Meta-analyses and reviews of the literature on child-centered and family programs to prevent crime have also shown these programs are effective (see Matjasko et al. 2012; Tremblay and Craig 1995; Yoshikawa 1995). One review (Manning, Homel, and Smith 2010) examined 11 programs that included some in schools, homes, and day care. The effects of the programs were highest for educational progress followed by deviance (medium effect). In Farrington and Welsh's (2003) meta-analysis, while parent training was found to be most effective in preventing child misbehavior, day care and home visiting programs were also effective.

Another review of child and family programs sought to examine whether early prevention efforts were effective in preventing adult crime (e.g., whether the programs had long-lasting results). Overall, the programs studied (which included the NFP and the social development model) did have effects on adult crime, but they were small (Deković et al. 2011). One study compared behavioral parent training to CBT for youths, finding a stronger effect for parent training than for youth CBT. However, CBT did have an overall positive effect on antisocial behavior (McCart et al. 2006).

Child- and family-centered programs have thus proven effective in reducing behavioral problems. It is difficult to determine which approach (parent training or child/family functioning) is superior, but as is clear from the select program descriptions above (listed in Table 8.2), programs often combine elements of both. It is likely that child and youth outcomes depend on individual as well as family/parenting factors. Thus, comprehensive approaches would be preferable. In their review, Kumpfer and Alvarado (2003) wrote that family skills training programs have lower rates of dropout than programs targeting only parents, in part because the youths helped make sure their parents were involved in programming. It is likely that the inverse also holds true, that if parents are part of programming, they will help ensure children are following through.

Table 8.2 Parenting and Family Programs	
Type of Program	**Example Programs**
Parent training	Triple P
	Nurse–Family Partnership
	Incredible Years
Family/child-centered	Yale Child Welfare Research Program
	Syracuse Family Development Research Program
	Social development model
	Functional Family Therapy
	Multisystemic Therapy

HOW DO PARENT/FAMILY PROGRAMS WORK?

Why do parenting and family- or child-centered programs work? Theoretically, as discussed at the outset of this chapter, parenting programs could be effective because parents are trained to supervise and discipline their children more effectively. It is also possible that programs addressing child cognitive problems prevent later antisocial behavior through improving mental health. Some scholars have argued that family programs are effective if they address multiple risk factors, each of which combines to increase the chances a youth will get into trouble (Sherman et al. 1997; Tremblay and Craig 1995; Yoshikawa 1995).

Generally, family programs are thought to work primarily through social processes (social control, social learning, increased resources, etc.). However, it may also be the case that these programs work through biosocial mechanisms (Rocque, Welsh, and Raine 2012; Vaske, Galycan, and Cullen 2011). For example, programs that reduce parental conflict and improve nutrition may help facilitate cognitive (brain) development in youths, which in turn may promote prosocial behaviors down the line.

PREVENTING FAMILY VIOLENCE

This chapter has mostly discussed the prevention of crime by youths using parenting and family approaches. Yet the family is also pertinent to crime prevention because it is the site of much violence in its own right. For example, domestic violence, which generally refers to violence between romantic couples (e.g., husband and wife), is prevalent in the United States. Research indicates that up to a quarter of women have experienced violence at the hands of a partner. Men are not exempt from such victimization, with estimates that around 14% have been physically attacked by a partner (https://ncadv .org/statistics).

Violence, both physical and sexual, is also directed at children in the family. According to a recent report, in 2015, there were 3.4 million children involved in reports to child protective services. Most child victims experienced neglect, while 17.2% experienced physical abuse. In 2015, there were 1,585 reported child deaths attributed to maltreatment (U.S. Department of Health and Human Services 2017). Data also indicate that sexual abuse is relatively common, with 11% of girls and about 2% of boys suffering abuse by an adult (who is usually related to them) (rainn.org/statistics/ children-and-teens).

So what works to prevent family violence? In a famous study led by Lawrence Sherman called the Minneapolis Domestic Violence Experiment, researchers had officers randomly assigned to one of three conditions when met with a call for service involving possible domestic violence. The first condition was mandatory arrest, the second was offering to counsel the couple, and the third was temporarily removing the perpetrator from the home. The initial results favored mandatory arrest (Sherman and Berk 1984). The study influenced police policy very soon after, as departments began to increase use of arrest as a response to domestic violence (Sherman and Cohn 1989). Another study in Milwaukee found slightly different results. Here, arrest was found to be effective for some but not all types of perpetrators (Sherman et al. 1992). Who were more likely to reduce their violent behavior after arrest? "Those who are employed, high school graduates, white, or married and those who have cohabitated for over two years" (Sherman et al. 1992:159).

Programs have also been developed to rehabilitate domestic abusers. Often called **batterer intervention programs**, these may take place in prison or in the community. As Babcock, Green, and Robie (2004) note, these programs are relatively new, as domestic violence was not seen as a public health issue (rather, more of a private family matter) until the 1980s. Babcock and colleagues examined 22 evaluations of such programs and concluded that they have small effects on recidivism. Another meta-analysis similarly found that while treatment effects showed some promise of effectiveness, the effect size was not statistically significant (Arias, Arce, and Vilariño 2013). With respect to court-ordered batterer programs, Feder and Wilson (2005) also found a lack of evidence that such approaches reduce or prevent violence.

With respect to preventing domestic violence before it starts, Wolfe and Jaffe (1999) presented two such models: first, an approach that seeks to reduce the contributing factors leading to domestic violence, and, second, an approach that addresses the three types of prevention (primary, secondary, and tertiary). Primary prevention that attempts to improve healthy development and reduce antisocial behavior should, in theory, reduce later perpetration of domestic violence.

An example of a program that seeks to reduce dating violence is called Safe Dates. Safe Dates was initiated in North Carolina and focuses on gender and conflict dynamics that can lead to violence in adolescent relationships (Foshee et al. 1996). Research evaluating the program found that initial first-year progress in improving behavior evaporated but the program did influence individuals' ideas about dating violence and how to manage conflict (Foshee et al. 2000). A later evaluation found that after 4 years, the students who received the intervention committed and experienced less dating violence (Foshee et al. 2004). Interestingly, though, the program included a "booster" for 50% of the treatment group, which was ineffective in reducing violence.

There are a large number of programs that have been developed to prevent child abuse and mistreatment. An early review found that most programs in the literature had not been evaluated properly, but those that had showed promise (Helfer 1982). One of the programs discussed previously, the Nurse–Family Partnership, is effective at reducing child abuse even 15 years later (Eckenrode et al. 2000). Interestingly, in that study, families of mothers who were visited during pregnancy but not after the birth of the child did not have fewer incidences than the control group. It appears that home visits during early childhood are vital. A meta-analysis of secondary programs (N = 40 studies) found that prevention programs have a small but statistically significant effect on child maltreatment (d = .29) (Geeraert et al. 2004). Another meta-analysis looked specifically at parenting programs and found that such programs reduced child abuse (d = .45) (Lundahl, Nimer, and Parsons 2006). A more recent meta-analysis similarly found that parenting programs reduce child maltreatment (random effect size .30) and also reduce risk factors for such outcomes (Chen and Chan 2016). However, one meta-analysis that focuses specifically on randomized trials found less convincing evidence that parent programs can reduce child maltreatment (overall effect size .13). Yet some programs in their review did work. Parent support programs were not as effective as parent training programs in reducing child maltreatment (Euser et al. 2015).

With respect to sexual abuse specifically, some programs have sought to educate the family as a way to reduce incidence, with home visits to address risk factors (Putnam 2003). School-based child sexual abuse programs have been subject to meta-analysis, indicating that they are effective at improving children's awareness of sexual misconduct. Rispens, Aleman, and Goudena (1997) found large effects of such programs for improving knowledge of sexual abuse terms and ability to protect oneself. They did not look at whether the programs actually reduced abuse. Another meta-analysis similarly showed that child comprehension and ability to protect themselves increased after participating in school programs (Davis and Gidycz 2000). Some work has examined whether programs reduce the occurrence of child sex abuse. Gibson and Leitenberg (2000) asked college students about whether they had participated in a particular program ("good touch–bad touch"). Those who had participated had a lower rate of sexual abuse (8%) than those who had not (14%).

CONCLUSION

The first and most important domain of life is the family. Parents and caretakers provide food, shelter, security, and socialization to children. Children are also at a developmental stage at which programs may have the most impact. It is not surprising, then, that parenting and family programs have shown strong effects on child behavior. Parenting has long been considered an important factor in repressing or preventing delinquency among juveniles. While it is very likely that past research overestimated the effects of parenting, since it did not take genetic factors into account, it seems clear that effective parenting does reduce child misbehavior.

In addition, family- and child-centered programs have shown evidence of crime prevention effects. Family programs may offer parent training in addition to other services, such as job training and therapy to reduce stress. Child programs teach social skills and management of behavior. It is likely that programs that combine more than one form of service have the strongest and most consistent effects.

SUMMARY

1. Parenting has long been implicated in theories of crime and delinquency. Parents are often blamed when youth act out or misbehave, even being blamed for acts such as mass shootings in schools.

2. In recent years, some have argued that parenting in fact does not affect child outcomes and previous estimates have been overstated because genetic effects were not accounted for.

3. Yet some parenting programs that have measured genes find parenting matters differently depending on genetic profiles (Beach et al. 2010). One psychologist argued that instead of one or the other, genes and parenting work together to produce outcomes in children (Maccoby 2000).

4. A number of parenting programs have been evaluated using rigorous randomized trials. These programs, including the Nurse–Family Partnership and Triple P, have been found to have strong effects on child behavior. Meta-analyses of parenting programs also show parenting is effective for crime prevention.

5. Family and child programs also show important effects. Family programs include the social development model and Functional Family Therapy.

6. One study examined the difficulties with recruitment for a universal program. The study found that only 31% of families participated in the program (Triple P) and certain factors such as low socioeconomic status decreased involvement (Heinrichs et al. 2005; see also Kaminski et al. 2008). Work remains to be done to determine how best to increase access and participation in such programs, given their demonstrated effectiveness.

7. Programs seem to have promise addressing family violence; however, programs aimed at domestic abusers have not shown strong results. Programs to address child sexual abuse seem to improve knowledge and behaviors to avoid becoming a victim, but there currently appears to be a lack of evidence that such programs reduce the incidence of child abuse.

KEY TERMS

attachment 165
authoritarian 166
authoritative 166
batterer intervention
   programs 176
blueprints 173
cognitive behavioral therapy
   (CBT) 174

developmental crime
   prevention 168
differential association
   theory 165
equal environments
   assumption 168
lax 166
neglectful 166

parens patriae 165
quasi-experimental 168
social control theory 165
targeted 168
twin studies 167
universal 168

REFERENCES

Agnew, Robert. 1992. "Foundation for a General Strain Theory of Crime and Delinquency." *Criminology* 30(1):47–88.

Arias, Esther, Ramón Arce, and Manuel Vilariño. 2013. "Batterer Intervention Programmes: A Meta-Analytic Review of Effectiveness." *Psychosocial Intervention* 22(2):153–160.

Avinun, Reut, and Ariel Knafo. 2014. "Parenting as a Reaction Evoked by Children's Genotype: A Meta-Analysis of Children-as-Twins Studies." *Personality and Social Psychology Review* 18(1):87–102.

Babcock, Julia C., Charles E. Green, and Chet Robie. 2004. "Does Batterers' Treatment Work? A Meta-Analytic Review of Domestic Violence Treatment." *Clinical Psychology Review* 23(8):1023–1053.

Baumrind, Diana. 1971. "Current Patterns of Parental Authority." *Developmental Psychology* 4(1p2):1–103.

Baumrind, Diana. 1991. "The Influence of Parenting Style on Adolescent Competence and Substance Use." *Journal of Early Adolescence* 11(1):56–95.

Beach, Steven R. H., Gene H. Brody, Man-Kit Lei, and Robert A. Philibert. 2010. "Differential Susceptibility to Parenting Among African American Youths: Testing the DRD4 Hypothesis." *Journal of Family Psychology* 24(5):513–521.

Besharov, Douglas J., Peter Germanis, Caeli A. Higney, and Douglas M. Call. 2011. *Syracuse Family Development Research Program.* Retrieved September 15, 2019 (http://www .welfareacademy.org/pubs/early_education/ pdfs/Besharov_ECE%20assessments_ Syracuse.pdf).

Bokhorst, Caroline L., Marian J. Bakermans-Kranenburg, Peter Fonagy, and Carlo Schuengel. 2003. "The Importance of Shared Environment in Mother–Infant Attachment Security: A Behavioral Genetic Study." *Child Development* 74(6):1769–1782.

Boutwell, Brian B. 2015. "Why Parenting May Not Matter and Why Most Social Science Is Wrong." *Quillette Magazine.* December 1. Retrieved September 15, 2019 (http://quillette. com/2015/12/01/why-parenting-may-not-matter-and-why-most-social-science-research-is-probably-wrong/).

Bretherton, Ingc. 1992. "The Origins of Attachment Theory: John Bowlby and Mary Ainsworth." *Developmental Psychology* 28(5):759–775.

Brody, Gene H., Velma McBride Murry, Lily McNair, Yi-Fu Chen, Frederick X. Gibbons, Meg Gerrard, and Thomas Ashby Wills. 2005. "Linking Changes in Parenting to Parent–Child Relationship Quality and Youth Self-Control: The Strong African American Families Program." *Journal of Research on Adolescence* 15(1):47–69.

Burt, S. Alexandra, Matt McGue, Robert F. Krueger, and William G. Iacono. 2007. "Environmental Contributions to Adolescent Delinquency: A Fresh Look at the Shared Environment." *Journal of Abnormal Child Psychology* 35(5):787–800.

Chen, Mengtong, and Ko Ling Chan. 2016. "Effects of Parenting Programs on Child Maltreatment Prevention: A Meta-Analysis." *Trauma, Violence, & Abuse* 17(1):88–104.

Davis, M. Katherine, and Christine A. Gidycz. 2000. "Child Sexual Abuse Prevention Programs: A Meta-Analysis." *Journal of Clinical Child Psychology* 29(2):257–265.

de Graaf, Ireen, Paula Speetjens, Filip Smit, Marianne de Wolff, and Louis Tavecchio. 2008. "Effectiveness of the Triple P Positive Parenting Program on Behavioral Problems in Children: A Meta-Analysis." *Behavior Modification* 32(5):714–735.

Deković, Maja, Meike I. Slagt, Jessica J. Asscher, Leonieke Boendermaker, Veroni I. Eichelsheim, and Peter Prinzie. 2011. "Effects of Early Prevention Programs on Adult Criminal Offending: A Meta-Analysis." *Clinical Psychology Review* 31(4):532–544.

Derks, Eske M., Conor V. Dolan, and Dorret I. Boomsma. 2006. "A Test of the Equal Environment Assumption (EEA) in Multivariate Twin Studies." *Twin Research and Human Genetics* 9(3):403–411.

Eckenrode, John, Mary Campa, Dennis W. Luckey, Charles R. Henderson, Robert Cole, Harriet Kitzman, Elizabeth Anson, Kimberly Sidora-Arcoleo, Jane Powers, and David Olds. 2010. "Long-Term Effects of Prenatal and Infancy Nurse Home Visitation on the Life Course of Youths: 19-Year Follow-Up of a Randomized Trial." *Archives of Pediatrics & Adolescent Medicine* 164(1):9–15.

Eckenrode, John, Barbara Ganzel, Charles R. Henderson Jr., Elliott Smith, David L. Olds, Jane Powers, Robert Cole, Harriett Kitzman, and Kimberly Sidora. 2000. "Preventing Child Abuse and Neglect With a Program of Nurse Home Visitation: The Limiting Effects of Domestic Violence." *JAMA* 284(11):1385–1391.

Euser, Saskia, Lenneke RA Alink, Marije Stoltenborgh, Marian J. Bakermans-Kranenburg, and Marinus H. van Ijzendoorn. 2015. "A Gloomy Picture: A Meta-Analysis of Randomized Controlled Trials Reveals Disappointing Effectiveness of Programs Aiming at Preventing Child Maltreatment." *BMC Public Health* 15(1):1068.

Farrington, David P., and Brandon C. Welsh. 2003. "Family-Based Prevention of Offending: A Meta-Analysis." *Australian & New Zealand Journal of Criminology* 36(2):127–151.

Feder, Lynette, and David B. Wilson. 2005. "A Meta-Analytic Review of Court-Mandated Batterer Intervention Programs: Can

Courts Affect Abusers' Behavior?" *Journal of Experimental Criminology* 1(2):239–262.

Filges, Trine, Ditte Andersen, and Anne-Marie Klint Jørgensen. 2015. Functional Family Therapy (FFT) for Young People in Treatment for Non-Opioid Drug Use: A Systematic Review. Campbell Systematic Reviews. Retrieved September 15, 2019 (https://www.campbellcollaboration.org/library/functional-family-therapy-youth-drug-use-treatment.html).

Foshee, Vangie A., Karl E. Bauman, Susan T. Ennett, G. Fletcher Linder, Thad Benefield, and Chirayath Suchindran. 2004. "Assessing the Long-Term Effects of the Safe Dates Program and a Booster in Preventing and Reducing Adolescent Dating Violence Victimization and Perpetration." *American Journal of Public Health* 94(4):619–624.

Foshee, Vangie A., Karl E. Bauman, Wendy F. Greene, Gary G. Koch, George F. Linder, and James E. MacDougall. 2000. "The Safe Dates Program: 1-Year Follow-Up Results." *American Journal of Public Health* 90(10):1619–1622.

Foshee, Vangie A., G. Fletcher Linder, Karl E. Bauman, Stacey A. Langwick, Ximena B. Arriaga, Janet L. Heath, Pamela M. McMahon, and Shrikant Bangdiwala. 1996. "The Safe Dates Project: Theoretical Basis, Evaluation Design, and Selected Baseline Findings." *American Journal of Preventive Medicine* 12(5):39–47.

Geeraert, Liesl, Wim Van den Noortgate, Hans Grietens, and Patrick Onghena. 2004. "The Effects of Early Prevention Programs for Families With Young Children at Risk for Physical Child Abuse and Neglect: A Meta-Analysis." *Child Maltreatment* 9(3):277–291.

Gibson, Laura E., and Harold Leitenberg. 2000. "Child Sexual Abuse Prevention Programs: Do They Decrease the Occurrence of Child Sexual Abuse?" *Child Abuse & Neglect* 24(9):1115–1125.

Goodman, Andy. 2006. *The Story of David Olds and the Nurse Home Visiting Program*. Princeton, NJ: Robert Wood Johnson Foundation.

Gottfredson, Michael R., and Travis Hirschi. 1990. *A General Theory of Crime*. Stanford, CA: Stanford University Press.

Harris, Judith Rich. 2011. *The Nurture Assumption: Why Children Turn Out the Way They Do*. New York, NY: Simon & Schuster.

Hawkins, J. David, Rick Kosterman, Richard F. Catalano, Karl G. Hill, and Robert D. Abbott. 2005. "Promoting Positive Adult Functioning Through Social Development Intervention in Childhood: Long-Term Effects From the Seattle Social Development Project." *Archives of Pediatrics & Adolescent Medicine* 159(1):25–31.

Heinrichs, Nina, Heike Bertram, Annett Kuschel, and Kurt Hahlweg. 2005. "Parent Recruitment and Retention in a Universal Prevention Program for Child Behavior and Emotional Problems: Barriers to Research and Program Participation." *Prevention Science* 6(4):275–286.

Helfer, Ray E. 1982. "A Review of the Literature on the Prevention of Child Abuse and Neglect." *Child Abuse & Neglect* 6(3):251–261.

Hennessy-Fiske, Molly. 2018. "Florida Shooting Timeline: Deputy Held Officers Back From Classrooms Where Shots Were Heard." *Los Angeles Times*. March 9. Retrieved September 15, 2019 (http://www.latimes.com/nation/la-na-florida-shooting-timeline-20180309-story.html).

Hidalgo, Louise. 2011. "Dr Spock's Baby and Child Care at 65." *BBC News*. August 23. Sec. US & Canada. Retrieved September 15,

2019 (http://www.bbc.com/news/world-us-canada-14534094).

Hirschi, Travis. 1969. *Causes of Delinquency*. Berkeley: University of California Press.

Hoeve, Machteld, Arjan Blokland, Judith Semon Dubas, Rolf Loeber, Jan RM Gerris, and Peter H. van der Laan. 2008. "Trajectories of Delinquency and Parenting Styles." *Journal of Abnormal Child Psychology* 36(2):223–235.

Hoeve, Machteld, Judith Semon Dubas, Veroni I. Eichelsheim, Peter H. Van Der Laan, Wilma Smeenk, and Jan RM Gerris. 2009. "The Relationship Between Parenting and Delinquency: A Meta-Analysis." *Journal of Abnormal Child Psychology* 37(6):749–775.

Hoeve, Machteld, Judith Semon Dubas, Jan RM Gerris, Peter H. van der Laan, and Wilma Smeenk. 2011. "Maternal and Paternal Parenting Styles: Unique and Combined Links to Adolescent and Early Adult Delinquency." *Journal of Adolescence* 34(5):813–827.

Huey, Stanley J., Jr., Scott W. Henggeler, Michael J. Brondino, and Susan G. Pickrel. 2000. "Mechanisms of Change in Multisystemic Therapy: Reducing Delinquent Behavior Through Therapist Adherence and Improved Family and Peer Functioning." *Journal of Consulting and Clinical Psychology* 68(3):451–467.

Kaminski, Jennifer Wyatt, Linda Anne Valle, Jill H. Filene, and Cynthia L. Boyle. 2008. "A Meta-Analytic Review of Components Associated With Parent Training Program Effectiveness." *Journal of Abnormal Child Psychology* 36(4):567–589.

Kazdin, Alan E., Debra Bass, Todd Siegel, and Christopher Thomas. 1989. "Cognitive-Behavioral Therapy and Relationship Therapy in the Treatment of Children Referred for Antisocial Behavior." *Journal of Consulting and Clinical Psychology* 57(4):522–535.

Kumpfer, Karol L., and Rose Alvarado. 2003. "Family-Strengthening Approaches for the Prevention of Youth Problem Behaviors." *American Psychologist* 58(6–7):457–465.

Lally, J. Ronald, Peter Mangione, and Alice Honig. 1987. "The Syracuse University Family Development Research Program: Long-Range Impact of an Early Intervention With Low-Income Children and Their Families." Retrieved September 15, 2019 (https://eric.ed.gov/?id=ED293637).

Landenberger, Nana A., and Mark W. Lipsey. 2005. "The Positive Effects of Cognitive–Behavioral Programs for Offenders: A Meta-Analysis of Factors Associated With Effective Treatment." *Journal of Experimental Criminology* 1(4):451–476.

Littell Julia H., Burnee Forsythe, and Melania Popa. 2005. "Multisystemic Therapy for Social, Emotional, and Behavioral Problems in Youth Aged 10–17." *Campbell Systematic Reviews*. Retrieved September 15, 2019 (https://www.campbellcollaboration.org/library/multisystemic-therapy-social-emotional-behavioral-problems.html).

Lundahl, Brad W., Janelle Nimer, and Bruce Parsons. 2006. "Preventing Child Abuse: A Meta-Analysis of Parent Training Programs." *Research on Social Work Practice* 16(3):251–262.

Lundahl, Brad, Heather J. Risser, and M. Christine Lovejoy. 2006. "A Meta-Analysis of Parent Training: Moderators and Follow-Up Effects." *Clinical Psychology Review* 26(1):86–104.

Maccoby, Eleanor E. 2000. "Parenting and Its Effects on Children: On Reading and Misreading Behavior Genetics." *Annual Review of Psychology* 51(1):1–27.

Manning, Matthew, Ross Homel, and Christine Smith. 2010. "A Meta-Analysis of the Effects of Early Developmental Prevention Programs in At-Risk Populations on Non-Health Outcomes in Adolescence." *Children and Youth Services Review* 32(4):506–519.

Matjasko, J. L., A. M. Vivolo-Kantor, G. M. Massetti, K. M. Holland, M. K. Holt, and J. D. Cruz. 2012. "A Systematic Meta-Review of Evaluations of Youth Violence Prevention Programs: Common and Divergent Findings From 25 Years of Meta-Analyses and Systematic Reviews." *Aggression and Violent Behavior* 17(6):540–552.

McCart, Michael R., Paul E. Priester, W. Hobart Davies, and Razia Azen. 2006. "Differential Effectiveness of Behavioral Parent-Training and Cognitive-Behavioral Therapy for Antisocial Youth: A Meta-Analysis." *Journal of Abnormal Child Psychology* 34(4):525–541.

Mendiola-Washington, Guadalupe, and Traqina Q. Emeka. 2014. "History of Juvenile Justice." Pp. 2191–2199 in *Encyclopedia of Criminology and Criminal Justice*, edited by Gerben Bruinsma and David Weisburd. New York, NY: Springer.

Menting, Ankie T. A., Bram Orobio de Castro, and Walter Matthys. 2013. "Effectiveness of the Incredible Years Parent Training to Modify Disruptive and Prosocial Child Behavior: A Meta-Analytic Review." *Clinical Psychology Review* 33(8):901–913.

Miller, Ted R. 2015. "Projected Outcomes of Nurse-Family Partnership Home Visitation During 1996–2013, USA." *Prevention Science* 16(6):765–77. https://doi.org/10.1007/s11121-015-0572-9.

Moyer, Melinda Wenner. 2018. "A New Pro-Gun Talking Point Blames Lax Parenting for Mass Murders. Here's How Wrong That Is." *Slate*. February 16, 2019 (https://slate.com/human-interest/2018/02/its-ridiculous-to-blame-lenient-parenting-for-school-shootings.html).

Neiderhiser, Jenae M., David Reiss, E. Mavis Hetherington, and Robert Plomin. 1999. "Relationships Between Parenting and Adolescent Adjustment Over Time: Genetic and Environmental Contributions." *Developmental Psychology* 35(3):680.

Nowak, Christoph, and Nina Heinrichs. 2008. "A Comprehensive Meta-Analysis of Triple P-Positive Parenting Program Using Hierarchical Linear Modeling: Effectiveness and Moderating Variables." *Clinical Child and Family Psychology Review* 11(3):114.

Olds, David L. 2006. "The Nurse–Family Partnership: An Evidence-Based Preventive Intervention." *Infant Mental Health Journal* 27(1):5–25.

Olds, D. L., C. R. Henderson, R. Tatelbaum, and R. Chamberlin. 1986. "Improving the Delivery of Prenatal Care and Outcomes of Pregnancy: A Randomized Trial of Nurse Home Visitation." *Pediatrics* 77(1):16–28.

Piquero, Alex R., David P. Farrington, Brandon C. Welsh, Richard Tremblay, and Wesley G. Jennings. 2009. "Effects of Early Family/Parent Training Programs on Antisocial Behavior and Delinquency." *Journal of Experimental Criminology* 5(2):83–120.

Piquero, Alex R., Wesley G. Jennings, Brie Diamond, David P. Farrington, Richard E. Tremblay, Brandon C. Welsh, and Jennifer M. Reingle Gonzalez. 2016. "A Meta-Analysis Update on the Effects of Early Family/Parent Training Programs on Antisocial Behavior and Delinquency." *Journal of Experimental Criminology* 12(2):229–248.

Putnam, Frank W. 2003. "Ten-Year Research Update Review: Child Sexual Abuse." *Journal of the American Academy of Child & Adolescent Psychiatry* 42(3):269–278.

Reilly, Kate. 2018. "'This Is the New Normal Unless We Stop It.' Teachers Are Fighting for Gun Control After Parkland." *Time*. Retrieved September 15, 2019 (http://time.com/5167305/florida-shooting-teachers-gun-control-activism/).

Rescorla, Leslie A., and others. 1979. "The Yale Child Welfare Research Program: Description and Results." Paper presented at the Biennial Meeting of the Society for Research in Child Development, San Francisco, California, March 15–18.

Rescorla, Leslie A., and Edward Zigler. 1981. "The Yale Child Welfare Research Program: Implications for Social Policy." *Educational Evaluation and Policy Analysis* 3(6):5–14.

Reyno, Sandra M., and Patrick J. McGrath. 2006. "Predictors of Parent Training Efficacy for Child Externalizing Behavior Problems—A Meta-Analytic Review." *Journal of Child Psychology & Psychiatry* 47(1):99–111.

Rispens, Jan, Andre Aleman, and Paul P. Goudena. 1997. "Prevention of Child Sexual Abuse Victimization: A Meta-Analysis of School Programs." *Child Abuse & Neglect* 21(10):975–987.

Rocque, Michael, Brandon C. Welsh, and Adrian Raine. 2012. "Biosocial Criminology and Modern Crime Prevention." *Journal of Criminal Justice* 40(4):306–312.

Rousseau, Jean-Jacques. 1762/1889. *Emile or Concerning Education. Extracts.* Boston, MA: D.C. Heath.

Sanders, Matthew R. 1999. "Triple P-Positive Parenting Program: Towards an Empirically Validated Multilevel Parenting and Family Support Strategy for the Prevention of Behavior and Emotional Problems in Children." *Clinical Child and Family Psychology Review* 2(2):71–90.

Sanders, Matthew R., James N. Kirby, Cassandra L. Tellegen, and Jamin J. Day. 2014. "The Triple P-Positive Parenting Program: A Systematic Review and Meta-Analysis of a Multi-Level System of Parenting Support." *Clinical Psychology Review* 34(4):337–357.

Sanders, Matthew R., Carol Markie-Dadds, and Karen M. T. Turner. 2003. *Theoretical, Scientific and Clinical Foundations of the Triple P-Positive Parenting Program: A Population Approach to the Promotion of Parenting Competence.* Parenting Research and Practice Monograph No. 1.

Scott, Stephen, Carolyn Webster-Stratton, Quentin Spender, Moira Doolan, Brian Jacobs, and Helen Aspland. 2001. "Multicentre Controlled Trial of Parenting Groups for Childhood Antisocial Behaviour in Clinical Practice." *BMJ* 323(7306):194–197.

Serketich, Wendy J., and Jean E. Dumas. 1996. "The Effectiveness of Behavioral Parent Training to Modify Antisocial Behavior in Children: A Meta-Analysis." *Behavior Therapy* 27(2):171–186.

Sexton, Thomas, and Charles W. Turner. 2010. "The Effectiveness of Functional Family Therapy for Youth With Behavioral Problems in a Community Practice Setting." *Journal of Family Psychology* 24(3):339.

Sherman, Lawrence W., and Richard A. Berk. 1984. "The Minneapolis Domestic Violence Experiment." *Police Foundation Reports*.

Sherman, Lawrence W., and Ellen G. Cohn. 1989. "The Impact of Research on Legal Policy: The Minneapolis Domestic Violence Experiment." *Law and Society Review* 23(1):117–144.

Sherman, Lawrence W., Denise C. Gottfredson, Doris L. MacKenzie, John Eck, Peter Reuter, and Shawn Bushway. 1997. *Preventing Crime: What Works, What Doesn't, What's Promising: A Report to the United States Congress*. Washington, DC: U.S. Department of Justice, Office of Justice Programs.

Sherman, Lawrence W., Janell D. Schmidt, Dennis P. Rogan, and Douglas A. Smith. 1992. "The Variable Effects of Arrest on Criminal Careers: The Milwaukee Domestic Violence Experiment." *Journal of Criminal Law & Criminology* 83: 137–169.

Somech, Lior Y., and Yoel Elizur. 2012. "Promoting Self-Regulation and Cooperation in Pre-Kindergarten Children With Conduct Problems: A Randomized Controlled Trial." *Journal of the American Academy of Child & Adolescent Psychiatry* 51(4):412–422.

Spera, Christopher. 2005. "A Review of the Relationship Among Parenting Practices, Parenting Styles, and Adolescent School Achievement." *Educational Psychology Review* 17(2):125–146.

Spock, Benjamin. 1966. *The Common Sense Book of Baby and Child Care*, Revised ed. New York, NY: Duell, Sloan, and Pearce.

Sukhodolsky, Denis G., Howard Kassinove, and Bernard S. Gorman. 2004. "Cognitive-Behavioral Therapy for Anger in Children and Adolescents: A Meta-Analysis." *Aggression and Violent Behavior* 9(3):247–269.

Sutherland, Edwin. 1939. *Principles of Criminology*. Chicago, IL: Lippincott.

Thomas, Rae, and Melanie J. Zimmer-Gembeck. 2007. "Behavioral Outcomes of Parent-Child Interaction Therapy and Triple P—Positive Parenting Program: A Review and Meta-Analysis." *Journal of Abnormal Child Psychology* 35(3):475–495.

Tremblay, Richard E., and Wendy M. Craig. 1995. "Developmental Crime Prevention." *Crime and Justice* 19: 151–236.

U.S. Department of Health and Human Services. 2017. *Child Maltreatment 2015*. Retrieved September 15, 2019 (http://www.acf.hhs.gov/programs/cb/research-data-technology/statistics-research/child-maltreatment).

Vaske, Jamie, Kevan Galyean, and Francis T. Cullen. 2011. "Toward a Biosocial Theory of Offender Rehabilitation: Why Does Cognitive-Behavioral Therapy Work?" *Journal of Criminal Justice* 39(1):90–102.

Wagner, David V., Charles M. Borduin, Aaron M. Sawyer, and Alex R. Dopp. 2014. "Long-Term Prevention of Criminality in Siblings of Serious and Violent Juvenile Offenders: A 25-Year Follow-Up to a Randomized Clinical Trial of Multisystemic Therapy." *Journal of Consulting and Clinical Psychology* 82(3):492–499.

Walker, Samuel. 1998. *Popular Justice: A History of American Criminal Justice*, 2nd ed. New York, NY: Oxford University Press.

Webster-Stratton, Carolyn and Jamila Reid (2003). "The Incredible Years Parents, Teachers, and Children Training Series: A Multifaceted Treatment Approach for Young Children with Conduct Problems" In *Evidence-Based Psychotherapies for Children and Adolescents*, edited by Alan E. Kazdin and John R. Weisz. New York, NY: Guilford Press.

Webster-Stratton, Carolyn H., and M. Jamila Reid. 2010. "The Incredible Years Parents, Teachers and Children Training Series: A Multifaceted Treatment Approach for Young Children With Conduct Problems." Pp. 194–210 in *Evidence-Based Psychotherapies for Children and Adolescents*, 2nd ed., edited by Alan E. Kazdin and John R. Weisz. New York, NY: Guilford Press.

Webster-Stratton, Carolyn H., and M. Jamila Reid. 2011. "The Incredible Years Program for Children From Infancy to Pre-Adolescence: Prevention and Treatment of Behavior Problems." Pp. 117–138 in *Clinical Handbook of Assessing and Treating Conduct Problems in Youth*, edited by Rachael C. Murrihy, Antony D. Kidman, and Thomas H. Ollendick. New York, NY: Springer.

Wilson, Philip, Robert Rush, Susan Hussey, Christine Puckering, Fiona Sim, Clare S. Allely, Paul Doku, Alex McConnachie, and Christopher Gillberg. 2012. "How Evidence-Based Is an 'Evidence-Based Parenting Program'? A PRISMA Systematic Review and Meta-Analysis of Triple P." *BMC Medicine* 10(1):130.

Wolfe, David A., and Peter G. Jaffe. 1999. "Emerging Strategies in the Prevention of Domestic Violence." *The Future of Children* 9(3):133–144.

Wright, John, Kevin Beaver, Matt Delisi, and Michael Vaughn. 2008. "Evidence of Negligible Parenting Influences on Self-Control, Delinquent Peers, and Delinquency in a Sample of Twins." *Justice Quarterly* 25(3):544–569.

Yoshikawa, Hirokazu. 1995. "Long-Term Effects of Early Childhood Programs on Social Outcomes and Delinquency." *The Future of Children* 5(3):51–75.

Zigler, Edward, Cara Taussig, and Kathryn Black. 1992. "Early Childhood Intervention: A Promising Preventative for Juvenile Delinquency." *American Psychologist* 47(8):997–1006.

9

SCHOOLS AND CRIME PREVENTION

In the previous chapter, we opened by discussing a school mass shooting (sometimes called a "rampage shooting") that occurred in the winter of 2018. Extreme events such as rampage shootings, characterized by large body counts and lack of an obvious explanation—Is it mental illness? Parenting?—capture our collective attention. The social media movement led by several students from Marjory Stoneman Douglas High School, using #neveragain, helped ensure that school rampage shootings would remain in the public consciousness longer than previous incidents had.

Yet rampage shootings at schools are relatively rare. In fact, recent research has shown that there have been only 16 mass shootings at schools extending over the past 20-plus years. What is more common is non-rampage-style violence in schools, but even these events do not happen often. James Alan Fox and Emma Fridel (2018) found that shooting deaths at schools have decreased since the 1990s. The National Center for Education Statistics publishes a report on crime in schools each year, called *Indicators of School Crime and Safety.* According to the 2016 report, 12 youths ages 5 to 18 were murdered in schools. This the authors compared with the number of homicides outside of school for the same age group, which was 1,053. The number of homicides in schools has also decreased over time, from a high of 34 (which happened in 1992–1993 and 1997–1998) (Musu-Gillette et al. 2017).

Chapter Outline

- Schools and Risk Factors for Crime
- Preventing Crime in the School
  - Bullying
  - School Violence
- Crime Prevention Programs in Schools: Developmental Approaches
  - Substance Use Programs
  - General Delinquency Programs
  - Preschool Approaches
  - Extracurricular Activities
- Conclusion

Learning Questions

1. What do we know about crime in schools?

2. How do our schools fail our children?

3. How can we prevent school violence?

4. Do school prevention programs affect crime outside of the schools?

Thus, schools are a relatively safe place for students compared with the world outside of schools. But that does not mean crime is low within the schoolhouse. The school safety report found that there were *more* nonfatal victimizations of students (ages 12–18) at school than away, with more than three-quarters of a million incidents. In addition, nearly a quarter of students were bullied at school.

Crime, including violence, does happen in schools, so it is important to examine methods of preventing it. At the same time, developmental crime prevention programs, which seek to improve or facilitate healthy youth growth and maturation, have often taken place in school settings. Both types of crime prevention (school crime and developmental programs) are the focus of this chapter. We begin with a discussion of schools and the issues they face, which may increase criminal behavior of students. We then describe school prevention efforts aimed at reducing school crime and delinquency. The final section of the chapter reviews crime prevention programs that have taken place in school settings.

SCHOOLS AND RISK FACTORS FOR CRIME

From the time children are around age 5 all the way until they are legal adults (and, at least for you and your colleagues, far beyond age 18), schools are an all-encompassing environment. Students spend upward of 7 hours a day (more if they engage in extracurricular activities) within schoolhouse walls, interacting with other students, staff, and teachers. It is instructive to examine how the school provides an important context for crime from the viewpoint of several criminological theories.

One perspective, called **strain theory**, suggests that crime happens when individuals want to obtain something but are not able to do so in socially approved ways. The first version of strain theory (Merton 1938) was concerned with adult crime, suggesting that individuals who could not obtain the American Dream (get a nice job, house, etc.) legitimately would need to turn to illegitimate means to do so (e.g., robbery). This theory has been applied to the school, replacing the American Dream with the goal of obtaining good grades (see, e.g., Cohen 1955; Farnworth and Leiber 1989).

Resources are not evenly distributed across schools in the United States, as has long been known. In the late 1980s, Jonathon Kozol documented the stark differences he noticed as he traveled the country. His first experience with inequality in education came in the 1960s when he started as an elementary school teacher in Boston in a poor school, was fired, and then was hired at a wealthier school outside of the city. His later career took him to schools across the nation, and he was struck by the extreme segregation he saw in urban areas, where schools were often "95–99% nonwhite" (Kozol 2012:3). And things were not "separate but equal." Far from it. In the schools where nonwhites were concentrated, neighborhoods were marked by poverty and schools had to make do with few and often old resources.

A look at spending per student can give an idea of the sort of inequality that exists. In 2013, the U.S. Census found that spending per student ranged from nearly $20,000 in New York to $6,555 in Utah (U.S. Census 2015). What sorts of effects does this type of inequality have? In Connecticut, where there are large differences in spending across school districts, poorer districts "tend to have more students in need of extra help, and yet they have fewer guidance counselors, tutors, and psychologists, lower-paid teachers, more dilapidated facilities and bigger class sizes than wealthier districts, according to an ongoing lawsuit" (Semuels 2016). In 2014–2015, states varied in terms of high school graduation rates, ranging from a low of 69% in Washington, D.C., and Nevada to a high of 91% in Iowa. In that same year, rates for different races also varied, with a high of 90% for Asian/Pacific Islanders and a low of 72% for Native Americans (National Center for Education Statistics 2018). Inequality in education outcomes is also linked to crime (Groot and van den Brink 2010; Lochner and Moretti 2004). For example, those who drop out of school are more likely to engage in antisocial behavior, but the reason is unclear (Sweeten, Bushway, and Paternoster 2009). It could be, for example, that people who drop out of school are those who are at higher risk for delinquency, regardless of school achievement.

Resources for schools generally reflect the resources available in the communities in which those schools are located. Thus, inequality in America leads to inequality across schools. And in the United States, there are large differences in school outcomes by socioeconomic status (Garcia and Weiss 2017). These disparities have implications for crime, as criminological research has shown inequality is a strong predictor of crime and violence (Blau and Blau 1982; Hagan 1995; Morenoff, Sampson, and Raudenbush 2001).

Control theory, which argues that social ties restrain us from deviance, also is relevant to the school. Teachers act as supervisors and also prosocial adults with whom students can bond. Hirschi's (1969) original specification of social bond theory argued that being involved in prosocial activities (such as extracurricular activities) and being committed to school can help prevent student antisocial behavior. In addition, belief in the moral validity of authority acts as a restraint on such behavior. If students feel unfairly singled out, that the rules do not apply equally across groups, they may be more likely to engage in delinquency. This suggests that the troubling persistence of racial disparities in school discipline (Rocque 2010; Welch and Payne 2012) may have criminogenic consequences. If people feel that the law or ruling body is not legitimate, they are more likely to engage in criminal behavior (Tyler 1990).

Labeling theory (further discussed in Chapter 10) implies that our behavior can be traced to our self-concept, which is influenced by how others treat and perceive us. If someone thinks of us as smart, hardworking, and dedicated to completing tasks, we may internalize that label and actually become more hardworking than we were before! Some research has found that being punished for misbehavior can increase later misbehavior (Paternoster and Iovanni 1989). Those who are punished in schools may be more likely to engage in delinquency and crime later in their school careers.

Learning theory can help explain deviance in the school context because of the interactions students have with one another on a daily basis (see Gottfredson 1997). To the extent that students have contact with delinquent role models, they may be at risk for developing antisocial attitudes and behaviors themselves. One theory in particular, Moffitt's (1993) developmental typology, argues that for the vast majority of students who will be delinquent in youth but not in adulthood (she calls these youths "adolescent-limited offenders"), the school is the context where they begin to take on antisocial proclivities. Often, this occurs through social mimicry, in which the delinquency is a result of imitating the behavior of more popular but also more troubled youths.

Finally, the recent attention to life-course criminology (see Chapter 4) helps make sense of crime in the schools. Life-course criminology focuses on crime and antisocial behavior throughout the life span, beginning with childhood. This work has shown that antisocial behavior tends to peak in adolescence and early adulthood, indicating that the school years are ripe for delinquency (Rocque, Posick, and Hoyle 2015).

PREVENTING CRIME IN THE SCHOOL

Approaches to preventing crime in schools often seek to reduce opportunities to engage in deviance or to remove offenders. As discussed in Chapter 7, several situational crime prevention techniques have been implemented in schools. However, these approaches, such as using metal detectors and conducting random locker sweeps, do not seem to be effective in reducing crime (O'Neill and McGloin 2007). In recent years, in response to a perception of increased crime in schools, especially violent crime, so-called **zero-tolerance** approaches have emerged. Zero-tolerance policies are a way to ensure punishment is meted out consistently, no matter the degree of egregiousness. They are a one-size-fits-all approach, which means that no infraction, no matter the context, will escape punishment. In theory, such approaches will act as a deterrent to would-be offenders and thus reduce crime. However, the evidence to date does not support such a supposition (Kang-Brown et al. 2013; Skiba and Knesting 2001). Additionally, there are anecdotal stories of students being punished for making gun gestures with their hands or for bringing butter knives to school, which clearly seem to be examples of overreach with respect to the policies (Cuevas 2014; Gates 2013).

Other approaches seem to have more merit. Chapter 5 of Sherman and colleagues' congressional report on "What Works" to prevent crime covers the school. In that chapter, Gottfredson (1997) described many school-related factors that may influence crime and delinquency. These include the individual factors such as attitudes and peers, and school factors such as rules, regulations, and support. In her chapter, Gottfredson found that school prevention can improve the safety and functioning of schools. We will examine programs that address different types of misconduct in the following sections.

In asking school principals what strategies they embark on to prevent crime in schools, one study found that schools do several things. These include having clear rules that are strongly enforced, improving monitoring of students, and attempting to change the environment of the school to one that is conducive to safety (Gottfredson and Gottfredson 2001). According to the authors of the survey, though, most strategies lack empirical evidence. There are specific programs that have shown effectiveness, however. Often, these programs focus on particular types of behavior. In what follows, we discuss programs designed to prevent certain forms of antisocial behaviors that take place in schools.

Bullying

Bullying has been a persistent problem in schools for decades. **Bullying** can be defined as behaviors targeting a student or group of students meant to harass, intimidate, or humiliate. Bullying can range from name-calling to jokes to online harassment. One of your authors distinctly remembers being threatened with a beating unless he mimicked a Michael Jackson dance move on the elementary school playground. Certain school programs have been designed specifically to reduce bullying. One program, called the **Olweus Bullying Prevention Program (OBPP)**, was developed in the early 1980s in Norway. This program addresses components of several criminological theories, including control and learning perspectives. For example, the program trains adults in schools to react appropriately when they see misbehavior and to improve relationships with students, demonstrating proper behavior. Staff and teachers are not the only target of the program; there are community-, classroom-, and student-focused parts of the program as well (Hazelden Foundation 2016).

Research on the OBPP has shown promise in reducing bullying. The first evaluation was not a randomized one, but the schools that received the program showed reductions in bullying behavior (Olweus and Limber 2010). Other evaluations have similarly indicated that the program is effective outside of Norway. The studies show that the program reduces bullying from around 30% to 50%. The Blueprints for Healthy Youth Development organization rates the Olweus program as "promising."

A "model" program rated by the Blueprints group is called **Positive Action**, which was created in the late 1970s. Positive Action targets more than just bullying and is directed at childhood and adolescence. The program involves active learning on the part of students, with numerous lessons for each grade level. Positive Action seeks to instill a healthy self-image through positive actions. "The program teaches children what actions are positive, that they feel good when they do positive actions, and that they then have more positive thoughts and future actions" (Flay, Allred, and Ordway 2001:75). As described above, labeling theory suggests that how one views oneself can influence behavior. Evaluations have demonstrated positive effects on children's behavior (including bullying) and mental health (Guo et al. 2015; Li et al. 2011).

How effective are programs to reduce bullying overall? Meta-analytic methods, discussed in previous chapters, can help us answer this question by combining the results of many studies, in a systematic manner, into one metric. One meta-analysis combined the results of 53 evaluations, finding that overall, bullying programs reduce the incidence of bullying behavior as well as bullying victimization. It is important to note, though, that of the nine randomized trials (which have the strongest designs to isolate causality) in their review, eight did not show statistically significant effects of the program (Ttofi and Farrington 2011). Another meta-analysis examined the ability of programs to increase the tendency for people to do something when they see bullying (called **bystander intervention**). The meta-analysis of 12 programs showed that they are effective in increasing bystanders' actions when confronted with bullying (they also counted studies that examined whether bystanders increased reporting of intending to intervene). The meta-analysis indicated that intervening is positively affected by programs but empathy toward victims is not (Polanin, Espelage, and Pigott 2012).

School Violence

School violence has long been a concern for policymakers and parents alike. That concern ramped up after the April 1999 massacre at Columbine High School, when Dylan Klebold and Eric Harris killed and wounded more than 30 individuals. The FBI developed a "threat assessment" protocol that covered four different areas: personality, family dynamics, school dynamics, and social dynamics (O'Toole 1999). Each of these domains included warning signs (e.g., the individual let it be known that they wanted to be violent) that could be used to assess when intervention was necessary (see also Reddy et al. 2001; Twemlow et al. 2002). One study found that after a threat assessment training, school staff demonstrated more knowledge about how to reduce violence in schools (Allen et al. 2008). Another study showed that after implementation of the Virginia threat assessment approach, students noted changes in the school climate and indicated that they would be more likely to intervene if need be (Cornell et al. 2009). Research is clearly needed to assess the efficacy of these approaches in terms of influencing school safety.

One model for preventing school violence uses a multilevel approach, which would target individual students, particular groups, and also the entire school. This approach, then, encapsulates all three types of prevention (primary, secondary, and tertiary). Thus, while some estimate that less than 10% of students have ingrained, problematic behaviors, it is important to ensure that all students (those at risk and those not demonstrating any issues) receive some form of intervention to keep them on the right track. Sugai and colleagues (2000) drew on this model to show how school office referral data could be used to determine what level of intervention would be most effective at particular schools. Schools with relatively high discipline referral rates should focus on creating a new universal intervention or altering their current approach. If a school has a low number of problem students but those problem students have a large number of referrals, then a new secondary approach may be called for. Finally, if analysis of the office discipline records indicates a small number of chronic misbehaving youths, then tertiary approaches are needed.

An example of a universal program to reduce school violence is called **PeaceBuilders**. PeaceBuilders is offered to young children (elementary school students). The program seeks to improve student outcomes through changing the way the school operates and addressing student behavior.

> For example, staff and students are encouraged to use "praise notes" to pay attention to and reinforce positive, prosocial behavior in the classroom, at school, and at home, seemingly related to learning theories. "Peace feet" might be placed by the drinking fountains to encourage children not to cut in line while waiting their turn, and students are sometimes sent to the principal for kind acts or good

deeds rather than just for discipline problems (principal "preferrals"). (Flannery et al. 2003:294)

In their randomized study of eight schools, four of which received the program after a delay, Flannery et al. (2003) found that the program reduced student aggression and increased social competence.

In the aftermath of the Parkland, Florida, school mass shooting in early 2018, many strategies to reduce school violence have risen to the fore. In Parkland, for example, students were told that they had to use clear backpacks so they could not easily hide weapons (Dube 2018). After the Parkland shooting, another school shooter, this time in Maryland, was confronted by a school resource officer. It later turned out that the shooter, a student named Austin Rollins, had turned his gun on himself (Haag 2018). The question of whether or not the school resource officer stopped Rollins from hurting anyone else is important for current debates regarding how to prevent such incidents.

School resource officers (SROs) are officers who serve schools, often having the ability to make arrests (Theriot 2009). After the 2012 shooting at Sandy Hook Elementary School, in which a shooter named Adam Lanza killed 26 people, including 20 children (CBS News 2019), the president asked for funding to increase the number of SROs (James and McCallion 2013). The use of SROs initially was in large part a reaction to school shootings in the 1990s (James and McCallion 2013; Theriot 2009).

Do SROs improve safety? Theoretically, SROs could act as a deterrent and also interrupt crimes in progress. They could also arrest problem students, thus removing them from the pool of potential student criminals. One study found that violence declined after SROs were put in schools in a southern U.S. city (Johnson 1999).

Na and Gottfredson (2013) examined the School Survey on Crime and Safety data to determine whether SROs affected safety across the United States. In their analysis, Na and Gottfredson were able to take advantage of multiple years of data collection in the survey to determine what happened to schools when they increased their number of officers. They found that weapon/drug offenses went up when more police were in schools. Interestingly, this was not due to an increase in the severity of discipline in schools associated with an increase in officer numbers. The key takeaway from the study was that there was "no evidence suggesting that SRO or other sworn law-enforcement officers contribute to school safety. That is, for no crime type was an increase in the presence of police significantly related to decreased crime rates" (Na and Gottfredson 2013:642).

Another study examined the same data set and came to a different conclusion. Owens (2017) argued that schools with SROs may have more arrests because schools with more crime are likelier to use SROs. Examining the question of how SROs influenced school safety by using data on "Cops in Schools" federal grants, Owens found that these grants lowered school crime as recorded by school administrators. However, schools did see an increase in police-reported crime (violent and weapons related), which is consistent with Na and Gottfredson's (2013) work. Owens (2017:30) described her findings this way: "When compared to the school survey results, this tells us that, even if school safety is increasing, the response to incidents that do occur is such that, on net, police observe more offenses than before SROs were put in place."

An often overlooked type of crime in schools is that which targets educators. Victimization in schools generally focuses on students, but teachers can and do become victims as well. Much discussion has ensued regarding whether teachers should be armed in schools, to protect themselves as well as their students. As we have argued, more guns on campus will likely lead to more, not less, tragedy (Barkan and Rocque 2017). Several factors are related to the likelihood of teachers being victimized, including gender (males are more likely), as well as school climate, including harsher discipline (Yang et al. 2018). One study looked at factors that are related to teacher victimization specifically. Another study (Gregory, Cornell, and Fan 2012) found that school characteristics such as the availability of support in the case of trouble arising predicted teacher victimization across schools.

CRIME PREVENTION PROGRAMS IN SCHOOLS: DEVELOPMENTAL APPROACHES

The evidence for crime prevention programs or strategies with respect to reducing school crime or violence thus appears inconsistent. However, much of the crime prevention that takes place within schools is geared toward reducing crime and delinquency generally (e.g., out of the school context) for the youths who take part in the programs. Sometimes, the programs address behaviors within schools and outside of schools. For example, the "What Works" (Gottfredson 1997) chapter on school prevention included programs and approaches that reduced school misbehavior and behavior in general. Under the "managing classes" approach, programs targeted behavior in classes as well as drug use and delinquency. These approaches fall under the developmental perspective because they generally are focused on healthy youth development and maturation. Developmental crime prevention assumes that early intervention can lead to better life-course outcomes as the individual grows up.

Substance Use Programs

Programs in schools have often targeted substance use. Some notorious examples mark this literature. For example, the Drug Abuse Resistance Education (D.A.R.E.) model was initiated in the early 1980s. D.A.R.E. focuses on teaching students to refuse to engage in drugs and to respond appropriately to peer influence. Interestingly, the program is taught by a police officer in the school. Despite its seemingly sound basis, evaluations of D.A.R.E. have not been favorable (Ennett et al. 1994; Pan and Bai 2009). D.A.R.E. is based on a theory that was popularized during the Reagan administration—that if we provide education about drugs and motivation to "say no," students will not partake in substances. It turns out that these approaches do not do as much as those that emphasize positive interactions with peers. As Lilienfeld and Arkowitz (2014) stated, "Merely telling participants to 'just say no' to drugs is unlikely to produce lasting effects because many may lack the needed interpersonal skills."

So how can school-based programs reduce substance use? Gottfredson and Wilson (2003) performed a meta-analysis of 94 studies to determine what elements of the programs (including sample factors) were associated with effectiveness. Overall, higher effect sizes were found for middle school students (compared with elementary or senior high school students) and peer-led programs.

One program with demonstrated effectiveness is called **Unplugged** (Faggiano et al. 2010). This program would fall under the norm reinforcement or reorientation category in Sherman et al.'s (1997) report on "What Works" to prevent crime. There are 12 units in all that take place in three stages. First, teachers provide knowledge about substances and students also work on their own to learn information about them. In addition, the program seeks to change student attitudes toward substances and to correct incorrect estimates about how many of their peers are using substances. The third component focuses on resisting peer influence and the appropriate way to deal with peers. In other words, saying "no thanks" is not a response to be ridiculed but complimented. The program was evaluated in a randomized trial in Europe. Middle schools were assigned to receive the program or not (three experimental groups and one control group, N = 170). Interestingly, substance use increased across all groups from baseline to 18 months, but the increase was larger in the control group. For cigarette smoking, the effect was limited to 6 months, however (Faggiano et al. 2010). That substance use increased for all groups may suggest limited effectiveness of the Unplugged program.

As with other forms of crime prevention, several meta-analyses of substance abuse programs exist. Tobler and colleagues (2000) meta-analyzed the results of more than 200 studies, seeking in particular to find out what elements of programs are more effective than others. There was a lot of variation in the studies, with effect sizes as low as $-.71$ and as high as 1.46 (mean .18). Programs that had some element of interaction were more effective overall. Higher effect sizes were found for programs that addressed tobacco compared with alcohol or other drugs. Interestingly, having clinicians run the program was associated with higher effect sizes than peer-run programs (see also Tobler and Stratton 1997). An earlier meta-analysis found that smoking and alcohol programs can affect student behavior, with smoking programs having a longer-term impact (Rundall and Bruvold 1988).

A systematic review was conducted to examine specific components of drug prevention programs in schools. Pim Cuijpers (2002) argued that there is great variability in the effect of drug prevention programs. It is important to systematically identify the elements or components that effective programs have in common. In his review, Cuijpers (2002:1019–1020) argued that when deciding which program to implement, stakeholders should ensure that the program

1. is effective, and has a high degree of evidence showing it as such;

2. uses some form of interaction;

3. is based on the "social influence model";

4. addresses attitudes toward drug use;

5. expands beyond the school into the community;

6. uses peers as leaders of the program; and

 7. incorporates skills beyond drug use.

So we know a bit about what types of programs work best to reduce or prevent substance use for students. Does that mean schools are implementing this knowledge and following advice? One study examined what researcher Nancy Tobler and colleagues had found to be effective via meta-analyses over the years:

> The Tobler meta-analyses make evident that school-based substance use prevention programs can have positive short-term effects. . . . Specifically, programs with *content* focused on social influences' knowledge, drug refusal skills, and generic competency skills and with *delivery* (i.e., instructional approach) that emphasizes participatory teaching strategies are more effective than programs that focus simply on drug-related knowledge and attitudes and that favor traditional, didactic instructional approaches. (Ennett et al. 2003:1–2)

Ennett and colleagues surveyed school staff (mostly teachers), and found that across the content types, most schools emphasized the four content domains, but the delivery style was much more likely to be noninteractive. In all, 14% of the respondents both implemented the appropriate content and used the appropriate delivery method.

General Delinquency Programs

Some programs focus on delinquency in general. One recent analysis of a randomized trial of the Ability School Engagement Program found that truant children who received the program reduced their delinquency. The program, in partnership with police, focused on procedural justice and ensuring that parents understand the importance of their children attending school (Mazerolle et al. 2018). In a meta-analysis of school programs to reduce problem behavior, Wilson, Gottfredson, and Najaka (2001) gathered data from 165 evaluations. These studies examined everything from crime to substance use to truancy to dropping out. Overall, the programs were effective, but the effects were not large. Effects were larger for dropout and truancy than for delinquency. For delinquency, the average effect size was .04; for dropout/truancy it was .16. For this meta-analysis, larger effects were found in older grades, which is opposite of what was found for preventing crime in schools. In addition, programs focusing on "high-risk" samples were more effective.

Much as was the case for substance use prevention programs, research has examined what elements of crime prevention programs in schools are most effective. Since we know generally what elements seem to work, it makes sense to examine why some schools go all in on implementing evidence-based programs and others do not. Payne, Gottfredson, and Gottfredson (2006) examined "intensity of implementation" of programs across schools, which included things like the number and length of sessions, whether the program was created by someone outside of the school, and the like. On the community level, the authors found that large schools in urban areas had higher levels of program intensity.

After-school crime prevention programs take place on school grounds but after school is out of session. These **after-school programs** can function by providing needed education and therapy but also by giving youths a place to be once school lets out. One report showed that three o'clock in the afternoon was the prime time for juvenile crime; this is the time when students leave school, but often their parents are not yet home (Newman et al. 2000).

Newman and colleagues reviewed after-school programs such as Quantum Opportunities to demonstrate their effectiveness in reducing crime. This program was evaluated using freshmen boys whose families were on welfare. "The program combined academics, personal development, community service, and monetary incentives" (Newman et al. 2000:10). The study was a random clinical trial and found that participants were much less likely to be convicted of a crime than nonparticipants. Results like these led Newman and colleagues to argue that "after-school programs are now proven to greatly reduce the terrible prospect that children and teens will be caught up in behaviors that can ruin their lives and devastate thousands of innocent families" (p. 3).

It is important to examine the data on when juvenile crime is likely to occur. Soulé, Gottfredson, and Bauer (2008) argued that much of the literature on when juvenile crime peaks is from official sources (e.g., arrests, convictions). Using a self-report survey, which was directed toward participants in an after-school program, they found that the likeliest time when a victimization or delinquency took place was during school. However, in terms of specific violent crimes, simple assault was most likely during school, but other types of crime increased after school. The researchers also found that substance use delinquency was most likely to happen on the weekend.

Northeastern University researchers Sema Taheri and Brandon Welsh (2016) reviewed after-school programs to determine their overall effect on delinquency. They located 17 studies on after-school programs and categorized them as academic, recreation, and skills training/mentoring. The programs seemed to reduce crime, but the effect size was not statistically significant. The weighted average effect size was only .062. However, they were quick to point out that their results did not mean after-school programs are without value. Even if these programs do not reduce crime, they have other functions, such as providing supervision when parents are still at work.

Preschool Approaches

What about before school starts? During President Johnson's War on Poverty, a program called **Head Start** was developed that was meant to help give children from families in need a hand up early in life (Garces, Thomas, and Currie 2002). The program seeks to make sure all children start off on the same level in school, when they begin kindergarten around age 5. In 2015–2016, there were more than 1 million children enrolled in Head Start programs. Head Start is not just about education but also about providing needed resources for families (housing, job readiness, insurance, etc.) (Head Start 2018).

Some research has examined whether Head Start has lasting effects on children. Garces and colleagues (2002) examined the Panel Study of Income Dynamics and found that those who completed Head Start had a greater chance of completing high school and were less likely to have a charge for a crime; this latter effect was especially strong for African Americans.

One of the most well-known school-based prevention programs is called the **Perry Preschool Project**. The program was initiated in 1962 and geared toward participants with multiple areas of deficits. All 123 children who were included were African Americans ages 3 to 4 at the time of enrollment, with 58 being given the treatment and the remainder representing a control group. The program focused on cognitive development and interpersonal skills development. Children spent 5 days a week at the school, and parents also participated at times. Long-term follow-ups have shown that at age 19, the treatment group had fewer arrests and court petitions. Additionally, teacher and self-report data indicated that the treatment group was better behaved than the control group, lending support to the idea that preschool programs can be an effective crime prevention tool over the life course (Parks 2000).

As with most approaches, preschool programs have been subject to reviews and meta-analyses. In Tremblay and Craig's (1995) review of developmental crime prevention programs, they discussed the Perry Preschool Program and the Syracuse University Family Development Research Program (discussed in the previous chapter). Both of these programs showed effects on later antisocial behavior. One such meta-analysis examined preschool programs in relation to a variety of outcomes, such as cognitive and social development, finding they had moderate effects (Nelson, Westhues, and MacLeod 2003). To the extent that social and cognitive development are linked to antisocial behavior, it is reasonable to assume these programs may positively influence behavior.

Extracurricular Activities

One final school-related approach that may be linked to a reduction in antisocial behavior is extracurricular activities and/or sports programs. We already discussed sports in relation to crime prevention in the community context. Here, we are concerned with programs that occupy youths during after-school hours. Extracurricular activities also include activities that are not formal or organized. On the macro level, Cohen and colleagues (2007) found that antisocial behavior was lower in places with more extracurricular athletics. On the individual level, results are a bit more mixed, with some data suggesting that certain activities (such as religious-oriented activities) reduce antisocial behavior (Linville and Huebner 2005) while other activities, such as sports, increase such behavior (Burton and Marshall 2005; Linville and Huebner 2005). Past research found that extracurricular activities do not prevent delinquency. For example, Hirschi (1969) found that "involvement" in conventional activities was not negatively related to antisocial behavior; in fact, some activities (like riding around in a car) were associated with an increase in antisocial behavior.

A more recent review argued that physical activity programming can reduce crime, but a one-size-fits-all approach is not likely to succeed. Describing the HSBC/Outward Bound project and Youth Sport Trust/BSkyB "Living for Sport" program, Sandford,

Duncombe, and Armour (2008) analyzed whether such activities have benefits for youth participants. Evaluations of the programs have shown positive effects on participants' observed behavior over time. Not every feature of the programs was effective, and the authors pointed out important factors such as ensuring that student needs are addressed by the program content. The authors noted these approaches are promising. Additional research is certainly warranted.

CONCLUSION

Crime prevention in the school setting has a long history. Many different types of approaches have been attempted, with some having more success than others. Certain approaches, such as D.A.R.E., seem clearly not to work, while others, such as preschool programs, have much promise. The school is an ideal setting for crime prevention to take place, as the entire purpose of schools is education. Much of crime prevention, it seems, is also about education, about the appropriate responses to strain, about the effect of attitudes toward deviance, and on and on. Programs that involve some sort of interaction with peers seem to be more effective. Scholars know more about the elements of effective school-based crime prevention than ever before, and we hope that knowledge is put to good use as schools expand their repertoire of programming.

SUMMARY

1. Youths spend much of their day in the school environment. They are a captive audience for which prevention programs can be effectively deployed, reaching otherwise difficult-to-reach populations.

2. Crime prevention in schools can take two forms: (1) programs aimed at reducing crime and delinquency within the school and (2) programs that take place in schools but are meant to address student behavior within and without the school context.

3. For the first type of crime prevention approach, situational techniques do not seem to be effective. Much more promising are programs that seek to identify school and student factors that may be uniquely related to problem behavior.

4. With respect to types of school misbehavior, programs addressing bullying have had some success.

5. With respect to the second type of crime prevention, several approaches seem promising and/or effective. For substance use, programs that are interactive (not just lecturing) and that involve some peer leadership are most effective, but one study did find that clinicians may be more effective directing programs.

6. Evaluations of after-school programs, which ostensibly work by occupying youths in the

period of time between when school ends and their parents get home, show mixed evidence.

7. Perhaps more promising are preschool and Head Start–type programs, which begin before school starts. One of the most well-known and effective programs for crime prevention over the life course is the Perry Preschool Program, which took place in the 1960s.

KEY TERMS

after-school programs 197
bullying 191
bystander intervention 191
control theory 189
Head Start 197
labeling theory 189

learning theory 189
Olweus Bullying Prevention
   Program (OBPP) 191
PeaceBuilders 192
Perry Preschool Project 198
Positive Action 191

school resource officers
   (SROs) 193
strain theory 188
Unplugged 195
zero-tolerance 190

REFERENCES

Allen, Korrie, Dewey Cornell, Edward Lorek, and Peter Sheras. 2008. "Response of School Personnel to Student Threat Assessment Training." *School Effectiveness and School Improvement* 19(3):319–332.

Barkan, Steven E., and Michael Rocque. 2017. "More Guns Won't Make Our Universities and Colleges Any Safer." *Bangor Daily News.* June 4. Retrieved September 21, 2019 (https://bangordailynews.com/2017/06/04/opinion/contributors/more-guns-wont-make-our-universities-and-colleges-any-safer/).

Blau, Judith R., and Peter M. Blau. 1982. "The Cost of Inequality: Metropolitan Structure and Violent Crime." *American Sociological Review* 47(1):114–129.

Burton, Jodi M., and Lisa A. Marshall. 2005. "Protective Factors for Youth Considered at Risk of Criminal Behaviour: Does Participation in Extracurricular Activities Help?" *Criminal Behaviour and Mental Health* 15(1):46–64.

CBS News. 2019. "A Look Back: Sandy Hook Elementary School Shooting." Retrieved September 21, 2019 (https://www.cbsnews.com/pictures/a-look-back-sandy-hook-elementary-school-shooting/2/).

Cohen, Albert. 1955. *Delinquent Boys.* New York, NY: Free Press.

Cohen, Deborah A., Stephanie L. Taylor, Michela Zonta, Katherine D. Vestal, and Mark A. Schuster. 2007. "Availability of High School Extracurricular Sports Programs and High-Risk Behaviors." *Journal of School Health* 77(2):80–86.

Cornell, Dewey, Peter Sheras, Anne Gregory, and Xitao Fan. 2009. "A Retrospective Study of School Safety Conditions in High Schools Using the Virginia Threat Assessment

Guidelines Versus Alternative Approaches." *School Psychology Quarterly* 24(2):119–129.

Cuevas, M. 2014. "10-Year-Old Suspended for Making Fingers Into Shape of Gun." CNN. Retrieved September 21, 2019 (https://www.cnn.com/2014/03/04/us/ohio-boy-suspended-finger-gun/index.html).

Cuijpers, Pim. 2002. "Effective Ingredients of School-Based Drug Prevention Programs: A Systematic Review." *Addictive Behaviors* 27(6):1009–1023.

Dube, Dani-Elle. 2018. "How Parkland Students Are Protesting the Mandatory Clear Backpacks—And Why Parents Need to Listen." *Global News*. Retrieved September 21, 2019 (https://globalnews.ca/news/4120674/how-parkland-students-are-protesting-the-mandatory-clear-backpacks-and-why-parents-need-to-listen/).

Ennett, Susan T., Christopher L. Ringwalt, Judy Thorne, Louise Ann Rohrbach, Amy Vincus, Ashley Simons-Rudolph, and Shelton Jones. 2003. "A Comparison of Current Practice in School-Based Substance Use Prevention Programs With Meta-Analysis Findings." *Prevention Science* 4(1):1–14.

Ennett, Susan T., Nancy S. Tobler, Christopher L. Ringwalt, and Robert L. Flewelling. 1994. "How Effective Is Drug Abuse Resistance Education? A Meta-Analysis of Project DARE Outcome Evaluations." *American Journal of Public Health* 84(9):1394–1401.

Faggiano, Fabrizio, Federica Vigna-Taglianti, Gregor Burkhart, Karl Bohrn, Luca Cuomo, Dario Gregori, Massimiliano Panella, Maria Scatigna, Roberta Siliquini, and Laura Varona. 2010. "The Effectiveness of a School-Based Substance Abuse Prevention Program:

18-Month Follow-Up of the EU-DAP Cluster Randomized Controlled Trial." *Drug & Alcohol Dependence* 108(1):56–64.

Farnworth, Margaret, and Michael J. Leiber. 1989. "Strain Theory Revisited: Economic Goals, Educational Means, and Delinquency." *American Sociological Review* 54(2):263–274.

Flannery, Daniel J., Alexander T. Vazsonyi, Albert K. Liau, Shenyang Guo, Kenneth E. Powell, Henry Atha, Wendy Vesterdal, and Dennis Embry. 2003. "Initial Behavior Outcomes for the Peacebuilders Universal School-Based Violence Prevention Program." *Developmental Psychology* 39(2):292–308.

Flay, Brian R., Carol G. Allred, and Nicole Ordway. 2001. "Effects of the Positive Action Program on Achievement and Discipline: Two Matched-Control Comparisons." *Prevention Science* 2(2):71–89.

Fox, James Alan, and Emma E. Fridel. 2018. "The Three R's of School Shootings: Risk, Readiness, and Response." In *The Wiley Handbook on Violence in Education: Forms, Factors, and Preventions*, edited by H. Shapiro. New York, NY: Wiley/Blackwell.

Garces, Eliana, Duncan Thomas, and Janet Currie. 2002. "Longer-Term Effects of Head Start." *American Economic Review* 92(4):999–1012.

Garcia, Emma, and Elaine Weiss. 2017. "Education Inequalities at the School Starting Gate: Gaps, Trends, and Strategies to Address Them." Economic Policy Institute. Retrieved September 21, 2019 (https://www.epi.org/publication/education-inequalities-at-the-school-starting-gate/).

Gates, S. 2013. "Student Suspended for Butter Knife She Brought to Middle School in Packed Lunch." *Huffington Post*. Retrieved

September 21, 2019 (https://www.huffpost
.com/entry/student-suspended-butter-knife-
lunch_n_2979808).

Gottfredson, Denise C. 1997. "School-Based Crime
Prevention." In *What Works, What Doesn't,
What's Promising: A Report to the United States
Congress*, edited by Lawrence W. Sherman,
Denise C. Gottfredson, Doris L. MacKenzie,
John Eck, Peter Reuter, and Shawn Bushway.
Retrieved September 21, 2019 (https://www
.ncjrs.gov/pdffiles1/Digitization/165366
NCJRS.pdf).

Gottfredson, Gary D., and Denise C. Gottfredson.
2001. "What Schools Do to Prevent Problem
Behavior and Promote Safe Environments."
*Journal of Educational and Psychological
Consultation* 12(4):313–344.

Gottfredson, Denise C., and David B. Wilson. 2003.
"Characteristics of Effective School-Based
Substance Abuse Prevention." *Prevention Science*
4(1):27–38.

Gregory, Anne, Dewey Cornell, and Xitao Fan.
2012. "Teacher Safety and Authoritative School
Climate in High Schools." *American Journal of
Education* 118(4):401–425.

Groot, Wim, and Henriëtte Maassen van den Brink.
2010. "The Effects of Education on Crime."
Applied Economics 42(3):279–289.

Guo, Shenyang, Qi Wu, Paul R. Smokowski, Martica
Bacallao, Caroline B. R. Evans, and Katie
L. Cotter. 2015. "A Longitudinal Evaluation of
the Positive Action Program in a Low-Income,
Racially Diverse, Rural County: Effects on
Self-Esteem, School Hassles, Aggression, and
Internalizing Symptoms." *Journal of Youth
and Adolescence* 44(12):2337–2358.

Haag, Matthew. 2018. "Maryland School Gunman
Confronted by Officer Shot Himself,
Authorities Say." *New York Times*, March 26, sec.

U.S. Retrieved September 21, 2019 (https://
www.nytimes.com/2018/03/26/us/maryland-
school-shooting.html).

Hagan, John. 1995. *Crime and Inequality*. Stanford,
CA: Stanford University Press.

Hazelden Foundation. 2016. "Core Components
of the Olweus Bullying Prevention
Program." Violence Prevention Works.
Retrieved September 21, 2019 (http://www
.violencepreventionworks.org/public/olweus_
scope.page).

Head Start. 2018. "Head Start Program Facts:
Fiscal Year 2016." Head Start Early Childhood
Learning and Knowledge Center. Retrieved
September 21, 2019 (https://eclkc.ohs.acf.hhs
.gov/about-us/article/head-start-program-facts-
fiscal-year-2016).

Hirschi, Travis. 1969. *Causes of Delinquency*.
Berkeley: University of California Press.

James, Nathan, and Gail McCallion. 2013. "School
Resource Officers: Law Enforcement in
Schools." Congressional Research Service.
Retrieved September 21, 2019 (https://fas.org/
sgp/crs/misc/R43126.pdf).

Johnson, Ida M. 1999. "School Violence: The
Effectiveness of a School Resource Officer
Program in a Southern City." *Journal of
Criminal Justice* 27(2):173–192.

Kang-Brown, Jacob, Jennifer Trone, Jennifer
Fratello, and Tarika Daftary-Kapur. 2013. *A
Generation Later: What We've Learned About Zero
Tolerance in Schools*. Brooklyn, NY: Vera Institute
of Justice, Center of Youth Justice.

Kozol, Jonathan. 2012. *Savage Inequalities: Children in
America's Schools*. New York, NY: Broadway Books.

Li, Kin-Kit, Isaac Washburn, David L. DuBois,
Samuel Vuchinich, Peter Ji, Vanessa Brechling,
Joseph Day, Michael W. Beets, Alan C. Acock,

and Michael Berbaum. 2011. "Effects of the Positive Action Programme on Problem Behaviours in Elementary School Students: A Matched-Pair Randomised Control Trial in Chicago." *Psychology and Health* 26(2):187–204.

Lilienfeld, Scott O., and Hal Arkowitz. 2014. "Why 'Just Say No' Doesn't Work." *Scientific American Mind.* Retrieved September 21, 2019 (https://www.scientificamerican.com/article/why-just-say-no-doesnt-work/? redirect=1).

Linville, Deanna C., and Angela J. Huebner. 2005. "The Analysis of Extracurricular Activities and Their Relationship to Youth Violence." *Journal of Youth and Adolescence* 34(5):483–492.

Lochner, Lance, and Enrico Moretti. 2004. "The Effect of Education on Crime: Evidence From Prison Inmates, Arrests, and Self-Reports." *American Economic Review* 94(1):155–189.

Mazerolle, Lorraine, Sarah Bennett, Emma Antrobus, Stephanie M. Cardwell, Elizabeth Eggins, and Alex R. Piquero. 2018. "Disrupting the Pathway From Truancy to Delinquency: A Randomized Field Trial Test of the Longitudinal Impact of a School Engagement Program." *Journal of Quantitative Criminology* 35(138):1–27.

Merton, Robert K. 1938. "Social Structure and Anomie." *American Sociological Review* 3(5):672–682.

Moffitt, Terrie E. 1993. "Adolescence-Limited and Life-Course-Persistent Antisocial Behavior: A Developmental Taxonomy." *Psychological Review* 100(4):674.

Morenoff, Jeffrey D., Robert J. Sampson, and Stephen W. Raudenbush. 2001. "Neighborhood Inequality, Collective Efficacy, and the Spatial Dynamics of Urban Violence." *Criminology* 39(3):517–558.

Musu-Gillette, Lauren, Anlan Zhang, Ke Wang, Jizhi Zhang, and Barbara Oudekerk. 2017. "Indicators of School Crime and Safety: 2016." NCES 2017-064/NCJ 250650. Washington, D.C.: National Center for Education Statistics.

Na, Chongmin, and Denise C. Gottfredson. 2013. "Police Officers in Schools: Effects on School Crime and the Processing of Offending Behaviors." *Justice Quarterly* 30(4):619–650.

National Center for Education Statistics. 2018. "Public High School Graduation Rates." Retrieved September 21, 2019 (https://nces.ed.gov/programs/coe/indicator_coi.asp).

Nelson, Geoffrey, Anne Westhues, and Jennifer MacLeod. 2003. "A Meta-Analysis of Longitudinal Research on Preschool Prevention Programs for Children." *Prevention & Treatment* 6(1):31a.

Newman, Sanford A., James Alan Fox, Edward A. Flynn, and William Christeson. 2000. "America's After-School Choice: The Prime Time for Juvenile Crime, or Youth Enrichment and Achievement." A Report From *Fight Crime: Invest in Kids.* Retrieved September 21, 2019 (https://files.eric.ed.gov/fulltext/ED445823.pdf).

Olweus, Dan, and Susan P. Limber. 2010. "Bullying in School: Evaluation and Dissemination of the Olweus Bullying Prevention Program." *American Journal of Orthopsychiatry* 80(1):124–134.

O'Neill, Lauren, and Jean Marie McGloin. 2007. "Considering the Efficacy of Situational Crime Prevention in Schools." *Journal of Criminal Justice* 35(5):511–523.

O'Toole, Mary Ellen. 1999. *The School Shooter: A Threat Assessment Perspective.* Quantico, VA: Federal Bureau of Investigation.

Owens, Emily G. 2017. "Testing the School-to-Prison Pipeline." *Journal of Policy Analysis and Management* 36(1):11–37.

Pan, Wei, and Haiyan Bai. 2009. "A Multivariate Approach to a Meta-Analytic Review of the Effectiveness of the DARE Program." *International Journal of Environmental Research and Public Health* 6(1):267–277.

Parks, Greg. 2000. "The High/Scope Perry Preschool Project." *Juvenile Justice Bulletin* 11: 1–8.

Paternoster, Raymond, and Leeann Iovanni. 1989. "The Labeling Perspective and Delinquency: An Elaboration of the Theory and an Assessment of the Evidence." *Justice Quarterly* 6(3):359–394.

Payne, Allison Ann, Denise C. Gottfredson, and Gary D. Gottfredson. 2006. "School Predictors of the Intensity of Implementation of School-Based Prevention Programs: Results From a National Study." *Prevention Science* 7(2):225–237.

Polanin, Joshua R., Dorothy L. Espelage, and Therese D. Pigott. 2012. "A Meta-Analysis of School-Based Bullying Prevention Programs' Effects on Bystander Intervention Behavior." *School Psychology Review* 41(1):47.

Reddy, Marisa, Randy Borum, John Berglund, Bryan Vossekuil, Robert Fein, and William Modzeleski. 2001. "Evaluating Risk for Targeted Violence in Schools: Comparing Risk Assessment, Threat Assessment, and Other Approaches." *Psychology in the Schools* 38(2):157–172.

Rocque, Michael. 2010. "Office Discipline and Student Behavior: Does Race Matter?" *American Journal of Education* 116(4):557–581.

Rocque, Michael, Chad Posick, and Justin Hoyle. 2015. "Age and Crime." In *The Encyclopedia of Crime and Punishment*, edited by Wesley G. Jennings. New York, NY: Wiley.

Rundall, Thomas G., and William H. Bruvold. 1988. "A Meta-Analysis of School-Based Smoking and Alcohol Use Prevention Programs." *Health Education Quarterly* 15(3):317–334.

Sandford, Rachel A., Rebecca Duncombe, and Kathy M. Armour. 2008. "The Role of Physical Activity/Sport in Tackling Youth Disaffection and Anti-Social Behaviour." *Educational Review* 60(4):419–435.

Semuels, Alana. 2016. "Good School, Rich School; Bad School, Poor School. The Inequality at the Heart of America's Education System." *The Atlantic*. August 25. Retrieved September 21, 2019 (https://www.theatlantic.com/business/archive/2016/08/property-taxes-and-unequal-schools/497333/).

Sherman, Lawrence W., Denise C. Gottfredson, Doris L. MacKenzie, John Eck, Peter Reuter, and Shawn Bushway. 1997. *What Works, What Doesn't, What's Promising: A Report to the United States Congress*. Retrieved September 21, 2019 (https://www.ncjrs.gov/pdffiles1/Digitization/165366NCJRS.pdf).

Skiba, Russell J., and Kimberly Knesting. 2001. "Zero Tolerance, Zero Evidence: An Analysis of School Disciplinary Practice." *New Directions for Student Leadership* 2001(92):17–43.

Soulé, Dave, Denise Gottfredson, and Erin Bauer. 2008. "It's 3 P.M. Do You Know Where Your Child Is? A Study on the Timing of Juvenile Victimization and Delinquency." *Justice Quarterly* 25(4):623–646.

Sugai, George, Jeffrey R. Sprague, Robert H. Horner, and Hill M. Walker. 2000. "Preventing School Violence: The Use of Office Discipline Referrals to Assess and Monitor School-Wide Discipline Interventions." *Journal of Emotional and Behavioral Disorders* 8(2):94–101.

Sweeten, Gary, Shawn D. Bushway, and Raymond Paternoster. 2009. "Does Dropping Out of School Mean Dropping Into Delinquency?" *Criminology* 47(1):47–91.

Taheri, Sema A., and Brandon C. Welsh. 2016. "After-School Programs for Delinquency Prevention: A Systematic Review and Meta-Analysis." *Youth Violence and Juvenile Justice* 14(3):272–290.

Theriot, Matthew T. 2009. "School Resource Officers and the Criminalization of Student Behavior." *Journal of Criminal Justice* 37(3):280–287.

Tobler, Nancy S., Michael R. Roona, Peter Ochshorn, Diana G. Marshall, Andrei V. Streke, and Kimberly M. Stackpole. 2000. "School-Based Adolescent Drug Prevention Programs: 1998 Meta-Analysis." *Journal of Primary Prevention* 20(4):275–336.

Tobler, Nancy S., and Howard H. Stratton. 1997. "Effectiveness of School-Based Drug Prevention Programs: A Meta-Analysis of the Research." *Journal of Primary Prevention* 18(1):71–128.

Tremblay, Richard E., and Wendy M. Craig. 1995. "Developmental Crime Prevention." *Crime and Justice* 19: 151–236.

Ttofi, Maria M., and David P. Farrington. 2011. "Effectiveness of School-Based Programs to Reduce Bullying: A Systematic and Meta-Analytic Review." *Journal of Experimental Criminology* 7(1):27–56.

Twemlow, Stuart W., Peter Fonagy, Frank C. Sacco, Mary Ellen O'Toole, Eric Vernberg, and Michael S. Jellinek. 2002. "Premeditated Mass Shootings in Schools: Threat Assessment." *Journal of the American Academy of Child & Adolescent Psychiatry* 41(4):475–477.

Tyler, Tom 1990. Why People Obey The Law. New Haven, CT: Yale University Press.

U.S. Census. 2015. "Public Education Finances: 2013." Educational Finance Branch. Retrieved September 21, 2019 (https://www.census.gov/content/dam/Census/library/publications/2015/econ/g13-aspef.pdf?eml=gd&utm_medium=email&utm_source=govdelivery).

Welch, Kelly, and Allison Ann Payne. 2012. "Exclusionary School Punishment: The Effect of Racial Threat on Expulsion and Suspension." *Youth Violence and Juvenile Justice* 10(2):155–171.

Wilson, David B., Denise C. Gottfredson, and Stacy S. Najaka. 2001. "School-Based Prevention of Problem Behaviors: A Meta-Analysis." *Journal of Quantitative Criminology* 17(3):247–272.

Yang, Chunyan, Lyndsay Jenkins, Stephanie S. Fredrick, Chun Chen, Jia-Shu Xie, and Amanda B. Nickerson. 2018. "Teacher Victimization by Students in China: A Multilevel Analysis." *Aggressive Behavior* 45(2):169–180.

10

PEERS, GANGS, AND YOUTH CRIME

Chapter Outline

Learning Questions

1. What is the evidence for the higher crime rates of young people?

2. Why do delinquent peers seem to have such a negative influence on other young people?

3. Why does the lack of random assignment hinder evaluations of the effectiveness of peer strategies?

In July 2019, New York City police arrested three youths and charged them with murdering a reputed gang member in a drive-by shooting. Police said the trio sprayed the victim with bullets from two cars shortly after he and a friend came out of a building. The victim died from a bullet in the head, while his friend survived two bullets in the stomach (Parascandola and Annese 2019).

To reduce crime, it is essential to reduce youth crime, deadly and less serious alike. Adolescents and young adults commit more than their fair share of crime, as this drive-by shooting illustrates, and the most serious juvenile offenders often continue to commit crime well into young adulthood. These facts mean that strategies that address the dynamics of youth crime will also help prevent adult crime. To set the context for these strategies, this chapter discusses the role of peer influences and the involvement of street gangs in youth crime before discussing various efforts to reduce these influences and to prevent gang-related criminal behavior.

A theoretical consideration underscores the need for this type of discussion in a text on crime prevention. This consideration comes from labeling theory, one of the most important theories in the study of criminology and deviant behavior, but one that did not fit neatly into the discussion of criminological theories in Chapters 3 and 4. A full discussion of labeling

4. What are the key features that characterize a delinquent group as a street gang and not just a delinquent group?

5. Why do gang suppression strategies seem ineffective in reducing gang membership and gang crime?

theory is beyond our scope here, but an important belief of labeling theory is that a *deviant label* (such as arrest) may lead to continued deviance rather than reducing such behavior. The idea here is that someone labeled deviant may come to accept the label, especially if and when, as often happens, other people begin treating the labeled person as a deviant.

To take a hypothetical example, if you had just emerged from prison for committing a string of burglaries and wanted to lead a law-abiding life, what if you had trouble finding a job because of your prison record and also had trouble finding new law-abiding friends (to replace your former lawbreaking companions) once they hear about this record? Would this experience embitter you, prompt you to resume spending time with your lawbreaking friends, and cause other problems that could lead you back into crime?

Labeling theory argues that this counterproductive result of labeling could well happen, especially among teenagers, who are generally much more impressionable than older persons (Mallett and Tedor 2019). Research supports this assumption. For example, a police record may reduce the likelihood of graduating high school and reduce employment prospects into young adulthood, increasing the chances that someone will turn to crime (Clear 2010; Sweeten 2006). The experience of living in prison or a juvenile detention center may lead young offenders to be more likely to commit crime once they return to society, as much research has found (Nieuwbeerta, Nagin, and Blokland 2009; Restivo and Lanier 2015).

These considerations mean that if our society simply relied on arresting young people who have (allegedly) committed crime, the resulting legal process may sometimes do more harm than good in terms of their continued criminality. Our society does not rely only on arresting young people, of course, and instead does engage in prevention efforts. But labeling theory underscores the need to increase these efforts and to enhance their effectiveness, precisely because a law enforcement approach to youth crime may sometimes prove counterproductive. This chapter's discussion of youth crime prevention thus proceeds with labeling theory in mind.

Table 10.1 summarizes specific programs and strategies discussed in this chapter.

YOUTH CRIME: FACTS AND FIGURES

The term *youth crime* often refers to criminal behavior committed by adolescents ages 12 to 17 and is also often used as a synonym for *juvenile delinquency*. It is important for legal and other purposes to have this distinction between crime committed by juveniles and

Table 10.1	Summarizing Peer and Gang Programs and Strategies
Domain	**Program or Strategy**
Peers	Peer risk intervention
	Teen courts
	Youth employment programs
	Mentoring
Gangs	Gang suppression
	Group violence intervention
	Functional Family Therapy
	Gang resistance education and training

crime committed by adults ages 18 and older. At the same time, however, this distinction obscures four facts about age and crime:

1. Young people as a whole (ages 15–24) commit crime far out of proportion to their representation in the national population, as we will demonstrate shortly.

2. At least some gang members are 18 and older and thus not juveniles in the eyes of the law. National surveys of law enforcement agencies yield estimates that 60% of street gang members are 18 and older (National Gang Center 2018), while other research concludes that young adults are only a small minority of gang members (Pyrooz 2014). While the true proportion of young adult gang members thus remains unknown, the presence of at least some young adults in gangs reminds us that not all "youth crime" is committed by adolescents.

3. Adolescents (ages 12–17) and young adults (ages 18–24) generally commit crime in the same types of circumstances (e.g., time and place) and also have very similar risk factors for doing so (Circo, Pizarro, and McGarrell 2018).

4. Finally, and as Chapter 4 explained, brains are not fully mature in most people even when they become legal adults at age 18.

These facts mean to us that it is rather arbitrary to define youth crime as being committed only by youths under age 18. A legal distinction may be necessary, but we find it more useful when thinking about peer influences and gang involvement in youth crime to conceive of **youth crime** as crime committed by people ages 15 to 24. Any such age range is admittedly somewhat arbitrary, but this age range is often what criminologists have in mind when they consider the crime that young people commit.

With this definition in crime, it is important to now show that young people ages 15 to 24 do, in fact, commit crime far out of proportion to their representation in the national population. To do so, we will use data from the U.S. Census and Uniform Crime Reports (UCR), respectively. Drawing on the census, the 15-to-24 age group constituted 13.4% of the national population in 2017 (U.S. Census Bureau 2018). Drawing on the UCR, this age group accounted for 30.0% of all violent crime arrests in 2017 and 32.9% of all property crime arrests. Looking at these percentages, the 15-to-24 age group is greatly overrepresented among arrests for both violent crime and property crime.

To illustrate this overrepresentation another way, it is useful to divide the number of arrests for the 15-to-24 age group by its population size and then multiply by 100,000 to yield its arrest rate per 100,000 population. Doing so with data again from the census and UCR yields young-people arrest rates of about 281 per 100,000 for violent crime and 745 per 100,000 for property crime. In contrast, the arrest rate for the remainder of the population is about 101 per 100,000 for violent crime and 235 per 100,000 for property crime. Doing a little math, the violent and property crime arrest rates for young people are thus roughly three times higher than those for the remainder of the population.

As all these numbers illustrate, young people clearly commit far more than their fair share of violent and property crime. If so, it is critical to develop and implement crime prevention strategies aimed specifically at youth crime. As mentioned earlier, such effective strategies would help not only reduce crime among the 15-to-24 age group but also reduce the number of young people who continue to commit crime as they age beyond this age group. Many of the strategies discussed in other chapters of this book hold great promise for reducing young people's crime. Accordingly, this chapter focuses specifically on the *social nature* of their crime: the fact that young people tend to commit crime in groups, either groups of peers or the type of groups that criminologists call *street gangs*. We first discuss peer influences on youth crime before turning to gangs and gang violence.

PEERS AND YOUTH CRIME

A fundamental aspect of youth crime is that it is decidedly *social*. Youths seldom commit crime alone. Instead, they tend to commit crime along with at least one, two, or more other youths. This fact of youth crime reflects the importance of peers in all aspects of young people's lives. Just as they seldom see a film, go to a concert, or dine out alone, so do they seldom commit crime alone. It is probably only a small exaggeration to say that most young people crave the friendship, admiration, and respect of other people their age. This is no less true of young people who break the law than of those who obey the law. So just as young people tend to engage in all types of law-abiding behavior in small groups, so do they tend to commit crime in small groups.

Criminologists have long recognized this essential "social side of delinquent behavior" (Warr 2012:226). Reflecting this recognition, Mark Warr (2012:226–227) observes that "when young people break the law, they usually do so in the company of others their age." Another way of saying this is that youth crime is largely a group phenomenon rather than an individual phenomenon. Youths acting alone commit only about one-fifth of all delinquent acts, while groups of two to four youths commit about three-fourths of all delinquent acts (Warr 2012).

These latter *delinquent groups* are much more prevalent than the street gangs described later in this chapter, and also smaller and less organized (Warr 2012). They commit less serious crime than street gangs do but still commit more than their fair share of a wide range of lawbreaking, including burglary, trespassing, vandalism, and other property crime; marijuana use, underage drinking, and other illegal drug use; and some acts of violence.

These groups tend to lack clear roles (such as who specializes in this task or that task), and their membership changes frequently. Young offenders tend to belong to different delinquent groups at different times and sometimes to more than one delinquent group at the same time. As a result of this dynamic, they tend to have different accomplices at different times. The key point, though, is that they do in fact have accomplices rather than acting alone, reflecting and illustrating the social side of delinquency. Peer influences on antisocial behavior seem most weighty during adolescence but still matter to some extent during young adulthood (Warr 2012).

The group nature of most youth crime highlights the importance of peer influences for involvement in such crime, as social learning theories remind us (see Chapter 4). As Warr (2012:230–231) observes, "Most offenders have friends who also engage in delinquency . . . , and the number of delinquent friends an adolescent has is one of the strongest known predictors of delinquent behavior." Adolescents are more likely to have delinquent friends and also to be influenced by them when they have family problems (Elliott, Huizinga, and Ageton 1985). These problems, which include marital conflict, ineffective parenting, and harsh discipline, weaken the parent–child bond. Consistent with social bonding theory as described in Chapter 4, these weakened bonds open the door for influences of delinquent friends to take hold.

Explaining the Influence of Delinquent Peers

How and why do these influences occur? Several dynamics are possible (Warr 2002). First, and as Edwin Sutherland maintained in his theory of differential association (see Chapter 8), adolescents may commit delinquency because they learn and adopt the beliefs and attitudes of delinquent friends that justify breaking the law. Second, they may commit delinquency because they want to earn and maintain their delinquent peers' friendship and respect and the sense of status and self-esteem that stems from their peers' approval. Third, and related, they commit delinquency because they fear ridicule and other negative reactions from delinquent peers if they decline to break the law. Fourth, they may feel a sense of loyalty to their delinquent group of friends and thus an obligation to join in their illegal activities. Fifth, young people often consider illegal behavior exciting precisely because it is illegal; engaging in such behavior with their friends thus provides them this excitement.

This set of reasons generally helps explain why peers can and do influence young people to break the law. However, the exact reasons and the relative strength of this or that reason vary from individual to individual. The most important reasons overall remain unclear in the peer and youth crime literature, although there is some evidence that attitude change, the first reason listed in the previous paragraph and one highlighted by Sutherland, is not an important reason for peer influence (Warr 2012). If so, adolescents copy their peers' misbehaviors for one or more of the other reasons we have listed, but not because their peers have convinced them to change their beliefs about the morality of lawbreaking.

Methodological Considerations

We have mentioned that the number of delinquent friends is a very important predictor of delinquency involvement. This conclusion reflects the rather strong correlation in the self-report research literature between the number of delinquent friends and respondents' own delinquency. Many studies yield this finding, and its strength and consistency underscore the significance of peer influences on delinquency.

Even so, two important methodological issues remain in interpreting this common finding (see Chapter 4). The first issue is one of possible *spuriousness*. In this possibility, the number of delinquent friends and one's own delinquency may be statistically associated only because of the influence of a third factor, such as poverty: Being poor prompts more friendships with delinquent peers (because, for example, a poor family may live in a higher-crime area), and, for different reasons, being poor may produce more delinquent behavior (for reasons discussed in Chapter 5). Fortunately, research finds that a strong correlation between delinquent friends and one's own delinquency persists even when poverty and other possible confounding factors are taken into account statistically. The connection between delinquent friends and one's own delinquency does not appear to be spurious.

The second methodological issue is one of *causal order*. Most criminologists interpret the strong correlation we have cited as confirming the importance of delinquent peers for one's own delinquency. However, it is also possible, reflecting the old adage that "birds of a feather flock together," that one's own delinquency affects the number of delinquent friends. In this interpretation, adolescents with an affinity for illegal behavior may gravitate toward and actually seek out peers with the same affinity, just as young people with certain tastes in music, video games, and other interests may gravitate toward peers with similar interests.

It is difficult to rule out this alternative explanation. The best way to do so would be to conduct an experiment in which adolescents are randomly assigned to have either delinquent friends or law-abiding friends, and then to see whether those in the former situation end up being more delinquent than those in the latter situation. While methodologically desirable, this sort of experiment is undoubtedly both impractical and unacceptable for ethical reasons.

Absent this type of study, scholars have instead relied on longitudinal research to assess the timing of delinquency involvement vis-à-vis that of association with delinquent peers. Finding that delinquency involvement tends to occur after initial contacts with delinquent peers, not before, this line of research concludes that having delinquent peers does in fact promote one's own delinquency (Elliott and Menard 1996). Once this dynamic develops, the relationship between delinquent peers and one's own delinquency then proceeds in a reciprocal fashion, with the increased delinquency stemming from acquiring delinquent friends leading to associations with additional delinquent peers

(Matsueda and Anderson 1998; Thornberry et al. 1994). These new associations might then produce even more delinquency in a sort of vicious cycle.

Although we cannot randomly assign adolescents to have delinquent friends, other experimental evidence confirms the impact of peer influences on one's own risky behavior (Warr 2012). Some of this evidence involves young people playing video games: When they are in the presence of peers, subjects are more likely to engage in risky behavior in the games, such as driving through a yellow light, than when they are playing the game alone (Gardner and Steinberg 2005).

A real-life experimental study involved new first-year students at a large state university who were randomly assigned roommates, as happens at many colleges and universities. This random assignment meant that some students ended up with a roommate who drank alcohol before entering college, while other students ended up with a roommate who had abstained from alcohol. Taking advantage of this situation, two researchers investigated the impact of having a drinking roommate on one's own grades (Kremer and Levy 2008), and they found that male students with a drinking roommate ended up with lower grades at the end of the next year or two than those with a nondrinking roommate. For reasons beyond the scope of our discussion here, the researchers attributed this unfortunate effect to the likelihood of more frequent drinking by students with a drinking roommate rather than to any disruption in study opportunities caused by such a roommate.

Experimental studies like these lead Warr (2012:234) to conclude that they "provide compelling evidence of peer influence" and that "they leave little room for doubt that peer influence is real, and that it can be very strong." To the extent this is true, strategies that effectively reduce negative peer influences hold great promise for reducing youth crime for the many offenders who break the law in delinquent groups but do not belong to more troublesome street gangs. We now examine several such strategies. Other chapters in this book also describe strategies that may indirectly reduce negative peer influences, but our focus in the next section is on strategies that specifically target these influences.

Peer Strategies

To reduce negative peer influences, it makes sense to try to accomplish one or more of the following objectives: (1) to reduce the contact that a youth may have with delinquent peers; (2) to limit the opportunity for groups of peers to get into trouble; (3) to increase contact with, and thus influence by, **prosocial** friends and adults; and (4) to counter in other ways (such as enhancing communication and problem-solving skills) the harmful attitudinal and behavioral influences that delinquent peers may exert. Peer strategies generally aim to accomplish one or more of these objectives. As Warr (2012:241) states, "There are good reasons to believe that regulating exposure to peers can be an effective strategy for delinquency prevention."

Of course, conscientious parents realize this intuitively. They thus try to take reasonable measures to reduce their teenagers' contact with "bad kids" and in other ways to practice parenting that helps reduce the influence of any delinquent friends their adolescent children may have (see Chapters 4 and 8). Often they achieve this worthy goal, and research finds that teens who spend more time with their families tend to be less delinquent, in part because they presumably spend less time with potentially delinquent friends (Warr 1993). But parents sometimes fail to achieve this goal, in part because their teenagers may conceal delinquent peers from their parents (Warr 2007). Although parenting practices are certainly important for limiting negative peer influences, our discussion in this section focuses on formal strategies by various policymakers rather than on the more informal strategies practiced by parents, family members, and neighbors who have daily or regular contact with youths.

Some specific formal strategies seem more effective than others in preventing youth crime. In the next few pages, we summarize some of the more notable types of strategies that have been tried, and comment on their effectiveness. Before doing so, we should acknowledge the difficulty in assessing the exact mechanisms underlying the effectiveness of at least some of the strategies we will be discussing. Although we consider these peer strategies because they aim to achieve one or more of the four peer-based objectives we listed just above, it is possible that they may succeed for other reasons, for example, by increasing attachment to parents. We will return to this conceptual issue as it arises for specific strategies. Our examination of peer strategies covers four types or examples: (1) peer risk intervention programs; (2) teen courts; (3) youth employment programs; and (4) mentoring.

Peer Risk Intervention Programs

A diverse collection of programs has attempted to help youths develop skills in communication, conflict resolution, decision-making, problem-solving, and other areas, with the direct aim of countering the negative influences of delinquent peers. As such, these diverse programs are called **peer risk intervention programs** (also called *peer group intervention programs*). These programs take many forms and are found in many types of settings, but their common focus and main purpose is to try to reduce the risk that peer influences often pose. They are specifically designed to help youths "resist developing attachments to undesirable peers" and to resist any influences from such peers (Sullivan and Jolliffe 2012:207). Some programs focus on preventing substance abuse, while others focus on preventing property and/or violent crime or other forms of delinquency. Many programs are based in schools in high-crime urban areas and involve either all youths or just middle school students or high school students in these areas.

Not surprisingly, some programs involve youths who have already come to the attention of the juvenile justice system. Some programs also involve group discussions, others involve role-playing, and still others involve instruction by trained professionals. Whatever form they take, all these programs try to help at-risk youths develop the ability to resist peer pressure from delinquent peers. Sometimes this is their only focus, but many programs also try to help youths avoid getting into trouble by addressing other risk factors they may have, such as poor school performance.

The Effectiveness of Peer Risk Intervention Programs How effective are all these programs? It would certainly be encouraging to be able to say they are all very effective, but the actual answer seems to be that they are somewhat effective. This restrained conclusion reflects a recent review of evaluations of these programs that reported what it called "mixed effects," with some programs judged to be very effective in reducing negative peer influences and delinquency or related outcomes, but with other programs having "positive outcomes on some measures but no effects on others" (Sullivan and Jolliffe 2012:214–215).

One of the more successful programs is the Aban Aya Youth Project, a 4-year program involving African American students in Grades 5 through 8. (The name Aban Aya comes from the Ghanaian term for "protection and self-determination.") In this program, students in 12 Chicago, Illinois, schools were randomly assigned to one of three conditions:

- A social development classroom curriculum (SDC) involving cognitive-behavioral skills designed to help students resist peer pressure, develop positive relationships, resolve conflicts and settle problems productively, and handle anxiety and stress effectively. An important goal of this curriculum was to have students develop a sense of cultural pride in their African American history and backgrounds.

- A school/community intervention (SCI) that included the SDC but also a school–community task force and activities, as well as parental training.

- A health enhancement curriculum (HEC), which promoted good nutrition and physical activity and served as the control condition for this program. This curriculum also aimed to develop cultural pride.

Although the program had no beneficial effects for girls, boys in the SCI and SDC subsequently had lower rates of violence, school delinquency, substance use, and sexual activity than boys in the HEC (Flay et al. 2004; Ngwe et al. 2004). Because the HEC aimed to develop cultural pride, the researchers speculated it may have also helped reduce delinquent behaviors more than a "true" control condition would have. If so, this circumstance might explain why the SCI and SDC did not appear to help girls more than the HEC did.

Another, similar program was somewhat less successful. This program, called Responding in Peaceful and Positive Ways (RIPP), was conducted in three schools in high-crime areas in Richmond, Virginia, and involved students in Grades 6 through 7 who were randomly assigned to either take or not take a violence prevention curriculum. This situation yielded two groups for comparison: the intervention curriculum and the control curriculum. The intervention curriculum featured role-playing, problem-solving, and group and critical-thinking exercises all aimed at helping students enhance their ability to avoid negative peer influences and avoid interpersonal violence. Students' behaviors and attitudes were measured via self-report surveys at the beginning of the experiment in October (the pretest survey), at the end of the school year in May (the posttest survey), and then 6 months and 12 months afterward.

At the end of the school year, students in the intervention curriculum had lower rates of school disciplinary problems than students in the control curriculum and also reported fewer fight-related injuries. At the 6-month follow-up, intervention boys self-reported lower levels of verbal aggression but no other behavioral benefits (Farrell et al. 2003). At the 12-month follow-up, intervention girls, but not intervention boys, were less likely than their control counterparts to say they had threatened to harm a teacher. But neither sex in the intervention curriculum reported lower rates than their control curriculum counterparts of other types of aggressive and antisocial behavior, such as threatening to hurt someone with a weapon, bringing a weapon to school, or being injured in a fight.

Although these overall results were discouraging, there was evidence that the intervention curriculum did help students in the most need of help: Among the students who reported higher pretest levels of aggression and other antisocial behaviors, those in the intervention curriculum reported lower levels of these behaviors than those in the control curriculum at the 6-month and 12-month follow-ups (Farrell et al. 2003). In other encouraging results, the RIPP program was also implemented among sixth graders at a rural school, with random assignment into the intervention and control curriculums. At the end of the school year, the intervention students reported lower peer pressure to use drugs, greater peer support for nonviolent conflict resolution, and, perhaps for these reasons, lower levels of physical aggression and drug use themselves (Farrell et al. 2002).

Despite some mixed evidence overall, then, peer risk intervention programs do seem to hold considerable promise for reducing delinquency. One methodological problem in assessing these programs is that many and perhaps most of the programs lack good measures, or even any measures, of peer-risk intervening mechanisms (Sullivan and Jolliffe 2012). This lack makes it difficult to assess whether any reductions in delinquent behavior these programs may achieve stem from their effects on negative peer contact and influences. This problem notwithstanding, these programs do seem to be worth implementing, and they do seem to exert at least some of their beneficial effects by reducing negative peer effects.

In this regard, teen drug treatment programs that involve older, non-drug-using teens ("peer leaders") engaging with younger at-risk teens about how to resist peer pressure seem to be rather successful in reducing underage drinking, smoking, and other drug use (Tobler et al. 1999). Experimental evidence also shows that having prosocial teens interact with at-risk teens in activity groups helps improve the latter's behavior compared with groups composed only of at-risk teens (Feldman, Wodarski, and Caplinger 1983). This type of evidence indicates that "the influence of prosocial peers can be harnessed to reduce offending" (Welsh 2012:405).

Teen Courts

A peer strategy that relies heavily on the influence of prosocial peers aims to prevent recidivism by adolescents who have become involved in the juvenile justice system. This strategy involves the use of **teen courts** (Butts, Roman, and Lynn-Whaley 2012). With the help of federal funding, these courts are found across the nation in hundreds of cities and number more than 1,200. There were only 80 teen courts in the nation in the early

1990s, but their number reached 1,100 by 2006, thanks to increased interest in their potential and especially to federal funding from the U.S. Department of Justice's Office of Juvenile Justice and Delinquency Prevention. Teen courts are used primarily for first-time offenders who have committed low-level crimes such as shoplifting, vandalism, marijuana use and underage drinking, and minor assaults. Instead of a juvenile court judge deciding the offender's legal fate, other teens, on a volunteer basis, decide this fate by acting as judges and/or jurors in an actual juvenile courtroom. Juvenile offenders and their parents must agree to participate in a teen court; their participation is therefore voluntary, not mandated.

How teen courts work varies across the nation. Some teen courts have a teen judge and teen jurors who hear the evidence, with teens also serving as prosecuting and defense attorneys and as bailiffs and clerks; many and perhaps most teen courts have an adult judge, with teens serving in the other roles just listed; and some teen courts have a tribunal of three teen judges who hear the evidence and determine the outcome and any sanctions, with no jury involvement. These are the most common formats, but other formats also exist. The sanctions imposed by teen courts vary but include community service, restitution, fines, and/or letters of apology.

Teen courts are widely considered a peer strategy because prosocial peer influences form the rationale for their creation and popularity. As Donna M. Bishop and Barry Feld (2012:914) note, the thought is that "being sanctioned by one's peers . . . can have a more powerful impact than sanctioning by an adult." Jeffrey A. Butts and colleagues (2012:610) add that "the dominant presence of other youths in teen court demonstrates to young offenders that most young people are law abiding, that breaking the law has consequences, and that law breakers are not admired."

The Effectiveness of Teen Courts An essential question is how well teen courts prevent recidivism. Relatively few studies try to answer this question, in part because teen courts typically rely on offenders and parents volunteering to participate in them rather than on random assignment. This situation means that the offenders and parents who do agree to participate in teen courts might somehow be different (e.g., perhaps they are more motivated to be law-abiding in the future) than those who do not agree to participate in them. This *selectivity* factor makes it difficult to interpret the recidivism rate of offenders who go to teen courts. For example, if they end up with a low recidivism rate, did this low rate reflect their extra motivation to "toe the line," or did it reflect the effectiveness of the teen court process? Would this rate have been higher if they had not gone to a teen court? Studies without comparison groups can only report the recidivism rate of teen court offenders, and it is difficult to know what to make of this rate in the absence of a comparison group rate (Vose and Vannan 2013).

For the best assessment of teen court effectiveness, random assignment would be ideal, with offenders randomly assigned to either teen court or traditional juvenile justice. In the absence of random assignment, researchers have sometimes compared the recidivism of teen court offenders with offenders in traditional juvenile court who are *matched* on such criteria as the seriousness of the offense, prior record, age, ethnicity, sex, family structure, and other variables. If the youth court offenders have a lower recidivism rate than this type of comparison group, researchers reasonably conclude that the teen court was effective in reducing recidivism. In view of the selectivity issue, however, it is still possible that the youth court teens and families were different from their comparison-group counterparts in ways that account for the recidivism differences between the two groups.

With this methodological issue in mind, what does the research evidence say about the effectiveness of teen courts? Overall, the evidence is mixed, just as it was for peer risk intervention programs. Some studies conclude that teen courts are indeed more effective in reducing recidivism (Gase et al. 2016), but other studies conclude that they are no more effective in doing so (Norris, Twill, and Kim 2011). That said, Butts and colleagues (2012:613) conclude that "the overall impression one gets from the evaluation literature is positive," although other researchers dispute this optimistic conclusion (Norris et al. 2011).

Echoing the latter researchers, a recent systematic review (called a *meta-analysis*) of the youth court research concluded that teen courts are not more effective in reducing recidivism than traditional juvenile justice processing (Bouchard and Wong 2017). This meta-analysis's authors speculated that because teen courts typically process low-risk, first-time offenders, these offenders' chances of recidivism are low in any event. If so, it is difficult for teen courts to lower their recidivism beyond this already low probability. The authors also noted that some of the studies they assessed found lower recidivism rates for youth courts that processed repeat offenders instead of just first-time offenders. This set of findings led the authors to speculate that youth courts might in fact become more effective if they began to process repeat offenders and other higher-risk offenders, rather than just first-time, low-risk offenders.

Despite the generally pessimistic assessment of this meta-analysis, one especially positive study of teen courts' effectiveness is worth noting; this was one of the studies just cited in which teen courts processed some repeat offenders. This particular study examined teen courts in four states (Alaska, Arizona, Maryland, and Missouri) and involved more than 500 offenders matched with a comparison group from traditional juvenile justice (Butts, Buck, and Coggeshall 2002). Teen courts had lower recidivism rates than the comparison group in three of the four states. In Alaska, the teen court recidivism rate was 6%, while the comparison group recidivism rate was 23%; in Missouri, the teen court recidivism rate was 9%, while the comparison group recidivism rate was 27%.

The mixed evidence overall does not provide a strong conclusion for the use of teen courts to reduce recidivism. Still, some studies do find positive effects: Teen courts are no less effective in reducing recidivism than traditional processing, and they are very inexpensive because the teens who participate in them as jurors, judges, and other roles are volunteers. We agree with other observers that more research is needed on which specific teen court formats are most effective and on whether teen courts might generally be more effective for repeat offenders than for first-time offenders (Bouchard and Wong 2017; Butts et al. 2002).

Youth Employment Programs

There is an old saying that "idle hands are the devil's workshop." Two very similar sayings are that "the devil finds work for idle hands" and that "the devil makes work for idle hands to do." These statements all mean that people who have too much time on their hands are more likely to get into trouble. Although many old sayings are not supported by sound social science research, these particular sayings are actually consistent with *opportunity explanations* of crime, which say that crime is more likely to occur when there is more opportunity for this to happen (see Chapter 4). Regarding the "idle hands" sayings, the presumed effect on crime of having too much time on one's hands occurs because people who are not busy working or doing something else have more time and opportunity to get into trouble, and so they do. As John Laub and Robert Sampson (2003:47) observe, "The simple fact is that people who work are kept busy and are less likely to get into trouble."

Since the 1960s, many youth employment programs—those that train youths for jobs and those that provide actual jobs—have been based largely or partly on the belief that keeping youths busy at work helps keep them out of trouble. The idea here is that employment (after school, in the summer, and/or following high school graduation or dropout) limits their opportunities to hang out with potentially delinquent peers, with this limited opportunity in turn reducing their likelihood of breaking the law.

The Effectiveness of Youth Employment Programs Despite this reasonable expectation, research on adolescent employment and delinquency reports inconsistent findings, with some studies finding the expected reduction in delinquency from employment, but other studies actually finding an *increase* in delinquency (Uggen and Wakefield 2008). To the extent the unfortunate latter effect may occur, it may be because employment increases the contact that youths may have with delinquent peers away from supervision by their parents or other adults (Ploeger 1997).

Complicating the situation, some research suggests that the type of employment may affect whether employment decreases or increases delinquency (Staff and Uggen 2003). For example, jobs that are intensive (i.e., working at least 20 hours weekly) are apt to increase delinquency, in part because these jobs' many working hours impair school performance and limit family interaction. Jobs that offer higher wages (which can then be used to purchase illegal drugs or alcohol for underage drinking) are also likely to increase delinquency. And jobs that increase contact with delinquent peers may have the same effect. In contrast, jobs that are not intensive in terms of work hours, that offer lower wages, and that limit contact with delinquent peers may reduce delinquency or at least not increase it. All things equal, then, and to focus only on contact with delinquent peers, a 17-year-old who works at a fast-food restaurant in a high-crime area (and thus interacts with customers who may be offenders) may become more delinquent because of this type of job, while someone of the same age working at an upscale department store in an upscale mall may become less delinquent because of this type of job.

Although the research results on adolescent employment and delinquency are equivocal, research on young adult employment more consistently reports a crime-reduction effect of gainful employment during young adulthood (Uggen and Wakefield 2008).

This research reinforces the idea that employment is an important "turning point" that more often than not helps young adults desist from crime or not begin committing it in the first place (Apel and Horney 2017). As Chapter 5 explained, employment has this effect for one or more of several reasons. It may reduce the time and opportunity for offending, as our discussion in this chapter has stressed; it may help lift individuals out of poverty; it may give them a sense of responsibility and a "stake in conformity"; and it may increase their self-esteem and self-worth.

This last point reminds us of the conceptual issue discussed earlier in this chapter. To the extent that youthful employment reduces delinquency and youth crime to at least some degree, if not always consistently, why does it do so? We have considered youth employment programs as a peer strategy because gainful employment might limit contact with deviant peers. But if employment reduces deviant behavior for reasons other than limiting contact with deviant peers, then youth employment programs are not really a peer strategy after all.

Unfortunately, the research on employment and crime has focused much more on the effects of employment than on the reasons for why it has these effects. This situation leads Robert Apel and Julie Horney (2017:308) to observe that "surprisingly little is known about the mechanisms through which work lowers individual involvement in crime." Fortunately, some research does conclude that the limited contact with peers that employment sometimes produces is indeed a factor, if not the only factor, for its crime-reduction effect (Apel and Horney 2017). Youth employment programs may thus indeed be considered a peer strategy, even if their effects occur for reasons in addition to reduced contact with deviant peers.

Mentoring

A final strategy that aims at reducing negative peer influences involves **mentoring** by an adult who volunteers to spend much one-on-one time over many weeks or months with an at-risk youth. The Big Brothers Big Sisters program is probably the most familiar mentoring program. The idea here is that the prosocial influence of the adult mentor will help an at-risk youth resist negative influences of delinquent peers (Sullivan and Jolliffe 2012). A good mentor can help a youth resist these influences through conversations about conflict resolution and problem-solving. As well, and as social bonding theory posits, the attachment a youth might form with a mentor may lead the youth to be less likely to break the law, to avoid the mentor's disappointment and disapproval. A good mentor can also help improve an at-risk youth's self-esteem and certain personality traits, and this type of improvement, too, could help the youth avoid committing delinquency. The mentoring may also help a youth in other ways; for example, the mentor could help the youth fill out a job application or seek financial assistance for postsecondary education. For all these reasons, mentoring has been a popular strategy for reducing delinquency and for helping at-risk youths in other ways.

The Effectiveness of Mentoring We saw earlier that teen courts have also been popular but perhaps not as effective as their advocates might expect. How effective, then, has mentoring been in reducing delinquency? As with the other peer strategies already discussed in this chapter, mentoring programs often lack random assignment, making it difficult to draw sound conclusions from evaluations of their effectiveness. The best mentoring studies either do include random assignment or else include a matched comparison group of at-risk youths who did not have a mentor (Sullivan and Jolliffe 2012).

One such study examined the Big Brothers Big Sisters program in eight cities across the United States (Grossman and Tierney 1998). Almost 500 boys and girls were randomly assigned to receive a "big brother" or "big sister," while a similar number were randomly assigned to be on the waiting list. At the end of the 11-month study period, the mentored youths were less likely than the waiting-list youths to have used alcohol or other drugs. However, the two groups did not differ in their commission of theft, vandalism, or violence.

Another study compared randomly assigned mentored or unmentored at-risk youths in a program called the Buddy System (O'Donnell, Lydgate, and Fo 1979). Rearrest rates for the two groups of youths were similar 2 years after the end of the program. This overall similarity obscured some interesting other results. First, mentored youths with no arrests at the beginning of the program ended up with fewer arrests by the 2-year follow-up period than unmentored youths with no arrests at the beginning of the program. Second, mentored youths who had been arrested before the beginning of the program ended up with *more* arrests at follow-up than unmentored youths who had been arrested before the program's start. This surprising latter result may have reflected the fact that the mentored youths interacted with other at-risk youths during the program (McCord 2003).

Because these are only two of the studies that have evaluated mentoring, it is helpful to note the results of a meta-analysis of the mentoring research (Jolliffe and Farrington 2008), which concluded that mentoring does indeed reduce delinquency to a moderate degree. Two other systematic reviews of mentoring research reached a similar conclusion (Tolan et al. 2008, 2013). The reviews also concluded that the most successful mentoring programs were those that were the best designed, for example, by involving more frequent and enduring (time spent per meeting) visits between mentors and mentees, and using mentors who were experienced and well-trained (Matz 2014). Because mentoring appears more effective when it involves more frequent and enduring contact, this suggests that the emotional bond that developed between mentors and mentees was stronger than in situations where the meetings were less frequent and/or less enduring (Sullivan and Jolliffe 2012).

The conclusions of the reviews by Jolliffe and Farrington (2008) and by Tolan et al. (2008) differed in at least one important respect (Sullivan and Jolliffe 2012). In some mentoring programs, mentoring is the only strategy used to help an at-risk youth; in other mentoring programs, mentoring is just one of several efforts used to help a particular youth, with other strategies including counseling and employment. The review by Tolan and colleagues (2008) found that mentoring was effective whether or not it was the only effort used, while the review by Jolliffe and Farrington (2008) found that mentoring was effective only if it was part of a more diverse set of efforts. Considering all the research evidence, Sullivan and Jolliffe (2012:219) conclude that "there is some evidence to suggest that mentoring might be beneficial, especially if a strong relationship can be fostered (through persistent contact) between mentor and mentee."

One difficulty in reaching any firm conclusions regarding mentoring's effectiveness is that mentoring programs differ in many ways, for example, in terms of what mentors actually do with their mentees (Sullivan and Jolliffe 2012). Furthermore, within any one mentoring program, different mentors may do different things with their mentees. For example, one mentor may prefer to spend their time together just talking about the mentee's life, while another mentor may take the mentee to see a film or sports event or for a walk in a park. All this variation might be unavoidable, but it does make it difficult to draw a strong conclusion about mentoring programs.

To the extent that mentoring may be effective, the exact reasons for any such effectiveness also remain unclear. Further, because, as already noted, many mentoring programs include other efforts in addition to mentoring, this combination of efforts makes it difficult to assess the effectiveness of mentoring itself (Sullivan and Jolliffe 2012). Still, the systematic reviews of mentoring leave us with a fairly optimistic conclusion overall: Mentoring is at least moderately effective in reducing delinquency, and the best-designed mentoring programs are the most effective. The task for crime prevention, then, is to improve the mentoring programs that already exist, and to develop and implement new well-funded and well-designed programs, especially those that include experienced and well-trained mentors (Matz 2014).

GANGS AND CRIME

Street gangs (also called *youth gangs* or *juvenile gangs*) are certainly a type of delinquent group as described at this chapter's outset. But they differ in several key ways from the typical delinquent group that gets into minor trouble once in a while. In their most notable aspects, street gangs are larger and more organized, and their members commit much more violence and other crime than do nonmembers (Thornberry et al. 2018). Street gangs are found in all our major cities and also in many smaller towns and even some rural areas. They can dominate whole neighborhoods of a city, their violence and drug trafficking strike fear among community residents, and their gun violence regularly leads to the wounding and deaths of gang members and the same for innocent bystanders caught by a stray bullet. To reduce crime, it certainly helps to be able to reduce street gang crime. As Cheryl L. Maxson and Kristy N. Matsuda (2012:262) note, "The volume and seriousness of juvenile delinquency could be decreased substantially if levels of gang association, gang joining, and the length of active gang participation could be reduced." At the same time, there is a noticeable lack of research, says Abigail A. Fagan (2018:945), "about how to prevent youth from joining gangs, reduce offending by gang members, and eliminate existing gangs."

Many of the strategies and specific programs already discussed in this chapter might target individual gang members or at least try to help prevent someone from joining a gang. But they do not target the gang itself. One such approach involves **gang suppression** strategies that rely on the threat of arrest and punishment to reduce gang violence, gang involvement in drug trafficking and other illegal activity, and gang membership. To provide a context for understanding and evaluating these strategies, we first describe the major features of gangs. We shall see that suppression strategies seem ineffective in reducing gang membership and crime, and that *multidimensional approaches* offer more promise in this regard. But we shall also see that the nature and prevalence of gangs make it very difficult for any efforts to reduce their membership and to prevent their crime.

Understanding Gangs and Gang Membership

We start our discussion by trying to define the basic term *gang*. This is only a four-letter word (and one that inspires gang critics to use other four-letter words!), but criminologists and criminal justice officials and policymakers have spent much time and effort trying to define exactly what a (street) gang is. A good definition is critical to allow us to know how many gangs exist and where they flourish, and also to be able to assess the effectiveness of gang suppression strategies. So many definitions of gangs exist that the National Institute of Justice (2011) states that "there is no universally agreed-upon definition of 'gang' in the United States."

Compounding this problem, different federal agencies have different definitions of gangs, and so do the different states. In the absence of a universal definition, we rely here on the National Gang Center's definition, which states that a delinquent group is a gang if it features the following criteria (taken verbatim from National Gang Center 2018):

- The group has three or more members, generally aged 12–24.

- Members share an identity, typically linked to a name, and often other symbols.

- Members view themselves as a gang, and they are recognized by others as a gang.

- The group has some permanence and a degree of organization.

- The group is involved in an elevated level of criminal activity.

With this definition in mind, how many gangs and how many gang members are there in the United States? To try to answer this question, the National Gang Center regularly conducts the National Youth Gang Survey, which is administered to law enforcement agencies throughout the United States. Responses to the survey, which at the time of this writing was last conducted in 2012, yield the following estimates (Egley, Howell, and Harris 2014):

- There are 30,700 gangs in 30% of law enforcement jurisdictions across the nation.

- There are 850,000 gang members.

- Gangs are found in 85% of larger cities, 50% of suburban counties, and 15% of rural counties.

Beyond these numbers, other research estimates that between 6% and 30% of youths join a street gang at some point during their adolescence, with the higher percentages found in the larger urban areas (Maxson 2011). The typical age for first joining a gang is between 13 years and 15 years, and many members stay in a gang for no more than 1 year. Slightly more than one-third of adolescent members of gangs quit their gang every year, with this number being replaced by new members (Pyrooz and Sweeten 2015). As these numbers suggest, gang membership is rather fluid, with a hard core of members staying in a gang over time and a larger number of fringe members joining and leaving within a given year.

It is certainly better for many reasons to aim prevention programs at young adolescents so that they never join a gang in the first place. Once they do join a gang, and certainly reflecting extremely negative peer influences, their violence and other illegal activity markedly increase (Pyrooz et al. 2016), and their chances of being victimized by violence and theft also increase (Wu and Pyrooz 2016).

Beyond these basic facts of gang membership, research finds that gang membership is very "sticky" for the hard core of gang members (Maxson 2011). By this we mean that these gang members consider their membership to be very important and may deem their gang to be their second family, or even the first family they never really had. Gangs attract youths from homes filled with family conflict, and they attract youths who are not doing well at school. Gangs fill a void by giving these youths close friendships, a strong sense of group identity and group belonging, increased self-esteem, and considerable excitement, and they also may provide a source of income through the gangs' drug trafficking and other illegal activities. Once in a gang, some youths develop a deep sense of loyalty to the gang for these reasons and cannot imagine leaving it. They form the hard core of gang membership that helps any one gang persist despite the dangers of being in a gang and despite law enforcement efforts to thwart gangs.

All these dynamics underscore the difficulty of reducing gang membership as a way of decreasing the power of gangs and the violence and other crime they commit. As a result, they also underscore the importance of trying to keep young adolescents from joining gangs in the first place, which is not only one aim of the strategies discussed earlier in this chapter but also of many of the strategies discussed in other chapters.

Despite these strategies, gangs certainly continue to exist and to attract hundreds of thousands of new members every year, as we have seen. Gang suppression strategies relying on the threat of arrest and punishment therefore remain popular. The next section examines several such strategies and comments on their effectiveness.

Gang Suppression Strategies

To first provide some background, efforts to thwart street gangs take three forms: *primary gang prevention*, *secondary gang prevention*, and *tertiary gang prevention*. These three forms parallel primary, secondary, and tertiary crime prevention, respectively (see Chapter 2).

Primary gang prevention involves efforts to reduce poverty, improve schools, and address the other underlying factors that produce delinquency and crime. If successful, these efforts would help prevent young adolescents from ever joining a street gang. These efforts include the strategies discussed in Chapter 6 and several of the strategies discussed in other chapters.

Secondary gang prevention (also called *intervention strategies*) focuses on youths who are thought to be especially at risk for possible gang involvement but who are not already in gangs. These strategies include the peer strategies discussed earlier in this chapter and several of the strategies discussed in other chapters.

Tertiary gang prevention focuses on youths already in gangs and on the gangs themselves. These strategies include some of the peer strategies discussed earlier in this chapter and the gang suppression strategies relying on law enforcement that are the subject of this section. In a typical strategy, law enforcement officials, often with the use of police gang units, try to gather information on gang members and leaders and their crimes, and then try to arrest them and have them legally punished.

The Effectiveness of Gang Suppression

Unfortunately, evaluations of these suppression strategies conclude that they tend to be fairly ineffective (Greene and Pranis 2007; Klein and Maxson 2006). Several reasons help account for their general ineffectiveness.

First, and as we have already suggested, suppression strategies face a difficult task because of the nature of "sticky" gang membership for the hard core of gang members. As one criminologist observes, "Tertiary prevention involves convincing youths to give up their gang affiliation and become responsible members of the community. This is difficult to do, because a committed gang member considers the gang to be the primary institution in his or her life, replacing even the family. To lure youths away from an organization that has such a strong grip on loyalty is difficult" (Fuller 2013:341).

An additional problem is that gang suppression strategies may ironically increase the sense of group cohesion that characterizes many gangs (Maxson 2011). A long-standing maxim from the social science literature is that external threats to a group may increase its internal cohesion (Markides and Cohn 1982; Pepitone and Kleiner 1957). This is no less true for street gangs than it is for sports teams, rival high schools, or whole nations at war. By "going after" a gang, law enforcement personnel may strengthen social bonding within the gang and thereby strengthen the gang itself, as scholars of gangs have long recognized (Decker 1996; Klein 1971). This possibility further underscores the difficulty of achieving effective gang suppression strategies.

A third problem concerns the nature of gang leadership. Although gangs are generally more organized and more hierarchical than "mere" delinquent groups, most are still not very organized or very hierarchical. Not only do many members come and go, but so do their leaders in terms of who is a gang's leader at any one time. Contrary to popular perceptions, leadership in a gang tends to be transitory because gang members value their autonomy and dislike authority. As a result, research finds that gang leadership tends "to be unstable, shifting and shared among many gang members" (Maxson 2011:168). This dynamic means that law enforcement practices that focus on gang leaders are not apt to be effective because these "leaders" may not have much influence on the gang in the first place and are likely to be quickly replaced by other leaders.

A final problem is that gang suppression strategies rely on deterring criminal behavior by gang members by making them concerned about the possibility of arrest and prosecution. But as Chapter 3 discussed, such deterrence does not seem to occur for most offenders, and gang members are no exception. Like other offenders, they simply do not consider or else ignore their prospects of arrest and prosecution, and their loyalty to their gang proves more compelling than any concerns they might have about getting arrested (Hennigan and Sloane 2013).

Civil Gang Injunctions

An additional suppression strategy that has been tried is the **civil gang injunction (CGI)**. CGIs are popular throughout the United States and involve civil lawsuits against whole gangs or specific gang members for allegedly violating state codes banning public nuisances. The aim of this type of lawsuit is to have a judge issue an injunction prohibiting gang involvement (including engaging in gang-related illegal activity but also including any signs of gang membership, such as wearing gang colors) within a particular location (called a *safety zone*) in a city. Depending on a specific injunction, either all members of a gang might be targeted or just the hard-core members of a gang. Gang members who violate this injunction may then be arrested and prosecuted for doing so. Despite their popularity, CGIs raise some important legal and other issues. Among other concerns, critics say they violate the right to freedom of association and may be overly broad by targeting youths who are not actually active gang members (ACLU of Northern California 2010; Crawford 2009).

The Effectiveness of CGIs

A key question for crime prevention involves whether CGIs effectively reduce gang membership and gang crime. Research on this issue is rather limited but again reports mixed results, with some studies suggesting that CGIs reduce gang violence (Grogger 2002) but with other studies finding no crime reduction (Goulka et al. 2009). A recent review of this literature concluded that "these mixed findings suggest that gang injunctions may be modestly effective in reducing crime and fear [of crime] 6 months or a year after, but not uniformly so" (Hennigan and Sloane 2013:8).

At least two reasons help explain why CGIs may be rather ineffective (Hennigan and Sloane 2013). First, and like the other gang suppression strategies discussed earlier, they rely on the principle of deterrence, which simply does not work well in practice. Second, and again like other suppression strategies, CGIs may ironically increase gang cohesion. These reasons suggest that CGIs may be more effective if they rely less on arrest and prosecution and more on providing social services (such as counseling and job training) to youths who violate a CGI.

To test this hypothesis, a study compared gang members' offending in a CGI zone that provided these forms of help to specific gang members with their offending in a CGI zone that relied on arrest and prosecution (Hennigan and Sloane 2013).

Supporting the hypothesis, violence and other crime reduced in the former zone but not in the latter zone, in part because the social services and other help provided reduced individual gang members' sense of identification with their gang. The study's authors concluded that multidimensional "gang programs are both needed and difficult to achieve" (p. 34).

Beyond Gang Suppression

The ineffectiveness of gang suppression has led criminologists, community leaders, police, and other parties to develop and favor other types of approaches (Howell and Griffiths 2019). This section discusses three such efforts.

Group Violence Intervention

Group violence intervention (GVI) is a multidimensional tertiary prevention approach for addressing gangs and gang crime. This approach involves coalitions of community leaders and members, clergy and other church members, outreach workers who talk with gang members and try to have them receive various services, and other agencies and individuals who all work together on the gang problem in their locations. These coalitions may also include so-called **violence interrupters** who try to intervene at the street level in gang conflicts to try to diffuse anger and reduce potential gang violence. Many violence interrupters are former gang members, and they rely on this experience when they talk with gang members.

An example of this approach was the Chicago CeaseFire program, which was established in 1999 and eventually involved 25 locations in Chicago and other places in Illinois. Evaluation of Chicago CeaseFire found that it significantly reduced fatal and nonfatal shootings by gang members in several but not all of the neighborhoods in which the program operated (Ritter 2009). The Phoenix, Arizona, TRUCE Project, a program modeled on Chicago CeaseFire, similarly reduced gang shootings in the neighborhoods in which it was implemented (Fox et al. 2015).

A related example was Boston's Operation CeaseFire, implemented in 1996. This program used local and federal prosecutors; police; outreach workers and community leaders, including clergy; leaflets and other pre-Internet publicity; and public forums to make it very clear to gang members (often in face-to-face meetings) that arrest and severe punishment would be certain consequences for any further gang violence. This has since become known as a *pulling levers* approach. Evaluation of this program concluded that it significantly reduced fatal and nonfatal gun violence (Braga et al. 2001). Funding by the U.S. Department of Justice enabled expansion of the Boston model to several other cities, and research finds that these areas also experienced a drop in gang violence after implementing this model (Rosenbaum and Schuck 2012).

GVI approaches are costly and difficult to implement, especially in a way that lends itself to sound research evaluation. For example, random assignment of gang members to a treatment (e.g., a CeaseFire approach) or control condition (e.g., a traditional law enforcement suppression strategy and/or no contact at all) is difficult to achieve, confounding good evaluation of the effectiveness of these approaches. Still, these multidimensional gang strategies do seem to help reduce gang violence, and policymakers would be wise to help ensure that they are developed, well-funded, and properly implemented.

The Functional Family Therapy Program

In addition to this type of approach, certain programs for other types of adolescent problems might be successfully adapted to work with gangs. One such program is called Functional Family Therapy (FFT). In its use for problematic adolescent behaviors more generally, FFT involves a dozen or so weekly sessions (or more sessions or more frequent sessions as necessary), usually at home, during which trained family therapists meet with at-risk youths and their parents or caregivers. The therapists work with the families on improving such processes as family communication, parenting skills, problem-solving, and conflict resolution. FFT has proven very successful in helping at-risk teens reduce their delinquent actions, substance use, and other problematic behaviors (Hartnett et al. 2017; see Chapter 8), but it has not traditionally focused on gangs and gang members themselves.

In an adaptation of FFT for gangs, Terence P. Thornberry and colleagues (2018) were permitted to randomly assign adjudicated (as delinquent) youths from a family court judge's courtroom in Philadelphia, Pennsylvania, to either undergo FFT (which was modified to include a gang-related component and thus called FFT-G) or not to do so. This latter control group received regular juvenile probation and certain family services that were less intense and impactful than FFT-G.

The effects of this experimental intervention depended on the level of risk the youths posed for gang membership. Compared with their counterparts in the control group, FFT-G youths at high risk for gang membership (by being either current or former gang members or having family members or close friends in the same circumstance) were less likely to recidivate during an 18-month follow-up period. However, a similar comparison for youths at low risk for gang membership found no such difference. To explain the different results for high-gang-risk and low-gang-risk teens, the authors speculated that "higher risk youth and their families have more and greater needs that effective services can improve, thereby yielding a larger impact on recidivism" (Thornberry et al. 2018:979). (See Chapter 13 for similar evidence in community corrections crime prevention that programs and services are more effective for higher-risk individuals.)

The Gang Resistance Education and Training Program

A third gang prevention program that has been shown to be effective is Gang Resistance Education and Training (G.R.E.A.T.). G.R.E.A.T., which involves a curriculum focusing on social skills training and emphasizing negative aspects of gangs, has been used for some 30 years and has involved more than 7 million middle school and elementary school students nationwide. In one of several evaluations of G.R.E.A.T., students in 31 schools in seven cities were randomly selected to receive or not to receive this program. During a 4-year follow-up period, youths who took this curriculum were less likely to join a gang than youths who did not take it (Esbensen et al. 2013).

Addressing Community Conditions

Earlier chapters in this book emphasized that poverty and the deteriorating conditions of urban neighborhoods help generate street crime and thus need to be addressed for effective crime reduction to be achieved. If street crime is rooted in these structural conditions, so, then, are street gangs. Criminologists stress that gangs flourish in the same types of neighborhoods that give rise to street crime more generally (Howell 2015). As Fagan (2018:948) observes, "Gangs are especially prevalent in economically disadvantaged, inner-city neighborhoods." Criminologically speaking, this prevalence is no accident and is even to be expected. Gang prevention efforts that target whole gangs or individual members of gangs leave untouched the structural conditions that give rise to gangs in the first place. To maximize gang prevention, then, our society must pursue the types of strategies discussed elsewhere in this book that target these structural conditions.

CONCLUSION

Peers matter greatly for involvement in delinquency and youth crime, and they especially matter for members of street gangs. Strategies based on reducing negative peer influences are often effective in reducing these influences and thus delinquency, but the mixed evidence of their effectiveness points to the need for scholars and policymakers to formulate and implement the most effective strategies possible. Because the research evidence is rather clear that street gang suppression strategies are ineffective, multidimensional gang programs should be the preferred approach. Such programs are needed because gang members have a history of many risk factors for their gang involvement and criminal behavior. As one scholar has observed, "Youth involved in gangs regularly harbor numerous risk factors for antisocial development that cut across a number of domains, including family, education, peers, and personality. It only seems logical, therefore, to call for a comprehensive strategy to help youth deal with these myriad social and psychological deficits" (Melde 2013:45). It is also logical to try to address the negative structural conditions that help produce delinquency, youth gangs, and street gangs.

SUMMARY

1. Youth ages 15 to 24 commit crime far out of proportion to their numbers. Crime prevention efforts should thus focus on this age group and also on younger children to help prevent them from committing crime when they reach this age group.

2. Peer influence matters greatly for youth crime, as it does for so many other aspects of the lives of young people. This fact has inspired many crime prevention strategies aimed at limiting negative peer influences and at providing young people prosocial models.

3. Peer strategies to reduce crime include peer risk intervention programs, teen courts, youth employment programs, and mentoring by prosocial adults. These strategies are often effective, but the research evidence overall provides a mixed assessment of their effectiveness. The lack of random assignment in the many programs and practices involving peer strategies complicates assessments of their effectiveness.

4. Street gangs are a major problem in many American cities. The various rewards they offer their members and their members' sense of loyalty to their gang makes it difficult for gang prevention efforts to succeed.

5. Gang suppression strategies involving law enforcement and the threat of arrest and prosecution have proven to be ineffective for many reasons, while the evidence on civil gang injunctions is mixed. Multidimensional efforts to reduce gang membership and gang crime offer more promise.

KEY TERMS

civil gang injunction (CGI) 225
gang suppression 222
mentoring 219
peer risk intervention
    programs 213

primary gang prevention 224
prosocial 212
secondary gang prevention 224
street gangs 221
teen courts 215

tertiary gang prevention 224
violence interrupters 226
youth crime 208

REFERENCES

ACLU of Northern California. 2010. "Gang Injunctions Fact Sheet." Retrieved September 23, 2019 (https://www.aclunc.org/article/gang-injunctions-fact-sheet).

Apel, Robert, and Julie Horney. 2017. "How and Why Does Work Matter? Employment Conditions, Routine Activities, and Crime Among Adult Male Offenders." *Criminology* 55(2):307–343. doi: 10.1111/1745-9125.12134.

Bishop, Donna M., and Barry C. Feld. 2012. "Trends in Juvenile Justice Policy and Practice." Pp. 898–926 in *The Handbook of Juvenile Crime and Juvenile Justice*, edited by B. C. Feld and D. M. Bishop. New York, NY: Oxford University Press.

Bouchard, Jessica, and Jennifer Wong. 2017. "A Jury of Their Peers: A Meta-Analysis of the Effects of Teen Court on Criminal Recidivism." *Journal of Youth & Adolescence* 46(7):1472–1487.

Braga, Anthony A., David M. Kennedy, Elin J. Waring, and Anne Morrison Piehl. 2001. "Problem-Oriented Policing, Deterrence, and Youth Violence: An Evaluation of Boston's

Operation Ceasefire." *Journal of Research in Crime and Delinquency* 38: 195–225.

Butts, Jeffrey A., Janeen Buck, and Mark Coggeshall. 2002. *The Impact of Teen Court on Young Offenders*. Washington, DC: Urban Institute.

Butts, Jeffrey A., John K. Roman, and Jennifer Lynn-Whaley. 2012. "Varieties of Juvenile Court: Nonspecialized Courts, Teen Courts, Drug Courts, and Mental Health Courts." Pp. 606–635 in *The Oxford Handbook of Juvenile Crime and Juvenile Justice*, edited by B. C. Feld and D. M. Bishop. New York, NY: Oxford University Press.

Circo, Giovanni M., Jesenia M. Pizarro, and Edmund F. McGarrell. 2018. "Adult and Youth Involvement in Gun-Related Crime: Implications for Gun Violence Prevention Interventions." *Criminal Justice Policy Review* 29(8):799–822. doi: 10.1177/0887403416655431.

Clear, Todd R. 2010. "Policy and Evidence: The Challenge to the American Society of Criminology: 2009 Presidential Address to the American Society of Criminology." *Criminology* 48: 1–25.

Crawford, Lindsey. 2009. "No Way Out: Analysis of Exit Processes for Gang Injunctions." *California Law Review* 38: 1253–1274.

Decker, Scott H. 1996. "Collective and Normative Features of Gang Violence." *Justice Quarterly* 13: 243–264.

Egley, Arlen, Jr., James C. Howell, and Meena Harris. 2014. *Highlights of the 2012 National Youth Gang Survey*. Washington, DC: Office of Juvenile Justice and Delinquency Prevention.

Elliott, Delbert S., David Huizinga, and Suzanne S. Ageton. 1985. *Explaining Delinquency and Drug Use*. Beverly Hills, CA: Sage.

Elliott, Delbert S., and Scott Menard. 1996. "Delinquent Friends and Delinquent Behavior: Temporal and Developmental Patterns." Pp. 28–67 in *Delinquency and Crime: Current Theories*, edited by J. D. Hawkins. Cambridge, UK: Cambridge University Press.

Esbensen, Finn-Aage, D. Wayne Osgood, Dana Peterson, Terrance J. Taylor, and Dena C. Carson. 2013. "Short- and Long-Term Outcome Results From a Multisite Evaluation of the G.R.E.A.T. Program." *Criminology & Public Policy* 12: 375–411.

Fagan, Abigail A. 2018. "A Roadmap for Advancing the Science of Gang Prevention." *Criminology & Public Policy* 17(4):945–951.

Farrell, Albert D., Aleta L. Meyer, Terri N. Sullivan, and Eva M. Kung. 2003. "Evaluation of the Responding in Peaceful and Positive Ways (RIPP) Seventh Grade Violence Prevention Curriculum." *Journal of Child & Family Studies* 12(1):101–120.

Farrell, Albert D., Robert F. Valois, and Aleta L. Meyer. 2002. "Evaluation of the RIPP-6 Violence Prevention Program at a Rural Middle School." *Journal of Health Education* 33: 167–172.

Feldman, Ronald A., John S. Wodarski, and Timothy E. Caplinger. 1983. *Conundrum: The Effective Treatment of Antisocial Youth*. Englewood Cliffs, NJ: Prentice Hall.

Flay, Brian R., Sally Graumlich, Eisuke Segawa, James L. Burns, and Michelle Y. Holiday. 2004. "Effects of Two Prevention Programs on High-Risk Behaviors Among African-American

Youth." *Archives of Pediatric and Adolescent Medicine* 158(4):377–384.

Fox, Andrew M., Charles M. Katz, David E. Choate, and E. C. Hedberg. 2015. "Evaluation of the Phoenix Truce Project: A Replication of Chicago Ceasefire." *Justice Quarterly* 32(1):85–115. doi: 10.1080/07418825.2014.902092.

Fuller, John Randolph. 2013. *Juvenile Delinquency: Mainstream and Crosscurrents*. New York, NY: Oxford University Press.

Gardner, Margo, and Laurence Steinberg. 2005. "Peer Influence on Risk Taking, Risk Preference, and Risky Decision Making in Adolescence and Adulthood: An Experimental Study." *Developmental Psychology* 41: 625–635.

Gase, Lauren, Tony Kuo, Elaine Lai, Michael Stoll, and Ninez Ponce. 2016. "The Impact of Two Los Angeles County Teen Courts on Youth Recidivism: Comparing Two Informal Probation Programs." *Journal of Experimental Criminology* 12(1):105–126.

Goulka, Jeremiah, Paul Heaton, George Tita, Carl Matthies, Alyssa Whitby, and Alexia Cooper. 2009. "FY 2006 Anti-Gang Initiative Grants in the Central District of California." Santa Monica, CA: RAND Corporation.

Greene, Judith, and Kevin Pranis. 2007. *Gang Wars: The Failure of Enforcement Tactics and the Need for Effective Public Safety Strategies*. Washington, DC: Justice Policy Institute.

Grogger, Jeffrey. 2002. "The Effects of Civil Gang Injunctions on Reported Violent Crime: Evidence From Los Angeles County." *Journal of Law & Economics* 4: 69–90.

Grossman, Jean Baldwin, and Joseph P. Tierney. 1998. "Does Mentoring Work? An Impact Study of the Big Brothers Big Sisters Program." *Evaluation Review* 22: 404–426.

Hartnett, Dan, Alan Carr, Elena Hamilton, and Gary O'Reilly. 2017. "The Effectiveness of Functional Family Therapy: A Meta-Analysis." *Family Process* 56: 607–619.

Hennigan, Karen M., and David Sloane. 2013. "Improving Civil Gang Injunctions: How Implementation Can Affect Gang Dynamics, Crime, and Violence." *Criminology & Public Policy* 12(1):7–41.

Howell, James C. 2015. *The History of Street Gangs in the United States: Their Origins and Transformations*. Lanham, MD: Lexington Books.

Howell, James C., and Elizabeth Griffiths. 2019. *Gangs in America's Communities*. Thousand Oaks, CA: Sage.

Jolliffe, Darrick, and David P. Farrington. 2008. *The Influence of Mentoring on Reoffending*. Stockholm, Sweden: Swedish National Council on Crime Prevention.

Klein, Malcolm W. 1971. *Street Gangs and Street Workers*. Englewood Cliffs, NJ: Prentice-Hall.

Klein, Malcolm W., and Cheryl Maxson. 2006. *Street Gang Patterns and Policies*. New York, NY: Oxford University Press.

Kremer, Michael, and Dan Levy. 2008. "Peer Effects and Alcohol Use Among College Students." *Journal of Economic Perspectives* 22(3):189–206.

Laub, John H., and Robert J. Sampson. 2003. *Shared Beginnings, Divergent Lives: Delinquent Boys to Age 70*. Cambridge, MA: Harvard University Press.

Mallett, Christopher A., and Miyuki Fukushima Tedor. 2019. *Juvenile Delinquency: Pathways and Prevention*. Thousand Oaks, CA: Sage.

Markides, Kyriacos C., and Steven F. Cohn. 1982. "External Conflict/Internal Cohesion: A Reevaluation of an Old Theory." *American Sociological Review* 47: 88–98.

Matsueda, Ross L., and Kathleen Anderson. 1998. "The Dynamics of Delinquent Peers and Delinquent Behavior." *Criminology* 36: 269–308.

Matz, Adam K. 2014. "Commentary: Do Youth Mentoring Programs Work? A Review of the Empirical Literature." *Journal of Juvenile Justice* 3(2):83–101.

Maxson, Cheryl. 2011. "Street Gangs." Pp. 158–182 in *Crime and Public Policy*, edited by J. Q. Wilson and J. Petersilia. New York, NY: Oxford University Press.

Maxson, Cheryl L., and Kristy N. Matsuda. 2012. "Gang Delinquency." Pp. 246–271 in *The Oxford Handbook of Juvenile Crime and Juvenile Justice*, edited by B. C. Feld and D. M. Bishop. New York, NY: Oxford University Press.

McCord, Joan. 2003. "Cures That Harm: Unanticipated Outcomes and Crime Prevention Programs." *Annals of the American Academy of Political & Social Science* 587: 16–30.

Melde, Chris. 2013. "The Practicalities of Targeted Gang Interventions." *Criminology & Public Policy* 12(1):43–48.

National Gang Center. 2018. "Demographics: Age of Gang Members." Retrieved September 22, 2019 (https://www.nationalgangcenter.gov/survey-analysis/demographics).

National Institute of Justice. 2011. "What Is a Gang? Definitions." September 23, 2019 (https://www.nij.gov/topics/crime/gangs/pages/definitions.aspx).

Ngwe, Job E., Li C. Liu, Brian R. Flay, Eisuke Segawa, and Aban Aya Investigators. 2004. "Violence Prevention Among African American Adolscent Males." *American Journal of Health Behavior* 28(Suppl.):S24–S37.

Nieuwbeerta, Paul, Daniel Nagin, and Arjan Blokland. 2009. "Assessing the Impact of First-Time Imprisonment on Offenders' Subsequent Criminal Career Development: A Matched Samples Comparison." *Journal of Quantitative Criminology* 25(3):227–257. doi: 10.1007/s10940-009-9069-7.

Norris, Michael, Sarah Twill, and Chigon Kim. 2011. "Smells Like Teen Spirit: Evaluating a Midwestern Teen Court." *Crime & Delinquency* 57(2):199–221.

O'Donnell, Clifford R., Tony Lydgate, and Walter S. O. Fo. 1979. "The Buddy System: Review and Follow-Up." *Child Behavioral Therapy* 1: 161–169.

Parascandola, Rocco, and John Annese. 2019. "Three Charged in 2017 Killing of Brooklyn Gang Member." *New York Daily News*. July 3. Retrieved September 22, 2019 (https://www.nydailynews.com/new-york/nyc-crime/ny-three-men-busted-in-brooklyn-gang-member-killing-2017-20190703-fnlqgleip5crznh4xd7x36izoe-story.html).

Pepitone, Albert, and Robert Kleiner. 1957. "The Effects of Threat and Frustration on Group Cohesiveness." *Journal of Abnormal and Social Psychology* 54(2):192–199.

Ploeger, Matthew. 1997. "Youth Employment and Delinquency: Reconsidering a Problematic Relationship." *Criminology* 35: 659–675.

Pyrooz, David C. 2014. "'From Your First Cigarette to Your Last Dyin' Day': The Patterning of Gang Membership in the Life Course." *Journal of Quantitative Criminology* 30:349–372.

Pyrooz, David C., and Gary Sweeten. 2015. "Gang Membership Between Ages 5 and 17 Years in the United States." *Journal of Adolescent Health* 56: 414–419.

Pyrooz, David C., Jillian J. Turanovic, Scott H. Decker, and Jun Wu. 2016. "Taking Stock of the Relationship Between Gang Membership and Offending." *Criminal Justice & Behavior* 43(3):365–397.

Restivo, Emily, and Mark M. Lanier. 2015. "Measuring the Contextual Effects and Mitigating Factors of Labeling Theory." *Justice Quarterly* 32(1):116–141. doi: 10.1080/07418825.2012.756115.

Ritter, Nancy. 2009. "CeaseFire: A Public Health Approach to Reduce Shootings and Killings." *NIJ Journal.* November. Retrieved September 23, 2019 (https://www.nij.gov/journals/264/pages/ceasefire.aspx).

Rosenbaum, Dennis P., and Amie M. Schuck. 2012. "Comprehensive Community Partnerships for Preventing Crime." Pp. 226–246 in *The Oxford Handbook of Crime Prevention*, edited by B. C. Welsh and D. P. Farrington. New York, NY: Oxford University Press.

Staff, Jeremy, and Christopher Uggen. 2003. "The Fruits of Good Work: Early Work Experiences and Adolescent Deviance." *Journal of Research in Crime and Delinquency* 40: 263–290.

Sullivan, Christopher J., and Darrick Jolliffe. 2012. "Peer Influence, Mentoring, and the Prevention of Crime." Pp. 207–225 in *The Oxford Handbook of Crime Prevention*, edited by B. C. Welsh and D. P. Farrington. New York, NY: Oxford University Press.

Sweeten, Gary. 2006. "Who Will Graduate? Disruption of High School Education by Arrest and Court Involvement." *Justice Quarterly* 23: 462–480.

Thornberry, Terence P., Brook Kearley, Denise C. Gottfredson, Molly P. Slothower, Deanna N. Devlin, and Jamie J. Fader. 2018. "Reducing Crime Among Youth at Risk for Gang Involvement: A Randomized Trial." *Criminology & Public Policy* 17(4):953–989.

Thornberry, Terence P., Alan J. Lizotte, Marvin D. Krohn, Margaret Farnworth, and Sung Joon Jang. 1994. "Delinquent Peers, Beliefs, and Delinquent Behavior: A Longitudinal Test of Interactional Theory." *Criminology* 32(1):47–83.

Tobler, Nancy S., Terri Lessard, Diana Marshall, Peter Ochshorn, and Michael Roona. 1999. "Effectiveness of School-Based Drug Prevention Programs for Marijuana Use." *School Psychology International* 20: 105–137.

Tolan, Patrick, David Henry, Michael Schoeny, and Arin Bass. 2008. *Mentoring Interventions to Affect Juvenile Delinquency and Associated Problems*. Oslo, Norway: Campbell Systematic Reviews.

Tolan, Patrick, David Henry, Michael Schoeny, Arin Bass, Peter Lovegrove, and Emily Nichols. 2013. *Mentoring Interventions to Affect Juvenile Delinquency and Associated Problems: A Systematic Review*. Oslo, Norway: Campbell Collaboration.

Uggen, Christopher, and Sara Wakefield. 2008. "What Have We Learned From Longitudinal Studies of Adolescent Employment and Crime?" Pp. 191–219 in *The Long View of Crime: A Synthesis of Longitudinal Research*, edited by A. Liberman. New York, NY: Springer.

U.S. Census Bureau. 2018. "Annual Estimates of the Resident Population for Selected Age Groups by Sex for the United States, States, Counties, and Puerto Rico Commonwealth and Municipios: April 1, 2010 to July 1, 2017." Retrieved September 22, 2019 (https://factfinder.census.gov/faces/tableservices/jsf/pages/productview.xhtml?src=bkmk).

Vose, Brenda, and Kelly Vannan. 2013. "A Jury of Your Peers: Recidivism Among Teen Court Participants." *Journal of Juvenile Justice* 3(1):97–109.

Warr, Mark. 1993. "Parents, Peers, and Delinquency." *Social Forces* 72: 247–264.

Warr, Mark. 2002. *Companions in Crime: The Social Aspects of Criminal Conduct*. New York, NY: Cambridge University Press.

Warr, Mark. 2007. "The Tangled Web: Delinquency, Deception, and Parental Attachment." *Journal of Youth and Adolescence* 36: 607–622.

Warr, Mark. 2012. "The Social Side of Delinquent Behavior." Pp. 226–245 in *The Oxford Handbook of Juvenile Crime and Juvenile Justice*, edited by B. C. Feld and D. M. Bishop. New York, NY: Oxford University Press.

Welsh, Brandon C. 2012. "Delinquency Prevention." Pp. 395–415 in *The Oxford Handbook of Juvenile Crime and Juvenile Justice*, edited by B. C. Feld and D. M. Bishop. New York, NY: Oxford University Press.

Wu, Jun, and David Pyrooz. 2016. "Uncovering the Pathways Between Gang Membership and Violent Victimization." *Journal of Quantitative Criminology* 32(4):531–559.

PART IV

TERTIARY CRIME PREVENTION

Focus on Criminal Justice

11

POLICING AND CRIME PREVENTION

The police are the most visible and familiar of the three branches of the criminal justice system (the other two being courts and corrections). Relatively few of us have had to go to court for a criminal offense, and even fewer have experienced supervision in the correctional system (although in the United States, this figure is larger than in other, similar nations). But most of us have had interactions with police officers, whether that be in our schools, on the roads after traveling a bit too fast, or at an event. The police are the "first line" of defense in the criminal justice system; they are who we call when we are in trouble or after we have been victims of crime. Entire industries have been built up around police as a form of entertainment, from the show *Cops* to fictional police procedurals.

In this chapter, we describe the effectiveness of police in terms of reducing or preventing criminal conduct. We should note that preventing crime is only *one* aspect of policing. Police are also responsible for responding to crime when it occurs and for helping keep order in our neighborhoods, schools, and events. Increasingly, with the advent of community-oriented policing (which we discuss further below), police are involved in more routine, everyday aspects of life in communities, building trust and legitimacy with citizens.

In the 1970s and 1980s, the idea that the police were effective at reducing or preventing crime came under fire. The political scientist James Q. Wilson (1985:61) wrote, "The average citizen thinks of the police as an organization primarily concerned with preventing crime and catching criminals. . . .

Chapter Outline

- History of Policing
- Deterrence Theory and Policing
- What Does Not Work?
  - Broken Windows Policing
- What Seems to Work?
  - Community-Oriented Policing
  - Problem-Oriented Policing
  - Hot Spot Policing
- Controversies in Police Crime Prevention
- Conclusion

Learning Questions

1. What is deterrence?
2. Which types of policing do not work?
3. Which types of policing strategies are effective in preventing crime?
4. Which types of policing strategies are effective in reducing crime?
5. What are hot spots?
6. What are some controversies associated with policing?

[But] this public conception is misleading." Most of their work, he argued, was about maintaining order and responding to crime. Some degree of crime prevention could be gained by "massive" (p. 73) increases in numbers of police in the streets, but the evidence was not strong that police had a large effect on preventing crime.

Theorists Michael Gottfredson and Travis Hirschi (1990) went further, arguing that the police do not do much to affect crimes (other than being called after the fact). "The police are simply not a factor in the overwhelming number of robberies, burglaries, assaults, homicides, thefts or drug deals. . . . In the bulk of these offenses, the offender does not know or care about the probability of being observed by the police" (p. 270). In other words, even if police presence was high in particular areas, certain individuals would go ahead and commit the crimes they intended to commit since their behavior was driven by something other than a rational calculation (e.g., impulsivity).

Part of this lack of faith in policing was theoretical, but part of it was also empirical. Research had emerged during this time showing that varying police numbers did not seem to affect crime rates (Levine 1975). One well-known study was conducted in Kansas City, seeking to determine whether increasing the number of police on patrols would decrease crime. The logic was simple: The more police present in a particular area, the more likely that they would be seen and thus able to deter would-be offenders from committing crimes. This was thought to be the primary way the police prevent crime. Yet the idea had not been subject to strong empirical evaluation. The Kansas City Preventive Patrol Experiment did just that. **Police beats** (areas in which police patrol) were randomly assigned to control conditions—reactive only (police did not patrol but did respond to crime) and proactive beats, in which more police than usual were patrolling the area.

What did the findings show? Interestingly, there were no differences in victimization reports across the conditions, and minimal differences in other reported crimes to police. And the differences that were found "showed no consistent pattern" in terms of whether the proactive beats fared better (Kelling et al. 1974). In addition, citizen fear of crime was barely affected by changing the level of patrol in particular areas (Kelling et al. 1974). This was a truly stunning set of results that called into question just how much the police can affect crime.

Since that time, the science of policing has advanced tremendously. Not only that, but in the 1990s, crime in America began to decline, and some attributed it to the new strategies that police were using (Kelling and Bratton 1998; Levitt 2004). In addition, new technologies such as crime mapping have allowed police and researchers to pinpoint areas that are "hot" with criminal activity so police can more effectively deploy resources.

In this chapter, we discuss crime prevention from the standpoint of the police. We begin with a brief history of policing and then discuss ways police can prevent crime from occurring in the first instance and ways police can prevent reoccurrence of criminal activity.

HISTORY OF POLICING

Some argue that the foundation for the role of police in preventing crime was laid by Henry Fielding in 1751. In that year, Fielding published *Enquiry Into the Causes of the Late Increase of Robbers* (Dodsworth 2008). Fielding, just a couple of years prior, had formed a band of men to help identify offenders in the community. They were located at Bow Street, in London, and later called the Bow Street Runners. While initially these men were not paid, Fielding would come to argue that they should be paid for their work, ushering in the era of a paid police force (Beattie 2012).

The first "official" police force was created in the early 1800s in London. The officers of the **Metropolitan Police**, under the leadership of Robert Peel, were militaristic in appearance, with sharp uniforms and billy clubs, and a hat that also functioned as a step to stand on "for peering over walls" (Miller 1999:33). Peel developed nine principles of policing, which proved influential for the establishment of a professional police force in England and elsewhere. These principles stated in part that police exist to prevent crime, that public approval and cooperation is vital, that the police should be unbiased, and that decreases in crime should be the test of how effective the police are in their jobs (Williams 2003). Thus, from the time when police were first organized, crime prevention has been a primary goal. However, this does not mean policing in any form was nonexistent prior to this time. In fact, in the United States, constables were charged with bringing suspects to court. In addition, a form of self-policing, called **night watch**, was common, in which community members took turns supervising towns (Monkkonen 1992). The idea was that if something, such as a crime, happened in town overnight, the night watch would see it and warn others. Unfortunately, some claimed "that they slept, used their noisy rattles to warn off potential offenders, and ran from real dangers" (Monkkonen 1992:549).

After the establishment of the Metropolitan Police in 1829, similar formal organized agencies followed in the United States. According to Monkkonen (1992), these formal agencies were much better equipped to fight crime than the informal watches. Specifically, they were sophisticated agencies with a clear organizational structure, which meant that officers knew who to report to and with whom ultimate authority rested. In addition, the police were no longer part of the court system, which meant that they could focus on criminal, rather than civil, activity. Police were also uniformed and easily recognizable, which sped up time to reporting. Finally, Monkkonen argues that one of the goals of the police—as opposed to the informal watches—was to prevent crime, to take actions to make communities safer, not just react when something happened.

In the United States, police agencies spread out across large and small cities. Scholars of police recognize several eras of policing (see Figure 11.1), including the **political era** in the late 1800s, when police were entrenched in local politics, and the **professional era** in the early 1900s, when reformers such as August Vollmer strove to make police more accountable, educated, and qualified. The last era has been called the **community policing era** (Greene 2000; Walker 1998).

Police in America have often been linked to varying degrees of controversy. In the early 1990s, the acquittal of a group of officers caught on videotape beating a man named

Figure 11.1 Stages of Policing

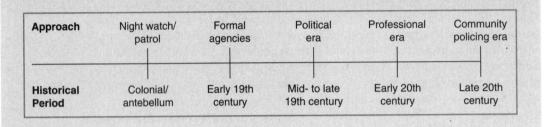

Approach	Night watch/ patrol	Formal agencies	Political era	Professional era	Community policing era
Historical Period	Colonial/ antebellum	Early 19th century	Mid- to late 19th century	Early 20th century	Late 20th century

Rodney King for an extended period of time led to a sustained riot in Los Angeles (Sastry and Bates 2017). The use of police as an instrument of racial social control has deep roots in the United States, with the slave patrol—a precursor to police—serving as a method of ensuring slaves did not wander or try to escape (Spruill 2016). Recently, highly publicized cases of police shooting unarmed black citizens resulted in much unrest and a social movement called **Black Lives Matter**. Black Lives Matter, and other forms of protest, including NFL players kneeling during the national anthem, sought to hold police accountable for perceived racial discrimination. These actions were opposed by those who believed they were anti-American and unfair to police.

Thus, policing has a long and intriguing history in the United States and abroad. It is important to keep in mind that policing has different connotations and implications for different groups as well. Research indicates that, overall, people are confident in the police and feel that they do a good job protecting us. For example, a 2016 Gallup poll found that 76% of Americans have "a great deal of respect" for police (McCarthy 2016). However, this overall pattern masks disparities by race. Whites overwhelmingly support the police; people of color, however, are more circumspect. That same Gallup poll found that 80% of whites but only 67% of people of color said they respect police in their area. In fact, some work has suggested that racial prejudice is linked to whites' support of police use of force (Barkan and Cohn 1998).

DETERRENCE THEORY AND POLICING

One way police may prevent crimes is to act as a deterrent. Would-be criminals know police are or may be in the area and thus decide not to commit a crime they may have been contemplating. Even the not seriously criminal among us intuitively understand this logic. Who has not slowed down upon seeing a parked state trooper on the side of the highway? **Deterrence theory** (see Chapter 3) has a long history in criminology and is associated with the classical and neoclassical schools of criminology. These schools of thought are based on the premise that humans are rational creatures who weigh (if implicitly) the costs and benefits of any course of action before taking it (Schram and

Tibbetts 2018). Thus, to prevent crime, the cost/benefit calculus must be tipped in the direction of not choosing such courses of action. Police presence or operations in particular areas may be such a tipping mechanism, according to the theory.

Deterrence theory in criminology has an interesting history. After its initial appearance with the classical school in the 18th century, it was pushed aside in favor of the **positive school** of criminology, which argued that rational choices were not the primary reason for crime. Rather, outside factors (sometimes beyond the control of the individual) were the cause of the behavior. Deterrence theory made a comeback in the 1970s with the rise of the neoclassical school of criminology, which brought back the idea of choice and decision-making. Early deterrent research focused on simple analyses of whether harsher punishments in particular areas led to less criminal behavior. For several reasons (including the inability to parse out whether the harsher punishments led to different levels of crime or vice versa), this research was not very conclusive. Some scholars were not optimistic that costs/benefits could tell us much about offending, particularly in the context of murder and the death penalty (Zeisel 1976). If people really weigh the costs and benefits of committing a crime, so the logic goes, then they will be less likely to commit murder in places where they could be put to death. Research was and continues to be equivocal on this point (Nagin and Pepper 2012).

The Kansas City Preventive Patrol study in the mid-1970s seemed to indicate that the police can have a minimal effect on crime before it occurs. Other research seemed to confirm this finding (Wellford 1974). Some scholars provided sophisticated equations to model the effect of police patrols on crime detection. But in terms of direct deterrence (the presence of police stopping a would-be criminal by removing the opportunity to commit a crime), Riccio (1974:216) argued that "police patrol at the levels most departments operate poses very little direct deterrence and the increase in direct deterrence caused by doubling the patrol force might be insignificant." The explanation for this finding seemed to be that the police, to prevent a crime, must be visible to would-be offenders, requiring them to be in all places where crimes may occur, which is clearly not possible. Research on deterrence and the criminal justice system overall in the mid-1970s was simply not convincing (Nagin 1975).

Yet scholarship on deterrence in the late 1970s and early 1980s found that criminals can be deterred and the criminal justice system can play a role in this process (Blumstein, Cohen, and Nagin 1978; Cook 1980). Cook (1980:223–224) expanded on this logic, with respect to police: "If the police are seen frequently in an area, potential criminals may be persuaded that there is a high likelihood of arrest in that area due to presumed police response time and the chance that they will happen on the scene while a crime is in progress." While he acknowledged the null effects in Kansas City, he noted several other studies that seemed to show police can deter crime. By 1992, Lawrence Sherman's review noted that much had been learned about how police can be most effective, such as focusing on the places in which crime is concentrated. Yet he admitted that the research on how much the police can reduce crime was mixed. But there was more evidence that police could reduce crime than existed in the past. One particular strategy Sherman noted was called "hot spots" policing, in which officers would concentrate their efforts on small locations where crime was high. We will discuss this in more detail later.

WHAT DOES NOT WORK?

Today, we have a better idea of what works in policing to reduce crime. At the same time, we have a good idea of what does not work. One interesting strategy has to do with domestic violence. Prior to the 1980s, domestic violence was viewed quite differently than it is today. Some felt that it was a "family" issue, not best dealt with by the criminal justice system. Social movements helped change this narrative, and then discussion turned to what *was* the best method for preventing family violence.

Sherman and his collaborator, Richard Berk, conducted an influential study to try to answer this question. Using random selection, they tested whether mandatory arrest after a domestic violence allegation would prevent recurrence of such violence. When police were called to a home due to this type of allegation, they were assigned to one of three conditions: (1) mandatory arrest, (2) mediation, or (3) removing the offender from the home temporarily. Their results showed the first condition reduced later offending (Sherman and Berk 1984).

So does mandatory arrest work? It turns out, not in general. Studies were conducted to replicate the Sherman and Berk experiment, but their findings suggested that mandatory arrest is not a one-size-fits-all solution. For example, some studies showed mandatory arrest did not reduce subsequent offending; others showed it did for particular subgroups (white, married, employed) (Mills 1998).

In the *What Works* report to Congress, Sherman (1997) identified four strategies that do not appear effective in preventing crime: First, simply adding more officers to be deployed when called; second, random patrols that are not directed at specific areas; third, reactive arrests; and fourth, community policing alone lacked evidence that they reduce crime. These ineffective approaches to policing are what Weisburd and Eck (2004:44) refer to as the **Standard Model**. Practices falling under the Standard Model include "such strategies as increasing the size of police agencies, random patrol across all parts of the community, rapid response to calls for service, generally applied follow-up investigations, and generally applied intensive enforcement and arrest policies."

Broken Windows Policing

One somewhat controversial method of policing that does not fall within the scope of standard approaches is called *broken windows*, *disorder*, or *aggressive order maintenance policing*. These are not identical strategies, and there are important differences among them, but they all focus on attempting to reduce crime by paying particular attention to smaller issues like vandalism, graffiti, or turnstile hopping in the subway. The idea is that disorder (broken windows) leads to the message that no one cares about the area, and crime will ensue.

Braga, Welsh, and Schnell (2015) conducted a meta-analysis of disorder policing evaluations and found that they do reduce crime somewhat. Community-oriented problem-solving policing techniques, in which police integrate themselves into a neighborhood and become partners with the community, appear to work when targeting disorder. What is clear is that aggressive order strategies do not, with an average effect size of only .06. Aggressive order maintenance policing does seek to reduce disorder but does so in a way that may be alienating or downright upsetting to community members. Certain groups may feel targeted and thus become hostile toward the police (RAND n.d.).

Currently, the Center for Evidence Based Crime Policy at George Mason University lists broken windows policing as unknown in terms of effectiveness (Center for Evidence-Based Crime Policy n.d.). As discussed in Chapter 6, broken windows theory is the idea that signs of disorder in a community can signal to would-be criminals that they can get away with criminal behavior. Consequently, broken windows policing is a strategy of policing that focuses on cleaning up disorder and minor offenses in an effort to reduce more serious crime. This brand of policing, though, has not been without controversy. One study found that while disorder does lead to fear of crime among the populace—suggesting that if police can reduce disorder, they will reduce fear of crime—police actions actually increase fear of crime (Hinkle and Weisburd 2008). A recent review concluded that disorder does not increase aggression in neighborhoods, which puts a damper on the key mechanism proposed by the theory (O'Brien, Farrell, and Welsh 2019).

Others have criticized broken windows policing as discriminatory toward disadvantaged social groups and as having minimal empirical support (Collins 2007; Harcourt 2001). One reason broken windows theory may be associated with discrimination is that aggressive order maintenance policing—an offshoot of broken windows strategies that we feel is distinct from general broken windows approaches—may be disproportionately targeted toward disadvantaged groups. For example, Fagan and Davies (2000:457) conclude that "policing is not about disorderly places, nor about improving the quality of life, but about policing poor people in poor places." Other research has shown that these policing strategies can reduce police legitimacy (Gau and Brunson 2010).

A well-known tragic case—while not typical of order maintenance approaches—illustrates what can go wrong with them. In the summer of 2014, Eric Garner, an African American male, was placed in a choke hold by a New York City police officer who was tasked with policing quality-of-life issues (such as sales of loose cigarettes). Garner was videotaped in the hold, pleading with the officers that he could not breathe. He later died from the encounter (Goodman 2018; Sisak 2019).

Certain approaches to reduce substance use among youths are also known not to work. Among these are the Drug Abuse Resistance Education (D.A.R.E.) program. While D.A.R.E. takes place in the school setting, it is a police-led program. Numerous meta-analyses have indicated that D.A.R.E. simply does not reduce drug-using behavior on the part of students (Ennett et al. 1994; West and O'Neal 2004). One of the reasons that D.A.R.E. may have been ineffective, according to some, is that it "exaggerated" the ill effects of certain drugs such as marijuana (Lopez 2014). Anecdotally, one of your authors recalls when "Officer Friendly" would come to his school to educate students about drugs as part of D.A.R.E. It was a fun day (because it meant less work!) but not one his classmates tended to take seriously.

WHAT SEEMS TO WORK?

There is now substantial evidence that police can effectively reduce crime, contrary to earlier pessimistic conclusions. As mentioned above, in the 1990s and 2000s, some research began to indicate that new police approaches and strategies had a hand in the crime decline that began in the early part of that decade. Franklin Zimring's (2007) book on the crime decline in the United States argues that there are two ways policing could have affected crime rates over time: (1) through an increase in police numbers (as was called for in President Clinton's 1994 Federal Crime Bill) and (2) through improvements in police strategies. He was not convinced by the evidence on the first possibility and argued the differences in strategies vary so widely across the country that improved approaches likely did not affect national crime rates. However, he wrote that place-based changes may have led to crime decreases in those areas (e.g., New York).

Community-Oriented Policing

One method that has gained popularity is called *community-oriented policing*, or COP. This, recall, is the label for the third era of policing. The idea was that police should be more integrated within their communities, forge ties with the citizens, and build partnerships rather than being seen as outside invaders. As Sherman (1997) wrote, COP was a response to the fear that police had become divorced from those who most need protection. The police car patrol, in which police officers would simply drive around a community and have little direct contact with citizens, was replaced by the foot patrol.

Sherman suggested that COP may reduce crime in four ways:

- By increasing legitimacy of police in the eyes of the community
- By increasing community knowledge about crime
- By using the community as a source of information for the police
- By encouraging neighborhood watches

Contradicting the Campbell Collaboration report referenced in Chapter 6, Sherman argued that neighborhood watches are ineffective. The idea of community policing leading to improved legitimacy and of using the public to inform police Sherman marks as "promising." The evidence that COP can work by informing the public about crime is not supportive of crime prevention effects. COP, while perhaps not reducing crime, does seem to positively affect views toward the police (Gill et al. 2014).

Problem-Oriented Policing

A perhaps more well-accepted approach is called **problem-oriented policing**, or POP. POP as an approach emerged from the work of the 2018 Stockholm Symposium

Award winner in criminology, Herman Goldstein, in the late 1970s. To effectively reduce crime, Goldstein suggested police engage in a process of "identifying . . . problems in more precise terms, researching each problem, documenting the nature of the current police response, assessing the adequacy of existing authority and resources, engaging in a broad exploration of alternatives to present responses, weighing the merits of these alternatives, and choosing from among them" (Goldstein 1979, as cited in Braga 2008a:1–2).

Sherman (1997:8–30) argued two decades ago that "tests of [the problem-oriented policing] hypothesis are generally more positive than the tests of community policing." He reviewed two strategies under POP, addressing "gun carrying" and "separating potential victims and offenders," and found the former to have more evidence than the latter.

POP has gained further support since Sherman's (1997) assessment. In one randomized trial, Braga and colleagues (1999) examined the effect of a program in New Jersey that identified places with high rates of violent crime and used the well-known **SARA** approach, which stands for *scan*, *analyze*, *respond*, and *assess*. Each place is analyzed closely for the reasons behind and types of crime, and solutions are attempted. In this project, 56 high-crime areas were matched with 28 control areas. Of the high-crime areas, 28 were randomized to receive treatment. The responses differed across the areas but often resembled disorder policing—cleaning up the areas. The evaluation of the project showed both disorder and crime were reduced in treatment areas.

POP and related strategies have now been evaluated enough to have been subject to systematic reviews. Weisburd and colleagues (2010), in a Campbell Collaboration report, found that POP strategies did reduce crime and disorder, but the effect was not altogether large.

Hot Spot Policing

POP sometimes uses a form of policing that relies on the identification of hot spots (much like the Braga et al., 1999, study did). Hot spot policing recognizes that, as is the case for individuals, crime is clustered within particular places. In other words, there are some areas in which crimes are much more likely to occur. This idea can be traced to pioneering work by researchers such as Lawrence Sherman, who, along with his colleagues, found that 50.4% of police calls came from just 3.3% of addresses and intersections in Minneapolis, Minnesota (Sherman, Gartin, and Buerger 1989). The clustering was even more extreme for certain crimes such as robbery, where all 4,166 robbery calls were from 2.2% of the total areas.

The concept of "hot spots" is so ingrained in criminology today that at the annual meeting of the American Society of Criminology, researchers were once treated to a rock show put on by a band called, you guessed it, the Hot Spots, featuring criminologists Lawrence Sherman, Alex Piquero, Brenda Blackwell, and Wayne Osgood, among others. Unfortunately, the band has broken up.

How much more efficient, then, to deploy police in those areas rather than in random patrols? Braga, Papachristos, and Hureau (2012:9) describe the logic of identifying characteristics of places that facilitate crime and then addressing them this way:

For example, a poorly lit street corner with an abandoned building, located near a major thoroughfare, provides an ideal location for a drug market. The lack of proper lighting, an abundance of "stash" locations around the derelict property, a steady flow of potential customers on the thoroughfare, and a lack of informal social control (termed defensive ownership) at the place generates an attractive opportunity for drug sellers. In many such cases, the police spend considerable time and effort arresting sellers without noticeably impacting the drug trade. The compelling criminal opportunities at the place attract sellers and buyers, and thus sustain the market. If the police want to be more efficient at disrupting the market, this suggests they should focus on the features of the place which cause the drug dealing to cluster at that particular location

In **hot spot policing**, various tactics are used to address the clustering of crime in particular places. Hot spot policing is premised on the theory that crime clusters in particular locations. This is likely because there are areas in which crimes are more likely to happen, due to the characteristics of those locations. Research has found that places that have been victimized (e.g., by a burglary) are more likely to be victimized later, and often by the same offender(s) (Bernasco 2008). So if crime clusters in particular areas, it makes sense to have police focus their attention on these areas, rather than randomly patrol neighborhoods and cities. But does it reduce crime?

Braga (2005) reviewed randomized trials of hot spot policing, finding five such studies. Four of those studies indicated that such policing tactics can reduce crime, with a mean effect size of .35. Braga and colleagues' (2012:13) Campbell Collaboration review included "traditional tactics such as directed patrol and heightened levels of traffic enforcement as well as alternative strategies such as aggressive disorder enforcement and problem-oriented policing." Their review found that hot spot policing reduced crime somewhat (effect size = .23) but also that crime was not forced "just around the corner," which is called displacement. In other words, focused crime prevention approaches did not simply move crime hot spots from one place to another. In addition, they noted that community members were positive toward the approaches but that caution should be used so the tactics do not become too aggressive.

Figure 11.2 shows a hot spot map created with mapping software. Software such as ArcGIS allows users to layer data files over geographic areas to indicate where, for example, crimes are concentrated. Users can specify different rules to identify what a hot spot is and how it is illustrated. The map in Figure 11.2 shows Washington, D.C., and plots the number of homicides. As can be seen, the more homicides, the more "hot" the map. Hot spots are found in the southeast and mid-south sections of the map.

An additional way hot spot scholarship has advanced crime prevention knowledge is through forecasting. In brief, forecasting involves using statistical models to predict where crime will be concentrated, or how much crime a particular area will have in the future. In 2017, the National Institute of Justice offered a challenge to researchers to come up with the best prediction for hot spots covering various crime types. One of the top prediction approaches was submitted by George Mohler and Michael Porter (2018). It is likely that future developments in this area will improve prediction and forecasting even further, resulting in more crime-reducing benefits.

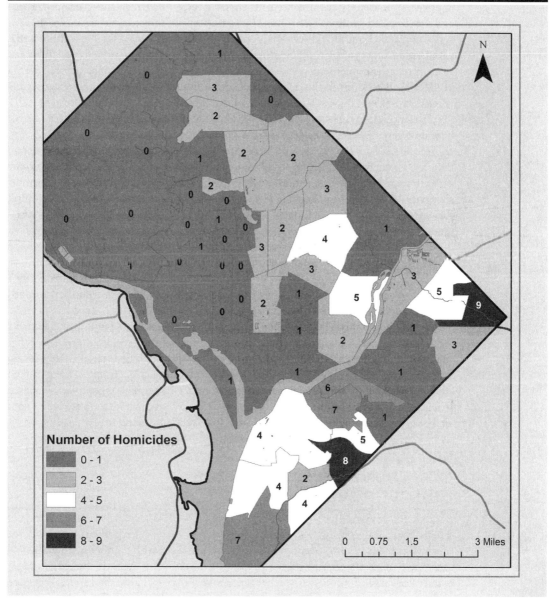

Figure 11.2   2017 Homicides in Washington, D.C.

Number of Homicides
- 0 - 1
- 2 - 3
- 4 - 5
- 6 - 7
- 8 - 9

0   0.75   1.5   3 Miles

Source: Map produced by and used with permission from David Mazeika.

In Telep and Weisburd's (2016:151–153) review of reviews, the authors identified several other strategies that "work" to reduce crime. These include focused deterrence strategies, strategies to reduce illegal possession and carrying of firearms, drug law enforcement, police patrols to prevent drunk driving, and intensive police programs to reduce traffic accidents (see also Telep and Weisburd 2012). With respect to the first approach, "focused deterrence," they discussed a review by Braga and Weisburd (2012) and the so-called **pulling levers** strategy. In this type of policing, the goal is to prevent crime via "understanding underlying crime-producing dynamics and conditions that sustain recurring crime problems and implementing an appropriately focused blended strategy of law enforcement, community mobilization, and social service actions" (Braga 2014:4174). The levers in this approach refer to different strategies used to reduce crime (Braga 2008b). As can be seen from this definition, pulling levers is a new form of POP.

Braga (2008b) reported on one example of pulling levers POP in Stockton, California. There, gun crime had been traced to gang wars, and a strategy was devised to address these issues that was tailored to the particular context in Stockton. The program that developed, called Operation Peacekeeper, worked like this: First, a unit within the police department was assigned to deal exclusively with gang crime. Second, partnerships were formed across organizations that deal with gang crime and violence. Third, social services were deployed so that youths had other options (e.g., jobs, education assistance). "The Operation Peacekeeper pulling levers focused deterrence strategy involved deterring violent behavior by chronic gang offenders by reaching out directly to gangs, saying explicitly that gun violence would no longer be tolerated, and backing that message by 'pulling every lever' legally available when violence occurred (Kennedy, 1997, p. 461)" (Braga 2008b:335). Braga's evaluation indicated that murders using guns decreased after the implementation of Operation Peacekeeper.

In sum, today much is known about what strategies police can employ to effectively reduce and prevent crime. Random, unfocused approaches (e.g., traditional policing that relies on simply having police "out there") do not appear to be effective. Neither do simple educational approaches for drug prevention. Focused, geographically restricted strategies seeking to work *with* the community on specific problems, however, do appear to work. As more is discovered and new technologies are implemented to aid in the fight against crime, the effectiveness of the police will likely only increase.

CONTROVERSIES IN POLICE CRIME PREVENTION

The police, as we have discussed in this chapter, play many roles in the community, one of which is reducing or preventing crime. They also work with community members to accomplish other shared goals such as "improving the quality of life in our neighborhoods," as indicated on the homepage of the Bangor, Maine, Police Department website. Police are a vital part of community safety, which includes fear and disorder. Police are supposed to make each community member feel safe and secure. Yet certain controversies and strategies have had the opposite effect. Above, we discussed the cases of Rodney King and recent police shootings of unarmed African Americans that have caused unrest and protests.

Police **use of force** refers to police officers using their hands or weapons to elicit compliance from citizens. For example, a police officer might grab a suspect or might need to use a Taser to stop someone from resisting. Or a police officer, in the most extreme form of use of force, may be compelled to use a weapon, such as their gun, to protect themselves or the public. Several factors influence use of force, including whether an agency requires officers to prepare a form on their use of force or not (Alpert and MacDonald 2001) and whether they are in areas marked by higher homicide numbers and more disadvantage (unemployment, poverty, female-headed households, etc.; Terrill and Reisig 2003).

The use of force (along with other actions taken by police) involves quick decision-making. Often, police must decide what to do within seconds, which complicates analysis of these decisions. In addition, bias may creep in when information concerning what is the most appropriate course of action is limited. Do police use force indiscriminately or disproportionately against particular groups? Research on **implicit bias** would suggest that our unconscious tendencies to believe certain groups are more likely to be dangerous (Welch 2007) mean police may perceive black males as more threatening and thus use more force against them even when unwarranted. Research on shootings is somewhat mixed. Some studies find racial bias in decisions to shoot, but others do not (Correll et al. 2014). Race seems to predict lesser forms of use of force more clearly (Fryer 2016; Willits and Makin 2018). Obviously, demographic factors should not influence whether force is used. To the extent that force is used or perceived to be used differentially by race, the police may be seen as less legitimate in the eyes of particular groups.

Another controversy with respect to policing involves lack of attention to criminal events. Research has indicated that reporting practices by police are not consistent (Berger et al. 2015; Black 1970). For example, research has found that the social status of the individual reporting a possible crime matters with respect to whether police make an official report. In addition, **clearance rates**, or the proportion of crimes known to police that have reached resolution (e.g., the offender was arrested or detained), vary widely. Keel, Jarvis, and Muirhead (2009) found a number of factors predicted homicide clearance rates, including politics (positive), crime rates (positive), and the proportion of the area that is nonwhite (negative). For example, with respect to political factors, cooperation by prosecutors and medical examiners/coroners was associated with higher clearance rates. Another study found that racial inequality and fewer homicides predicted higher clearance rates (Borg and Parker 2001).

Finally, a concerning trend involves the police becoming **militarized**, or coming to resemble military organizations preparing for war (Kraska 2007). Peter Kraska has documented this militarizing trend of the police, noting that police work with the military and train together, often sharing weapons. Kraska and Kappeler (1997) found that "police paramilitary units" are increasing in the United States. These units, they argued, use military language and weapons, resemble military structures, and are used in ways that traditional police units are not. Police operating as war-making units clearly is inconsistent with the notion that they are part of the community, there to "serve and protect." Military units occupy "hostile" territories, engaging with enemies. The police cannot be part of the community while at once viewing parts of it as hostile combatants. Some have argued this has facilitated a "war against the underclass" (Meeks 2006:33).

The public is wary of this move toward militarizing the police. Fox, Moule, and Parry (2018) found that 58% of people surveyed opposed police militarization.

Table 11.1 What Works and Does Not Work in Police Crime Prevention

Approach/Strategy	Description
Does Not Work	
D.A.R.E.	Drug Abuse Resistance Education for schoolchildren
Random patrols	Police patrols not focused on particular areas or groups
Reactive arrests	Reactive rather than proactive policing strategies
Disorder/aggressive order maintenance policing	Disorderly policing without community elements
Does Work	
Focused deterrence	Deterrence focused on specific groups or areas
Problem-oriented policing	Policing strategies seeking to identify and address underlying causes of problems in particular areas
Hot spot policing	Policing focused on "hot spots" of crime
Pulling levers policing	Using every available resource to reduce crime and disorder in communities
Directed patrol	Patrols focused on particular times and places

However, the wariness that the public feels toward militarization is tied to how people feel about the police in general. For example, Moule, Fox, and Parry (2019) recently found that those who are cynical toward the law and who do not view the police with legitimacy feel that the police are more militarized than others do. And those who view the police with less legitimacy are less likely to support such militarization.

Clearly the work of the police is complex, involving sometimes competing interests. They must protect the community but do so in ways that do not undermine trust and legitimacy. They must, at times, make split-second decisions that can mean life or death. It is all the more important that research on various tactics or strategies be conducted to determine what works—whether "working" means reducing crime, fear, or disorder (see Table 11.1).

CONCLUSION

Of the three levels of the criminal justice system, the police are the most visible and the ones with which most people have had at least some contact. The police are the only part of the justice system that deals with the community prior to the commission of crimes.

In that sense, it may be reasonable to believe that the police, rather than the courts or corrections, are best positioned to prevent crime. In fact, the earliest forms of policing, including the night watch, were implemented with the idea that having eyes and ears on communities at night might deter would-be offenders. For much of the history of policing, it was generally assumed that the presence of police would be enough to deter criminals. So the random patrol was a staple of "traditional" policing. Then in the 1970s, researchers began to evaluate this model of policing, finding it was less effective than previously thought.

The 1970s and 1980s were a period of skepticism in terms of the ability of the police to prevent crime. Some flat out argued the police did not reduce crime, while others argued that the evidence was simply too inconsistent. That began to change in the following years, with a consistent evidence base now accumulated that tells us quite convincingly that the police *can* and *do* prevent crime. Not all forms of policing are equal, however. Strategies that focus on specific people, places, and problems, and that work in collaboration with the community are effective. Specifically, problem-oriented policing, hot spots policing, focused deterrence, strategies to reduce gun violence and drunk driving, drug-targeted policing, and directed/focused patrol have been found to reduce crime.

At the same time, several controversies in policing remain. Police cannot focus on reducing crime to the detriment of individual rights and community well-being. Aggressive policing and use of force can undermine legitimacy, particularly within certain groups. Some scholars have also identified worrisome trends toward police militarization. These trends may negatively affect the ability of the police to reduce crime and make the community feel safe. It is very likely that the future will see new forms of policing emerge, and it remains essential to evaluate them for not only their deterrent impact but their overall effect on the community.

SUMMARY

1. In historical context, modern policing organizations are a relatively new development.

2. There have been several eras of policing, and the institution continues to evolve to this day. These include the political, professional, and community policing eras.

3. There was a period of time when scholars doubted that the police could have a significant impact on crime. Their job, it was argued, was to respond to crime and to do all they could to catch the perpetrator, *after* a crime had been committed. Scholars such as Gottfredson and Hirschi suggested that it would be a waste of time to try to prevent crime via police strategies.

4. However, in the 1980s and 1990s, evidence started to accumulate that certain approaches can have an effect on crime. By the University of Maryland's 1997 *What Works* report to Congress, Sherman was able to identify several

types of policing that evidence indicated "worked," and others that were "promising."

5. Under the "what works" category, he included focused police patrolling, proactive arrests, and arrests of domestic violence offenders if they are employed. Community policing and problem-oriented policing were considered "promising." Since that time, we have learned more about what does not work (aggressive policing, D.A.R.E.) and what does reduce crime (hot spot policing, focused deterrence strategies).

6. What the strategies that work or are promising have in common appears to be police working with the community in ways that increase trust and legitimacy, and using strategies focused on people and places that have disproportionately high crime rates.

KEY TERMS

Black Lives Matter 240
clearance rates 249
community policing era 239
deterrence theory 240
hot spot policing 246
implicit bias 249

Metropolitan Police 239
militarized 249
night watch 239
police beats 238
political era 239
positive school 241

problem-oriented policing 244
professional era 239
pulling levers 248
SARA 245
Standard Model 242
use of force 248

REFERENCES

Alpert, Geoffrey P., and John M. MacDonald. 2001. "Police Use of Force: An Analysis of Organizational Characteristics." *Justice Quarterly* 18(2):393–409.

Barkan, Steven E., and Steven F. Cohn. 1998. "Racial Prejudice and Support by Whites for Police Use of Force: A Research Note." *Justice Quarterly* 15(4):743–753.

Beattie, J. M. 2012. *The First English Detectives: The Bow Street Runners and the Policing of London, 1750–1840*. New York, NY: Oxford University Press.

Berger, Ronald J., Marvin D. Free, Melissa Deller, and Patrick K. O'Brien. 2015. *Crime, Justice, and Society: An Introduction to Criminology*, 4th edition. Boulder, CO: Lynne Reinner.

Bernasco, Wim. 2008. "Them Again? Same-Offender Involvement in Repeat and Near Repeat Burglaries." *European Journal of Criminology* 5(4):411–431.

Black, Donald J. 1970. "Production of Crime Rates." *American Sociological Review* 35(4):733–748.

Blumstein, Alfred, Jacqueline Cohen, and Daniel Nagin. 1978. "Deterrence and Incapacitation." Washington, DC: National Academy of Sciences.

Borg, Marian J., and Karen F. Parker. 2001. "Mobilizing Law in Urban Areas: The Social

Structure of Homicide Clearance Rates." *Law and Society Review* 35(2):435–466.

Braga, Anthony A. 2005. "Hot Spots Policing and Crime Prevention: A Systematic Review of Randomized Controlled Trials." *Journal of Experimental Criminology* 1(3):317–342.

Braga, Anthony A. 2008a. *Problem-Oriented Policing and Crime Prevention*, 2nd edition. Monsey, NY: Willow Tree Press.

Braga, Anthony A. 2008b. "Pulling Levers Focused Deterrence Strategies and the Prevention of Gun Homicide." *Journal of Criminal Justice* 36(4):332–343.

Braga, Anthony A. 2014. "Pulling Levers Policing." Pp. 4174–4185 in *Encyclopedia of Criminology and Criminal Justice*, edited by Gerben Bruinsma and David Weisburd. New York, NY: Springer.

Braga, Anthony, Andrew Papachristos, and David Hureau. 2012. "Hot Spots Policing Effects on Crime." *Campbell Systematic Reviews* 8(8):1–96.

Braga, Anthony A., and David L. Weisburd. 2012. "The Effects of 'Pulling Levers' Focused Deterrence Strategies on Crime." *Campbell Systematic Reviews* 8(6).

Braga, Anthony A., David L. Weisburd, Elin J. Waring, Lorraine Green Mazerolle, William Spelman, and Francis Gajewski. 1999. "Problem-Oriented Policing in Violent Crime Places: A Randomized Controlled Experiment." *Criminology* 37(3):541–580.

Braga, Anthony A., Brandon C. Welsh, and Cory Schnell. 2015. "Can Policing Disorder Reduce Crime? A Systematic Review and Meta-Analysis." *Journal of Research in Crime and Delinquency* 52(4):567–588.

Center for Evidence-Based Crime Policy. N.d. "Broken Windows Policing." Retrieved September 27, 2019 (https://cebcp.org/evidence-based-policing/what-works-in-policing/research-evidence-review/broken-windows-policing/).

Collins, Reed. 2007. "Strolling While Poor: How Broken-Windows Policing Created a New Crime in Baltimore." *Georgetown Journal on Poverty Law & Policy* 14: 419–439.

Cook, Philip J. 1980. "Research in Criminal Deterrence: Laying the Groundwork for the Second Decade." *Crime and Justice* 2: 211–268.

Correll, Joshua, Sean M. Hudson, Steffanie Guillermo, and Debbie S. Ma. 2014. "The Police Officer's Dilemma: A Decade of Research on Racial Bias in the Decision to Shoot." *Social and Personality Psychology Compass* 8(5):201–213.

Dodsworth, Francis M. 2008. "The Idea of Police in Eighteenth-Century England: Discipline, Reformation, Superintendence, c. 1780–1800." *Journal of the History of Ideas* 69(4):583–604.

Ennett, Susan T., Nancy S. Tobler, Christopher L. Ringwalt, and Robert L. Flewelling. 1994. "How Effective Is Drug Abuse Resistance Education? A Meta-Analysis of Project DARE Outcome Evaluations." *American Journal of Public Health* 84(9):1394–1401.

Fagan, Jeffrey, and Garth Davies. 2000. "Street Stops and Broken Windows: Terry, Race, and Disorder in New York City." *Fordham Urban Law Journal* 28: 457–504.

Fox, Bryanna, Richard K. Moule Jr., and Megan M. Parry. 2018. "Categorically Complex: A Latent Class Analysis of Public Perceptions of Police Militarization." *Journal of Criminal Justice* 58: 33–46.

Fryer, Roland G., Jr. 2016. "An Empirical Analysis of Racial Differences in Police Use of Force."

No. 22399. Cambridge, MA: National Bureau of Economic Research.

Gau, Jacinta M., and Rod K. Brunson. 2010. "Procedural Justice and Order Maintenance Policing: A Study of Inner-City Young Men's Perceptions of Police Legitimacy." *Justice Quarterly* 27(2):255–279.

Gill, Charlotte, David Weisburd, Cody W. Telep, Zoe Vitter, and Trevor Bennett. 2014. "Community-Oriented Policing to Reduce Crime, Disorder and Fear and Increase Satisfaction and Legitimacy Among Citizens: A Systematic Review." *Journal of Experimental Criminology* 10(4):399–428.

Goldstein, Herman. 1979. "Improving Policing: A Problem-Oriented Approach." *Crime & Delinquency* 25(2):236–258.

Goodman, J. David. 2018. "Eric Garner Died in a Police Chokehold. Why Has the Inquiry Taken So Long?" *New York Times*. Retrieved September 27, 2019 (https://www.nytimes.com/2018/11/07/nyregion/eric-garner-trial-nypd.html).

Gottfredson, Michael, and Travis Hirschi. 1990. *A General Theory of Crime*. Stanford, CA: Stanford University Press.

Greene, Jack R. 2000. "Community Policing in America: Changing the Nature, Structure, and Function of the Police." *Criminal Justice* 3(3):299–370.

Harcourt, Bernard E. 2001. *Illusion of Order: The False Promise of Broken Windows Policing*. Cambridge, MA: Harvard University Press.

Hinkle, Joshua C., and David Weisburd. 2008. "The Irony of Broken Windows Policing: A Micro-Place Study of the Relationship Between Disorder, Focused Police Crackdowns and

Fear of Crime." *Journal of Criminal Justice* 36(6):503–512.

Keel, Timothy G., John P. Jarvis, and Yvonne E. Muirhead. 2009. "An Exploratory Analysis of Factors Affecting Homicide Investigations: Examining the Dynamics of Murder Clearance Rates." *Homicide Studies* 13(1):50–68.

Kelling, George L., and William J. Bratton. 1998. "Declining Crime Rates: Insiders' Views of the New York City Story." *Journal of Crime, Law & Criminology* 88(4):1217–1232.

Kelling, George L., Tony Pate, Duane Dieckman, and Charles E. Brown. 1974. "The Kansas City Preventive Patrol Experiment." Washington, DC: Police Foundation.

Kennedy, David M. 1997. "Pulling Levers: Chronic Offenders, High-Crime Settings, and a Theory of Prevention." *Valparaiso University Law Review* 31: 449–484.

Kraska, Peter B. 2007. "Militarization and Policing—Its Relevance to 21st Century Police." *Policing: A Journal of Policy and Practice* 1(4):501–513.

Kraska, Peter B., and Victor E. Kappeler. 1997. "Militarizing American Police: The Rise and Normalization of Paramilitary Units." *Social Problems* 44(1):1–18.

Levine, James P. 1975. "The Ineffectiveness of Adding Police to Prevent Crime." *Public Policy* 23(4):523–545.

Levitt, Steven D. 2004. "Understanding Why Crime Fell in the 1990s: Four Factors That Explain the Decline and Six That Do Not." *Journal of Economic Perspectives* 18(1):163–190.

Lopez, German. 2014. "Why Anti-Drug Campaigns Like DARE Fail." *Vox*. Retrieved September 27,

2019 (https://www.vox.com/2014/9/1/5998571/why-anti-drug-campaigns-like-dare-fail).

McCarthy, Justin. 2016. "Americans' Respect for Police Surges." Gallup. Retrieved September 26, 2019 (https://news.gallup.com/poll/196610/americans-respect-police-surges.aspx).

Meeks, Daryl. 2006. "Police Militarization in Urban Areas: The Obscure War Against the Underclass." *The Black Scholar* 35(4):33–41.

Miller, Wilbur R. 1999. *Cops and Bobbies: Police and Authority in New York and London, 1830–1870*, 2nd edition. Columbus: Ohio State University Press.

Mills, Linda G. 1998. "Mandatory Arrest and Prosecution Policies for Domestic Violence: A Critical Literature Review and the Case for More Research to Test Victim Empowerment Approaches." *Criminal Justice and Behavior* 25(3):306–318.

Mohler, George, and Michael D. Porter. 2018. "Rotational Grid, PAI-Maximizing Crime Forecasts." *Statistical Analysis and Data Mining* 11(5):227–236.

Monkkonen, Eric H. 1992. "History of Urban Police." *Crime and Justice* 15: 547–580.

Moule, Richard K., Jr., Bryanna Hahn Fox, and Megan M. Parry. 2019. "The Long Shadow of Ferguson: Legitimacy, Legal Cynicism, and Public Perceptions of Police Militarization." *Crime & Delinquency* 65(2):151–182.

Nagin, Daniel. 1975. *General Deterrence: A Review of the Empirical Evidence*. Pittsburgh, PA: Carnegie-Mellon University, School of Urban and Public Affairs.

Nagin, Daniel S., and John V. Pepper (Eds.). 2012. "Deterrence and the Death Penalty."

Committee on Deterrence and the Death Penalty. Washington, DC: National Academies Press.

O'Brien, Daniel T., Chelsea Farrell, and Brandon C. Welsh. 2019. "Looking Through Broken Windows: The Impact of Neighborhood Disorder on Aggression and Fear of Crime Is an Artifact of Research Design." *Annual Review of Criminology* 2: 53–71.

RAND. N.d. "Zero Tolerance and Aggressive Policing (and Why to Avoid It) in Depth." Retrieved September 27, 2019 (https://www.rand.org/pubs/tools/TL261/better-policing-toolkit/all-strategies/zero-tolerance/in-depth.html).

Riccio, Lucius J. 1974. "Direct Deterrence—An Analysis of the Effectiveness of Police Patrol and Other Crime Prevention Technologies." *Journal of Criminal Justice* 2(3):207–217.

Sastry, Anjuli, and Karen Grigsby Bates. 2017. "When LA Erupted in Anger: A Look Back at the Rodney King Riots." NPR. Retrieved September 26, 2019 (https://www.npr.org/2017/04/26/524744989/when-la-erupted-in-anger-a-look-back-at-the-rodney-king-riots).

Schram, Pamela J., and Stephen G. Tibbetts. 2018. *Introduction to Criminology: Why Do They Do It?* 2nd ed. Thousand Oaks, CA: Sage.

Sherman, Lawrence W. 1992. "Attacking Crime: Police and Crime Control." *Crime and Justice* 15: 159–230.

Sherman, Lawrence W. 1997. "Policing for Crime Prevention." In *Preventing Crime: What Works, What Doesn't, What's Promising: A Report to the United States Congress*, edited by Lawrence W. Sherman, Denise C. Gottfredson, Doris L. MacKenzie, John Eck, Peter Reuter, and Shawn.

Washington, DC: U.S. Department of Justice, Office of Justice Programs.

Sherman, Lawrence W., and Richard A. Berk. 1984. "The Specific Deterrent Effects of Arrest for Domestic Assault." *American Sociological Review* 49(2):261–272.

Sherman, Lawrence W., Patrick R. Gartin, and Michael E. Buerger. 1989. "Hot Spots of Predatory Crime: Routine Activities and the Criminology of Place." *Criminology* 27(1):27–56.

Sisak, Michael R. 2019. "NYPD Officer Says He Inflated Charge Against Eric Garner." *AP News*. Retrieved September 27, 2019 (https://www.apnews.com/ce589240fb884eceab7eaba2bfdff9e2).

Spruill, L. 2016. "Slave Patrols, 'Packs of Negro Dogs' and Policing Black Communities." *Phylon* 53(1):42–66.

Telep, Cody W., and David Weisburd. 2012. "What Is Known About the Effectiveness of Police Practices in Reducing Crime and Disorder?" *Police Quarterly* 15(4):331–357.

Telep, Cody W., and David Weisburd. 2016. "Policing." Pp. 137–168 in *What Works in Crime Prevention and Rehabilitation*, edited by David Weisburd, David Farrington, and David P. Gill. New York, NY: Springer.

Terrill, William, and Michael D. Reisig. 2003. "Neighborhood Context and Police Use of Force." *Journal of Research in Crime and Delinquency* 40(3):291–321.

Walker, Samuel. 1998. *Popular Justice: A History of American Criminal Justice*. New York, NY: Oxford University Press.

Weisburd, David, and John E. Eck. 2004. "What Can Police Do to Reduce Crime, Disorder, and Fear?" *Annals of the American Academy of Political and Social Science* 593(1):42–65.

Weisburd, David, Cody W. Telep, Joshua C. Hinkle, and John E. Eck. 2010. "Is Problem-Oriented Policing Effective in Reducing Crime and Disorder? Findings From a Campbell Systematic Review." *Criminology & Public Policy* 9(1):139–172.

Welch, Kelly. 2007. "Black Criminal Stereotypes and Racial Profiling." *Journal of Contemporary Criminal Justice* 23(3):276–288.

Wellford, Charles R. 1974. "Crime and the Police: A Multivariate Analysis." *Criminology* 12(2):195–213.

West, Steven L., and Keri K. O'Neal. 2004. "Project DARE Outcome Effectiveness Revisited." *American Journal of Public Health* 94(6):1027–1029.

Williams, Keith L. 2003. "Peel's Principles and Their Acceptance by American Police: Ending 175 Years of Reinvention." *The Police Journal* 76(2):97–120.

Willits, Dale W., and David A. Makin. 2018. "Show Me What Happened: Analyzing Use of Force Through Analysis of Body-Worn Camera Footage." *Journal of Research in Crime and Delinquency* 55(1):51–77.

Wilson, James Q. 1985. *Thinking About Crime*, rev. ed. New York, NY: Basic Books.

Zeisel, Hans. 1976. "The Deterrent Effect of the Death Penalty: Facts v. Faiths." *The Supreme Court Review* 1976: 317–343.

Zimring, Franklin E. 2007. *The Great American Crime Decline*. New York, NY: Oxford University Press.

12

PRISONS AND CRIME PREVENTION

"Monsters! This is what they create in here, monsters. And then they drop you into society and tell you go ahead be a good boy. Can't conduct yourself like a human being when they treat you like an animal."

Those are the words of Ronald Joncas, an inmate at Maine State Prison in Warren, Maine. In 2014, the Public Broadcasting Service show *Frontline* aired a documentary on solitary confinement, having filmed in Maine previously. Joncas was discussing the treatment he received in solitary confinement, or **administrative segregation**. Administrative segregation, or "ad seg," is used to keep an inmate away from others (either for their own or others' protection), or for punishment purposes. In ad seg, inmates are kept in isolation, without contact, for 23 hours (1 hour a day is allowed for recreation, in a confined environment). To Joncas, if prisons are dehumanizing, they will end up hardening inmates, who will fail to integrate into society upon release.

Administrative segregation has long drawn criticism for its ill effects on inmates (Arrigo and Bullock 2008; Smith 2006). After all, environments in which individuals are isolated from virtually all social contact cannot be expected to help them improve socially, psychologically, or physically. Yet prisons in general have also come under scrutiny throughout history regarding their ability to improve public safety, or prevent crime among released offenders. Is cutting a person off from their social supports, job, and community network the best way to reduce reoffending (or what is referred to as recidivism)?

Learning Questions

1. What is the history of prisons in the Western world?

2. How has rehabilitation been viewed as a crime prevention strategy throughout history?

3. What is the RNR approach to correctional offender management?

(Continued)

(Continued)

4. How effective are educational and vocational programming in corrections?

5. What factors are associated with correctional program success?

The history of prisons and in particular of crime prevention within prisons is marked by oscillating views on the best way to manage those who have broken the law. Can prisons be effective in reducing future criminal behavior? This is the question we delve into in this chapter. We begin with a brief history of corrections and an overview of the ways prisons have been viewed over time with respect to their effects on future behavior.

PRISONS: A BRIEF HISTORY

Corrections represents the final component of the criminal justice system after police and the courts. Once an individual is found guilty and sentenced, they are handed over to correctional agencies, where they may be placed on probation, remanded to treatment, or sent to prison. Believe it or not, the emergence of prisons as the primary way to punish people who have broken the law was considered humanitarian at the time. Prior to the widespread use of prisons, individuals were punished in somewhat gruesome ways, from public stockades to hangings. Of course, incarceration, namely in jails and dungeons, had existed since the Middle Ages (Schmalleger and Atkin-Plunk 2015).

During the Enlightenment period (1600s–1800s), particular prison designs were proposed by philosophers such as **Jeremy Bentham** as a way to ensure inmates were always supervised and kept in line. Bentham called his design the **Panopticon**—circular in structure, with guards stationed above cells out of view of inmates (Bentham 1787). In addition, prisons were a form of punishment beyond the view of the public; previously, punishments took place in full view of the public, with the idea that such visibility would increase shame and thus aid in preventing reoccurrence of bad behavior. Yet during the Enlightenment, this public punishment was seen as archaic. As the philosopher Michel Foucault argued, "The monotonous tumbling of locks and the shadow of the cell block have replaced the grand ceremonial of flesh and blood. The condemned culprit's body is concealed rather than being placed on exhibition" (Pol Droit 1975).

Prisons were not only more humane than torture or public forms of punishment; their purpose was different as well. Whereas harsh, repressive punishments were meant either as deterrence or as retribution for social/personal harms, prisons were a place where those who had committed crimes were supposed to reflect on what they had done, take in religion, and do penance. Hence one of the original terms for prison: the **penitentiary**. The two basic systems of modern prisons emerged in the United States in the early 1800s (Walker 1998).

In the first system, called the New York or Auburn model, inmates intermingled with other inmates but were not allowed to interact. In the Pennsylvania system, inmates were kept away from others for 23 hours a day, much like solitary confinement or administrative segregation today. Samuel Walker (1998:81) described how these systems signified a change in the prevailing theories about criminality. "Both reflected a new environmental theory of criminal behavior: Crime was the product of corrupting external influences. This was a radical shift from the colonial era, when crime was equated with sin: a personal moral failing. The prison was designed to reform offenders by isolating them from bad influences and subjecting them to a 'prison discipline' of total silence, work, and religious instruction."

Prisons, like the police, also have ties to America's past racial injustices. For example, it is widely known that the 13th Amendment to the Constitution eliminated slavery in the United States. However, this statement is not wholly correct, as a provision allowed an exception "as a punishment for crime." In other words, slavery was no longer legal, unless it was for punishment. In the book *Slavery by Another Name*, the historian Douglas Blackmon (2012) describes how prisons effectively replaced slavery in parts of the South. Blacks were incarcerated for such things as not having a job (having been displaced from farms) and then forced to work on farms. One of the most infamous was Parchman Farm in Mississippi, which David Oshinsky (1996:2) called "the closest thing to slavery that survived the Civil War."

Mass Incarceration

Today, the "great American invention" of prison (Walker 1998:80) continues to be linked with the United States in the form of mass incarceration. As discussed in Chapter 1, mass incarceration refers to the dramatic increase in prison and jail rates (and also probation and parole rates) in the United States since the early 1970s. Blumstein and Cohen (1973) argued that incarceration rates were stable in the United States, after examining relatively small fluctuations across the 20th century. After that, however, the incarceration rate exploded. Some argue that this was a result of the war on drugs, in which the government began to take a punitive stance toward drug offenders, seeking to lock up more users and traffickers. This increase in incarceration hit some communities harder than others, leading to widening inequalities in prison rates by race and disrupting families in criminogenic ways (Alexander 2012; Blumstein and Beck 1999).

The United States has the highest incarceration rate in the world, at 2.2 million people in 2016 (and that is a decrease from 2.3 in 2008; Gramlich 2018). In the United States, 655 people per 100,000 are incarcerated (see Figure 12.1 for the incarceration rate by race), compared with 140 per 100,000 in the United Kingdom, and 107 per 100,000 in Canada (Institute for Criminal Policy Research 2019). Mass incarceration, to the extent that it disproportionately affects particular groups and damages public safety, is a significant social issue. Michele Alexander's (2012) *The New Jim Crow* argues that mass incarceration is simply a new iteration of racial social control, replacing **Jim Crow** laws, which legally mandated segregation, and slavery before that.

The ability of prisons to realize the original goal of reforming inmates continues to be the subject of debate and scientific research. Historically, as well, there have been phases when confidence was high in the ideal of reform or rehabilitation, and phases when confidence was low. We next discuss these trends.

Figure 12.1   Incarceration Rate per 100,000 by Race in the United States

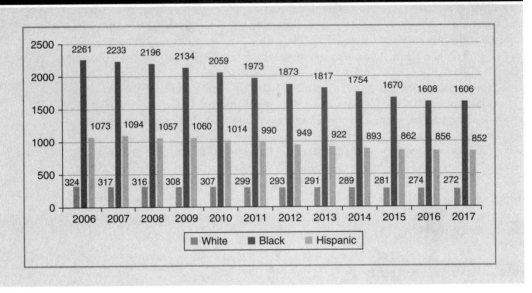

Source: Carson (2018).

FROM WE THINK IT WORKS, TO NOTHING WORKS, TO WHAT WORKS

Prisons were developed with the intention of reforming those who had done wrong. Punishment justifications range from **retribution** to deterrence to incapacitation to **rehabilitation**. Cutting off offenders from their negative influences was thought to be a requirement of helping them become more prosocial (Walker 1998). The ideal of rehabilitation was also used as a justification for putting inmates to work, on farms and in **prison industries** (Walker 1998). Inmates would be trained to work in a specialized industry, where they would learn discipline and the value of money. In Maine, prison industries specialize in woodworking. In Thomaston, there is a shop where inmate goods are sold.

The Martinson Report

The belief in the prison's ability to reform, through isolation, education, or vocational training, persisted until the 1970s. During that time, there was a decided shift toward conservative views in America. People began to question whether the prevailing punishment orientation was, in fact, doing any good. The big blow, however, came when a group of researchers evaluated the effectiveness of prison programs on recidivism.

Their publication, which came to be known as the **Martinson Report**, was surprising to those who believed prison programs worked. In a famous line, Robert Martinson

(1974:25) wrote, "With few and isolated exceptions, the rehabilitative efforts that have been reported so far have had no appreciable effect on recidivism." Thus ushered in the era of "**nothing works**," in which rather than the belief that prison reformed offenders, the prevailing view was that nothing was able to do so. Prisons, then, could affect crime only via deterrence or incapacitation—locking up dangerous souls and keeping them out of society. The latter philosophy was summed up perfectly by the political scientist James Q. Wilson in his *Thinking About Crime* (1975/1985:260) when he wrote, "Wicked people exist. Nothing avails except to set them apart from innocent people."

By the mid-1970s, the pendulum had swung all the way to the other side: Prisons, it was decided, did not really affect whether people were more or less likely to commit crimes. Yet, interestingly, that one line from the Martinson Report did not capture the reality that the researchers had found many studies to be of poor quality, not designed in such a way as to isolate treatment effects (e.g., randomized clinical trials). In fact, he wrote, "It is just possible that some of our treatment programs *are* working to some extent, but that our research is so bad that it is incapable of telling" (Martinson 1974:49). Yet he did not believe that was the case; rather, he believed that programs, as they were constituted then, did not work.

The view that "nothing works" persisted until the late 1980s when a group of scholars began to argue that, while it is true that not everything works for everybody, *some* approaches could be effective. The key was to figure out which approaches and for whom. This led to the "what works" movement that dominates today. The idea is to rigorously evaluate programs and policies in ways that allow us to know more fully which approaches to support. This movement has identified a wealth of programs that reduce recidivism for the formerly incarcerated as well as those on **community supervision** (probation or parole). These programs are the focus of the next section.

PAROLE: From Rehabilitation to Incapacitation

Parole is a mechanism for early release from incarceration that grew in popularity in the United States during the early 1900s. Generally, in what's called an indeterminate sentencing scheme, inmates become "eligible" to be released. When that happens, on a yearly basis, they come before a parole board composed of administrators and community members and plead their case. In determinate systems, inmates are released after having served their sentence and then sometimes put on parole. Once on parole, an individual is supervised in the community, reporting to a parole officer. In the 1970s, a shift in correctional ideology led to a movement away from indeterminate toward determinate sentencing and the abolishing of parole in certain states (including Maine) (Solomon, Kachnowski, and Bhati 2005; Travis and Lawrence 2002). Rather than let inmates out "early," the idea was to ensure they served a full and appropriate sentence. Research seems to indicate that parole does not have a substantial effect on reoffending (Solomon et al. 2005).

EXHIBIT 12.1

WHAT WORKS IN PRISON CORRECTIONS?

Entire volumes have been written about what works in corrections (see, for example, Gendreau, Little, and Goggin 1996; MacKenzie 2000; Seiter and Kadela 2003). Scholars have advanced theoretical perspectives to enhance the effectiveness of correctional treatment. One such perspective is called the **risk-need-responsivity (RNR)** approach, developed by James Bonta and Don Andrews, psychologists working in the social learning theory tradition.

The *risk* part of the RNR approach implies that individuals vary in terms of how much risk they present of committing new crimes. Risk factors include things like antisocial attitudes, a lack of employment, and drug use. The RNR approach also recognizes that offenders have needs that need to be addressed, such as education or cognitive behavioral treatment to target antisocial attitudes. Responsivity suggests that we need to match offenders' learning styles to modes of treatment (Bonta and Andrews 2007). Ideally, the process would go like this: A person commits a crime, is assessed for risk and **criminogenic needs** as well as learning style, then is matched to treatment according to those factors. After probation or a stint in prison, if the individual is given appropriate treatment, the end result should be that their risk has been lowered and they present less of a risk to the community.

The RNR approach is associated with a well-known **risk assessment tool** called the Level of Service Inventory (LSI). The LSI has undergone revisions over the years and also includes a version for youths called the Youth Level of Service/Case Management Inventory. The Level of Service Inventory–Revised, which is used in every state in the United States (Caroline Gauvin, MHS, personal communication, May 31, 2019), is a 54-item assessment tool that correctional staff use to rate the risk score and level of offenders. The LSI-R is also supposed to be used to guide supervision and treatment of these offenders.

What are some programs that are used in corrections? We begin with programs for juveniles and focus on those that scholars and practitioners have deemed evidence-based. **Evidence-based practices** or programs are those for which a high degree of support has been found: Using rigorous evaluation techniques, research in more than one location has found that the programs reduce recidivism or otherwise produce positive outcomes (e.g., reducing antisocial attitudes).

An important note about evaluating prison programs or approaches to rehabilitation is that they all hinge on measuring behavioral change, either within prisons or on the outside. Determining whether a program reduced criminal behavior after release from prison means that recidivism must be measured and operationalized. This is not as easy as it may sound. Should recidivism be measured by new convictions? Arrests? Arrests for serious crime? Self-reported criminal behavior?

We might assume that self-reported behavior would be the most accurate way to assess new crimes, because the other approaches may miss undetected crimes. However, this approach requires us to follow offenders after release and collect data directly from them, which is a costly and resource-intensive endeavor. In addition, the length of time of follow-up is important. We know that most recidivism, if it is going to occur, happens relatively close to release. But if we collect data on the first year after release only, we may miss offending after that window and incorrectly conclude a program was successful (see Harris, Lockwood, and Mengers 2009). Issues in defining recidivism for the evaluation of correctional practices were noted long ago by Alfred Blumstein and Richard Larson (1971).

Youth Programs

The juvenile justice system formally emerged with the opening of the Cook County juvenile court in 1899. This court signified that juveniles (those under age 18) who had broken the law would not be lumped in with adults and treated the same way (Thompson and Morris 2016). Juveniles, it was beginning to be recognized, were not simply young adults. Adolescence, the life stage between childhood and adulthood in which individuals are biologically maturing but still socially immature, was a new idea, one described in G. Stanley Hall's 1904 book by the same name.

The initial purpose of the juvenile justice system was to treat juveniles who had broken the law or were at risk of doing so. Juveniles were not "offenders" but "delinquents." In addition, they were not "found guilty" of crimes but "adjudicated." The state, under the juvenile justice system, was to care for the individual, under the auspices of the parens patriae doctrine, which meant that the government would act as the child's guardian (Custer 1978). The pendulum swing from rehabilitation to punitive orientation took place in the juvenile system as well as the adult system in the 1970s (Rocque, Serwick, and Plummer-Beale 2017).

In 1989, scholarship was beginning to question the "nothing works" mantra of the 1970s. A meta-analysis of juvenile correctional programs that year sought to provide systematic evidence on the question of whether treatment for youths can reduce recidivism. Whitehead and Lab's (1989:289) results were "far from encouraging for advocates of correctional intervention." While they did find some studies showing programs can reduce recidivism, they also found many that showed an *increase* in recidivism. The type of intervention that fared the best was **diversion**, in which youths are funneled out of the system altogether. Interestingly, a meta-analysis in 2012 found that diversion was not effective for juveniles who had committed crimes (Schwalbe et al. 2012), with 31.4% of the treatment group recidivating compared with 36.3% of the control group.

Since the "nothing works" period, much has been learned about what works in corrections for juveniles. There are several programs that we have already discussed in this book for youths who have found themselves in trouble with the law. These include the Blueprints programs (i.e., programs deemed effective by Blueprints for Healthy Youth Development), multisystemic therapy (MST), Functional Family Therapy (FFT), and Positive Action, among others. MST, FFT, and multisystemic therapy for problem sexual behavior can all take place within correctional facilities as well as in the community.

Other programs seek to place youths in foster homes instead of other types of placement (e.g., residential or correctional). Multidimensional Treatment Foster Care, now called **Treatment Foster Care Oregon**, is one such program. Families are selected and trained to help guide the youths through the program, and therapy is also used.

One goal of the program is to cut youths off from their delinquent peers ("Treatment Foster Care Oregon" 2019). Research has shown that the program reduces later incarceration, arrests, and criminal conduct (Chamberlain 2003).

What types of programming seem to be most effective? A year after Whitehead and Lab's study, a meta-analysis found that juvenile programs that are cognitively oriented are much more effective than those that are not (Izzo and Ross 1990). Cognitive behavioral therapy is a form of treatment that focuses on changing attitudes and negative thinking patterns related to problem behavior. In a review of meta-analyses, Manchak and Cullen (2015) found that programs for juveniles that are consistent with the RNR approach described above are more likely to be effective. Manchak and Cullen (2015) reviewed a study by Lipsey (2009), who had delineated the components of effective juvenile interventions. In that study, Lipsey had found that treatment worked better than punishment, treatment was effective whether it took place in the community or in a facility, and different types of treatment had varying effects. For example, counseling treatment was most effective, in his review.

What does *not* work with juveniles, it seems clear, are purely punitive, punishment-oriented approaches, meant to "scare" them into conformity (Manchak and Cullen 2015). For a time, **scared straight** was a popular approach aimed at deterring at-risk youth. The general idea was that a group of juveniles who were either in trouble with the law or at risk for such trouble would be exposed to the harsh realities of prison life—what awaited them if they continued their ways. Often, inmates would share stories or otherwise attempt to intimidate the juveniles. This approach is somewhat similar to the sex education model of having high school students take home dolls programmed to cry at particular times and needing to be changed and fed, to dissuade youths from having children too early. Research has shown unequivocally that scared-straight programs are ineffective at reducing antisocial behavior, and in fact may make things worse (Petrosino et al. 2013).

Adult Programs

Throughout the 1970s and 1980s, scholars and practitioners alike were by and large happy to conclude that nothing worked to reduce recidivism. The state could not be trusted to fairly and effectively design treatment programs for offenders. The only thing to do, therefore, was lock people up. This mindset led, in no small part, to the system of mass incarceration the United States is currently experiencing (Manchak and Cullen 2015).

Canadian psychologists who had been working in corrections did not take well to the prevailing wisdom that "nothing worked." According to Cullen (2013:335), "When Paul Gendreau, at the time a regional psychologist at Rideau Corrections Centre in Ontario, heard the claims that nothing works, he was appalled. He knew that many interventions could change behavior."

The Canadian school of criminologists began to demonstrate that certain approaches were effective in corrections. In 1990, Don Andrews and colleagues published a meta-analysis on treatment programs for offenders. They showed that "appropriate" correctional treatment was statistically more effective than inappropriate treatment. What did they mean by appropriate? The principles of effective intervention formed the basis of their RNR approach: Treatment should be given to those most at risk, should address deficits related to criminal behavior, and should be appropriate for the individuals.

The RNR approach is very popular in North America, with books and dozens of articles written in support of it. However, there is a rival model, called **Good Lives Model (GLM)**, which emphasizes slightly different factors in seeking to improve correctional outcomes. The approach was created to address some of the issues the authors found with the RNR perspective. For example, the Good Lives scholars argued that practitioners needed to focus not only on what was wrong with offenders but also on their strengths. The GLM aims to help offenders live a purposeful life with strong relationships as the backbone of success.

According to the GLM, there are several "human goods" that must be addressed in any program.

> The list of nine primary human goods is: (1) life (including healthy living and optimal physical functioning, sexual satisfaction), (2) knowledge, (3) excellence in play and work (including mastery experiences), (4) excellence in agency (i.e. autonomy and self-directedness), (5) inner peace (i.e. freedom from emotional turmoil and stress), (6) relatedness (including intimate, romantic and family relationships) and community, (7) spirituality (in the broad sense of finding meaning and purpose in life), (8) happiness, and (9) creativity. (Ward and Brown 2004:247)

Clearly needs and goods are related. The question is, does the GLM offer anything useful over and above RNR? Not surprisingly, the authors of RNR do not think so. In large part, this was a result of their rejection of the GLM authors' interpretation of the RNR approach and its limitations.

In general, what sorts of approaches work for adults? Two in particular, educational and vocational, merit specific consideration. One notion about what it takes to successfully reenter society upon release from prison is the ability to support oneself. Thus, meaningful employment is paramount. From that perspective, then, it would make sense that prisons should focus on ensuring inmates are as prepared as possible with the skills needed in the job force. Education is a key component of these skills, particularly in a postmodern world in which technological and academic knowledge is at a premium for many careers. For juveniles, one of the precursors to correctional facilities was reform schools (Schlossman 1995). In other words, the most appropriate form of incarceration was thought to be in an educational environment.

Education and Vocational Programs

Research has long examined the effect of education on recidivism. Martinson's report on rehabilitation noted "that there is very little empirical evidence to support" the effectiveness of education or skills building programs in prison (Martinson 1974:25). Just over 20 years later, research was beginning to show that education is helpful. One study compared recidivism rates of those who had obtained a degree in prison with the general recidivism rate (after 3 years) of the state, finding the educated inmates had a lower rate

(5% of the 60 who had obtained a degree recidivated with a violent crime compared with 40% of the general state prison population; Stevens and Ward 1997).

Of course, this sort of study cannot specifically determine that education is effective, because those who obtained a degree likely differ in important ways from the rest of the prisoner population. A team of researchers conducted a meta-analysis of 33 studies evaluating correctional education and vocational programs, and found that many were not methodologically rigorous. However, they concluded that overall, these programs reduced recidivism. Their calculated mean odds ratio of 1.52 meant that on average, program participants had a recidivism rate of 33% given a 50% rate for control group participants (Wilson, Gallagher, and MacKenzie 2000).

More recent work has continued to find that education programs are beneficial to inmates. A meta-analysis found that such programs reduce recidivism (Chappell 2004). Chappell looked specifically at postsecondary education programs (in other words, education beyond high school). In Minnesota, correctional researchers Grant Duwe and Valerie Clark (2013) reported that while those receiving secondary education degrees did better with employment upon release, they did not have lower recidivism rates. With postsecondary degrees, however, recidivism rates were lower.

Within the past few years, scholars have continued to conduct meta-analyses and systematic reviews on education and vocational programs. Bozick and colleagues (2018) found that correctional education did not improve employment, but studies using rigorous methods did show reduced recidivism. A systematic review of 12 experimental or quasi-experimental vocational programs provided to offenders upon release from prison found that not enough is known about such programs to make firm conclusions (Newton et al. 2018).

With respect to vocational programs in particular, one issue is that different populations may respond to treatment differently. For example, in the systematic review of vocational programs, a study by Christopher Uggen of the University of Minnesota was analyzed. This study is interesting because it reassessed the data from a previous study that had concluded the work program was not effective. Uggen thought that perhaps the program might be more appropriate for older offenders and found that for those age 27 and older, the program worked, while it was ineffective for those younger than 27 (Uggen 2000).

Another issue with employment of formerly incarcerated individuals is the stigma such persons face. Those of us who have applied for a job are familiar with the question about past convictions. Research has demonstrated that a criminal history does, in fact, harm one's chances of employment (Pager 2007). In an effort to help formerly incarcerated individuals, the **Ban the Box** movement began in the early 2000s to remove the criminal history information from job applications ("About: The Ban the Box Campaign" n.d.). This initiative was supported by then President Barack Obama, who advocated banning the box for federal employment (Lam 2016). Yet one paper (Doleac and Hansen 2016) found that ban-the-box policies actually hurt African Americans and Hispanics, lowering their chances of obtaining an interview. Why? The authors hypothesize that when criminal histories are not known, employers may use race as a shortcut for such information and be more likely to interview whites.

Programs That Do Not Work

What about novel programs that do not work? **Correctional boot camps** came into vogue in the 1980s in the United States. The idea was disarmingly simple: Army boot camp can be a transformative period for young adults who previously lacked structure and purpose. Boot camp provides regimentation and discipline and thus may help wayward souls turn their lives around. So why not provide a similar environment for those convicted of criminal behavior?

Unfortunately, much of the work on correctional boot camps does not show that they reduce later recidivism (Cullen et al. 2005; Wilson, MacKenzie, and Mitchell 2005). It turns out that yelling at "recruits" and inducing short-term discipline and regimentation does not fix what was criminogenic for the individuals in the community. Frank Cullen and colleagues (2005) describe this sort of approach as "common sense" corrections, which does not necessarily match "empirical" corrections (or what actually works).

Substance Use Programs

Employment is thought to be a necessary part of the reintegration process for ex-offenders. There are also factors known to impede or make this process more difficult, including the use of substances such as drugs and alcohol. The connection between drugs and alcohol and criminal behavior was touched on earlier in this book. Substance use can facilitate criminal behavior, but it can also make it more difficult for individuals who want to give up such behavior (called desistance) to actually do so (Rocque 2017). In addition, the majority of those in prison have an addiction or substance use disorder ("Report Finds Most U.S. Inmates Suffer From Substance Abuse or Addiction" 2010). Thus, programming that targets substance use and abuse is an important part of correctional treatment.

Therapeutic Communities

There are many varieties of substance use programs in prisons and in the community. We discussed community programs in Chapter 6; so we focus on prison programs here. One type of substance use programming that has been used in prisons is called **therapeutic communities (TCs)**. In TCs, individuals are separated from those not in treatment and work on the factors that led to substance use in the first place. TCs have been around since the 1950s and are linked to Alcoholics Anonymous (Center for Substance Abuse Treatment 1999). Participants work together to change their lives, learn to control their behavior, and become healthy. Often those in charge or providing treatment and therapy are former addicts themselves.

Research on TCs is encouraging. Wexler and colleagues have described one TC called Stay 'N Out that is used in prisons (Wexler and Williams 1986). The program operates separately from other inmates to reduce social influence. There are three phases of the program as the inmate moves through initiation to treatment to preparation for release. Days are regimented for participants, with work, counseling, and other events. The program encourages participants to open up to one another in a family-like environment (Wexler 1995). An evaluation of the program has shown it to be effective in lowering recidivism once inmates are released (Wexler, Falkin, and Lipton 1990). Evaluations of TCs overall tend to indicate they are beneficial (Inciardi, Martin, and Butzin 2004; Knight, Simpson, and Hiller 1999; Martin et al. 1999; Wexler et al. 1999).

Meta-analyses on prison substance use programs have been conducted. One done in 1999 found that, as discussed above, therapeutic communities work (Pearson and Lipton 1999). A 2007 meta-analysis showed that in addition to TCs, an approach called residential substance abuse treatment (RSAT) and group counseling are effective forms of correctional substance use treatment in reducing later criminal behavior. However, the review found that RSAT and group counseling did not clearly seem to reduce drug use. RSAT is similar to TCs in that they are conducted apart from the rest of the population of inmates. RSAT falls under the TC model, but as the authors of the review note, "RSAT-funded programs are essentially TCs, but not all TCs are RSAT-funded programs" (Mitchell, Wilson, and MacKenzie 2007:355).

Drug Courts

Entire systems have been built up to address substance use, with the notion that perhaps the criminal justice system is best equipped to deal with criminal behavior. **Drug courts** are systems that are oriented toward treatment and ensuring that those who broke the law remain drug-free, rather than focusing on punishment. The structure is different than with criminal courts, where the judge seeks to facilitate proceedings to determine guilt and appropriate sanctions. In drug courts, the goal is to ensure that the offender receives the support and treatment necessary to address the causes of the substance use. The entire premise is rehabilitation, rather than punishment (Wilson, Mitchell, and MacKenzie 2006). As Wilson and colleagues explain, "Typically, a judge closely monitors the progress of a drug offender (generally referred to as a client) and doles out sanctions for drug use relapse, failure to attend treatment, or other drug court infractions. The judge also reinforces successes through praise and encouragement and, possibly, a reduction in formal requirement or other reward" (p. 460).

Wilson and colleagues' (2006) review found that drug court may reduce offending, but the results were not strong. A meta-analysis from a year earlier showed modest reductions in offending associated with drug courts (Lowenkamp, Holsinger, and Latessa 2005). Other meta-analyses have found that drug courts are associated with lower rates of incarceration (Sevigny, Fuleihan, and Ferdik 2013). Mitchell et al. (2012) echoed the above findings but concluded that the stronger the research design, the weaker the findings. Drug courts were more effective for adults, they found. In fact, a meta-analysis of juvenile drug treatment courts found that recidivism was similar for drug courts compared to normal courts (Tanner-Smith, Lipsey, and Wilson 2016).

Behavioral Programs

In terms of general behavioral programs and approaches to reducing recidivism, several have shown signs of being effective. One type of treatment, discussed above, called cognitive behavioral therapy (CBT) is associated with improvements for offenders. CBT seeks to change thought patterns that lead to negative behaviors. Patients learn to identify negative thoughts that have resulted in poor decisions, actions, or other unwanted outcomes (e.g., depression) (Martin 2019).

CBT has been subject to a vast amount of research and, predictably, meta-analyses. One review examined 269 meta-analyses of the use of CBT for everything from depression to alcohol use. The review identified four meta-analyses of CBT for crime, showing that the treatment worked to reduce such behavior. "Physical treatments, such as surgical castration and hormonal treatment" worked better for sex offenders, but CBT was effective as a psychological treatment. However, the results for domestic violence were not as supportive for CBT (Hofmann et al. 2012).

With respect to antisocial behavior, CBT can take several forms. For example, cognitive skills training is used to help offenders learn new thinking patterns and ways to deal with antisocial thoughts. Anger management is used to help offenders control their temper and recognize when they are misinterpreting situations. Example programs are Aggression Replacement Therapy, Thinking for a Change, and the Reasoning and Rehabilitation Program (Lipsey, Landenberger, and Wilson 2007:5). Lipsey and colleagues' (2007) review focused on offenders receiving treatment in the community or in a facility. About half the studies were of programs in a facility (47%). Overall, the review found CBT reduced recidivism by 25% and that there was no difference between community or facility programs in terms of effectiveness.

Prisons and Social Ties

Social ties have long been a staple of criminological theorizing. Certain perspectives argue that human beings have natural impulses that can lead to what are defined today as antisocial behaviors. Strong relationships can act as a form of social control, restraining those impulses. But when a person is incarcerated, they are cut off from any prosocial networks they may have had in the community. Thus, **prison visitation** may be a vital part of ensuring those social ties remain intact. How might visitation help? Perhaps inmates are able to maintain romantic relationships or relationships with their children. These relationships remind them that they have something to lose if they continue with their criminal ways and provide motivation to "make good." Some research, in fact, has demonstrated that visitation in prison leads to less recidivism upon release (Bales and Mears 2008; Cochran 2014; Duwe and Clark 2013; Mears et al. 2012).

Recidivism rates, however, are not only a function of what happens to inmates while in prison. How they are treated and supervised in the community also matters. A recent focus of correctional practitioners and researchers is on what is called **reentry**, or the processes individuals undergo to reassimilate into society after incarceration. Reentry programs seek to assist or facilitate this process, perhaps providing job placement or housing services. For example, if an inmate receives job training or an education while incarcerated, they still may need help finding employment they are suited for, or a place they can stay. Navigating the restrictions and legal limits can be a challenge. One study examined reentry programs and found that those who were involved remained arrest-free for longer. What the authors labeled "practical service" program

Table 12.1 What Works in Correctional Programming?	
Approach	**Target**
Educational/vocational programs	Skills/ability to obtain employment
Cognitive behavioral programs	Criminogenic attitudes
Therapeutic communities	Substance use
Prison visitation	Social ties/network
Family therapy	Juveniles' social networks
Treatment foster care	Juveniles' social environment

elements (such as job training) did not seem to reduce recidivism (some even were shown to increase recidivism). However, personal program elements, such as relationship training and anger management, did help (Visher et al. 2017). (See Table 12.1 for a list of correctional programmatic approaches to prevent crime and what area each targets.)

Incarceration or Community Sanctions?

In terms of the approach taken for punishment upon a finding of guilty, there are two main options for sentencing. First, an offender can be confined in a facility such as a prison. Second, they can serve their sentence in the community, perhaps on probation or some other type of supervision (see Chapter 13). According to deterrence perspectives, incarceration, with its removal of freedom, should be more effective in reducing later crime. Deterrence is a perspective that views the threat of harsh punishment as enough to dissuade would-be offenders from committing a crime. Faced with being locked up for years, the logic goes, an individual might think twice before committing armed robbery. Yet a Campbell Collaboration review (Villettaz, Gilliéron, and Killias 2015) indicated no difference between custodial and noncustodial punishments in terms of recidivism.

The finding that noncustodial sanctions do not increase crime is important for those wondering how mass incarceration can be reduced without compromising the safety of the community. If noncustodial sanctions do no more harm than locking people up, they may be more cost-effective. More evidence is accumulating that simply not locking up those we have in the past does not increase crime rates. In California, overcrowding in prisons led the government to order the release of inmates, under Proposition 47. Research has indicated that overall, the release of 13,000 inmates has not affected most crime, though it may have increased larceny and motor vehicle theft (Bartos and Kubrin 2018).

While it seems that incarceration may not reduce crime beyond a certain level, some research finds that incarceration increases recidivism (Cullen, Jonson, and Nagin 2011). How might prisons increase crime? As previously mentioned, prisons cut individuals off from their social networks. In addition, as Cullen and colleagues (2011) note, prisons may make individuals more antisocial, acting as "schools for crime." In other words, associating with riskier peers can, via social learning processes, make one more antisocial. However, not all research supports this idea. One study explored whether association with cell mates who had more "experience" with crime led to more antisocial behavior. The study found that these associations either did not matter or were linked with less antisocial behavior (Harris, Nakamura, and Bucklen 2018).

What about effects on children? In examining how prisons affect crime, some work has expanded to include social networks of those incarcerated. For example, what happens to children whose parents have been locked up? Certain work has indicated that parental incarceration is harmful for children (Wakefield and Wildeman 2013). However, nailing down causal effects of incarceration is difficult because, of course, we cannot use randomized trials. This means that there is a selection effect, whereby those whose parents are incarcerated are fundamentally different from those whose parents are not (Kirk and Wakefield 2018). A recent economics study, using a quasi-experimental design, found that addressing these selection factors shows incarceration is *beneficial* for children in terms of risk of future incarceration. However, the study also found that parental or sibling incarceration is positively associated with teenage pregnancy (Norris, Pecenco, and Weaver 2019). The effects of parental or sibling incarceration are not likely to be the same for everyone (Kirk and Wakefield 2018); removal of a supportive parent is likely to be more damaging to a child than removal of an abusive one, for example. It is clear much more work needs to be done in this area to truly understand the total effects of incarceration.

EXPERIENCES IN PRISON AND RECIDIVISM

Some research has examined the effect of sentence length on recidivism. Perhaps long sentences are more harmful, resulting in **prisonization**, or the acculturation of inmates to the prison life, and a more permanent destruction of social ties. Or perhaps longer sentences are a firm reminder of just what the individual stands to lose if they commit a serious crime. One study looked at data on a group of more than 1,000 serious juvenile offenders, seeking to determine whether being incarcerated reduced future crime and what sort of effect longer sentences had, if any. Much like previous research, incarceration did not seem to matter and neither did longer sentences. Interestingly, one study found that longer sentences do not harm later income from employment (Kling 2006).

What about the effect of type of custody while in prison? Recall our discussion earlier in this chapter of the adverse effects of perhaps the most severe sanction in prison—solitary confinement. Some work has demonstrated that where and how individuals are housed affects their later behavior.

In an interesting randomized experiment, one group of researchers evaluated the effect of sending similarly classified inmates to lower security levels. Typically, correctional agencies will classify inmates according to how risky they are and then house them accordingly. As Gaes and Camp (2009:140) describe, there are three justifications for basing security levels on risk.

Higher risk inmates are separated from lower risk inmates so that the former will not extort, assault, or intimidate the latter. Prison officials can use procedural and technological methods to impose greater constraints to suppress violence among the higher risk inmates. Finally, by limiting the extra security methods to only higher risk inmates, the overall system is more efficient and administrators do not need to squander scarce prison resources on inmates who do not need the additional security procedures.

Gaes and Camp (2009) found that those sent to a lower security level were less likely to recidivate. Misbehavior in prisons did not differ between the groups, though. In another study looking at inmates housed in minimum-security facilities (generally places that are less restrictive of inmates, sometimes without a "fence") versus higher security levels, Chen and Shapiro (2007) found similar inmates in minimum-security levels recidivated equal to or even less than those in more secure facilities (low/medium/maximum security). Another study found that negative experiences in prison (crowding, fights) increased recidivism (Drago, Galbiati, and Vertova 2011). This work is consistent with general strain theory in criminology, which suggests stressful experiences lead to criminal behavior, and this applies to experiences in prison as well (Listwan et al. 2012).

This research may point to the difficulty of using risk scores to properly supervise and treat inmates. Is it true that riskier individuals should be supervised more stringently, for example? Do people who score high on antisocial attitudes do better if they are matched with CBT?

To try to answer these questions, one study attempted to determine how well the LSI-R, which is a risk and needs instrument, funneled individuals to appropriate treatment, which then reduced their risk. In theory, an individual who scored "high" on need for education should experience a greater reduction in recidivism than one who received education but was not high need. Duwe and Rocque (2016) looked at Minnesota inmates and found no clear evidence of the LSI-R's effectiveness in driving appropriate programming. For example, they examined how participation in 16 programs influenced changes in LSI-R scores. If the LSI-R is effective in driving treatment, then programs addressing particular domains should have a significant effect on that domain score. While this was the case for some programs/domains, the overall pattern was not consistent.

Genetic Considerations

Another way to think about risk and responsivity with respect to correctional treatment, besides in social terms, is in genetic ones. Human beings are very genetically similar to one another, sharing 99.9% of their genes. Yet there are gene variants, called alleles, that differentiate people (Simons, Beach, and Barr 2012). Some **biosocial** scholars have looked at how genetic variants interact with the environment to influence behavior. For example, certain variants of genes are considered risk factors for antisocial behavior. Some environments are also considered risk factors for the same behavior (e.g., abuse, poverty). When an individual has both risky genetic variants and is in risky environments, they have an elevated chance of being involved in antisocial behavior (see

Caspi et al. 2002). This is called a **gene by environment interaction**, which suggests the effect of one factor depends on the level of the other factor. This model is referred to as the **diathesis stress hypothesis**.

Differential Susceptibility

Another possibility is what some researchers have referred to as **differential susceptibility** (Gajos, Fagan, and Beaver 2016). Under this model, genes are not "risky" per se, but they indicate who is more susceptible to environmental influence. In other words, they are "plasticity genes," not risky genes (Gajos et al. 2016:687). Thus, people with these alleles will be negatively influenced by negative environments but, conversely, will be positively influenced by positive environments. This notion has implications for correctional programming and could explain why some people respond to interventions while others do not. Research making use of knowledge about risky and/or plasticity alleles could help improve how we design and implement prevention programs in corrections (Gajos et al. 2016).

Also in the biosocial framework, scholars have sought to incorporate findings from this perspective into the RNR approach. Newsome and Cullen (2017) argued that biosocial research could be used to enhance knowledge on RNR. For example, biosocial work has shown that factors such as brain structure and function, hormones, and genes are associated with antisocial behavior. Yet the RNR approach has not paid attention to these factors, instead focusing on social and psychological components. They offered several recommendations to include biosocial research in all three areas (*risk, need,* and *responsivity*). For example, they discussed research indicating that brain function may influence whether a person completes a rehabilitation program. This information could help improve outcomes for such programs.

CONCLUSION

The idea that prisons can help prevent crime is an old one in criminology. The public, practitioners, and policymakers alike lost faith that prisons could rehabilitate offenders in the 1970s, when research began to question the effectiveness of correctional programs. However, beginning in the late 1980s, researchers started to identify particular practices and approaches that did reduce later recidivism. These include family programming for youths and cognitive behavioral programs for adults. The risk-need-responsivity approach has helped correctional workers better understand how to guide treatment and supervision for offenders.

Today, much is known about how prison programs can help individuals succeed in society upon release. We also know much about what does not seem to work. For example, punitive/harsh punishments without any element of rehabilitation seem misguided. Community supervision approaches seem to be as effective as incarceration. Particular types of community programs are the focus of the next chapter. More research is needed on why particular programs work and for whom, and why others do not.

SUMMARY

1. Prisons are a uniquely American form of punishment, originally intended to facilitate penance on the part of the offender.

2. After a period in which it was generally assumed that rehabilitation programs worked, research began to question this assumption and faith was lost in the rehabilitation ideal.

3. The "what works" movement started in the late 1980s and early 1990s, identifying approaches and programs that effectively reduced recidivism in corrections.

4. Today, evidence-based lists contain many programs that research has demonstrated to be effective.

5. Effective programs target substance abuse, antisocial attitudes, and prosocial relationships/community ties.

6. Harsh/punitive treatment does not seem effective.

7. More research is needed on why particular approaches work for some but not for others.

KEY TERMS

administrative segregation 257
Ban the Box 266
biosocial 272
community supervision 261
correctional boot camps 267
corrections 258
criminogenic needs 262
diathesis stress hypothesis 273
differential susceptibility 273
diversion 263
drug courts 268
evidence-based practices 262

gene by environment interaction 273
Good Lives Model (GLM) 265
Jeremy Bentham 258
Jim Crow 259
Martinson Report 260
nothing works 261
Panopticon 258
penitentiary 258
prison industries 260
prison visitation 269
prisonization 271

reentry 269
rehabilitation 260
retribution 260
risk assessment tool 262
risk-need-responsivity (RNR) 262
scared straight 264
therapeutic communities (TCs) 267
Treatment Foster Care Oregon 263

REFERENCES

"About: The Ban the Box Campaign." N.d. Retrieved September 28, 2019 (http://bantheboxcampaign.org/about/#.XZAs UDZKjIW).

Alexander, Michelle. 2012. *The New Jim Crow: Mass Incarceration in the Age of Colorblindness*. New York, NY: Free Press.

Arrigo, Bruce A., and Jennifer Leslie Bullock. 2008. "The Psychological Effects of Solitary Confinement on Prisoners in Supermax Units: Reviewing What We Know and Recommending What Should Change." *International Journal of Offender Therapy and Comparative Criminology* 52(6):622–640.

Bales, William D., and Daniel P. Mears. 2008. "Inmate Social Ties and the Transition to Society: Does Visitation Reduce Recidivism?" *Journal of Research in Crime and Delinquency* 45(3):287–321.

Bartos, Bradley J., and Charis E. Kubrin. 2018. "Can We Downsize Our Prisons and Jails Without Compromising Public Safety? Findings From California's Prop 47." *Criminology & Public Policy* 17(3):693–715.

Bentham, Jeremy. 1787. *Panopticon: Or, the Inspection House.* Dublin, Ireland: Thomas Byrne.

Blackmon, Douglas, A. 2012. *Slavery by Another Name: The Re-Enslavement of Black Americans From the Civil War to World War II.* London, UK: Icon Books.

Blumstein, Alfred, and Allen J. Beck. 1999. "Population Growth in US Prisons, 1980–1996." *Crime and Justice* 26: 17–61.

Blumstein, Alfred, and Jacqueline Cohen. 1973. "A Theory of the Stability of Punishment." *Journal of Criminal Law & Criminology* 64(2):198–207.

Blumstein, Alfred, and Richard C. Larson. 1971. "Problems in Modeling and Measuring Recidivism." *Journal of Research in Crime and Delinquency* 8(2):124–132.

Bonta, James, and Donald A. Andrews. 2007. "Risk-Need-Responsivity Model for Offender Assessment and Rehabilitation." *Rehabilitation* 6(1):1–22.

Bozick, Robert, Jennifer Steele, Lois Davis, and Susan Turner. 2018. "Does Providing Inmates With Education Improve Postrelease Outcomes? A Meta-Analysis of Correctional Education Programs in the United States." *Journal of Experimental Criminology* 14(4):1–40.

Carson, E. Ann. 2018. "Prisoners in 2016." Bureau of Justice Statistics. Retrieved September 28, 2019 (https://www.bjs.gov/index.cfm?ty=pbdetail&iid=6187).

Caspi, Avshalom, Joseph McClay, Terrie E. Moffitt, Jonathan Mill, Judy Martin, Ian W. Craig, Alan Taylor, and Richie Poulton. 2002. "Role of Genotype in the Cycle of Violence in Maltreated Children." *Science* 297(5582):851–854.

Center for Substance Abuse Treatment. 1999. "Chapter 5: Therapeutic Communities." *Treatment of Adolescents With Substance Use Disorders.* Treatment Improvement Protocol Series, No. 32. Rockville, MD: Substance Abuse and Mental Health Services Administration. Retrieved September 28, 2019 (https://www.ncbi.nlm.nih.gov/books/NBK64342/).

Chamberlain, Patricia. 2003. "The Oregon Multidimensional Treatment Foster Care Model: Features, Outcomes, and Progress in Dissemination." *Cognitive and Behavioral Practice* 10: 303–312.

Chappell, Cathryn A. 2004. "Post-Secondary Correctional Education and Recidivism: A Meta-Analysis of Research Conducted 1990–1999." *Journal of Correctional Education* 55(2):148–169.

Chen, M. Keith, and Jesse M. Shapiro. 2007. "Do Harsher Prison Conditions Reduce Recidivism? A Discontinuity-Based Approach." *American Law and Economics Review* 9(1):1–29.

Cochran, Joshua C. 2014. "Breaches in the Wall: Imprisonment, Social Support, and Recidivism." *Journal of Research in Crime and Delinquency* 51(2):200–229.

Cullen, Francis T. 2013. "Rehabilitation: Beyond Nothing Works." *Crime and Justice* 42(1):299–376.

Cullen, Francis T., Kristie R. Blevins, Jennifer S. Trager, and Paul Gendreau. 2005. "The Rise and Fall of Boot Camps: A Case Study in Common-Sense Corrections." *Journal of Offender Rehabilitation* 40(3–4):53–70.

Cullen, Francis T., Cheryl Lero Jonson, and Daniel S. Nagin. 2011. "Prisons Do Not Reduce Recidivism: The High Cost of Ignoring Science." *The Prison Journal* 91(3 suppl):48S–65S.

Custer, Lawrence B. 1978. "The Origins of the Doctrine of Parens Patriae." *Emory Law Journal* 27: 195–208.

Doleac, Jennifer L., and Benjamin Hansen. 2016. *Does "Ban the Box" Help or Hurt Low-Skilled Workers? Statistical Discrimination and Employment Outcomes When Criminal Histories Are Hidden* (No. 22469). Cambridge, MA: National Bureau of Economic Research.

Drago, Francesco, Roberto Galbiati, and Pietro Vertova. 2011. "Prison Conditions and Recidivism." *American Law and Economics Review* 13(1):103–130.

Duwe, Grant, and Valerie Clark. 2013. "Blessed Be the Social Tie That Binds: The Effects of Prison Visitation on Offender Recidivism." *Criminal Justice Policy Review* 24(3):271–296.

Duwe, Grant, and Michael Rocque. 2016. "A Jack of All Trades but a Master of None? Evaluating the Performance of the Level of Service Inventory–Revised (LSI-R) in the Assessment of Risk and Need." *Corrections* 1(2):81–106.

Gaes, Gerald G., and Scott D. Camp. 2009. "Unintended Consequences: Experimental Evidence for the Criminogenic Effect of Prison Security Level Placement on Post-Release Recidivism." *Journal of Experimental Criminology* 5(2):139–162.

Gajos, Jamie M., Abigail A. Fagan, and Kevin M. Beaver. 2016. "Use of Genetically Informed Evidence-Based Prevention Science to Understand and Prevent Crime and Related Behavioral Disorders." *Criminology & Public Policy* 15(3):683–701.

Gendreau, Paul, Tracy Little, and Claire Goggin. 1996. "A Meta-Analysis of the Predictors of Adult Offender Recidivism: What Works!" *Criminology* 34(4):575–608.

Gramlich, John. 2018. "America's Incarceration Rate Is at a Two-Decade Low." Pew Research Center. Retrieved September 28, 2019 (http://www.pewresearch.org/fact-tank/2018/05/02/americas-incarceration-rate-is-at-a-two-decade-low/).

Hall, G. Stanley. 1904. *Adolescence: Its Psychology and Its Relations to Physiology, Anthropology, Sociology, Sex, Crime, Religion, and Education* (Vol. I & II). New York, NY: D. Appleton.

Harris, Phil W., Brian Lockwood, and Liz Mengers. 2009. *Defining and Measuring Recidivism.* A CJCA White Paper. Council of Correctional Administrators. Retrieved September 28, 2019 (https://pbstandards.org/cjcaresources/15/CJCA-Recidivism-White-Paper.pdf).

Harris, Heather M., Kiminori Nakamura, and Kristofer Bret Bucklen. 2018. "Do Cellmates Matter? A Causal Test of the Schools of Crime Hypothesis With Implications for Differential

Association and Deterrence Theories." *Criminology* 56(1):87–122.

Hofmann, Stefan G., Anu Asnaani, Imke J. J. Vonk, Alice T. Sawyer, and Angela Fang. 2012. "The Efficacy of Cognitive Behavioral Therapy: A Review of Meta-Analyses." *Cognitive Therapy and Research* 36(5):427–440.

Inciardi, James A., Steven S. Martin, and Clifford A. Butzin. 2004. "Five-Year Outcomes of Therapeutic Community Treatment of Drug-Involved Offenders After Release From Prison." *Crime & Delinquency* 50(1):88–107.

Institute for Criminal Policy Research. 2019. "Highest to Lowest—Prison Population Rate." *World Prison Brief.* Retrieved September 28, 2019 (https://www.prisonstudies.org/highest-to-lowest/prison_population_rate?field_region_taxonomy_tid=All).

Izzo, Rhena L., and Robert R. Ross. 1990. "Meta-Analysis of Rehabilitation Programs for Juvenile Delinquents: A Brief Report." *Criminal Justice and Behavior* 17(1):134–142.

Kirk, David S., and Sarah Wakefield. 2018. "Collateral Consequences of Punishment: A Critical Review and Path Forward." *Annual Review of Criminology* 1: 171–194.

Kling, Jeffrey R. 2006. "Incarceration Length, Employment, and Earnings." *American Economic Review* 96(3):863–876.

Knight, Kevin, D. Dwayne Simpson, and Matthew L. Hiller. 1999. "Three-Year Reincarceration Outcomes for In-Prison Therapeutic Community Treatment in Texas." *The Prison Journal* 79(3):337–351.

Lam, Bourree. 2016. "Obama's Proposal to 'Ban the Box' for Government Jobs." *The Atlantic.* Retrieved September 28, 2019 (https://www .theatlantic.com/business/archive/2016/05/obama-memorandum-opm/480909/).

Lipsey, Mark W. 2009. "The Primary Factors That Characterize Effective Interventions With Juvenile Offenders: A Meta-Analytic Overview." *Victims and Offenders* 4(2):124–147.

Lipsey, Mark W., Nana A. Landenberger, and Sandra J. Wilson. 2007. "Effects of Cognitive-Behavioral Programs for Criminal Offenders." *Campbell Systematic Reviews* 6(1):1–27.

Listwan, Shelley Johnson, Christopher J. Sullivan, Robert Agnew, Francis T. Cullen, and Mark Colvin. 2012. "The Pains of Imprisonment Revisited: The Impact of Strain on Inmate Recidivism." *Justice Quarterly* 30(1):144–168.

Lowenkamp, Christopher T., Alexander M. Holsinger, and Edward J. Latessa. 2005. "Are Drug Courts Effective: A Meta-Analytic Review." *Journal of Community Corrections* 15(1):5–11.

MacKenzie, Doris Layton. 2000. "Evidence-Based Corrections: Identifying What Works." *Crime & Delinquency* 46(4):457–471.

Manchak, Sarah M., and Francis T. Cullen. 2015. "Intervening Effectively With Juvenile Offenders: Answers From Meta-Analysis." Pp. 477–490 in *The Development of Criminal and Antisocial Behavior*, edited by Julian Morizot and Lila Kazemian. Cham, Switzerland: Springer.

Martin, Ben. 2019. "In-Depth: Cognitive Behavioral Therapy." PsychCentral. Retrieved September 28, 2019 (https://psychcentral.com/lib/in-depth-cognitive-behavioral-therapy/).

Martin, Steven S., Clifford A. Butzin, Christine A. Saum, and James A. Inciardi. 1999. "Three-Year Outcomes of Therapeutic Community Treatment for Drug-Involved Offenders in

Delaware: From Prison to Work Release to Aftercare." *The Prison Journal* 79(3):294–320.

Martinson, Robert. 1974. "What Works? Questions and Answers About Prison Reform." *The Public Interest* 35: 22–54.

Mears, Daniel P., Joshua C. Cochran, Sonja E. Siennick, and William D. Bales. 2012. "Prison Visitation and Recidivism." *Justice Quarterly* 29(6):888–918.

Mitchell, Ojmarrh, David B. Wilson, Amy Eggers, and Doris L. MacKenzie. 2012. "Assessing the Effectiveness of Drug Courts on Recidivism: A Meta-Analytic Review of Traditional and Non-Traditional Drug Courts." *Journal of Criminal Justice* 40(1):60–71.

Mitchell, Ojmarrh, David B. Wilson, and Doris L. MacKenzie. 2007. "Does Incarceration-Based Drug Treatment Reduce Recidivism? A Meta-Analytic Synthesis of the Research." *Journal of Experimental Criminology* 3(4):353–375.

Newsome, Jamie, and Francis T. Cullen. 2017. "The Risk-Need-Responsivity Model Revisited: Using Biosocial Criminology to Enhance Offender Rehabilitation." *Criminal Justice and Behavior* 44(8):1030–1049.

Newton, Danielle, Andrew Day, Margaret Giles, Joanne Wodak, Joe Graffam, and Eileen Baldry. 2018. "The Impact of Vocational Education and Training Programs on Recidivism: A Systematic Review of Current Experimental Evidence." *International Journal of Offender Therapy and Comparative Criminology* 62(1):187–207.

Norris, Samuel, Matthew Pecenco, and Jeffrey Weaver. 2019. "The Effects of Parental and Sibling Incarceration: Evidence From Ohio." Working Paper. Retrieved September 28, 2019 (https://docs.google.com/viewer?a=v&pid=sites&srcid=ZGVmYXVsdGRvbWFpbnxzYW1ub3JyaXNlY29ufGd4OjVhYzlhZTTdiODY2MzgzOTk).

Oshinsky, David M. 1996. *Worse Than Slavery: Parchman Farm and the Ordeal of Jim Crow Justice.* New York, NY: Free Press Paperbacks.

Pager, Devah. 2007. *Marked: Race, Crime, and Finding Work in an Era of Mass Incarceration.* Chicago, IL: University of Chicago Press.

Pearson, Frank S., and Douglas S. Lipton. 1999. "A Meta-Analytic Review of the Effectiveness of Corrections-Based Treatments for Drug Abuse." *The Prison Journal* 79(4):384–410.

Petrosino, Anthony, Carolyn Turpin-Petrosino, Meghan E. Hollis-Peel, and Julia G. Lavenberg. 2013. "'Scared Straight' and Other Juvenile Awareness Programs for Preventing Juvenile Delinquency." *Cochrane Systematic Review*, Issue 4. doi:10.1002/14651858.CD002796.pub2.

Pol Droit, Roger. 1975. "Michel Foucault, on the Role of Prisons." *New York Times.* Retrieved September 28, 2019 (https://archive.nytimes.com/www.nytimes.com/books/00/12/17/specials/foucault-prisons.html?mcubz=3).

"Report Finds Most U.S. Inmates Suffer From Substance Abuse or Addiction." 2010. *The Nation's Health* 40(3):E11. Retrieved September 28, 2019 (http://thenationshealth.aphapublications.org/content/40/3/E11).

Rocque, Michael. 2017. *Desistance From Crime: New Advances in Theory and Research.* New York, NY: Palgrave-MacMillan.

Rocque, Michael, Agneiszka Serwick, and Judy Plummer-Beale. 2017. "Offender Rehabilitation and Reentry During Emerging Adulthood: A Review and Introduction of a New Approach." Pp. 510–531 in *Flourishing in Emerging Adulthood: Positive Development During the*

Third Decade of Life, edited by Laura M. Padilla-Walker and Larry J. Nelson. New York, NY: Oxford.

Schlossman, Steven L. 1995. "Delinquent Children: The Juvenile Reform School." Pp. 363–389 in *Oxford History of the Prison: The Practice of Punishment in Western Society*, edited by Norval Morris and David J. Rothman. New York, NY: Oxford University Press.

Schmalleger, Frank, and Cassandra Atkin-Plunk. 2015. "Prison History—Criminology." *Oxford Bibliographies*. Retrieved September 28, 2019 (http://www.oxfordbibliographies.com/view/document/obo-9780195396607/obo-9780195396607-0189.xml).

Schwalbe, Craig S., Robin E. Gearing, Michael J. MacKenzie, Kathryne B. Brewer, and Rawan Ibrahim. 2012. "A Meta-Analysis of Experimental Studies of Diversion Programs for Juvenile Offenders." *Clinical Psychology Review* 32(1):26–33.

Seiter, Richard P., and Karen R. Kadela. 2003. "Prisoner Reentry: What Works, What Does Not, and What Is Promising." *Crime & Delinquency* 49(3):360–388.

Sevigny, Eric L., Brian K. Fuleihan, and Frank V. Ferdik. 2013. "Do Drug Courts Reduce the Use of Incarceration? A Meta-Analysis." *Journal of Criminal Justice* 41(6):416–425.

Simons, Ronald L., Steven R. H. Beach, and Ashley B. Barr. 2012. "Differential Susceptibility to Context: A Promising Model of the Interplay of Genes and the Social Environment." Pp. 139–163 in *Biosociology and Neurosociology*, edited by W. Kalkhoff, S. Thye, and E. Lawler. Bingley, UK: Emerald Group.

Smith, Peter Scharff. 2006. "The Effects of Solitary Confinement on Prison Inmates: A Brief History and Review of the Literature." *Crime and Justice* 34(1):441–528.

Solomon, Amy L., Vera Kachnowski, and Avinash Bhati. 2005. "Does Parole Work? Analyzing the Impact of Postprison Supervision on Rearrest Outcomes." Urban Institute. Retrieved September 28, 2019 (http://webarchive.urban.org/UploadedPDF/311156_Does_Parole_Work.pdf).

Stevens, Dennis J., and Charles S. Ward. 1997. "College Education and Recidivism: Educating Criminals Is Meritorious." *Journal of Correctional Education* 48(3):106–111.

Tanner-Smith, Emily E., Mark W. Lipsey, and David B. Wilson. 2016. "Juvenile Drug Court Effects on Recidivism and Drug Use: A Systematic Review and Meta-Analysis." *Journal of Experimental Criminology* 12(4):477–513.

Thompson, Kristin C., and Richard J. Morris. 2016. "History of the Juvenile Justice System." Pp. 55–72 in *Juvenile Delinquency and Disability*. Advancing Responsible Adolescent Development. Cham, Switzerland: Springer (https://doi.org/10.1007/978-3-319-29343-1_5).

Travis, Jeremy, and Sarah Lawrence. 2002. "Beyond the Prison Gates: The State of Parole in America." Urban Institute Justice Policy Center. Retrieved September 28, 2019 (http://webarchive.urban.org/UploadedPDF/310583_Beyond_prison_gates.pdf).

"Treatment Foster Care Oregon." 2019. Blueprints for Healthy Youth Development. Retrieved September 28, 2019 (https://www.blueprintsprograms.org/programs/treatment-foster-care-oregon/).

Uggen, Christopher. 2000. "Work as a Turning Point in the Life Course of Criminals: A Duration Model of Age, Employment, and

Recidivism." *American Sociological Review* 65(4):529–546.

Villettaz, Patrice, Gwladys Gilliéron, and Martin Killias. 2015. "The Effects on Re-Offending of Custodial vs. Non-Custodial Sanctions: An Updated Systematic Review of the State of Knowledge." *Campbell Systematic Reviews* 11(1):1–92.

Visher, Christy A., Pamela K. Lattimore, Kelle Barrick, and Stephen Tueller. 2017. "Evaluating the Long-Term Effects of Prisoner Reentry Services on Recidivism: What Types of Services Matter?" *Justice Quarterly* 34(1):136–165.

Wakefield, Sara, and Christopher Wildeman. 2013. *Children of the Prison Boom: Mass Incarceration and the Future of American Inequality*. New York, NY: Oxford University Press.

Walker, Samuel. 1998. *Popular Justice: A History of American Criminal Justice*. New York, NY: Oxford University Press.

Ward, Tony, and Mark Brown. 2004. "The Good Lives Model and Conceptual Issues in Offender Rehabilitation." *Psychology, Crime & Law* 10(3):243–257.

Wexler, Harry K. 1995. "The Success of Therapeutic Communities for Substance Abusers in American Prisons." *Journal of Psychoactive Drugs* 27(1):57–66.

Wexler, Harry K., Gregory P. Falkin, and Douglas S. Lipton. 1990. "Outcome Evaluation of a Prison Therapeutic Community for Substance Abuse Treatment." *Criminal Justice and Behavior* 17(1):71–92.

Wexler, Harry K., Gerald Melnick, Lois Lowe, and Jean Peters. 1999. "Three-Year Reincarceration Outcomes for Amity In-Prison Therapeutic Community and Aftercare in California." *The Prison Journal* 79(3):321–336.

Wexler, Harry K., and Ronald Williams. 1986. "The Stay 'N Out Therapeutic Community: Prison Treatment for Substance Abusers." *Journal of Psychoactive Drugs* 18(3):221–230.

Whitehead, John T., and Steven P. Lab. 1989. "A Meta-Analysis of Juvenile Correctional Treatment." *Journal of Research in Crime and Delinquency* 26(3):276–295.

Wilson, James Q. 1975/1985. *Thinking About Crime*. New York, NY: Vintage.

Wilson, David B., Catherine A. Gallagher, and Doris L. MacKenzie. 2000. "A Meta-Analysis of Corrections-Based Education, Vocation, and Work Programs for Adult Offenders." *Journal of Research in Crime and Delinquency* 37(4):347–368.

Wilson, David B., Doris L. MacKenzie, and Fawn Ngo Mitchell. 2005. "Effects of Correctional Boot Camps on Offending." *Campbell Systematic Reviews* 6: 1–42.

Wilson, David B., Ojmarrh Mitchell, and Doris L. MacKenzie. 2006. "A Systematic Review of Drug Court Effects on Recidivism." *Journal of Experimental Criminology* 2(4):459–487.

13

COMMUNITY CORRECTIONS
Probation, Parole, and Reentry

Chapter 12 considered crime prevention programs and services for prisoners and jail inmates while they are still incarcerated. But many people convicted of a crime are not sentenced to incarceration. Instead, they are sentenced to probation and must comply with the terms of their probation. Because their sentence is served in the community, they experience **community corrections** rather than incarceration. How well does probation and whatever terms probationers must fulfill help prevent recidivism compared with incarceration? When people who do go to prison are released from incarceration, they ordinarily go on parole and often receive substance abuse counseling and other services designed to help them successfully reenter the community. They, too, experience community corrections. How well do parole and reentry services help prevent recidivism? Chapter 12 introduced these questions, and this chapter examines them further.

Because, as we shall see, so many people are released from prison every year or are sentenced to community corrections, these two questions are critical for successful crime prevention. This chapter examines the research evidence to try to answer these questions.

Regarding probation, a major focus will be how well this form of legal punishment prevents recidivism compared with incarceration, the other common legal punishment and the one with which Americans are most familiar. Chapter 1 explained that incarceration is very expensive, incurs many collateral consequences, and is rather ineffective

Chapter Outline

- Understanding Probation and Parole
  - History of Probation and Parole
  - Probation and Parole Today
- Probation and Crime Prevention
  - Intermediate Sanctions
- Parole and Crime Prevention
  - Prisoner Reentry
- Conclusion

Learning Questions

1. What is the difference between probation and parole?

2. About how many people are on probation, and how many leave prison every year?

3. Why is probation a reasonable alternative to incarceration for many offenders?

4. How effective are the different types of intermediate sanctions in preventing recidivism?

5. Why is it difficult to assess the effectiveness of prisoner reentry programs and services?

in preventing crime and recidivism. Given this context, if probation and community corrections are no worse than incarceration in preventing recidivism, then they constitute a very reasonable alternative to incarceration for many offenders by keeping the public at least as safe as incarceration in the long run while saving much money and reducing other problems compared with incarceration.

Regarding parole and reentry, a major focus will be how well parole and reentry services also prevent recidivism, and what types of parole practices and reentry services seem most effective in this respect. Because hundreds of thousands of prisoners are released back into their communities every year, it is important to have the best parole practices and reentry services possible to help prevent recidivism and ensure public safety.

UNDERSTANDING PROBATION AND PAROLE

Before exploring these matters, it will be helpful to present some basic facts about probation and community corrections and about parole and reentry. This discussion will provide a context for the later examination of their effectiveness in preventing recidivism.

Probation is a form of correctional supervision that takes place in the community. After defendants are found guilty of an offense, they may be sentenced to a period of supervision on probation, or their sentence may be split between prison and probation. Probationers are subject to conditions that they must follow, such as remaining crime-free, meeting regularly with a probation officer, refraining from alcohol and other drug use, and not leaving the community. If they violate these conditions, they may have their probation revoked and be placed in prison.

Parole, on the other hand, is supervised release after confinement in prison. Probation and parole are both forms of community supervision, but probation is the sentence, while parole is used after release from a prison sentence. Generally, a person sent to prison on an **indeterminate sentence** (meaning the range of years served can vary) may be eligible to go up for parole after a certain number of years, and a parole board will decide whether the individual is ready for life in the community. After release on parole, parolees must comply with the terms of parole for a set amount of time, often 1 or 2 years. States with **determinate sentencing** instead send convicted defendants to prison for set amounts of time, with these individuals often incurring 1 year of parole supervision after release from prison.

After being released from prison, formerly incarcerated people normally return to their home communities and in effect are reentering society. This process is called prisoner reentry, a term that applies to prisoners released on parole and also those released without parole supervision. The goal of the corrections system here is to help formerly incarcerated prisoners adjust back to society as successfully as possible. This is certainly a humane goal in terms of just helping these individuals, but it is also a goal aimed at preventing recidivism and keeping society safe.

In any event, achieving successful reentry is a very difficult task for a fundamental reason: Many and perhaps most released prisoners bring with them a host of problems that they had before entering prison, that they developed during prison, or that worsened during their incarceration (LaCourse et al. 2019). These problems include substance abuse, a history of being physically and/or sexually abused, and a range of mental and/or physical health problems. Successful reentry requires that these problems be addressed effectively. As criminologists Cheryl Leo Jonson and Francis T. Cullen (2015:522) observe, "Offenders face personal and situational risks that, if left unaddressed, will likely lead them back into crime. Reentering prisoners are thus seen as being at risk for recidivating—but not destined to this fate. The challenge is thus to develop programs that work—which are effective and evidence based."

History of Probation and Parole

Before proceeding further, it is useful to sketch the history of probation and parole. The origin of probation is actually an interesting story. A Boston, Massachusetts, cobbler named John Augustus took an interest in individuals convicted of crimes and personally vouched for them during the 1840s. He put up their bail and supervised them for a period of time with certain conditions in place. If the individuals stayed out of trouble, they would avoid incarceration (Taxman 2015). His example motivated Boston to pass a law in 1878 to become the first city to officially institute probation, in which probation officers would be responsible for supervising offenders in lieu of incarceration. The entire state of Massachusetts was using probation by 1891 (Walker 1998).

A few other states instituted probation by 1900, and most states were using probation within a few decades. All these systems of probation drew from Augustus's example and efforts. As criminologist Joan Petersilia (1997:156) writes, "Virtually every basic practice of probation was conceived by him. He was the first person to use the term 'probation'—which comes from the Latin term *probatio*, meaning a 'period of proving or trial.' He developed the ideas of the presentence investigation, supervision conditions, social casework, reports to the court, and revocation of probation."

Traditionally, the development of parole is also traced to one man, Alexander Maconochie, a Scottish superintendent of British penal colonies on an Australian island in the mid-1800s. Serving in this capacity, Maconochie developed a "tickets of leave" system allowing inmates to exit prison early under supervision. Although Maconochie is often considered the founder of parole, some scholars dispute this characterization; they argue that the elements of Maconochie's tickets-of-leave system were too different from those of modern systems of parole (in ways that need not concern us here) for him to be given this credit (White 1976).

In the United States, parole in effect began during the later 19th century, when severe prison crowding forced prison wardens and governors to release many prisoners before they had served their full terms of incarceration (Walker 1998). As this process began, prison authorities and legislators quickly realized the need to supervise this mass of early releasees. Parole boards developed by the early 20th century to decide which prisoners deserved parole and to help manage the system of parole. The first official parole system was established at the Elmira Reformatory in New York state in the 1870s. Prisoners received indeterminate sentences and then could win early release on parole if they behaved well. All the states had parole systems within a few decades. By the 1970s, almost three-fourths of all released prisoners were released to parole supervision (as opposed to no supervision), with most prisoners also serving indeterminate sentences (Petersilia 1998).

Within a decade, however, observers from both sides of the political system began to criticize parole (Rhine 2015). Liberals said parole release decisions were too arbitrary and racially discriminatory, while conservatives said parole was putting dangerous criminals back on the streets long before they should have been released. Led by Maine in 1976, several states responded to this two-pronged criticism by instituting determinate sentencing and abolishing **discretionary parole** (early release from prison for good behavior). About one-third of the states now follow these early examples by using determinate sentences and automatic release from prison after the determinate sentence has been served (Rhine, Watts, and Reitz 2018). Many released prisoners in these states still remain under **mandatory parole** supervision for at least 1 year.

Probation and Parole Today

To indicate the importance of having effective probation and parole programs and practices, it is helpful to appreciate how many people are on probation or parole at any one time.

In the latest year (year-end 2016) at the time of this writing, roughly 3.7 million adults were on probation (Kaeble and Cowhig 2018). Half of these adults had been convicted of either a property crime or drug offense, and one-fifth of a violent crime; 14% were convicted of drunk driving (Bonczar and Mulako-Wangota 2018). About 2 million people entered probation in 2016, while the same number exited probation (Kaeble 2018). Because some people may enter and/or exit probation more than once in 1 year, it is more accurate to say that there were about 2 million movements onto probation (*entries*) and 2 million movements out of probation (*exits*).

Another 875,000 adults were also on parole at (year-end 2016 (Kaeble 2018). Parole entries numbered about 457,000, while parole exits numbered about 456,000. Along with prisoners released without having to go on parole, the annual number of released prisoners exceeds 600,000 (Carson 2018) today and exceeded 700,000 in the late 2000s. The combined number of probationers and parolees at year-end 2016, more than 4.6 million, amounted to 1 of every 55 adults in the United States, or almost 2% of the adult population.

As we have already mentioned, when people go on probation, they normally must fulfill several conditions, with any violation of these conditions possibly leading to revocation of their probation and then incarceration. The threat of incarceration is intended to help induce probationers to follow all the conditions required of them.

Three general categories of conditions exist for probationers, as they also do for many parolees (Alarid 2019):

- *Standard conditions*, including meeting regularly with, or communicating by phone or other means with, a probation officer; not consuming alcohol or other drugs; not associating with known criminals; and looking for employment

- *Punitive conditions*, which consist of *intermediate sanctions* (to be described just below), which are imposed on offenders who were convicted of more serious crimes and/or who have more extensive prior criminal records

- *Treatment conditions*, which may be required for probationers with such personal problems as alcohol and other drug abuse or mental illness; these individuals may be required to receive appropriate counseling or other services

Intermediate Sanctions

As just noted, probationers deemed the highest risk in terms of their prior records or offense seriousness may incur one or more **intermediate sanctions** as part of their probation. These sanctions developed in the 1980s and are considered "intermediate" because they are harsher than *traditional* (also called *routine* or *standard*) probation but less harsh than incarceration. These sanctions include the following:

- Community service

- Day-reporting centers, at which probationers are required to be during the day and receive various services, including vocational training and substance abuse treatment; they then go home at night

- Fines, restitution, and forfeiture of assets such as personal property

- House arrest and electronic monitoring to ensure a person does not leave home

- Intensive supervision, which involves more frequent monitoring of probationers than routine probation

- Shock probation, which places probationers in a paramilitary setting similar to a military boot camp and is designed to enhance their respect for authority, among other aims

Having now completed our summary of probation and parole, we now examine the evidence on their effectiveness in preventing recidivism. We will see that probation is indeed at least as effective as incarceration in this regard—admittedly a low standard but still an important benchmark for criminal justice policy—while certain parole and reentry practices also show promise.

PROBATION AND CRIME PREVENTION

Because probation is so much less expensive than incarceration, evidence that it prevents incarceration at least as well as incarceration would argue for the continued use and even expansion of probation. On the other hand, if probationers in fact have a higher recidivism rate than prisoners, that type of evidence would argue against probation, at least in terms of public safety if not expense. So what does the evidence say?

One type of evidence is very clear, and that is the economic cost of probation compared with incarceration. Although we have already said that probation is much less expensive, some actual dollar figures will help illustrate this significant difference and provide a context for our discussion of the evidence on recidivism. The national average cost of incarceration was $33,274 per prisoner in 2015 according to New York's Vera Institute of Justice (Mai and Subramanian 2017). Meanwhile, the national average cost of probation for federal offenders was $3,347 per probationer in 2012 (Administrative Office of the U.S. Courts 2013); for the sake of argument, let's assume this latter estimate applies to all offenders and not just to federal offenders.

Adjusting for inflation, these amounts would have been $36,017 and $3,740, respectively, in 2019. Doing a little math reveals that incarceration costs 9.6 times more than probation per person. If all the people now on probation were instead incarcerated, the extra cost to the nation would be more than $100 billion annually, and this huge figure does not include the hundreds of billions of dollars it would cost to build the new prisons that would be necessary to hold them. Probation is clearly much less expensive than incarceration and therefore far more cost-effective.

From a pure crime prevention perspective, though, the key question is whether probation and the intermediate sanctions it sometimes involves are at least as effective as incarceration in preventing recidivism. Before commenting on the evidence on this point, we must first acknowledge that some probationers do commit new offenses while on probation. In 2016, 4% of the probationers who exited probation did so because they committed a new offense and were then incarcerated; most of the remainder completed probation successfully, while some had their probation revoked because they violated a term of their probation. If the 4% who committed a new offense had originally been incarcerated instead of being placed on probation, fewer crimes would have occurred and society would have been a bit safer. However, it is virtually impossible to predict accurately who might commit a new offense while on probation (Dressel and Farid 2018). The only way, then, to prevent all new offenses by probationers would be to do away with probation, which, as we have suggested, is not at all financially viable.

Turning finally to the evidence on recidivism, the best type of evidence would stem from random assignment of convicted offenders to either incarceration or probation. For ethical and practical reasons, such random assignment does not occur and would be difficult or impossible to implement in any event for research purposes. This methodological fact means that studies of probation and recidivism must rely on comparisons of the recidivism of probationers with that of released prisoners after matching the two groups on such criteria as offense seriousness, prior criminal record, and age. These types of comparisons generally find that the recidivism rate of probationers is no higher than, and sometimes lower than, the recidivism rate of released prisoners (Taxman 2015). Because probation is also so much less expensive than incarceration, this recidivism evidence underscores the benefits and importance of probation for today's criminal justice system.

Probation experts say that probation would be even more effective in preventing recidivism if probation caseloads were smaller and if probationers received better services and treatment for their many personal problems, which resemble those we described earlier for released prisoners (Petersilia 2002). If these improvements occurred, probationers' recidivism might reduce by an estimated 30% (Jalbert and Rhodes 2012).

Intermediate Sanctions

The foregoing discussion focused on probation generally, but many higher-risk probationers incur intermediate sanctions that are designed to help prevent their recidivism. How effective are intermediate sanctions in this respect? Researchers typically compare the recidivism of probationers on a particular intermediate sanction with that of matched released prisoners. Because intermediate sanctions vary somewhat in their effectiveness, we discuss them separately.

Community Service

Community service is used much more often in Western Europe, and studies there find that it produces recidivism that is about the same as, or sometimes lower than, that of matched offenders who were incarcerated (Andersen 2015; Klement 2015). Few U.S. studies examine community service, but those that do reach the same conclusion as the Western European research (McDonald 1992). Criminologist Michael Tonry (1998:697) concluded from all the evidence that community service "can serve as a meaningful, cost-effective sanction for offenders who would otherwise have been imprisoned."

Day-Reporting Centers

Day-reporting centers (DRCs) were first established in Britain in the 1960s and first appeared in the United States in Connecticut and Massachusetts in the 1980s. They are now used for both probationers and parolees who are thought to especially need various services. Because DRCs require daytime attendance, they also enable authorities to monitor their clients' behavior and thus reduce their opportunity for offending, at least during the day. Many DRCs also require their clients to submit to random drug testing. Because DRCs have these assumed benefits, they have become a popular intermediate sanction.

The research on the effectiveness of DRCs (also called *community resource centers*) examines this type of sanction for both probationers and parolees (more studies focus on the former than on the latter), with recidivism of either type of offender compared to matched counterparts who did not have to report to these centers. The results of this research are decidedly mixed: Some studies suggest that the DRCs reduce recidivism compared with traditional probation or incarceration (Champion et al. 2011), while other studies find that the centers produce similar recidivism rates or even higher rates (Marciniak 2000).

Several reasons probably account for these mixed results. DRCs operate differently across the nation: They take in different types of offenders with different risk levels, and they also differ in the services they offer and in other aspects of their operation. All these differences mean that some DRCs may simply be more effective than others, and some may be much less effective.

Methodological problems may also account for these mixed results. One problem is a familiar issue that we have already noted in this chapter and in earlier chapters: the lack of random assignment. Although researchers try to compensate for this problem by using matched samples, the matching process may be less than ideal. In a second problem, the probationers or parolees in some of the studies have certain characteristics, such as mental illness, that might mean these studies' results do not apply to probationers or parolees more generally.

It is worth noting that two methodologically sound studies of New Jersey DRCs found that DRC involvement actually *increased* recidivism. The first of these two studies used a well-matched comparison group and found that DRC parolee clients ended up with higher recidivism rates than matched parolees (Hyatt and Ostermann 2019). The second study was able to use random assignment; this study also found that DRC client parolees ended up with higher recidivism rates than the control-group parolees (Boyle et al. 2013). The first study's authors concluded that the DRCs "failed to produce the reduction in criminal behaviors and increases in community reintegration for which they were intended" (Hyatt and Ostermann 2019:112). Regarding crime prevention policy, they further concluded that their study's results "may also call into question the appropriateness of using day reporting centers . . . for either prison diversion or intermediate punishment" (p. 114).

Why might DRCs actually increase recidivism when the opposite consequence might well have been expected? The authors of the second study just mentioned visited the DRCs they studied and noticed problems in their operation that may have accounted for the increased recidivism their study found (Boyle et al. 2013). For example, they observed much unstructured time in the DRCs that allowed clients to interact with one another (and thus to negatively influence one another), whereas traditional parolees might not encounter many or any other parolees while waiting to meet with their parole officer. Their observations underscore our earlier point that some DRCs may simply operate more or less effectively than other DRCs in terms of preventing recidivism.

The very mixed results of the DRCs research suggest they are not a viable means of crime prevention for either probationers or parolees. However, because some studies have found positive results, future research should assess the characteristics of DRCs that might enhance or instead impair their ability to prevent recidivism, as criminologists urge (Duwe 2013; Steiner and Butler 2013).

Fines, Restitution, and Forfeiture

These intermediate sanctions are all used in the United States for offenders convicted of minor crimes, including traffic violations. These offenders probably have a low probability of committing new offenses, especially serious crimes. Perhaps because of this low probability, there is very little research on the crime prevention impact of these sanctions compared with routine probation.

However, a few studies suggest that restitution (such as regular payments to victims by offenders or doing yard work around the victim's home) reduces recidivism at least for some offenders (Ruback 2002; Sims 2000). That said, there is also evidence that restitution and other financial penalties may ironically increase recidivism if offenders feel compelled to commit crime to obtain the money they owe (Piquero and Jennings 2017).

Despite this inconsistent evidence, restitution has become a rather popular sanction in general, but perhaps especially for juveniles who have committed low-level offenses. If restitution does help lower recidivism by at least some offenders, it might be because continual restitution payments remind offenders of the harm they caused to their victims, and because their regular payments help them see themselves as law-abiding persons (Ruback et al. 2018). In this regard, it may be important for states and counties to have offenders pay their restitution amounts separately from other payments they may owe, such as fines and court fees (Cares and Haynes 2018). This suggested separation reflects the probability that offenders will consider restitution to be a fairer and more appropriate sanction for their illegal behavior than these other types of financial sanctions, which they may consider unfairly punitive.

Many states require restitution for some types of crimes and in some circumstances. However, many and probably most offenders do not always make their required regular payments, in part because doing so may aggravate the financial hardships many are already facing, and in part because they may not understand how much money to remit and where they should send the money. In an interesting experiment, R. Barry Ruback and colleagues (Ruback et al. 2014, 2018) randomly assigned offenders who were behind in their payments to either receive or not receive a monthly letter outlining the latter information. Those who did receive this letter ended up making more regular payments, and they also ended up with a lower recidivism rate within a 2-year follow-up period.

House Arrest and Electronic Monitoring

House arrest and electronic monitoring usually occur jointly: A probationer is required to stay home at all times, and an electronic ankle bracelet or other electronic measure is used to ensure compliance with this requirement. People under house arrest can still commit crimes at home, such as domestic violence and illegal drug use and trafficking, but at least they cannot commit crimes against the public, assuming they do in fact stay home all the time.

The relatively few studies on the effectiveness of this twin sanction find that people under house arrest and electronic monitoring do not have lower recidivism rates than those under routine probation (MacKenzie 2006). The fact that house arrest is typically used for low-level offenders, who might not have reoffended anyway, may account for these null results. One study did find that probationers under house arrest who were electronically monitored had lower recidivism rates than those under house arrest who were not electronically monitored (Padgett, Bales, and Blomberg 2006). Thus, even if house arrest itself does not reduce recidivism, electronic monitoring might do so.

Because, as just noted, electronic monitoring typically does accompany house arrest in today's high-tech society, this finding about electronic monitoring might be interesting, but it is also not actually very useful for crime prevention policy beyond what is now already occurring. Returning to our main point, though, house arrest and electronic monitoring as an intermediate sanction do not appear to reduce recidivism beyond what routine probation already accomplishes.

Intensive Supervision

Intensive supervision (also called *intensive supervised probation or parole*, or ISP) is intended for probationers or parolees who have committed more serious offenses, who have more extensive prior records, and/or who are thought to need more supervision to help them avoid reoffending. Compared with people on routine probation (or parole), those on ISP meet with their probation or parole officer much more often, both at the officer's workplace and also at the offender's home; they are also tested much more often for substance use, and they have to abide by curfews. The probation and parole officers who handle ISP have smaller caseloads than those who handle offenders on routine probation or parole.

Research on ISP sometimes involves random assignment and other times matched samples. This research finds that ISP does not reduce recidivism more effectively than routine probation or parole does (Hyatt and Barnes 2017; MacKenzie 2006). It also finds that ISP results in more observed violations of probation or parole conditions because of the greater scrutiny given to ISP offenders. This observation in turn leads to more revocations of probation or parole, and thus incarceration, for ISP offenders than for those on routine probation or parole. Because ISP is also more expensive than routine probation or parole, all these disadvantages suggest that it is not a sensible alternative to routine probation or parole.

Despite this pessimistic assessment, a new type of ISP offers much more optimism for reducing recidivism. This new model combines ISP with two additional features: (1) swift and certain punishment (hearings within 72 hours of a violation, followed by short jail stays) for any violation of ISP conditions and (2) substance abuse treatment and other services. The prototype for this new model is Hawaii's Opportunity Probation with Enforcement (HOPE), established in 2004. HOPE involves random assignment, and research finds it reduces recidivism compared with routine probation (Alm 2016). HOPE-style programs in other states also achieve this same benefit (DeVall et al. 2017). Based on this success, a review of these programs concluded that "the time is ripe for [them] to be embraced by politicians, criminal justice practitioners, and the general public" (p. 605).

Shock Probation

Unfortunately, the optimistic conclusions of the research on this new ISP model do not apply to **shock probation**, which resembles military boot camps by housing probationers, usually young men, in a paramilitary setting, emphasizing obedience to authority, military drills, rigorous exercise, and so forth. The goal of these boot camps is to have these young men learn respect for authority and to acquire a sense of responsibility. They are called "shock probation" because the relatively harsh experience of being in these boot camps is intended to shock offenders into obeying the law in the future. The first two boot camps were used in Georgia and Oklahoma in 1983, and many other states soon followed suit.

These boot camps have been popular, but they have also been a failure. According to much research, they do not reduce recidivism more effectively than routine probation (Bergin 2016), and they have also sometimes subjected their participants to abuse by the correctional officers who act as their paramilitary instructors (Hamilton, Parvini, and Knoll 2015). A review of the boot camp research concluded, "At this point in time, there is no evidence that correctional boot camps are effective in reducing the future criminal activities of adults or juveniles. . . . The military atmosphere of the boot camps is not effective in changing offender behavior" (MacKenzie 2006:296).

PAROLE AND CRIME PREVENTION

The goal of parole is to help prevent recidivism by supervising parolees and providing them with various services, including substance abuse treatment and vocational training. With hundreds of thousands of released prisoners going on parole every year, it is critical for parole to achieve this key goal. At the same time, the corrections system faces major obstacles in doing so, because, as we have emphasized, released prisoners typically have a history of offending and a history of personal problems and other circumstances that may easily lead them to reoffend.

In this regard, they pose more of a threat to public safety than probationers for at least three reasons: (1) They have usually committed more serious offenses than probationers, (2) they usually have a greater record of prior offenses than probationers, and (3) their prison experience may have damaged them in ways that make it even more likely that they will reoffend (Mears, Cochran, and Cullen 2015). When they reenter society, they often have trouble finding gainful employment, staying off drugs, and avoiding contact with criminal peers, and they experience other problems that make it difficult for them to desist from criminal behavior (Western 2018). The lack of correctional services for many prisoners helps guarantee they will not be able to overcome these problems (Jonson and Cullen 2015).

Because of all these circumstances, most released prisoners do reoffend. Evidence of this unfortunate fact comes from a study by the U.S. Bureau of Justice Statistics of the several hundred thousand state prisoners released in 2005 (Alper, Durose, and Markman 2018). This study found that two-thirds of these prisoners were rearrested within 3 years, 79% were rearrested within 6 years, and 83% were rearrested within 9 years. On the average, each person who was rearrested during the 9-year follow-up had committed six new offenses.

In addition to the reasons already stated for this high rate of recidivism, another circumstance also matters. When prisoners are released, they typically have little money and few possessions. As Jonson and Cullen (2015:527) note, "Most states release prisoners with little concern for their material welfare. Inmates are typically given $20–$100 in gate money, a bus ticket to an in-state location, the single set of clothes worn on their backs, and prescription medicine that will expire in 1 week to 60 days." Their conviction records may make it very difficult for them to secure public or private housing, and their conviction records, lack of education, and lack of stable work history also make it very difficult to find gainful employment.

Released prisoners, then, are far more likely to eventually be rearrested than to obey the law. Of course, perhaps an even greater proportion of released prisoners, most of whom go on parole, would be arrested if they had not experienced parole, or perhaps the recidivists would have committed an even greater number of new offenses per person. These hypothetical outcomes aside, parole cannot be considered to be very effective in preventing recidivism.

A study that compared the recidivism of released prisoners who went on parole with that of released prisoners who did not go on parole reinforces this conclusion (Solomon, Kachnowski, and Bhati 2005). This study found that the former group had roughly the same recidivism rate as the latter group.

Although this evidence on released prisoners' recidivism is discouraging, there is also some evidence that their recidivism is declining. This evidence comes from comparisons of the recidivism of prisoners released in 2005 and 2012, respectively (Gelb and Velázquez 2018). Of those released in 2005, 48% were readmitted to prison within 3 years; of those released in 2012, 37% were readmitted to prison within 3 years. Those released in 2012 were also less likely to reenter prison within 5 years. To the extent that parole has become more effective during the past decade or two, experts say it is because many states have improved the range of treatment programs and other services for released prisoners (National Reentry Resource Center 2017). Much of this improvement came in the wake of federal legislation, called the Second Chance Act, passed by Congress and signed by President George W. Bush in 2008. This legislation provided some $300 million for a variety of correctional and reentry programs and services across the nation.

Prisoner Reentry

Efforts to improve reentry programs and services reflect increasing recognition since this century began of the need for successful prisoner reentry to help ensure public safety (Middlemass 2017). As mass incarceration developed over the past several decades, many more people went to prison and many more people have been coming out of prison—more than 600,000 annually in recent years, as we have already noted. The sheer size of this released prisoner population has forced states and the federal government to increase their efforts to help them overcome the many problems that led to their initial offending and that make their recidivism so common. The goal here is to ease and enhance their reentry back into society, with the hope they will be less likely to commit new crimes as a result.

To increase the prospects for successful reentry, released prisoners need myriad well-funded, well-designed, and well-implemented programs and services, including vocational training and employment services, substance abuse treatment, anger management counseling, and so forth (Jonson and Cullen 2015; Visher et al. 2017). What kind of reentry programs and services seem most effective in preventing recidivism? This is certainly an important question. Because some programs and services may be more effective than others, it is essential to identify which such efforts are more effective and which are less effective.

Several problems make it difficult to assess the effectiveness of reentry programs and services. One problem in assessing the effectiveness of reentry programs and services is a definitional issue. Should the term *reentry programs and services* include only those programs and services that are provided for former prisoners (*postrelease* programs and services)? Should they include only those programs and services that are provided for current prisoners (*prerelease* programs and services), which were the subject of Chapter 12? Or should they include programs and services that are provided for both current and former prisoners? Some studies of reentry efforts focus only on postrelease efforts, other studies focus only on prerelease efforts, and still others focus on both postrelease and prerelease efforts. This situation means that not every scholar and policymaker has the same types of programs and services in mind when they study their effectiveness. While Chapter 12 discussed prerelease correctional services, the following discussion focuses on prerelease and postrelease programs and services combined.

A related problem is that the reentry category encompasses a diverse range of programs, services, and practices that makes it difficult to assess the relative effectiveness of all these efforts (Jonson and Cullen 2015). Adding to this difficulty is the fact that current and former prisoners may receive help from more than one program/service/practice at any one time, or help from more than one such effort over time. If these individuals then recidivate less often than prisoners with less or no such help, which specific effort should receive the credit? This type of question is difficult for research to answer.

Still another problem is that many reentry programs and services are not well-designed and well-implemented. Jonson and Cullen (2015:541) call this problem a "lack of integrity in program implementation." Examples of this problem include programs and services that do not last long enough, that involve group counseling for groups that are too large for effective intervention, and that do not meet the risk-need-responsivity criteria as described just below. Research may judge these flawed efforts to be ineffective, when in fact the fault might lie more in their design and implementation than in the efforts themselves were they not so flawed.

Another problem in assessing the effectiveness of reentry strategies is the familiar one of lack of random assignment, as well as some other methodological issues. These issues mean that "much remains unknown about what works for prisoners reentering society" (Visher et al. 2017:140).

With this context in mind, which types of reentry efforts seem more or less effective in preventing recidivism? Research that tries to answer this question yields several conclusions (Jonson and Cullen 2015; Visher et al. 2017). One bottom line is this: Efforts to *rehabilitate* offenders are much more effective at preventing recidivism than *control* efforts that focus on monitoring their behavior and threatening them with legal punishment.

Another finding is that treatment programs seem more effective regarding recidivism when they involve higher-risk offenders compared with lower-risk offenders (Andrews and Bonta 2017). The reason for this difference is probably that high-risk offenders simply have more room for improvement, while low-risk offenders are much less likely to reoffend in any event.

A third finding is that *individual change efforts*, which focus on helping prisoners and former prisoners become motivated to want to avoid offending (for example, to help them realize it is immoral to commit crime, or to help them control their anger) seem more effective than *practical needs efforts*, which focus on providing former prisoners jobs and helping them meet other practical needs (Lipsey and Cullen 2007; MacKenzie 2012). The latter efforts are sometimes helpful, research finds, but the former seem more helpful in terms of the size of their effects and also more helpful in terms of the consistency of research findings.

A fourth finding involves *continuity* (or *continuum*) *of care*. Research suggests that reentry programs and services are most effective if they begin during incarceration and then continue for offenders after release from prison. Offenders who receive programs and services only during incarceration or only after release are more likely to reoffend than those who receive this help at both time points.

A fifth finding, and one that both reflects and explains the findings just mentioned, is that programs and services are more effective if they rely on a *risk-need-responsivity* model (Andrews and Bonta 2017). This model assumes that reentry programs and services are most effective if they involve high-*risk* offenders, if they address the factors in the offenders' lives (their *needs*) that predict they will recidivate, and if they use treatment methods and procedures that are *responsive* to these needs. Programs and services that meet all these criteria are likely to be more effective in reducing recidivism than those that do not.

Beyond these general findings, the overall research on reentry strategies yields results that perhaps raise more questions than they answer, in part because of the methodological difficulties cited earlier, in part because of the great diversity of these strategies, and in part because the results themselves are inconsistent. As a recent review noted, "A wide diversity of programs fall under the rubric and only a limited number of rigorous evaluations have been conducted. Research suggests that, overall, reentry services reduce recidivism, but program effects are heterogeneous [varied] and at times criminogenic" (Jonson and Cullen 2015:517).

A recent investigation that uncovered heterogeneous and criminogenic effects examined prisoner reentry programs (prerelease) at sites in 12 states (Visher et al. 2017). Random assignment was used in some of the sites, while matched samples were used in the other sites. Within 6 years postrelease, most of the prisoners in the study were rearrested. Even so, this study found that some services were more effective than others in preventing recidivism. Those that focused on individual change, such as criminal attitude training, education classes, and personal relationship training, reduced recidivism slightly. On the other hand, services that focused on practical needs, such as employment services and life skills assistance, had no effect on recidivism or even increased recidivism slightly by evidently having criminogenic effects.

Why did these criminogenic effects occur? This study's authors speculated that practical services may raise prisoners' expectations that they will successfully reenter society and that when they fail to do so, as often happens, they respond with greater criminality: "When these individuals hit obstacles after release they may be particularly frustrated and go back to old patterns" (Visher et al. 2017:159–160). Their findings led them to recommend an increased focus on individual change programs and services to achieve successful reentry but also for more high-quality research on the effectiveness of a wide range of reentry strategies.

The reentry research literature is still limited, and so is the development of well-designed and well-funded reentry programs and services. This situation leads Jonson and Cullen (2015:565) to call for a new *criminology of reentry* to help better identify and evaluate the best reentry practices and the theories underlying these practices. If such a new criminological focus succeeds, reentry programs and services will become more effective in preventing recidivism, and society will be safer.

CONCLUSION

People on probation and those released from prison have a host of individual and structural problems that make it highly likely that they will reoffend, and so they do. A wide variety of programs, services, and practices try to reduce their recidivism. These efforts vary in their effectiveness, with some reducing recidivism, some having no effects, and some even increasing recidivism. It is critical for future research to identify the most effective strategies to help offenders desist from criminal behavior, and it is also critical for the criminal justice system to develop, fund, and implement the best such strategies. Success in these efforts will help lower the crime rate and ensure public safety.

SUMMARY

1. Probation and parole are both forms of community corrections. Probation is an alternative to incarceration, while parole provides supervision for prisoners after release from incarceration.

2. Offenders on probation or parole typically must comply with a set of standard conditions, and some also must comply with various punitive and/or treatment conditions.

3. Probationers thought to be at higher risk for reoffending sometimes incur intermediate sanctions, including such forms as community service, house arrest, and day-reporting centers.

4. Research finds that probationers have about the same recidivism rate as released prisoners. This fact means that probation keeps society no less safe than incarceration and does so at a much lower cost.

5. The different types of intermediate sanctions have inconsistent effects on recidivism. Those that combine the sanction with various program and treatment services seem most effective. Intensive supervision combined with swift and certain punishment for violation of conditions and with substance abuse treatment and other services shows promise for reducing recidivism.

6. Most released prisoners commit new crimes whether or not they were released to parole supervision. On a positive note, their recidivism rate seems to have declined slightly during the past decade.

7. Prisoner reentry is a critical issue for today's society because more than 600,000 prisoners are released every year and have a host of problems that put them at high risk for reoffending.

8. Many issues make it difficult to assess the effectiveness of reentry programs and services. Those that appear to be most effective conform to the risk-need-responsivity model.

KEY TERMS

community corrections 281
day-reporting centers
   (DRCs) 287
determinate sentencing 282

discretionary parole 284
indeterminate sentence 282
intensive supervision 290
intermediate sanctions 285

mandatory parole 284
parole 282
probation 282
shock probation 290

REFERENCES

Administrative Office of the U.S. Courts. 2013. "Supervision Costs Significantly Less Than Incarceration in Federal System." Retrieved September 29, 2019 (http://www.uscourts .gov/news/2013/07/18/supervision-costs-significantly-less-incarceration-federal-system).

Alarid, Leanne Fiftal. 2019. *Community-Based Corrections*. Boston, MA: Cengage.

Alm, Steven S. 2016. "Hope Probation." *Criminology & Public Policy* 15(4):1195–1214. doi: 10.1111/1745-9133.12261.

Alper, Mariel, Matthew R. Durose, and Joshua Markman. 2018. *2018 Update on Prisoner Recidivism: A 9-Year Follow-Up Period (2005–2014)*. Washington, DC: Bureau of Justice Statistics, U.S. Department of Justice.

Andersen, Signe. 2015. "Serving Time or Serving the Community? Exploiting a Policy Reform to Assess the Causal Effects of Community Service on Income, Social Benefit Dependency and Recidivism." *Journal of Quantitative Criminology* 31(4):537–563. doi: 10.1007/s10940-014-9237-2.

Andrews, D. A., and James Bonta. 2017. *The Psychology of Criminal Conduct*. Cincinnati, OH: Anderson.

Bergin, Tiffany. 2016. *The Evidence Enigma: Correctional Boot Camps and Other Failures in*

Evidence-Based Policymaking. New York, NY: Routledge.

Bonczar, Thomas P., and Joseph Mulako-Wangota. 2018. "Count of Year-End Probation Population by Most Serious Offense." Generated using the Corrections Statistical Analysis Tool (CSAT)—Probation at www.bjs.gov.

Boyle, Douglas J., Laura M. Ragusa-Salerno, Jennifer L. Lanterman, and Andrea Fleisch Marcus. 2013. "An Evaluation of Day Reporting Centers for Parolees." *Criminology & Public Policy* 12(1):119–143. doi: 10.1111/1745-9133.12010.

Cares, Alison C., and Stacy H. Haynes. 2018. "Restitution: A Different Kind of Economic Sanction?" *Criminology & Public Policy* 17(4):815–823.

Carson, E. Ann. 2018. *Prisoners in 2016.* Washington, DC: Bureau of Justice Statistics, U.S. Department of Justice.

Champion, David R., Patrick J. Harvey, and Youngyol Yim Schanz. 2011. "Day Reporting Center and Recidivism: Comparing Offender Groups in a Western Pennsylvania County Study." *Journal of Offender Rehabilitation* 50(7):433–446.

DeVall, Kristen E., Christina Lanier, David J. Hartmann, Sarah Hupp Williamson, and LaQuana N. Askew. 2017. "Intensive Supervision Programs and Recidivism: How Michigan Successfully Targets High-Risk Offenders." *The Prison Journal* 97(5):585–608.

Dressel, Julia, and Hany Farid. 2018. "The Accuracy, Fairness, and Limits of Predicting Recidivism." *Science Advances* 4(1). Retrieved September 29, 2019 (http://advances.sciencemag.org/content/4/1/eaao5580.full).

Duwe, Grant. 2013. "What's Inside the 'Black Box'?" *Criminology & Public Policy* 12(1):145–152. doi: 10.1111/1745-9133.12012.

Gelb, Adam, and Tracy Velázquez. 2018. "The Changing State of Recidivism: Fewer People Going Back to Prison." Pew Charitable Trusts. Retrieved September 29, 2019 (http://www.pewtrusts.org/en/research-and-analysis/articles/2018/08/01/the-changing-state-of-recidivism-fewer-people-going-back-to-prison).

Hamilton, Matt, Sarah Parvini, and Corina Knoll. 2015. "Children in Boot Camp Investigation Suffer Lasting Damage, Lawyer Says." *Los Angeles Times.* August 6. Retrieved September 29, 2019 (https://www.latimes.com/local/california/la-me-boot-camp-arrests-20150807-story.html).

Hyatt, Jordan M., and Geoffrey C. Barnes. 2017. "An Experimental Evaluation of the Impact of Intensive Supervision on the Recidivism of High-Risk Probationers." *Crime & Delinquency* 63(1):3–38.

Hyatt, Jordan M., and Michael Ostermann. 2019. "Better to Stay Home: Evaluating the Impact of Day Reporting Centers on Offending." *Crime & Delinquency* 65(1):94–121.

Jalbert, Sarah Kuck, and William Rhodes. 2012. "Reduced Caseloads Improve Probation Outcomes." *Journal of Crime & Justice* 35(2):221–238.

Jonson, Cheryl Lero, and Francis T. Cullen. 2015. "Prisoner Reentry Programs." *Crime and Justice* 44(1):517–575. doi: doi:10.1086/681554.

Kaeble, Danielle. 2018. *Probation and Parole in the United States, 2016.* Washington, DC: Bureau of Justice Statistics, U.S. Department of Justice.

Kaeble, Danielle, and Mary Cowhig. 2018. *Correctional Populations in the United States, 2016.*

Washington, DC: Bureau of Justice Statistics, U.S. Department of Justice.

Klement, Christian. 2015. "Comparing the Effects of Community Service and Imprisonment on Reconviction: Results From a Quasi-Experimental Danish Study." *Journal of Experimental Criminology* 11(2):237–261. doi: 10.1007/s11292-015-9231-1.

LaCourse, Ashleigh, Shelley Johnson Listwan, Shannon Reid, and Jennifer L. Hartman. 2019. "Recidivism and Reentry: The Role of Individual Coping Styles." *Crime & Delinquency* 65(1):46–88.

Lipsey, Mark W., and Francis T. Cullen. 2007. "The Effectiveness of Correctional Rehabilitation: A Review of Systematic Reviews." *Annual Review of Law and Social Science* 3: 297–320.

MacKenzie, Doris L. 2006. *What Works in Corrections: Reducing the Criminal Activities of Offenders and Delinquents*. New York, NY: Cambridge University Press.

MacKenzie, Doris L. 2012. "The Effectiveness of Corrections-Based Work and Academic and Vocational Education Programs." Pp. 492–518 in *The Oxford Handbook of Sentencing and Corrections*, edited by J. Petersilia and K. R. Reitz. New York, NY: Oxford University Press.

Mai, Chris, and Ram Subramanian. 2017. *Price of Prisons 2015: Examining State Spending Trends, 2010–2015*. New York, NY: Vera Institute of Justice.

Marciniak, Liz Marie. 2000. "The Addition of Day Reporting to Intensive Supervision Probation: A Comparison of Recidivism Rates." *Federal Probation* 64: 34–39.

McDonald, Douglas. 1992. "Punishing Labor: Unpaid Community Service as a Criminal Sentence." In *Smart Sentencing: The Emergence of Intermediate Sanctions*, edited by J. M. Byrne, A. J. Lurigio, and J. Petersilia. Newbury Park, CA: Sage.

Mears, Daniel P., Joshua C. Cochran, and Francis T. Cullen. 2015. "Incarceration Heterogeneity and Its Implications for Assessing the Effectiveness of Imprisonment on Recidivism." *Criminal Justice Policy Review* 26(7):691–712.

Middlemass, Keesha M. 2017. *Convicted and Condemned: The Politics and Policies of Prisoner Reentry*. New York: New York University Press.

National Reentry Resource Center. 2017. "Reducing Recidivism: States Deliver Results." Retrieved September 29, 2019 (https://csgjusticecenter.org/nrrc/publications/reducing-recidivism-states-deliver-results-2017/).

Padgett, Kathy G., William D. Bales, and Thomas G. Blomberg. 2006. "Under Surveillance: An Empirical Test of the Effectiveness and Consequences of Electronic Monitoring." *Criminology & Public Policy* 5: 61–92.

Petersilia, Joan. 1997. "Probation in the United States." *Crime and Justice: A Review of Research* 22: 149–200.

Petersilia, Joan. 1998. "Probation and Parole." Pp. 563–588 in *The Handbook of Crime and Punishment*, edited by M. Tonry. New York, NY: Oxford University Press.

Petersilia, Joan. 2002. *Reforming Probation and Parole in the 21st Century*. Alexandria, VA: American Correctional Association.

Piquero, Alex R., and Wesley G. Jennings. 2017. "Research Note: Justice System-Imposed Financial Penalties Increase the Likelihood of Recidivsm in a Sample of Adolescent

Offenders." *Youth Violence and Juvenile Justice* 15: 325–340.

Rhine, Edward E. 2015. "The Present Status and Future Prospects of Parole Boards and Parole Supervision." Pp. 637–656 in *The Oxford Handbook of Sentencing and Corrections*, edited by J. Petersilia and K. R. Reitz. New York, NY: Oxford University Press.

Rhine, Edward, Alexis Watts, and Kevin R. Reitz. 2018. "Parole Boards Within Indeterminate and Determinate Sentencing Structures." Robina Institute of Criminal Law and Criminal Justice. Retrieved September 29, 2019 (http://robinainstitute.umn.edu/news-views/parole-boards-within-indeterminate-and-determinate-sentencing-structures).

Ruback, R. Barry. 2002. *Restitution in Pennsylvania: A Multimethod Investigation*. Erie: Pennsylvania Commission on Crime and Delinquency.

Ruback, R. Barry, Andrew S. Gladfelter, and Brendan Lantz. 2014. "Paying Restitution: An Experimental Analysis of the Effects of Information and Rationale." *Criminology & Public Policy* 13: 405–436.

Ruback, R. Barry, Lauren K. Knoth, Andrew S. Gladfelter, and Brendan Lantz. 2018. "Restitution Payment and Recidivism: An Experimental Analysis." *Criminology & Public Policy* 17(4):789–813.

Sims, Barbara. 2000. "Victim Restitution: A Review of the Literature." *Justice Professional* 13(3):247–269.

Solomon, Amy, Vera Kachnowski, and Avi Bhati. 2005. *Does Parole Work? Analyzing the Impact of Postprison Supervision on Rearrest Outcomes*. Washington, DC: Urban Institute.

Steiner, Benjamin, and H. Daniel Butler. 2013. "Why Didn't They Work? Thoughts on the Application of New Jersey Day Reporting Centers." *Criminology & Public Policy* 12(1):153–162. doi: 10.1111/1745-9133.12014.

Taxman, Faye S. 2015. "Probation, Intermediate Sanctions, and Community-Based Corrections." Pp. 363–387 in *The Oxford Handbook of Sentencing and Corrections*, edited by J. Petersilia and K. R. Reitz. New York, NY: Oxford University Press.

Tonry, Michael. 1998. "Intermediate Sanctions." Pp. 683–711 in *The Handbook of Crime & Punishment*, edited by M. Tonry. New York, NY: Oxford University Press.

Visher, Christy A., Pamela K. Lattimore, Kelle Barrick, and Stephen Tueller. 2017. "Evaluating the Long-Term Effects of Prisoner Reentry Services on Recidivism: What Types of Services Matter?" *JQ: Justice Quarterly* 34(1):136–165. doi: 10.1080/07418825.2015.1115539.

Walker, Samuel. 1998. *Popular Justice: A History of American Criminal Justice*. New York, NY: Oxford University Press.

Western, Bruce. 2018. *Homeward: Life in the Year After Prison*. New York, NY: Russell Sage Foundation.

White, Stephen. 1976. "Alexander Maconochie and the Development of Parole." *Journal of Criminal Law & Criminology* 67: 72–88.

PART V

CONCLUSION
Final Thoughts on Crime Prevention

CHAPTER 14 **Epilogue: The Promise and Challenge of Crime Prevention**

14

EPILOGUE

The Promise and Challenge of Crime Prevention

This final chapter summarizes what readers have learned from this book and discusses crime prevention in other wealthy democracies. It ends with a brief essay on the future of crime prevention in the United States.

Chapter Outline

- What Have You Learned?
- Lessons From Canada and Western Europe
  - Germany's Correctional Model
- The Future of Crime Prevention in the United States

Learning Questions

1. What are any four things that you learned from reading this book?

2. Which crime prevention lessons should the United States learn from other wealthy democracies?

3. What happened after Canada did not follow the example of the United States of adopting a tough-on-crime approach during the 1970s and later?

4. How do Germany's correctional practices differ from those in the United States?

5. What three themes have guided this book's discussion of crime prevention?

WHAT HAVE YOU LEARNED?

Readers first learned that the United States has been following a tough-on-crime approach since the 1970s that has led to the rise of mass incarceration. This consequence has led millions of Americans to spend time behind bars and created numerous collateral consequences for their lives. These consequences have been especially numerous and severe for people of color. Mass incarceration has cost billions of dollars without appreciably preventing crime and keeping society safe. Crime prevention that instead follows a public health model offers much more promise than the punitive approach that the United States has been following for the past several decades.

You next became familiar with the many explanations of street crime offered by the fields of biology, psychology, and the social sciences. Crime has various causes, and the risk factors for crime all ideally need to be addressed for effective crime prevention to occur. Biological and psychological explanations say the roots of crime lie inside the individual, while sociological explanations emphasize the social environment. All these explanations combine to offer a more comprehensive understanding of crime, and thus effective crime prevention, than any one explanation by itself.

The chapters on crime prevention constituting the heart of this book alerted you to the kinds of strategies that seem to offer the most promise for preventing street crime. Strategies overall vary in their effectiveness, but some do seem more effective or promising than others. At the heart of any effective crime prevention must be primary crime prevention. This means that the federal, state, and local policymakers help reduce crime by enhancing efforts to attack the major structural roots of street crime: poverty and the criminogenic conditions of urban neighborhoods. Criminologically speaking, it is no accident that serious street crime rates are higher among low-income people and higher in the poorest and most socially disorganized urban neighborhoods. Although there are many reasons to reduce poverty and improve urban neighborhoods that have nothing to do with crime prevention, efforts that do address these problems will help prevent crime and victimization. Community strategies that address the situational factors that increase the opportunities for crime and victimization also hold great promise for crime prevention.

Beyond primary prevention, secondary crime prevention is also essential. As you learned, this includes efforts that improve family functioning, improve schools and education, reduce negative peer influences, and address gang membership. Criminologists and other scholars have identified myriad programs and practices at the secondary prevention level that show great promise for achieving these goals. To reduce crime and bring about numerous other benefits, it is long past time for the nation to fund and expand all these efforts.

As with disease in the public health model, it is also important for crime prevention to engage in tertiary prevention by focusing on the offenders among us. In this regard, criminologists and other scholars have also identified many strategies in the areas of policing, corrections, and community corrections that show promise for reducing crime and recidivism. Consistent with civil liberties, these practices should be funded, expanded, and well-designed and well-implemented to help keep society safe.

LESSONS FROM CANADA AND WESTERN EUROPE

To achieve effective crime prevention, the United States must learn from the examples of other wealthy democracies, including our neighbor to the north, Canada, and the nations of Western Europe. These nations feature and emphasize most of the practices summarized in the preceding section of this chapter and discussed throughout this book. Two particular kinds of practices stand out.

First, and as Chapter 5 stated, these nations provide their citizens many more forms of social supports than the United States does (Russell 2018). The nature of these supports and their extent vary by nation, but they include income payments to families, free or heavily subsidized childcare, paid parental leave, universal health care, and others. All these programs and policies help families and individuals generally, but especially those who have low incomes and thus are at the greatest risk for a host of personal problems such as illness, unemployment, and, yes, criminal behavior.

As this book has emphasized, children who grow up in low-income families are for many reasons more at risk for antisocial behavior during childhood, delinquency during adolescence, and criminal behavior during young adulthood. The social supports that other Western democracies provide help prevent their low-income children from ending up on this pathway. The United States would do well to follow its peer nations' example.

Second, these nations take a very different approach to fighting crime (Dammer and Albanese 2014; Reichel 2018). Instead of taking the punitive approach that has characterized U.S. crime and criminal justice policy since the 1970s, these nations place much greater emphasis on addressing the social roots of street crime and the factors in the damaging personal backgrounds of offenders that lead them to commit crime. These nations do have prisons and jails, but they also emphasize alternatives to corrections far more than the United States does, and they provide many more programs for their prisoners than the United States does. They also provide many more services for former prisoners and in other respects feature practices that help these individuals reenter society.

Canada's experience illustrates the advantages of this way of dealing with crime. When the United States adopted its punitive, tough-on-crime approach in the 1970s in the face of rising crime rates (see Chapter 1), Canada, which also faced rising crime, did not. Because both nations' crime rates declined after the early 1990s, these twin declines strongly suggest that the United States' punitive approach did not deserve credit for its crime decline (Zimring 2006). Meanwhile, because Canada did not emphasize stricter sentencing and mass incarceration, it saved untold numbers of dollars and avoided the collateral consequences that have beset the United States.

Germany's Correctional Model

One lesson that the United States can learn comes from Germany. Its correctional system provides a model, which Canada and other Western European nations (especially the Netherlands and the Scandinavian nations) also feature, that critics of American criminal justice policy say the United States should copy (Delaney et al. 2018; Subramanian and Shames 2013). Germany, whose cruel history does not suggest it would be soft on crime, emphasizes the need to treat prisoners humanely and to help reintegrate them into society. Reflecting this emphasis, the German Prison Act declares: "(1) Life in penal institutions should be approximated as far as possible to general living conditions, (2) any detrimental effects of imprisonment shall be counteracted, and (3) imprisonment shall be so designed as to help the prisoner reintegrate himself into life at liberty" (Delaney et al. 2018:52).

Toward these ends, Germany tries to avoid incarcerating convicted felons whenever possible by using community service, fines, and other alternatives. Only 6% of German convicted offenders are incarcerated, whereas 70% of American convicted felons are incarcerated; German prison sentences also tend to be much shorter than American sentences (Subramanian and Shames 2013). All these differences yield a German incarceration rate (number of prisoners per 100,000 population) that is only about one-tenth the U.S. rate, even though the two nations have roughly similar crime rates. German prisoners regularly receive home leave, a practice rare in the United States, to visit their families and/or to seek employment or find housing, and they consider the denial of home leave to be a severe punishment. Compared with the United States, Germany also places a far lower proportion of its prisoners in solitary confinement and for much shorter stays.

In another distinction from U.S. prisons, German prisons feature many more practices aimed at rehabilitating prisoners and preparing them for life after prison. As the Vera Institute of Justice (Subramanian and Shames 2013:11–12) observes, German prisoners "are allowed individual expression and a fair amount of control over their daily lives, including the opportunity to wear their own clothes and prepare their own meals; and, in order to instill self-worth, both work and education are required and remunerated. In addition, respect for prisoners' privacy is practiced as a matter of human dignity."

In yet another distinction, German correctional officers receive 2 years of education and training before beginning their jobs. During this time, they take courses in criminal law and constitutional law, psychology, conflict resolution, and other areas. This background gives them a far better appreciation than American correctional officers tend to have of prisoners' backgrounds and needs, and it also helps much better prepare them to interact with prisoners on a daily basis.

German prisons also look much different than American prisons. Many and perhaps most maximum- and medium-security American prisons feature long, dark hallways; many of them also lack air conditioning and become dangerously sweltering during the summer or even year-round in the warmer states (Chudzinski 2018). In contrast, German prisons have wide hallways, are well-lit with plenty of windows, and have good ventilation and temperature control.

Once they leave prison, German offenders do not face the restrictions that their American counterparts often face (Subramanian and Shames 2013). For example, and unlike many American released prisoners, German released prisoners are allowed to vote and are not prohibited from obtaining public housing, from receiving various social benefits and public sources of money for formal education, and from obtaining a license for various types of jobs.

As this short summary of the criminal justice policies of Germany and other Western democracies should indicate, the world's wealthy democracies deal with their crime problem in a more enlightened, less punitive manner than does the United States. They do not practice mass incarceration, they provide many social supports to their citizenry, and they treat their prisoners far more humanely and emphasize preparing them for reentry into society. When it comes to crime prevention, the United States has much to learn from their example.

THE FUTURE OF CRIME PREVENTION IN THE UNITED STATES

In a very informative book on correctional theory and correctional practices, Francis T. Cullen and Cheryl Lero Jonson (2017) write that three themes guided their discussion. Although their book is about corrections, they note that these themes also apply to criminal justice as a whole. Because these themes are thus also relevant for crime prevention more generally, we discuss them here because they also guided this book's discussion. The themes are as follows:

1. *Theory has consequences.*

2. *The social context has consequences.*

3. *Ignoring the evidence has consequences.*

The first theme, *theory has consequences*, means that criminal justice practices, correctional practices, and, for our purposes, crime prevention practices should all be based on theory. Theory is a strong guide to practice because it alerts us to the reasons for certain problems or situations and thus to the kinds of policies, programs, and practices that should deal with these issues most effectively. In the area of crime prevention and criminal justice more generally, theory tells us what should work to help prevent crime. It is because the authors of this book on crime prevention certainly agree that theory has consequences that we devoted two whole chapters (Chapter 3 and Chapter 4) to criminological theories, an uncommon feature in other crime prevention texts. These theories set the stage for all the subsequent chapters on crime prevention strategies for the simple reason that the most effective such strategies must rest on sound theory, while those that do not meet this standard are likely to fail.

The second theme, *the social context has consequences*, means that current events influence whether this theory or that theory about a social issue becomes popularly accepted or instead is dismissed as being unsound. Cullen and Jonson (2017) note that the tough-on-crime approach became popular in the 1970s because many events during the previous decade, including urban riots, campus unrest, the Vietnam War, the southern civil rights movement, and the assassinations of Dr. Martin Luther King, Jr., and the Kennedy brothers, had made Americans worry about social order and think that a tougher approach to crime and disorder was needed.

Regarding crime prevention, we now have a social context that has given rise to new interest in crime prevention. As many commentators have noted since a decade ago (Pew Charitable Trusts 2017; Richburg 2009), the declining crime rate and the huge cost of mass incarceration have helped motivate states to seek alternatives to incarceration and to give more thought to successful prisoner reentry and other crime prevention strategies. The time is thus favorable for crime prevention, and we hope that this book contributes to even greater interest in this important goal.

The third theme, *ignoring the evidence has consequences*, means that good social policy must be based on good evidence for its effectiveness, and any social policy that ignores this evidence is likely to fail. Regarding crime prevention, the research evidence tells us what is likely to help prevent crime and what is less likely to prevent crime. As Cullen and Jonson (2017:208) note regarding correctional policy, "To stubbornly use failed interventions when effective ones are available risks jeopardizing public safety." This observation underlies our effort throughout this book to both challenge the tough-on-crime approach and to evaluate the research evidence on crime prevention at the primary, secondary, and tertiary levels. Yes, much of this evidence is inconsistent, as we have emphasized in various chapters, and also lacking on many strategies. But the fact remains that sound crime prevention depends on sound evidence, and we trust that this book has given you a good idea of what works and what does not work in crime prevention.

Many and perhaps most criminologists think the United States should abandon its tough-on-crime approach and join the world's other wealthy democracies in emphasizing above all the need to prevent criminal behavior before it begins, as well as the need to rehabilitate the offenders among us. We hope that this book has alerted you to these needs while also alerting you to the types of crime prevention policies, programs, and practices that offer the best hope and promise for keeping our society safer.

SUMMARY

1. Readers learned many things from this book, including the cost and ineffectiveness of the tough-on-crime approach and mass incarceration, the numerous explanations for crime and criminal behavior, and some of the crime prevention strategies at the primary, secondary, and tertiary levels.

2. Canada and Western Europe feature criminal justice and crime prevention policies and

practices that offer more hope than those featured in the United States for prevention of crime.

3. Three themes guided this book's discussion of crime prevention and help explain the nature of crime prevention: Theory has consequences, the social context has consequences, and ignoring the evidence has consequences.

REFERENCES

Chudzinski, Kellie. 2018. "Why Temperatures in Prisons and Jails Matter." Vera Institute of Justice. August 10. Retrieved October 2, 2019 (https://www.vera.org/blog/why-temperatures-in-prisons-and-jails-matter).

Cullen, Francis T., and Cheryl Lero Jonson. 2017. *Correctional Theory: Context and Consequences.* Thousand Oaks, CA: Sage.

Dammer, Harry R., and Jay S. Albanese. 2014. *Comparative Criminal Justice Systems.* Belmont, CA: Wadsworth.

Delaney, Ruth, Ram Subramanian, Alison Shames, and Nicholas Turner. 2018. *Reimagining Prison.* New York, NY: Vera Institute of Justice.

Pew Charitable Trusts. 2017. *State Reforms Reverse Decades of Incarceration Growth.* Washington, DC: Author.

Reichel, Philip L. 2018. *Comparative Criminal Justice Systems: A Topical Approach.* New York, NY: Pearson.

Good Job
You Finished
*Love Simmons :)

Richburg, Keith B. 2009. "States Seek Less Costly Substitutes for Prison." *Washington Post.* July 13. Retrieved October 2, 2019 (http://www.washingtonpost.com/wp-dyn/content/article/2009/07/12/AR2009071202432.html).

Russell, James W. 2018. *Double Standard: Social Policy in Europe and the United States.* Lanham, MD: Rowman & Littlefield.

Subramanian, Ram, and Alison Shames. 2013. *Sentencing and Prison Practices in Germany and the Netherlands.* New York, NY: Vera Institute of Justice.

Zimring, Franklin E. 2006. *The Great American Crime Decline.* New York, NY: Oxford University Press.

GLOSSARY

administrative segregation Or "ad seg," also called solitary confinement. It is a form of incarceration in which inmates are kept in isolation for 23 hours a day with no human contact. It can be used for discipline or protection purposes.

after-school programs Programs to reduce delinquency by occupying students after school lets out until parents or caregivers return from work

antecedent variable A variable that affects both an independent variable and a dependent variable that are associated with each other

atavism The belief that criminals are evolutionary accidents born as throwbacks to earlier stages of evolution

attachment A concept indicating warm and stable relationships between parents and children, thought to be important in healthy child development and the basis of early parenting theories

authoritarian A style of parenting that is harsh and rigid, demanding obedience without much negotiation

authoritative A style of parenting that is considered firm but fair; seeks to explain rules and punishment to children

Ban the Box Movement to remove questions from employment applications asking about previous convictions, to make it easier for former offenders to obtain employment and reintegrate into society

batterer intervention program Program for individuals convicted of domestic abuse to prevent the reoccurrence of such abuse

Big Brothers Big Sisters Mentoring program that matches at-risk youths with older role models

biosocial Perspective that sees human outcomes (e.g., behavior) as the product of both environmental and biological influences in concert

biosocial criminology The view that criminal behavior has biological roots

Black Lives Matter Social movement sparked by police shootings of unarmed black men

blueprints Programs selected by the Blueprints for Healthy Youth Development organization that have shown promise for crime prevention. Model programs are those that have reached a high bar for demonstrating effectiveness.

broken windows policing Policing strategies to reduce disorder and incivilities rather than solely focusing on major crimes; policing strategy that seeks to ensure areas are clean and orderly, minimizing less serious issues to prevent larger ones from occurring

broken windows theory Theory put forth by Wilson and Kelling arguing that disorder in communities leads to crime; theory developed by George Kelling and James Q. Wilson suggesting that disorder and chaos in a community can lead to more serious criminal behavior by signaling that the community does not care and thus will not protect the place

bullying Behaviors targeting a student or group of students meant to harass, intimidate, or humiliate

bystander intervention An approach to reduce antisocial behavior by encouraging people who witness such behavior to do something to interrupt the event. In terms of bullying, research has shown that programs that teach students to intervene increase intervention behavior.

causal order problem A situation in which it is not clear, when there is an association between an apparent independent variable and an apparent dependent variable, whether the independent variable is affecting the dependent variable or vice versa

Chicago Area Project (CAP) Developed by Shaw to organize communities and utilize local organizations to reduce crime

child poverty The percentage of children living in families below the poverty line

civil gang injunction (CGI) A civil lawsuit against whole gangs or specific gang members for allegedly violating state codes banning public nuisances

civilian labor force All civilians 16 years of age or older who hold a paid job or are looking for work

classical school Criminological school of thought popular in the 18th century that focused on situations and cost benefits associated with crime rather than individual criminal traits; school of criminological thought that sees humans as rational beings and crime the result of decisions, not personal or environmental deficiencies

clearance rates Proportion of crimes "solved" via arrest or known perpetrator

closed-circuit television (CCTV) cameras Cameras located in strategic areas to deter and capture criminal behavior

cognitive behavioral therapy (CBT) Type of therapy that teaches individuals to recognize negative thinking patterns and prevent antisocial behavior from following those thoughts

collateral consequences The various social costs of mass incarceration that damage the lives of millions of Americans, many of them people of color

collective efficacy Theory developed by Sampson and colleagues that suggests communities with high trust and social cohesion have less crime

Communities That Care (CTC) Program developed by Hawkins and Catalano to facilitate communities in identifying needs and obtaining resources to address those needs to reduce risky behavior

community corrections Corrections that take place in the community rather than in prison or jail

community crime prevention Strategies and programs designed to reduce risk factors for criminal behavior in communities and neighborhoods

community factors Social aspects of neighborhoods that motivate persons to break the law or, instead, to obey it

community policing era Era of policing in which police tried to become a part of and work with the community to reduce crime

community supervision Form of correctional supervision that takes place in the community rather than in a prison. Examples are probation and parole.

concentrated poverty Census tracts with poverty rates above a certain level of poverty, usually 20%

control theory Theory of crime that suggests antisocial behavior is the result of a lack of restraints on humans;

assumes antisocial behavior is "natural" without sufficient controls

conventional crime Street crime

correctional boot camps In vogue in the 1980s and early 1990s, correctional boot camps seek to replicate the military boot camp experience to instill change in offenders.

corrections The component of the criminal justice system that deals with implementing sentencing, either in correctional facilities or in the community

cost-benefit analyses A type of analyses in which the costs of an approach are compared with the returns to determine if the approach is cost-effective

crime prevention through environmental design (CPTED) Approaches to crime reduction by altering the physical environment to discourage criminal behavior and encourage surveillance and ownership of areas

criminogenic Crime-causing

criminogenic needs Needs or deficits related to antisocial behavior. Examples include employment, family relations, and substance use.

cross-sectional surveys Surveys that study people at one point in time

cyberstalking A form of stalking that takes place online, primarily through chatrooms, social media, or e-mail

dark figure of crime Crimes that remain unknown to the police, mostly because victims do not report these crimes to the police

day-reporting centers (DRCs) Buildings at which probationers are required to be during the day to receive various services before going home at night

dependent variable A variable that is affected by an independent variable

determinate sentencing Prison sentences for a specific amount of time as determined by a judge

deterrence The idea that the threat of arrest and punishment reduces the crime rate because potential offenders do not want to risk being arrested, convicted, and incarcerated

deterrence theory The view that general deterrence and specific deterrence occur because potential offenders carefully weigh their chances of getting arrested, convicted, and incarcerated before they decide to commit a crime; theory of behavior that argues people calculate costs and benefits of possible lines of action, and to prevent crime, it is only necessary to raise the costs of such behavior above the rewards

developmental crime prevention Crime prevention approaches that seek to ensure healthy child and juvenile development in the family, school, and community

diathesis stress hypothesis The idea that risky genetic variants, in combination with risky environments, produce a higher likelihood of antisocial outcomes

differential association theory Edwin Sutherland's theory of crime that suggested crime results from associations with deviant peers

differential susceptibility The idea that certain genetic variants are not risky, but result in more susceptibility to environmental influence (whether good or bad)

diffusion of benefits The idea that situational crime prevention may reduce crime in surrounding areas because offenders do not know exactly where and when the techniques are being implemented

discretionary parole Early release from prison for good behavior

disorder Disarray, social disruption, and physical deterioration

displacement The idea that situational crime prevention may reduce crime in the immediate area but increase crime in surrounding locations, where the prevention techniques are not being implemented

dispositional theories Theories associated with the positive school of criminology that seek to discover the causes of crime within individual traits or deficiencies

diversion A process whereby juveniles who have committed a crime are placed outside of the justice system, either for treatment or to prevent them from being negatively influenced by the system

Drug Abuse Resistance Education (D.A.R.E.) Program developed in the 1980s to dissuade youths from engaging in substance use, with a police officer teaching students about the effects of drugs. Evaluations have demonstrated the program is not effective.

drug courts Courts designed specifically for drug offenders; often incorporate treatment requirements and reporting

effect size A standardized measure to illustrate the size of a statistical relationship. In general terms, .20 means a small effect, .50 means a medium effect, and .80 and above means a large effect

employment The condition of holding a paid job

environmental criminology A subfield of criminology that seeks to show how aspects of the built community affect crime patterns

episodic poverty The idea that families and individuals slip into and out of official poverty; defined by the Census Bureau as being officially poor for at least two consecutive months

equal environments assumption A key assumption in twin studies that children growing up in the same household are treated the same way (or experience the same environment)

eugenics The practice in the early 20th century of sterilizing immigrant women and women of color without their knowledge

evaluation research Research that assesses the effectiveness of a policy or program

event decision The decision-making process that prompts someone to decide to commit or not to commit a specific crime in a specific location at a specific time

evidence-based practices Practices that have been demonstrated to be effective in multiple independent experiments

experiments A research design in which subjects are divided into an experimental group and a control group

family functioning The quality of the social interaction among family members

family structure How a family is organized, including whether one parent or two parents are living in a household

felony disenfranchisement The denial of the right to vote for people convicted of a felony

funnel effect The idea that many more felonies are committed (the top of the funnel) than end in incarceration in prison for a felony (the bottom of the funnel)

gang suppression Strategies that rely on law enforcement and the threat of arrest and punishment to reduce gang violence, gang involvement in drug trafficking and other illegal activity, and gang membership

gene by environment interaction Type of biosocial scholarship that seeks to show how the effect of particular genetic traits vary according to different environments

general deterrence The situation that occurs when potential offenders in the general public decide not to commit crime because they fear legal punishment

general strain theory (GST) The view that many kinds of strains in people's lives lead to negative emotions and, in turn, criminal behavior

get-tough approach A policy of increased law enforcement and, especially, longer and more certain prison sentences, that has guided criminal justice policy in the United States since the 1970s

Good Lives Model (GLM) A supplement or alternative to the Risk Needs Responsivity approach that focuses on positive aspects of the offender's life and human goods

harm reduction A major component of the public health approach that focuses on trying as much as possible to reduce the harm to individual and social health arising from the causes of disease, illness, and injury

Head Start Program for disadvantaged youths to provide developmental assistance prior to the start of formal education

hidden crimes Crimes that remain unknown to the police, mostly because victims do not report these crimes to the police

hot spot policing The using of hot spot mapping to direct police resources and attention in a more efficient way to reduce crime

hot spots Areas with high rates of street crime; used to focus police resources and often identified via crime-mapping technologies

Implicit bias Prejudice against a group that is on an unconscious level

incapacitation Regarding mass incarceration, the idea that mass incarceration lowers the crime rate because convicted offenders are behind bars and not able to commit crimes against the public; punishment philosophy that views the goal of sanctions as removing the threat to society. Incarceration is a form of incapacitation.

incarceration boom The huge increase in incarceration since the 1970s

independent variable A variable that may affect or influence another variable

indeterminate sentences Prison sentences for a range of years

intensive supervision Probation that involves more frequent monitoring of probationers than routine probation involves

intermediate sanctions Sanctions that are harsher than traditional probation but less harsh than incarceration

Jeremy Bentham 18th-century philosopher who devised a new form of incarceration called the Panopticon

Jim Crow System of legalized discrimination in the United States in which segregation was mandated by race

labeling theory Theory of behavior that suggests that individuals' self-concepts are influenced by others' perceptions. These self-concepts, in turn, influence behavior.

lax A style of parenting in which parents are permissive and not strict when it comes to correcting misbehavior. These parents let their kids "get away with it."

learning theory Theory of crime that argues crime is learned in interactions with others who are delinquent

legitimacy The feeling that power is justified among particular groups

life-course criminology A set of theoretical explanations that examine how and why antisocial behavior develops during childhood and proceeds during adolescence and beyond

lifestyle theory The view that people's lifestyles make it more or less likely that they will commit crime

long arm of childhood The long-term impact of problems in children's lives that impair their cognitive and neurological development

longitudinal surveys Surveys that study the same people over time

mandatory parole Parole supervision that follows release after the end of a determinate sentence

Martinson Report Publication in the mid-1970s that found little evidence for the effectiveness of correctional programs; led to the decline in the belief in rehabilitation

mass incarceration The confinement of an incredibly large volume of Americans, more than 2.2 million on any given day, inside the nation's prisons and jails

mentoring Regarding crime prevention, intervention by an adult who volunteers to spend much one-on-one time over many weeks or months with an at-risk youth

meta-analysis A study that synthesizes, statistically, the results of several studies to provide an overall effect of a program or theory

methadone maintenance A program to help wean individuals addicted to opioids off the drug

Metropolitan Police First police agency, founded in London

Midnight Basketball A program in which at-risk youths play basketball, usually late at night, to engage them in prosocial activities

militarized The trend of police agencies coming to resemble military units in organization and weaponry

Mobilization for Youth (MFY) A program based on President Lyndon Johnson's war on poverty to provide resources in disadvantaged areas

Moving to Opportunity (MTO) A program that provided vouchers for people in disadvantaged communities to move to areas with less poverty, to assess the effect of place on outcomes

National Crime Victimization Survey (NCVS) A survey of a large random sample of the U.S. population carried out annually by the Bureau of Justice Statistics

near poverty Having an annual income above the government's poverty threshold but still having trouble making ends meet; often measured as having income up to twice as high as the poverty threshold

neglectful A style of parenting in which parents do not give much attention, supervision, or discipline to their children

neoclassical school Criminological school of thought that emerged in the late 20th century by drawing on rationality and contextual factors, much as the classical school did

night watch Early form of policing in which community members would keep watch over towns in case of trouble

nothing works Mantra held by politicians, practitioners, and researchers after the Martinson Report found little evidence for effectiveness of correctional programs

Olweus Bullying Prevention Program (OBPP) Bullying prevention program developed by Dan Olweus in the 1980s. The program includes community-, classroom-, and student-focused components.

opportunity In the criminal context, opportunity can be thought of as circumstances that allow for undetected and successful criminal conduct

Panopticon Correctional facility developed by Jeremy Bentham that would separate inmates and allow for the potential of 24-hour supervision

parens patriae The idea that the state can act as the parent of children in particular cases. This was the basis for the juvenile court in the United States.

parole Supervised release after confinement in prison

Part I crimes The term used in the Uniform Crime Reports for violent crime (homicide, aggravated assault, and rape) and property crime (burglary, larceny, motor vehicle theft, and arson)

Part II crimes The term used in the Uniform Crime Reports for crimes such as fraud, embezzlement, vandalism, prostitution, drug abuse, disorderly conduct, and several other offenses

PeaceBuilders Program to reduce school violence in elementary school by encouraging positive and discouraging negative behavior. Research has demonstrated that the program reduces aggression.

peer risk intervention programs A diverse collection of programs that attempt to help youths develop skills in communication, conflict resolution, decision-making, problem-solving, and other areas, with the direct aim of countering the negative influences of delinquent peers

penitentiary Early term for prisons that emphasized the idea that inmates were supposed to reflect and give penance

Perry Preschool Project Preschool program serving disadvantaged youths in the 1960s with demonstrated longitudinal positive benefits

phrenology The belief that the likelihood of criminal behavior can be determined from measuring the size and shape of the skull

police beats Geographic area assigned to police officers or units for patrol

political era Earliest era of policing, marked by corruption and political influence over police

population density The concentration of people within defined locations

Positive Action Bullying prevention program developed in the 1970s that seeks to teach children and adolescents how to engage in positive or prosocial behavior

positive school School of criminology thought that argued that rational choices were not the primary reason for crime; rather, outside factors (sometimes beyond the control of the individual) were the cause of the behavior

positivism School of criminological thought that supplanted the classical school, which argued that crime is caused by personal or environmental factors, not a result of purely a decision on the part of the offender

poverty As officially defined by the U.S. government, having an income below three times the cost of a minimally nutritious diet for a family depending on its size and composition

poverty areas Census tracts or neighborhoods that have concentrated poverty

prevalence rate Regarding criminal victimization as measured by the National Crime Victimization Survey, the percentage of people 12 and older who experienced at least one victimization during the past year

primary gang prevention Efforts to reduce poverty, improve schools, and address the other underlying factors that produce delinquency and crime; if successful, these efforts would help prevent young adolescents from ever joining a street gang

primary prevention In the field of public health, the prevention of health problems altogether by addressing features of the social, physical, and natural environments that help generate these problems

prison boom The huge increase in incarceration since the 1970s

prison industries Use of inmates to create products. Often, inmates can learn industries (e.g., woodworking, metalworking) as a way to build vocational skills for use upon release.

prison visitation Practice of allowing inmates visits with individuals who are not incarcerated so as to maintain important social ties

prisonization Adaptation to the prison culture that can be maladaptive

probation Correctional supervision that takes place in the community in lieu of incarceration

problem-oriented policing Policing that seeks to identify the source of problems in particular locations and address those root problems

professional era Policing era in which reformers such as August Vollmer tried to professionalize the police, introducing educational standards and meritocracy

prosocial Behavior and other influences that promote helping others and otherwise being a good member of society

public health All organized measures (whether public or private) to prevent disease, promote health, and prolong life among the population as a whole

pulling levers A method of problem-oriented or focused deterrence policing in which all available resources and strategies are used to prevent an identified problem

qualitative research A research method that involves two modes of gathering information: (1) observing people in their natural settings and (2) interviewing individuals one-on-one at length about their views, behaviors, and/or perceptions in regard to one or more topics

quasi-experimental Research design that does not use random allotment to treatment and control groups but does include some form of control group, either by matching or before-and-after comparisons

random drug testing Program in which eligible groups are subject to drug testing at unknown dates and times to make it more difficult to avoid detection

randomized clinical trial A study design meant to capture causality by randomly assigning a sample of individuals to a control or treatment group

rational choice theory (RCT) The view that crime is a rational act committed by rational individuals who calculate whether the potential rewards of their planned criminal behavior outweigh the potential risks of arrest, punishment, or other negative outcomes; theory developed by Derek Cornish and Ron Clarke that focuses on specific crime types and analyzes the decisions made by offenders

recidivism The act of engaging in criminal behavior after initially being caught (and often being involved in the justice system); typically defined as a new arrest or conviction after release from correctional supervision

reciprocal relationship A situation where both variables that are associated with each other are affecting each other

reentry The process by which former prisoners return to their home communities and in effect reenter society

rehabilitation Punishment philosophy that views the purpose of sanctions as inducing a change in the offender such that they are less likely to commit future criminal acts

relative deprivation The feeling that one's own situation is worse than those of other people

relative poverty As defined by many international agencies, the proportion of a nation's population with household incomes below half of the nation's median household income

respondents People who answer the questions on a questionnaire

retribution Punishment philosophy tied to the saying "an eye for an eye." Punishment, in this view, is to right a wrong and ensure the violator pays for their crime.

risk assessment tool Tool used to assess the risk offenders present with respect to committing new crimes. These tools help guide the level and type of supervision used.

risk-need-responsivity (RNR) Model for effective correctional intervention that argues it is important to assess offenders' risk for recidivism, their criminogenic needs (deficits causing antisocial behavior), and their learning styles

routine activities theory The view that crime and victimization are more likely when motivated offenders, attractive targets, and an absence of guardianship occur simultaneously; theory developed by Lawrence Cohen and Marcus Felson that argued crime results when three things come together: motivated offender, lack of capable guardian, and suitable targets

SARA Approach to policing that stands for *scan, analyze, respond, assess*. Linked to problem-oriented policing.

scared straight A type of juvenile-based deterrence program exposing youths who are at risk to what may be in store if they continue their ways. The goal is to scare the youths away from their current path.

school resource officers (SROs) Officers who serve schools, sometimes with the ability to make arrests, to maintain safety and security

secondary gang prevention Efforts that focus on youths who are thought to be especially at risk for possible gang involvement but who are not already in gangs

secondary prevention In the field of public health, the prevention of health problems by focusing on the many behaviors and practices that put people at greater risk for becoming ill or sustaining an injury

self-control theory The view that individuals with low self-control are more likely to be impulsive, to violate social norms, and to misbehave during childhood and commit delinquency during adolescence; theory advanced by Michael Gottfredson and Travis Hirschi stating that self-control (or lack thereof) is the primary cause of all crime

self-report surveys Surveys that ask respondents to indicate whether and how often they have committed various offenses during the past year or some other time frame

shock probation An intermediate sanction involving placement in a paramilitary setting

situational crime prevention (SCP) Efforts in specific locations that try to prevent the simultaneous occurrence of motivated offenders, attractive targets, and the absence of guardianship

situational factors Physical aspects of neighborhoods and elements of social interaction that help foster criminal behavior and victimization or, conversely, inhibit criminal behavior and victimization

social bonding theory The view that strong attachments to parents and schools help prevent delinquency from occurring

social control theory A theory of crime that suggests crime results from a lack of social or institutional controls

(associated with several criminologists, including Travis Hirschi)

social disorganization The weakening of social bonds and social control in a neighborhood due to structural conditions such as poverty and residential instability

social disorganization theory A theory developed by Shaw and McKay to explain community variation in crime rates based on three factors: poverty, population density, and ethnic heterogeneity

social learning explanations A set of explanations that emphasize that youths become delinquent because of the influence of deviant friends and acquaintances

specific deterrence The situation that occurs when convicted offenders who have already been legally punished decide not to commit a new crime because they do not want to risk a new incarceration

spuriousness A situation in which two variables are associated but only because a third variable, called an *antecedent variable*, is affecting each of the two variables

Standard Model Policing model that involves random patrols and largely reactive rather than proactive procedures

strain theory Theory of crime that suggests antisocial behavior is the result of strains or pressures (e.g., being blocked from attaining goals)

street crime A term that refers to violent crime and property crime, whether or not the crime actually occurs on a street, and to other offenses such as illegal gun possession and illegal drug trafficking

street gangs A delinquent group that conforms to the following characteristics: (1) They have three or more members, generally aged 12 to 14; (2) members share an identity; (3) members view themselves as a gang and are so recognized by others; (4) they have some permanence and a degree of organization; and (5) they are involved in an elevated level of criminal activity

survey research A research method that involves questionnaires administered to people over the phone, in person, by mail, or over the Internet

targeted Crime prevention approaches that are meant for individuals or groups with known risk factors (or who have already offended)

teen courts Juvenile court procedures involving teen volunteers acting as judges, jurors, and other roles, and deciding the sanction(s) for low-level juvenile offenders

tertiary gang prevention Efforts that focus on youths already in gangs and on the gangs themselves

tertiary prevention In public health, efforts to minimize or prevent short- and long-term consequences of a health problem

therapeutic communities (TCs) A form of substance use treatment that segregates participants from other inmates and uses group-based programming

toxic stress Severe, chronic stress that some children experience from stressors called adverse childhood experiences

Treatment Foster Care Oregon Type of correctional program for youths that involves placement in a foster home where the family is trained to help youths advance through programming

twin studies A research method in which twins are examined to separate the influence of genetics from the influence of shared and nonshared environment on outcomes

underemployment The condition of being unemployed, working part-time but wishing to work full-time, or having stopped looking for work because a job could not be found

unemployment The condition of looking for work but not being able to find a job

Uniform Crime Reports (UCR) The FBI's system by which it gathers crime data from police precincts around the country

universal Crime prevention approaches that impose no limits on the recipients of the programs (e.g., participants do not need to have demonstrated risk factors)

Unplugged A program to reduce substance use in schools by teaching norm reinforcement or reorientation. The program targets knowledge and attitudes about substances.

use of force Any use of physical tactics by police to gain compliance from citizens

utilitarianism The notion that society should promote actions that provide for the greatest amount of pleasure and the least amount of pain

variable In the study of people, any factor that can vary from one person to another person

violence interrupters People, often former gang members, who try to intervene at the street level in gang conflicts to try to diffuse anger and reduce potential gang violence

white-collar crime Crime committed by people in the course of their occupations, either for their own personal gain and/or for the gain of the corporations and other businesses for which they work

wilderness programs Programs for youths meant to engage them in challenges to build confidence and self-esteem

youth crime Crime committed by people ages 15 to 24

zero-tolerance Policies that do not take context into account for particular rule violations. All violations are treated with equal severity.

INDEX

genetics and crime, 42–45

prenatal and maternal problems and fetal development, 41–42

testosterone and, 44–45

Biosocial criminology, 40

Biosocial mechanisms, parent/family programs and, 175

Biosocial scholars, on genetic considerations and correctional treatment, 272–273

Bishop, Donna M., 216

Black Lives Matter, 240

Blackmon, Douglas, 259

Blackwell, Brenda, 245

Blueprints for Healthy Youth Development, 263

Blueprints program, 173

Blumstein, Alfred, 259, 263

Bonta, James, 262

Bonus effect, 153

Boot camps

correctional, 267

shock probation and, 285, 290–291

for youth, 127

Bowers, Kate J., 150, 153, 155

Bowlby, John, 165

Bow Street Runners, 239

Bozick, Robert, 266

Braga, Anthony A., 242–243, 245–246, 248

Brain, immaturity of youth, 75, 208

British Journal of Criminology, 143–144

Broken windows policing (order maintenance policing), 125–126, 242–243, 250 (table)

Broken windows theory, 120, 122 (table)

Buddy System program, 220

Building design, crime and, 131

Bullying

defined, 191

in schools, 188, 191–192

Bureau of Justice Statistics (BJS), 5

Bush, George W., 17, 292

Bushway, Shawn, 125

Butts, Jeffrey A., 216, 217

Bystander intervention, bullying reduction and, 191–192

California Youth Authority camp, 127

Camp, Scott D., 271–272

Canada

crime and incarceration rates in, 15

lessons from, 304–306

Case studies, evidence for situational crime prevention, 149–152

Catalano, Richard F., 132

Causal order, 30, 211

Causation, surveys and, 30

CCTV cameras, 130, 153

CeaseFire program, 226

Cell phone technology, crime reduction and, 149

Center for Evidence Based Crime Policy, 243

Centers for Disease Control and Prevention, 27

Chappell, Cathryn A., 266

Chen, M. Keith, 272

Chicago Area Project (CAP), 122–123

Chicago Housing Authority, moving away from low-income neighborhoods experiment, 102

Chicken or egg problem, 30

Child abuse and neglect, 71

preventing, 176, 177

Childcare subsidies, 110

Child-centered programs, how they work, 175

Childhood, negative personality traits in, 49

Child outcomes, parenting and, 164–168

Child poverty, 93, 94, 95, 110

Children

cognitive and neurological development of, 40–41

parental discipline and supervision of, 70

parental incarceration and, 271

at risk for growing up to commit delinquency and crime, 27

toxic stress, adverse childhood experiences, and, 96–97

Children's Defense Fund (CDF), 109

Child sexual abuse, preventing, 177

Chronic offenders, 14

Civil gang injunctions (CGIs), 225

effectiveness of, 225–226

Civilian labor force, 103

Clark, Valerie, 266

Clarke, Ronald V., 142, 143–144, 145 (table), 146, 147, 149, 152–153, 154–155

Classical school, 141

Clearance rates, 249

Clinton, Bill, 244

Clinton, Hillary, 118

Closed-circuit television (CCTV) cameras, 130, 153

Cloward, Richard, 123

Code of the street, 61

Cognitive behavioral therapy (CBT)

reduction of anger and, 174

reduction of recidivism and, 269

treatment for youthful offenders and, 264

Cognitive development, biological explanations of crime and, 40–41

Cognitive processes and motivation, crime and, 39 (table), 49–52

Cohen, Albert K., 73

Cohen, Deborah A., 198

Cohen, Jacqueline, 259

Cohen, Lawrence, 142, 144–145, 145 (table)

Collateral consequences, 8
  of mass incarceration, 16–17

Collective efficacy
  disadvantaged neighborhoods and lack of, 60
  disorder and, 126
  as risk factor for crime, 120, 122 (table)

Collective-efficacy policing, 126–127

Columbine High School shooting, 192

The Common Sense of Baby and Child Care (Spock), 165

Communities, effect of mass joblessness on, 107

Communities That Care (CTC), 132

Community and neighborhood approaches, 118–140
  community crime prevention and substance abuse, 131–133
  community risk factors for crime, 119–121
  contemporary community crime prevention approaches, 123–131
  difficulties with community crime prevention, 133
  early community crime prevention approaches, 121–123

Community conditions, street gangs and, 228

Community corrections, 281–299
  community service, 287
  day-reporting centers, 287–288
  fines, restitution, and forfeiture, 288–289
  history of probation and parole, 283–284
  house arrest and electronic monitoring, 289–290
  intensive supervision, 290
  intermediate sanctions, 285, 287–291
  parole and crime prevention, 291–295
  prisoner reentry, 282–283, 292–295
  probation and crime prevention, 286–291
  shock probation, 290–291
  understanding probation and parole, 282–285

Community crime prevention, defined, 118

Community disadvantage, 60

Community factors
  defined, 60
  risk factors for crime and, 58–61, 59 (table)

Community-oriented policing (COP), 242–243, 244

Community policing era, 239

Community resource centers. *See* Day-reporting centers (DRCs)

Community sanctions, incarceration *vs.*, 270–271

Community service, 285, 287

Community supervision, 261

Comte, August, 141

Concentrated disadvantage, as risk factor for crime, 122 (table)

Concentrated poverty, 94–95

Condordant behaviors, 43

Continuity of care, 294

Control group, 33

Control theory, 189

Conventional crime, 18

Conventional criminality, racial differences in, 102

Cook, Philip J., 241

Cornish, Derek, 142, 145 (table), 146

Correctional boot camps, 127, 267

Correctional model, German, 305–306

Correctional programming, what works, 270 (table). *See also* Prisons and crime prevention

Correctional supervision, 11

Corrections, 258
  cost of, 6, 7 (figure)
  See also Prisons and crime prevention

Cost
  of crime, 6
  of criminal justice, 6–8
  of street crime, 18
  of white-collar crime, 18
  See also Economic cost

Cost-benefit analysis
  of mass incarceration, 15
  of situational crime prevention, 150–151

Cost savings for society, from Nurse-Family Partnership, 170

Craig, Wendy M., 198

Crime, individual roots of, 37–57
  biological factors, 38–45
  cognitive processes and motivation, 49–52
  individual-level explanations of crime and antisocial behavior, 39 (table)
  psychological factors, 45–49

Crime and Everyday Life (Felson & Eckert), 129

Crime in the United States, 4

Crime mapping, 238, 246

Eck, John E., 151
Eckert, Mary, 129
Ecological variables, 28
Economic and employment strategies to prevent crime, 91–116
  employment and crime, 103–108
  poverty and crime, 92–102
  reducing poverty and promoting stable employment, 108–111
Economic cost
  of crime, 6
  of criminal justice system, 7 (figure)
  of probation, 286
  See also Cost
Educational attainment, unemployment rate and, 103, 104 (table)
Education programs, recidivism and adult, 265–266
Educators, as victims of school violence/crime, 194
Effect size, 125
Electronic monitoring, 285, 289–290
Elliott, Margaret C., 60–61
Emile (Rousseau), 165
Emotional health, as cost of crime, 6
Employment
  defined, 103
  desistance from crime and, 80
  reducing poverty and promoting stable, 108–111
Employment and crime, 103–108
  relevance of employment status for conventional crime, 105–107
  research on employment status and crime, 107–108
  in the United States, 103–105
The English Convict (Goring), 143
Enlightenment (Age of Reason), 49–50
Ennett, Susan T., 196
Enquiry Into the Causes of the Late Increase of Robbers (Fielding), 239
Environmental criminology, 121, 122 (table), 129
Environmental design, preventing crime through, 129–131
Environmental roots of crime, 58–87, 59 (table)
  community and situational factors, 58–66
  families, 66–71
  general strain theory, 78–79
  life-course criminology, 79–80
  need for multifaceted crime prevention, 78–80
  peer influences, 71–73
  schools and schooling, 73–75

sociodemographic correlates of crime, 75–78
Environmental toxins, antisocial behavior and, 100
Episodic poverty, 94
Episodic unemployment, 103
Equal environments assumption, 168
Erratic discipline, 70
Ethnicity
  concentrated poverty and, 95
  as correlate of crime, 77–78
  mass incarceration and, 12, 17, 259, 260 (figure)
  poverty rate by, 93, 94
  unemployment rate and, 104, 104 (table), 106 (table)
  See also Race
Ethnographic research, 32
Eugenics, 40
Evaluation research, 34
Event decision, 50
Evidence, consequences of ignoring, 307–308
Evidence-based crime prevention, 26
Evidence-based practices, 262
Exits, observing, 148 (table)
Experimental condition, 33
Experimental group, 33
Experimental research, 32–34
Experiments, 32–34
Extracurricular activities, crime prevention and, 198–199

Face-to-face survey, 29
Fagan, Abigail A., 228
Fagan, Jeffrey, 243
Families, effect of mass incarceration on, 16–17. *See also* Parenting/parents
Families, risk factors for crime and, 59 (table)
  family functioning and parenting, 69
  family structure, 66–69
Family/child-centered programs, 171–175, 175 (table)
  how they work, 175
Family functioning (family interaction)
  defined, 66
  employment and, 106–107
  nature and quality of, 69–70
  risk factors for crime and, 66
Family issues, delinquency and, 210
Family structure
  defined, 66
  risk factors for crime and, 66–69
Family violence, preventing, 175–177
Farrington, David P., 174, 220–221

Feder, Lynette, 176
Federal Bureau of Investigation (FBI), 4, 192
Federal Crime Bill (1994), 244
Feld, Barry, 216
Felony disenfranchisement, 17
Felson, Marcus, 129, 142, 144–145, 145 (table)
Ferri, Enrico, 143
Fetal development, biological explanations of crime
    and, 41–42
Fielding, Henry, 239
Field research, 32
Fines, 285, 288–289
Firm but fair discipline (authoritative discipline), 70
Flannery, Daniel, 193
Focused deterrence, 248, 250 (table)
Forfeiture, 285, 288–289
Foster homes, for youth offenders, 263–264
Foucault, Michel, 258
Fox, Bryanna, 249–250
Fox, James Alan, 187
Free rider effect, 153
Fridel, Emma, 187
Friedson, Michael, 123–124
Frontline (television program), 257
Functional Family Therapy (FFT), 173, 175, 227, 263
Funnel effect, 13, 46

Gaes, Gerald G., 271–272
Gall, Franz Joseph, 39
Gang Resistance Education and Training
    (G.R.E.A.T.), 227
Gangs
    age of members, 208
    defined, 222
    nature of leadership, 224
Gangs and crime, 221–228
    civil gang injunctions, 225–226
    community conditions and, 228
    functional family therapy program, 227
    Gang Resistance Education and Training, 227
    gang suppression strategies, 222, 223–226
    group violence intervention, 226–227
    understanding gangs and gang membership, 222–223
Garces, Eliana, 198
Garner, Eric, 243
Gender, correlated to crime, 76
Gendreau, Paul, 264
Gene by environment interaction, 272

General delinquency programs, 196–197
General deterrence, 51
Generalizing, 29
General strain theory (GST), 78–79
Genetics
    biological explanations of crime and, 42–45
    correctional treatment and, 272–273
    genetic factors in child outcomes, 167–168
Germany
    correctional model, 305–306
    German Prison Act, 305
Get-touch approach, 3, 8, 11
Gibson, Laura E., 177
Goddard, Henry H., 43
Goldstein, Herman, 245
Good Lives Model (GLM), 265
Gore, Al, 17
Goring, Charles, 143
Gottfredson, Denise C., 190, 193, 195, 196, 197
Gottfredson, Gary D., 196
Gottfredson, Michael R., 146, 171, 238
Goudena, Paul P., 177
Green, Charles E., 176
Group violence intervention (GVI), 226–227
Guardianship, 151
    routine activities theory and absence of, 62
Guerette, Rob T., 150, 153
Gun violence
    alcohol abuse and, 64
    preventing, 155–156

Habitual offenders, 14
Hall, G. Stanley, 263
Halo effect, 153
Handguns
    excessive alcohol use and, 64–66
    violence crime and, 155
Harm reduction
    preventing gun violence and, 155
    public health model and, 25–26
Harris, Eric, 192
Hartmann, Douglas, 128
Hawkins, J. David, 132, 172
Hayward, Keith, 154
Head Start, 197–198
Health enhancement curriculum (HEC), 214
Hemenway, David, 65
Hidden crimes, 4

Hirschi, Travis
    on extracurricular activities and crime
        prevention, 198
    on involvement in prosocial activities and crime
        reduction, 128
    on police and crime prevention, 238
    self-control theory, 69, 146, 171
    social bonding theory, 69, 73, 100, 189
    social control theory, 165–166
Hitkashrut program, 171
Hoeve, Machteld, 166
Homicides
    firearms and, 65, 155
    in schools, 187
    in Washington, D.C. (2017), 246, 247 (figure)
Hooton, Ernest A., 40
Hope, Tim, 133
Horney, Julie, 219
Hot spot policing, 238, 241, 245–248, 250 (table)
Hot spots, 125–126
House arrest, 285, 289–290
Housing subsidies, 110
HSBC/Outward Bound project, 198–199
Hureau, David, 245–246

Immigration, crime and, 78
Implicit bias, policing and, 249
Incapacitation
    conceptual issues regarding, 13–14
    defined, 13
Incapacitation effect, 13
Incarceration
    community sanctions *vs.*, 270–271
    as rite of passage, 52
    See also Mass incarceration
Incarceration boom, 11–12
Incredible Years parenting intervention, 169–170
Independent variable, 29
Indeterminate sentence, 282
Indicators of School Crime and Safety, 187
Individual change efforts, 294
Individual deterrence, 51
Individual roots of crime. *See* Crime, individual
    roots of
Inmates, mental illness among, 45–47
Intact household, 66–68
Intensive supervised probation or parole (ISP), 290
Intensive supervision, 285, 290

Intermediate sanctions, 287–291
    community service, 285, 287
    day-reporting centers, 285, 287–288
    fines, restitution, and forfeiture, 285, 288–289
    house arrest and electronic monitoring, 285, 289–290
    intensive supervision, 285, 290
    probation and, 285
    shock probation, 285, 290–291
Internet survey, 29
Interviews, 32

Jacobs, Jane, 121, 129
Jaffe, Peter G., 176
Jarvis, John P., 249
Jeffrey, C. R., 129
Jim Crow laws, 259
Job Corps, 125
Jobs programs, 110, 125
Johnson, Lyndon B., 123, 197
Jolliffe, Darrick, 220–221
Joncas, Ronald, 257
Jonson, Cheryl Lero, 283, 291–292, 295, 306–307
Judicial and legal system, cost of, 6, 7 (figure)
Juvenile delinquency. *See* Youth crime
Juvenile Justice and Delinquency Prevention, 216
Juvenile justice system, 263–264

Kallikak, Martin, 43
Kansas City Preventive Patrol Experiment, 238, 241
Kappeler, Victor E., 249
Keel, Timothy G., 249
Kindergeld, 108–109
King, Rodney, 240, 248
Klebold, Dylan, 192
Kobrin, Solomon, 123
Kozol, Jonathan, 188
Kraska, Peter, 249
Kumpfer, Karol L., 174

Lab, Steven P., 263, 264
Labeling theory, 189, 207
Lally, Ronald, 172
Lanza, Adam, 193
Larson, Richard, 263
Latinos, mass incarceration and, 12, 17
Laub, John, 218
Law enforcement, cost of, 6, 7 (figure). *See also* Policing
    and crime prevention

theoretical underpinnings of, 145 (table)

twenty-five techniques of, 148(table)

Situational factors

defined, 60

rational choice theory and, 50

risk factors for crime and, 58–60, 59 (table), 61–66

Skogan, Wesley, 120

Slave patrol, 240

Slavery, replaced by prisons in South, 259

Slavery by Another Name (Blackmon), 259

Social bonding theory, 69–70, 189

schools and, 73

Social bonds, 166

decision to commit crime and weak, 100

"Social Change and Crime Rate Trends"
(Cohen & Felson), 142

Social class

community crime prevention and, 133

correlated to crime, 76–77

unemployment rate and, 103

Social context, consequences of, 307

Social control, social disorganization
theory and, 119

Social control theory, parent-child
relationships and, 165–166

Social development curriculum (SDC), 214

Social development model, 172

Social disorganization, crime and, 60, 133

Social disorganization theory, 119, 122 (table)

Social learning explanations, 71–72

Social learning theory of crime, 146

Social mimicry, 190

Social problems approach to community crime
prevention, 124

Social roots of street crime, 305

Social side of delinquent behavior, 209

Social supports, to reduce poverty and promote
employment, 108–110

Social ties, prisons and, 269–270

Sociodemographic correlates of crime, 75–78

age, 75

gender, 76

race and ethnicity, 77–78

social class, 76–77

Solitary confinement. *See* Administrative segregation

Solnick, Sara J., 65

Soulé, Dave, 197

Specific deterrence, 51

Spelman, William, 12

Spock, Benjamin, 165

Sports, crime prevention and, 127–128, 198–199

Spuriousness, 31–32, 211

Standard conditions, probation and, 285

Standard Model, 242

Stark, Rodney, 62

States of mind, decision to commit crime and, 100

Steering column locks, crime prevention and, 149–150

Stockholm Symposium Award, 244–245

Strain theory, 188

Street crime, 18

African Americans and, 77

social roots of, 305

Street gangs, 209, 221. *See also* Gangs

Stress hormones, toxic stress and, 97

Strong African American Families Program, 171

Substance abuse

community crime prevention and, 131–133

deterrence and committing crimes, 51

fetal development and maternal, 42

mental illness, violence, and, 47

toxic stress and, 97

treatment programs, 293–294

Substance use

commission of crimes and, 63–64

parental, 71

Substance use programs, 267–268

drug courts, 268

in schools, 194

therapeutic communities, 267–268

Sugai, George, 192

Sullivan, Christopher, 221

Supplemental Nutrition Assistance Program (SNAP),
109, 110

Supplemental Poverty Measure, 93

Surveillance, criticism of use of SCP and, 154–155

Survey research, 29–30

causal order and, 30–31

spuriousness and, 31–32

Sutherland, Edwin, 165, 210

Syracuse University Family Development Research
Program, 172, 198

Taheri, Sema, 197

Targeted parenting programs, 168

Target hardening approaches, 147, 148 (table), 149

Targets, routine activities theory and, 62